The Films and Career of
ROBERT ALDRICH

The Films and Career of
ROBERT ALDRICH

Edwin T. Arnold and Eugene L. Miller

The University of Tennessee Press / Knoxville

Frontispiece: Robert Burgess Aldrich.
Used by permission of Adell Aldrich.

Publication of this book has been aided by a grant
from the American Council of Learned Societies
from funds provided by the Andrew W. Mellon Foundation.

The paper used in this book meets the minimum requirements
of the American National Standard for Permanence of Paper
for Printed Library Materials, Z39.48–1984.
Binding materials have been chosen for durability.

Library of Congress Cataloging in Publication Data

Arnold, Edwin T., 1947–
    The films and career of Robert Aldrich.

    "Filmography": p.
    Bibliography: p.
    Includes index.
    1. Aldrich, Robert, 1918–1983   . 2. Moving-picture
producers and directors—United States—Biography.
I. Miller, Eugene L., 1945–   . II. Title.
PN1998.A3A55927 1986   791.43′0233′0924 [B] 86–1499
ISBN 0–87049–504–6

For Ellen, Matthew, and Elizabeth
and June and Gene, Sr.,
Louise, Sarah, and Rachel

Contents

Preface xi

Acknowledgments xiii

1. The Man Without a Past 1

2. "Le Gros Robert" 23

3. Aldrich in Exile 76

4. Cannibal Time 99

5. A Better Mousetrap 140

6. At the Table 165

7. What Ever Happened
   to Robert Aldrich? 218

Epilogue 235

Notes 241

Filmography 257

Selected Bibliography 265

Index 269

Illustrations

Robert Burgess Aldrich   *frontispiece*
Carl Hubbell and Edward G. Robinson
        in *The Big Leaguer*   18
Dan Duryea in *World For Ransom*   20
John McIntire and Burt Lancaster in *Apache*   29
Ernest Borgnine, Burt Lancaster,
        and Gary Cooper in *Vera Cruz*   33
Jack Lambert, Ralph Meeker, and
        Jack Elam in *Kiss Me Deadly*   40
Gaby Rogers in *Kiss Me Deadly*   44
Ida Lupino and Jack Palance in *The Big Knife*   52
Joan Crawford, Ruth Donnelly, and
        Cliff Robertson in *Autumn Leaves*   56
Jack Palance, Steven Geray, Peter Van Eyck,
        and Richard Jaeckel in *Attack!*   70
Lee J. Cobb and Kerwin Mathews in *The Garment Jungle*   78
Jeff Chandler and Jack Palance in *Ten Seconds to Hell*   83
Robert Mitchum and Elizabeth Mueller
        in *The Angry Hills*   88
Kirk Douglas and Rock Hudson in *The Last Sunset*   92
Robert Aldrich directing *What Ever
        Happened to Baby Jane?*   101
Robert Aldrich and his wife Harriet with
        daughters Adell and Alida on the set of *Baby Jane*   103
Joan Crawford and Bette Davis in *Baby Jane*   106
Bette Davis, Jack Warner, Joan Crawford, and
        Robert Aldrich celebrate the success of *Baby Jane*   108
Olivia de Havilland and Bette Davis
        in *Hush . . . Hush, Sweet Charlotte*   113
Lee Marvin and *The Dirty Dozen*   126

Kim Novak and Peter Finch
    in *The Legend of Lylah Clare*   134
Dedication of the Aldrich Studios   142
Beryl Reid and Susannah York
    in *The Killing of Sister George*   145
Wesley Addy, Kim Darby,
    and Scott Wilson in *The Grissom Gang*   162
Burt Lancaster, Bruce Davison, and
    Jorge Luke in *Ulzana's Raid*   170
Burt Reynolds and Eddie Albert in *The Longest Yard*   184
Burt Reynolds and Catherine Deneuve in *Hustle*   190
Robert Aldrich, his son William, his daughter Adell,
    and his son Kelly on the set of *Hustle*   194
Burt Lancaster, Alvin Greenman, and Robert Aldrich
    on the set of *Twilight's Last Gleaming*   200
Burt Lancaster, Paul Winfield, and
    Charles Durning in *Twilight's Last Gleaming*   205
Don Stroud, Perry King, Burt Young, and
    James Woods in *The Choirboys*   212
Harrison Ford and Gene Wilder in *The Frisco Kid*   220
The championship match in . . . *All the Marbles*   226

Preface

When we began research for this book, we were soon embarrassed to discover how little we actually knew of Robert Aldrich; later we were amazed at how much there was to know. The book was at first intended to be a straightforward examination of Aldrich's films. Aldrich expressed his willingness to work with us in this study and to read an early version of the work; he offered numerous corrections and insights. Following his unexpected death in December 1983, our book of necessity took on a greater scope, and we felt impelled to expand our focus beyond the films to Aldrich himself. Thus, while we never intended to write a biography, the biographical facts have inevitably helped us form our opinions of the man and his achievements. What we here offer is a portrait of a professional filmmaker working in Hollywood from 1941 to 1983. We concentrate on Aldrich as artist, as businessman, and as politician—each an important facet of his career. In his personal life, he could be a complicated and demanding figure, and we have tried to capture some of that complexity. But, as one of his children succinctly summarized her father, "Above all, the gentleman was a director."

"Onward and upward" was Robert Aldrich's favorite salutation, and it completely captured his sense of joy and anticipation as he faced the challenge of making his films. For this book we have appropriated the slogan as our own.

ETA and ELM

Acknowledgments

Many people contributed to the making of this book. We would like especially to thank Robert Aldrich, who, before his death, read and responded to an early draft of this book; and his children—William, Adell, Kelly, and Alida—who spoke candidly with us about their father and his career. We are also grateful to Aldrich's friends and associates, who took the time to share with us their impressions of Aldrich the man and Aldrich the director: Eddie Albert, Joan Bennett, Joseph Biroc, Charles Durning, Mike Franklin, Alvin and Jean Greenman, Richard Jaeckel, Lukas Heller, Burt Lancaster, Mike Luciano, Lee Marvin, Burt Reynolds, and Burt Young.

For research assistance, we are particularly indebted to Howard Prouty at the American Film Institute who told us much we did not know about Aldrich's early work in television. We thank the staff members at the UCLA library, the Northwestern University library, the Library of Congress Film Division, and the American Film Institute (especially Ann Slassor) for helping us locate Aldrich materials. Mary Corliss and Terry Geesken of the Museum of Modern Art in New York assisted in the selection of the still photographs used in this book. And Sue Jeffe was our patient tour guide through the then uncatalogued Aldrich papers. Thanks to all of them.

Financial support for our trip to Los Angeles, where we conducted interviews with the Aldrich family and many of Aldrich's colleagues, was provided by a number of Appalachian State University administrative agencies: thanks in particular to Harvey Durham, Tom Bohannon, and Clinton Parker of the Office of Academic Affairs; to Bob Snead of the Development Office; to Greg Reck of the Graduate School; to William Strickland, former dean of the College of Arts and Sciences; to William Byrd, the present dean; and to Loyd Hilton of the Department of English. The National Endowment for the Humanities provided an NEH Summer Seminar Grant, which enabled us to complete much of the initial research for this book at Northwestern University.

For clerical assistance, we would like to thank Lois Stanbery, Betty Smith, Barb Winkler, Janet Wellborn, Shannon Jackson, and Mavis Goodheart. Ray Scantlin helped us find our way around Los Angeles;

Jim Stramm located a hard-to-find print of *The Last Sunset.* We owe them both.

For their support, advice, and encouragement, special appreciation is due Buck Gaston and Warren French, who got us started on this project; and T. J. Ross, Tom McLaughlin, Leon Lewis, and Karen Carmean, who kept us going. Charles Maland read an early draft of this book and offered valuable suggestions for revision. Our thanks also to Carol Orr, director of the University of Tennessee Press, and Katherine Holloway, our editor, who have been prompt and professional in their dealings with us.

Finally, we are grateful to our wives and children—to Ellen and Matthew and Elizabeth; to Louise and Sarah and Rachel—without whose love and faith and patience this book would not have been possible.

The Films and Career of
ROBERT ALDRICH

1. The Man Without a Past

The Aldriches of Rhode Island

There was always a sense of the outsider about Robert Aldrich, an acknowledgment that he played his own game, made his own rules, went his own way. He had come to Hollywood from the East. His friends and associates knew that he was a member of the Rhode Island Aldriches, perhaps the most prominent family in that state, and a cousin to the New York Rockefellers, whose influence and power spread worldwide and most definitely into the movie industry itself. Clearly it had been that Rockefeller-Aldrich connection that had gotten him, fresh out of college, his first job at RKO Studios in 1941. But his family was nothing he talked about, and certainly nothing he tried to use to his advantage. He had, for example, hired on at RKO as a production clerk—in his own words, "the lowest form of human life here, the guy below the book-keeper and below the tea-boy"[1]—rather than as an associate producer, the job first offered him as a rich man's son. He had started at the bottom and had worked his way through the various departments in the business of making movies until he reached his goal: director. It was this background that gave him such a thorough knowledge of both the art and the mechanics of film, and that accounted, in part, for his appreciation of and consideration for the crew on his set.

Still, his own political and social sympathies went far beyond any patrician sense of noblesse oblige. He had worked at the liberal and independent Enterprise Studios, on films like *Body and Soul* and *Force of Evil*, pictures that questioned the moral fabric of American society, that equated big business and politics with gangsterism long before *The Godfather*. There he had met and was influenced by such men as Abraham Polonsky, Robert Rossen, John Berry, John Garfield, and others who would suffer from the political blacklisting of the early 1950s. In his own statements and practices, both as a filmmaker and as a powerful figure in Hollywood politics, he proved himself defiantly at odds with the kind of conservative, aristocratic, status-quo mentality one might expect to find in a man with his background.

And there were his own films, whether made for hire or later for his own company and studio. On the one hand, they were commercial ventures aimed for the mass audience, meant to entertain and make money. But the films were also iconoclastic, anti-authoritarian, even revolutionary in message. They often depicted the courageous attempts of the individual to maintain or regain a sense of self-worth, of identity, in opposition to the crushing forces of authority. His truest protagonists would engage in battle with these forces in the foreknowledge that their efforts were probably doomed but with the conviction that the struggle was a form of affirmation, of vindication, in itself. The wealthy, the influential, the dominant were shown in Aldrich's works as figures of oppression, whether they be the military leaders in *Attack!* or *The Dirty Dozen*, the law officials in *Hustle* or *The Choirboys*, the studio heads in *The Big Knife* or *The Legend of Lylah Clare*, or the government in *Apache* or *Twilight's Last Gleaming*. In every case, the power of one man to make another act against his will, to modify another's freedom in any way, was presented as frightening and finally corruptive. Sometimes funny, sometimes cynical, sometimes angry or even a bit hysterical, Aldrich's films reflected the mind of the man who made them—a complex, contradictory, but always honest screen artist.

The Aldriches of Rhode Island were a family of wealth and influence. They had long been guiding forces in the political and cultural life of the state and country. They could trace their ancestry to Nathanael Greene, the Revolutionary War hero; to Roger Williams, the founder of Rhode Island; and even to one of the first settlers who came to the new world on the *Mayflower*.[2] In more recent times, the Aldrich family had produced other prominent members. Robert Aldrich's grandfather, Nelson Wilmarth Aldrich, was a self-made millionaire with a discriminating taste in art; his estate near Warwick, Rhode Island, was a showplace in the state. It was as a politician, however, that Nelson Aldrich had made his mark. After serving two terms in the state legislature, he refused the Republican nomination for governor and was elected instead to the United States House of Representatives. After serving there from 1878 to 1881, he was elected to the U.S. Senate and for the next thirty years was one of the most influential men in that body. For a time, he was considered the central figure in the national Republican party. With Senators Allison of Iowa, Platt of Connecticut, and Spooner of Wisconsin, Aldrich formed a group known as the "Big Four," which effectively voiced the interests of big business through numerous tarrif battles in Washington. He was also the author of the "Aldrich Plan," an important attempt at banking reform in the early part of the twentieth centry. By most accounts, he was a reasonably honorable man, although well-versed in the practice of politics.[3]

Nelson Aldrich was the father of eight children, all of whom achieved various degrees of success in their lifetimes. Of Nelson Aldrich's five sons, Edward (Robert Aldrich's father) was the eldest. After an early career as an industrialist, Edward became president and director of the Times Publishing Company in Rhode Island, which published *The Pawtucket Times*. He also acted a behind-the-scenes role in the state's Republican politics and was known to his followers as "Uncle Ned," an implicit acknowledgment of his authority.[4] Robert Aldrich's uncles were Stuart M. Aldrich, an investment broker and cattle breeder; William Truman Aldrich, a noted architect and yachtsman who studied at l'Ecole des Beaux Arts in Paris and taught at the Harvard School of Architecture, the Rhode Island School of Design, and the Museum of Fine Arts in Boston; Richard Steere Aldrich, who served in the Rhode Island House of Representatives from 1914 to 1916, in the state Senate from 1916 to 1918, and in the U.S. House from 1922 to 1933; and Winthrop William Aldrich, who acted as chairman of the Chase Manhattan Bank and was also U.S. ambassador to Great Britain under President Eisenhower from 1953 to 1957.[5] Among the three aunts were Lucy T. Aldrich, a determined and strongheaded (and nearly deaf) woman who was once captured by Chinese bandits on one of her many travels and who later wrote an engaging account of the adventure;[6] and Abby Greene Aldrich, who became the first wife of John D. Rockefeller, Jr., and the mother of his six children, including Nelson and Winthrop Rockefeller.[7]

Robert Burgess Aldrich surely gained a great deal as a member of this remarkable family, but such a heritage could prove a burden as well as a blessing. He was born in Cranston, Rhode Island, on 9 August 1918. In the opinion of his son, William, Robert Aldrich's position in the family was from the beginning a difficult one:

> If you really want to know who he was and why he did a lot of the things he did, you almost have to understand his relationship with that family. There was always a lot of competition, a lot of emphasis on achievement among the Aldriches and the Rockefellers. And Dad always felt that he had more to prove than anybody else. He had to be the star of the football team and the track team and the baseball team. He had to be president of his fraternity. He had to be president of all this to prove that he was every bit as good if not better than his cousins were. And when he had done it, he left.[8]

The Aldriches were elderly when the boy was born, and Lora Aldrich, whom Aldrich remembered with great affection, died when he was still a young child. The relationship with his father was apparently more restrained, for Edward Aldrich could be demanding and authoritative. In a 1977 letter to screenwriter Theodore Apstein, Aldrich described life among the Aldriches: " . . . there was little or no discussion of art or culture or theatre or music in my home when I was a child. Family conversations were predominately concerned with politics and power. Somewhere in mid-youth, I was puzzled why nobody every discussed money, but eventually I discovered that politics and power meant money. ERGO: No need to discuss it."[9]

Robert Aldrich always played down his impressive heritage. "He didn't talk about this very often, unless he got a little melancholy or something reminded him of Rhode Island," William Aldrich remembered. "He really didn't have much of a past. It was something he didn't pass on to his children, certainly. We met our grandfather, his father, once before he died. I barely remember him—just some old fellow in a wheelchair." In his entry in *Who's Who in America*, Aldrich omitted his parents' names and any mention of the Aldrich-Rockefeller connection.[10] After the 1971 Attica State Prison riots and deaths in New York, he renounced all relations with his first cousin Nelson Rockefeller who, as governor of New York, had refused to meet with the rebelling prisoners and had commanded the state militia to restore order by force. Given the anarchistic undercurrent found in almost all of his films, it is worth speculating just how much Aldrich's work was done in reaction to the kind of authority he found specifically embodied in the Aldrich and Rockefeller families. By extension, the number of destructive parental figures in his films, while representing another form of perverted authority, surely suggests the deeper element of rebellion at play within Aldrich's own character. Coming from such a family, and especially as the only son in his branch of the family, Aldrich must have felt a tremendous responsibility to follow family tradition. That he did not do so, that he in fact turned against it and what it represented, was an act of open defiance. As Aldrich's daughter Adell suggested, "He had these very democratic points of view, and that family was *very* Republican, right-wing, almost. If there was a conflict between him and his father, I think it had to be over social issues, caring for people." That his films further advocated this type of rebellion underlines the strong personal nature of his work.

Nevertheless, Aldrich initially followed the family tradition. Like his father he attended the Moses Brown School in Providence, where he was elected president of the senior class, business manager of the *Yearbook*, and captain of the track and football teams. (His father had also played football at Moses Brown.) He then went to the University of Virginia ("not being bright enough to get into Yale"),[11] ostensibly preparing for a career in publishing, finance, or politics. There he majored in economics, played on the varsity football team, and, as a freshman, ran track. He also served as president of the Intra-Fraternity Council, of his own fraternity, Delta Kappa Epsilon, and of the German Club, a campus dance society. As part of his position in the German Club, he booked a number of celebrity orchestras, and he found the work exciting and enjoyable—"more fun," he later observed, "than working in a bank or working on a newspaper."[12] As Aldrich remembered:

> I couldn't see myself in either banking or publishing like my father, but he had a brother who was involved in some New York banks and also had some movie interests in California. So I went to this uncle [Winthrop William Aldrich] and told him I would like to get into films.
>
> He pointed out that there were three divisions, production, exhibition, and distribution, and making up my mind quickly I naturally plumped for production. He gave me a job for six weeks at $25 per week saying, "I never want to see you again." And that's how I entered films.[13]

Thus it was, in 1941, after four years of college but without a degree, that Robert Aldrich left the University of Virginia and headed for Hollywood.[14]

Apprenticeship

RKO (Radio-Keith-Orpheum) was among the lesser of the major Hollywood studios at this time. It had been formed in 1928 by Joseph P. Kennedy as part of a business deal with RCA (Radio Corporation of America). Because of the Rockefeller interests in RCA, RKO Studios also came under their financial influence (hence the Aldrich connection). Despite its relatively small size (it was the smallest of the six major studios; MGM was the largest), RKO had during the 1930s achieved some impressive successes and was known for its willingness to take chances. In 1933, for example, it had released both *King Kong* (Merian C. Cooper and Ernest B. Schoedsack's classic fantasy-adventure) and George Cukor's stylish *Little Women*. In 1935, John Ford directed *The Informer* at RKO and won an Academy Award as best director. The studio was responsible for the series of Fred Astaire-Ginger Rogers musicals which appeared throughout the decade, among them *The Gay Divorcée* in 1934 and *Top Hat* in 1935. Howard Hawks's screwball comedy *Bringing Up Baby*, with Cary Grant and Katharine Hepburn (an RKO regular), was made in 1938, as was the Marx Brothers' *Room Service*. There were also the famous historical and costume dramas, such as *Mary of Scotland* in 1936, and, in 1939, both *The Hunchback of Notre Dame* and *Gunga Din*. In 1941, when Aldrich joined the studio, it had recently signed the young Orson Welles to a six-film contract; the first of his films, *Citizen Kane*, was released the year Aldrich arrived. RKO was an exciting place to be.[15]

Still, the position of production clerk at RKO was less than glamorous: "the lowest job in existence on a sound stage," in Aldrich's words.[16] For five months, Aldrich diligently dispensed coffee, kept time cards, made out call sheets, and completed production reports. A combination of hard work and good luck helped Aldrich to rise quickly through the ranks of the RKO organization. When World War II began, an old football injury led to his rejection by the Air Force Motion Picture Unit after only a few days' service, and he took full advantage of the chance to advance his career. For the next two years, he worked as a second assistant on over two dozen films directed by accomplished professionals such as Edward Dmytryk and Leslie Goodwins. Aldrich regarded these fledgling years of his career as invaluable for the practical experience they offered: "I've always thought that working your way up from third or fourth or fifth assistant is like getting paid to go to college. Working with great directors—and terrible directors—is the greatest education possible."[17] By 1944, he had been promoted to first assistant director to Goodwins on a series of Edgar Kennedy and Leon Errol comedy shorts. He soon saw, however, that he had gone as far as he could at RKO and decided to free-lance among the other studios. Thus he began a remarkable apprenticeship as first assistant to some of the world's most distinguished filmmakers.

Indeed, the years 1944 to 1952 provided Aldrich with an astonishing range of assignments during which time he watched and assisted and learned the fine art of direction. "During those nine years of being an Assistant Director I worked with/and for an extraordinary group of people—sometimes for long periods, sometimes for short periods—some of them made a profound lasting impression, some were boring and over-rated, but all of them had fascination," Aldrich remembered.[18] One of his first jobs was on Jean Renoir's *The Southerner* (1945). There he learned the importance of set location and atmosphere:

Renoir truly believed that a transfusion takes place from the physical surroundings to the performances and the picture itself. We would go on location,
and he would walk up and down a riverside, for example, where we were to
build the set, for two or three days. He would bring the actors there a week
early, get them into costumes, and have them walk around barefoot . . . getting the actors there, on location or on the set—or on the stage, for that
matter—and having them in costume, in their parts, seemed to me to make
great sense.[19]

Years later, as an experienced director, Aldrich said of himself: "I am
not one of those directors who can come on a set or location and immediately place his camera. I have to know it and analyze it thoroughly
beforehand. Then I know what I want."[20] While working on *The
Southerner* he also met William Faulkner, who worked on the screenplay
for the film. "He used to drive Faulkner to the studio back and forth,
and they started talking," William Aldrich recounted. "He was probably
the first *big* author that Dad started bullshitting with and finding out
why he thought a certain way. He was fascinated by Faulkner."

Still other directors added to his store of knowledge. From Lewis
Milestone, with whom he worked on *The Strange Love of Martha Ivers*
(1946), *Arch of Triumph* (1948), and *The Red Pony* (1949), he learned the
techniques of pre-planning a shot: Milestone was a "great pre-cutter"
who could "pre-edit in his mind" before ever beginning a shot.[21] Both
Milestone and William Wellman (*The Story of G. I. Joe*, 1945) taught him
how to rehearse action before filming to make it seem spontaneous
without being chaotic. From Joseph Losey, whom he assisted on *M* and
The Prowler (both in 1951), he learned the importance of communication with actors. "Losey has absolutely extraordinary rapport with actors," Aldrich said. "I don't think any other director I ever worked with
had that kind of personal communication."[22] And from Charles Chaplin,
whom he served as first assistant on *Limelight* (1952), he learned still
more: Chaplin approached his work with tremendous energy and enthusiasm, and he impressed on Aldrich the importance of the "visual
empathy" that must exist between camera and audience, the essential
element which comes before and goes beyond the dialogue—cinema
itself.[23] He did not always agree with Chaplin's manner of making films.
"I learned a lot of things you shouldn't do from Chaplin," he later said.[24]
He was disturbed by Chaplin's habit of shooting without a schedule,
a practice which resulted, in Aldrich's opinion, in *Limelight's* being im-
properly shot. He appreciated, however, Chaplin's genius and his recep-
tivity to ideas, which Chaplin would then make his own. Aldrich would

be noted for his willingness to listen to the suggestions of anyone on his set and was always generous with his credits. "Don't joke about the idea that the prop man comes up with," he said. "He may come up with the best idea in the picture. You will be surprised with the total contribution that is made to a film by people who are encouraged to contribute."[25]

But the most important lesson Aldrich learned came from the old pro Milestone, a man Aldrich came to admire greatly. Milestone impressed upon the apprentice director the need for control over the production. Milestone knew how the industry worked. "The game is power," he taught Aldrich, who later put the idea into his own words:

> The power is for the director to do what he wants to do. To achieve that he needs his own cutter, he needs his cameraman, he needs his own assistant and a strong voice in choice of writer; a very, very strong voice on who's the actor. He needs the power not to be interfered with and the power to make the movie as he sees it. Milestone had all the tools, but above all, he had the capacity to know when trouble was coming and how to deal with it. And it worked, really worked.[26]

It was this lesson that Aldrich best put to use in his own career. For him, power would be *the* essential aspect of creativity: without the power, you could not complete your vision. As a director, Aldrich brought together a team with which he worked, with some variations, on all of his films: Joseph Biroc would photograph twenty-two of Aldrich's twenty-nine pictures; Michael Luciano would edit nineteen; Frank DeVol would score sixteen; William Glasgow, as art director, would design eleven; Lukas Heller would script six. Aldrich would also assemble a remarkable group of actors, both leading men such as Burt Lancaster, Jack Palance, and Lee Marvin and supporting actors (some to become leading actors) such as Eddie Albert, Richard Jaeckel, Wesley Addy, Ernest Borgnine, and Charles Bronson. For Aldrich it would be a family, people he trusted and who trusted him. Loyalty was the key, and a sense of stability the result.

Other notable directors under whom Aldrich served as first assistant included Albert Lewin (*The Private Affairs of Bel Ami*, 1947), Richard Fleischer (*So This Is New York*, 1948), Richard Wallace (*A Kiss For Corliss*, 1949), Ted Tatzloff (*The White Tower*, 1950), Irving Reis (*Of Men and Music*, 1950; *New Mexico*, 1951), and Charles Lamont (*Abbott and Costello Meet Captain Kidd*, 1952). Aldrich's education, finally, involved a process of sorting out, in the case of each director, the good qualities from the bad: "I think what you probably learn is what not to do as well as what to do . . . . It's a matter of assimilation, and whose brain you can pick, trying to keep it for yourself later . . . . Of course, you would never be as good as that particular guy is in that particular field, but you try to make yourself a composite of what you like and stay away from the things you didn't like."[27]

Enterprise Studios

Of Aldrich's apprenticeship work, perhaps the most important is that which he did from 1946 to 1948 while under contract to Enterprise Productions, where he advanced from assistant director to unit production to, finally, studio manager. Enterprise was an independent studio set up by David L. Lowe, a producer known, in the words of Allen Eyles in his history of Enterprise, "as a maker of somewhat offbeat, distinguished and highly artistic pictures with restricted commercial potential . . . ."[28] He had been involved in two of the films Aldrich had worked on, *The Southerner* and *The Private Affairs of Bel Ami*. Lowe's partners in the undertaking were Charles Einfeld, A. Pam Blumenthal, the actor John Garfield, and Garfield's business manager Bob Roberts. Enterprise leased studio lots and financed its own pictures, largely through Lowe's connections. The films made at Enterprise were then distributed by larger companies, first United Artists and later MGM. Enterprise offered actors a chance to participate in their films' profits and attracted a number of big-name stars such as Garfield, Ingrid Bergman, Barbara Stanwyck, and Joel McCrea. Among the directors who were given the freedom to develop their own projects were André de Toth, Lewis Milestone, Robert Rossen, Abraham Polonsky, and Max Ophuls.

Enterprise was an idealistic attempt at independent filmmaking, and many of the creative people who gathered at the studio shared a liberal philosophy: for them a film could and should do more than entertain. A belief in the essential decency of the "common man" and a basic distrust of wealth and power were at the heart of many of their pictures. For Aldrich it was an enlightening experience. He remembered the studio as an "unequalled organization" experimenting with a "really brilliant idea of a communal way to make films."[29] In general, morale was high, interest and excitement were evident at all levels of production, and, most importantly, independent filmmakers could get the money they needed to make their pictures. Fringe benefits for employees ranged from small percs such as free coffee and donuts to big ones like life insurance policies, guaranteed vacations, and exceptionally high salaries. As film editor Robert Parrish remembered:

> Enterprise was designed to make the workers happy . . . . It was a very benign management: they said, we're all in this together, and it was the first time that I ever heard of in Hollywood that the management formed the studios with that in mind—they didn't wait until the pressure was on, they gave it to you rightaway. They would pay you more to get more—usually, if they didn't pay you very much they gave you more artistic freedom, but in this case they tried to do both.[30]

But there were also serious problems at Enterprise. A lack of strong leadership produced an unfortunate tendency for the studio to waste enormous sums of money, energy, and talent on weak material. In Aldrich's opinion, "The studio . . . had everything in the world in its favour except one thing: it didn't have anybody in charge who knew how to make pictures . . . there was no head of that studio. There were a lot of very talented, experienced, intelligent people among its various branches, but there was no knowledgeable guy to run the shop."[31] As a result, few of the films made at Enterprise were commercially profitable. These financial problems were compounded by the political backlash of the late 1940s, although Enterprise had closed its studios before the era of actual blacklisting began.

The first film Aldrich worked on at Enterprise was *Body and Soul* (1947), written by Abraham Polonsky, directed by Robert Rossen, and starring John Garfield. Garfield played the role of Charley Davis, a prizefighter (based in part on the fighter Barney Ross) who is corrupted by his own success and later tries to atone for his actions, to regain his self-respect, by refusing to throw a fight even though he has been ordered by gangsters to do so and faces almost certain death if he does not. This theme would become central to Aldrich's work, and *Body and Soul* must be seen as the pivotal artistic experience of his apprenticeship. Over and over again, even in his last film thirty-four years later, he would return to *Body and Soul* for inspiration. As Lukas Heller, who worked with Aldrich as writer throughout the sixties and seventies, remembered, "When we would have story problems, Aldrich would revert to the film *Body and Soul* and say, 'That ending was always right. Why don't we use that ending here?' And he tried to work the structure of that story into every other movie."[32] For Aldrich, the essential story, no matter what film, would be a testament to the possibility, however slim, of the kind of moral regeneration found in *Body and Soul*.

From a more practical point of view, *Body and Soul* taught Aldrich other lessons. "The picture cost a million dollars more than it should have cost because Rossen was given his head," Aldrich later said. "Polonsky, although he had written a marvellous script, really interfered too much. [Bob] Roberts . . . never really pretended to be a producer, and, as I said, there was nobody at the head of the studio to bring us all up short."[33] On his own films, Aldrich would always be the boss. He would become known for his dependability and consistency, and his pictures rarely ran over cost. Also, when he started his own independent studio in 1968, he used the Enterprise experience as an example of what to do and what not to do, although the Aldrich Studios proved no more successful than did Enterprise.

Aldrich next worked with Polonsky in 1948 on *Force of Evil*, which Polonsky wrote and directed. The film again starred John Garfield. *Body and Soul* had been Enterprise's one commercial success, and *Force of Evil* had Garfield in a role similar to that which he had played in the boxing film. Here Garfield was Joe Morse, a lawyer for the syndicate, who at first works for the gangsters but decides to inform on them after they murder his brother, a small-time numbers operator who refuses to join the organization. Allen Eyles describes *Force of Evil* as "probably the most worthwhile and original of the Enterprise pictures . . . . The dialogue was stylised, the fratricidal aspect given an intensity worthy of Greek drama, some of the characterisation mannered . . . and the images powerfully composed. *Force of Evil* offered a complex viewing experience; it was the kind of brave undertaking that the Enterprise set-up was ideally placed to encourage . . . ."[34]

Aldrich's friendship with Abraham Polonsky would prove to be one of the most important in his life. Although they never worked together after *Force of Evil*, they remained close and often got together to discuss the madness and corruption of the world they saw around them. In Polonsky's words, "It was an innate, intellectual friendship, based also on great affection for each other."[35] As Lukas Heller aptly put it, "I think it's fair to say that Abe Polonsky would be about the one person of whom [Aldrich] would think he was an intellectual inferior." Polonsky would deliver the warm and moving eulogy for Aldrich at the memorial service held by the Directors Guild of America shortly after his death.

The other films Aldrich worked on at Enterprise were Lewis Milestone's financially disastrous *Arch of Triumph* (1948), which cost $5 million to film and grossed only $1.5 million (perhaps the most direct cause of Enterprise's eventual collapse); Richard Fleischer's *So This Is*

New York (1948), a modest comedy based on a story by Ring Lardner; and the studio's last film, *Caught* (1949), directed by Max Ophuls. Aldrich was by this time studio production manager. "My work on *Caught* was short and abrasive," he remembered. Ophuls, the original director, became indisposed during filming with a bad case of shingles, and Aldrich's friend John Berry was brought in, as both he and Aldrich thought, to finish the picture. Soon it became clear, however, that Berry was hired only as an interim director. "About two-thirds of the way through filming I began to hear whispers to the effect that sketches and models of forthcoming sets and costumes yet to be photographed were being taken to Ophuls at night and that he was approving them and changing the script and so forth," Aldrich said. When Ophuls returned, it was Aldrich's job as studio manager to fire Berry, and Aldrich felt it was all badly handled. "However," he added,

> four or five months later, Ophuls had to come back for some retakes. We were really out of money then, so I was first assistant on *Caught* as well as studio production manager. I must say that it was with some sadistic delight that I gave Mr. Ophuls a very bad couple of days because the bank had vested in me much of the power of deciding what retakes to do or not to do. I never got even for the injustice Mr. Berry suffered but it was a pleasant two days.[36]

After Enterprise closed its doors, many of the people associated with the studio went on to illustrious careers in the industry. Some, however, were caught up in the hysteria and paranoia of the McCarthy witch-hunts. Enterprise earned a reputation of having been a left-wing organization. Among those called before the U.S. House Un-American Activities Committee were Robert Rossen, Abraham Polonsky, John Berry, John Garfield, and Carl Foreman. Aldrich carefully expressed himself on this matter:

> While Enterprise did have an orientation towards stories with "social significance," I think it would be unfair to say that that was its "aim." As the Irish say, this was just before the "troubles," and the talented people in that period . . . tended to be more liberal than the untalented people, and, because they were more liberal, they got caught up in social processes that had political manifestations which later proved to be economically difficult to live with. In its search for talented and interesting people, Enterprise hired a great many followers of that persuasion and its pictures consequently began to acquire more and more social content.[37]

Robert Rossen had been a member of the Communist party in the late 1930s and early 1940s, but he had become disillusioned and had ended his association in 1945. In 1951, when he was named as a communist by several witnesses in the hearings and was called to testify, he denied that he was at that time a member of the party and refused to discuss his former membership or to name others as members, past or present. For this refusal, he was blacklisted by the industry and for the next two years could not find work, despite the fact that his 1949 film *All the King's Men* had won the Academy Award as Best Picture. In 1953, Rossen requested a special hearing from the committee, at which time he explained, "I don't think, after two years of thinking, that any one individual can even indulge himself in the luxury of individual morality,"[38] and went on to name fifty people with party connections. Polonsky, also called in 1951, refused to affirm or deny party membership or to name names, and he stood by his decision, although it too resulted in his being blacklisted by the industry. John Garfield was likewise interrogated by the committee, on more than one occasion. Although Garfield cooperated with the committee to a point, he steadfastly refused to identify others as past or present members of the Communist party. As Abraham Polonsky explained in a now famous description: "[Garfield] said he hated Communists, he hated Communism, he was an American. He told the Committee what it wanted to hear. But he wouldn't say the one thing that would keep him from walking down his old neighborhood block. Nobody could say, 'Hey, there's the fucking stool pigeon.' "[39]

Despite his association with Enterprise and these men, Aldrich managed to emerge unscathed from the Hollywood witch-hunts. "I think Dad expected to be named at that time," William Aldrich felt. "Although he was not a member of the Party, he was certainly sympathetic to the cause. He was an assistant director, so maybe he wasn't *big* enough to be called." In 1982, Robert Aldrich put this time of his life in perspective:

During the 1940's and early 1950's I had the privilege of working with many, many people who were later black listed, some of whom even went to jail. It was my opinion then, it is my opinion forty-two years later that not one person I knew wanted to mount the barricades or overthrow the government by force. Of course, they were radicals. But so then were Washington and Jefferson. They made a variety of mistakes, not the least of which was pleading the wrong Amendment, nor defining fascism as a potential enemy long before Franco, Mussolini and Hitler.

I *was* fortunate. I was fortunate not to have come to California five years earlier. I was fortunate that nobody ever recruited me into the Party, and I was fortunate that I never volunteered. But over 40 + years later, were I asked to evaluate the patriotism of Dalton Trumbo and Ring Lardner [Jr.] as opposed to Martin Dies, Joe McCarthy and Ronald Reagan (then and now), I would have neither hesitancy nor difficulty in responding that Messrs. Trumbo and Lardner were more concerned with the welfare of their country than the latter-mentioned trio of horribles. One tends to forget over the years that the black list included the best and the brightest and only very few second-class citizens, second-guessers and opportunists were ostracized.[40]

Television and First Films

Aldrich earned his first credits as a director not with feature-length Hollywood movies but in filmed television in New York. Although generally regarded as the "golden age" of live television, the early 1950s also saw many soap operas and adventure serials being made on film. Given the economic disadvantages of relocation, few film directors chose to leave Hollywood for less lucrative work in New York, and television officials there soon found themselves faced with a serious shortage of trained, talented, and skilled personnel. Anxious to get experience as a director, Aldrich took advantage of the job opportunities available in the East and accepted a job arranged by a friend, Walter Blake.[41] In 1952 and 1953, Aldrich shot seventeen episodes of *The Doctor* in New York for NBC. *The Doctor* was an anthology series starring Warner Anderson in which emotional problems were often emphasized over physical ones. Aldrich wrote three of the screenplays himself, and the program anticipates his later psychological horror films such as *Autumn Leaves, What Ever Happened to Baby Jane?*, and *Hush . . . Hush, Sweet Charlotte.* "The sheer volume of these TV shows represented a marvelous internship," Aldrich recalled. "This director's crash course removed what I call the trauma of preciousness: No single project can make or break you, only the trend. Instant decisions reflect cumulative experience."[42]

Television gave Aldrich the chance to put into practice a number of the theories he had developed while working as first assistant director, the most important of which was his emphasis on rehearsals.

Even then it always seemed to me that the biggest advantage to be derived from a rehearsal period was in completely locking and freezing the conception for the actors and the director on how the story and the characters should unfold; and that once there was this creative meeting of the minds, and once the individual artist completely understood and concurred with the gradual development and interpretive building of his own performance, then that same artist would have no apprehensive feelings of misgiving or insecurity about any schedule juggling or out-of-continuity shooting that could facilitate and shorten the time it takes to shoot a feature and/or a TV show.[43]

The shooting schedule for *The Doctor* called for two episodes to be filmed per five-day week. Aldrich devoted from one-half to two-thirds of one of these days to rehearsal for each show filmed. After finishing *The Doctor*, he returned to California to work next on the *China Smith* show, an adventure series starring Dan Duryea. It was "a project that was considerably less classy, but one which physically presented a much more complex challenge."[44] Here Aldrich was required to shoot three shows in a six-day week, and again he insisted on devoting a portion of that time to rehearsal.

In addition to the more than twenty episodes of *China Smith* that Aldrich directed, he also worked as "guest director" on at least five episodes of *Four Star Playhouse* in late 1953 and early 1954. *Four Star Playhouse*, shown on CBS, was a thirty-minute anthology series shot on a three-to-four-day schedule. The "four stars" were Dick Powell, Charles Boyer, Ida Lupino, and David Niven, who took turns appearing on the program. Aldrich directed three episodes with Powell (in two of which Powell appeared as Willie Dante, a debonair gambler, a character created by Blake Edwards, who wrote both of these episodes) and two with Boyer (who had been the male lead in Milestone's *Arch of Triumph*).[45]

In 1959, during his exile from Hollywood, Aldrich would return to television to direct the pilots for *Adventures in Paradise*, based on an idea by James Michener, and for *The Sundance Kid* (retitled *Hotel de Paree*), a western starring Earl Holliman. The pilots sold easily, they gave Aldrich a "chance to show off a little," and he found them "an interesting way to make a living."[46]

While Aldrich was in New York directing *The Doctor*, MGM was in the process of forming a rather unique production unit. The idea was Louis B. Mayer's, who decided to express his gratitude to those who had helped him form Metro-Goldwyn-Mayer by organizing their sons into a production group which came to be called "The Sons of the Pioneers," a humorous reference to the country-western singing group started by Roy Rogers. Mayer and Dore Schary (studio production chief and, later, Mayer's successor at MGM) believed the unit would be an excellent way to bring along new talent,[47] and under Schary's leadership the unit made seven or eight low-budget pictures for MGM.[48] A combination of circumstances helped Aldrich get his first shot at directing one of these, a feature-length film called *The Big Leaguer* (1953). During his time at Enterprise, he had met and worked with Herbert Baker, who was now writing the screenplay for this baseball story to be produced by Matt Rapf, one of the aforementioned "sons." Baker enthusiastically recommended that Aldrich be hired as the director. Here was a man, he persuasively argued, with plenty of production and television directing experience, a lengthy apprenticeship as assistant director with the likes of Chaplin, and, most importantly for this film, a former career as an athlete. Aldrich got the job.

The Big Leaguer was made on location in Melbourne, Florida, at the New York Giants training camp. It was shot on a fourteen-day schedule. The film starred Edward G. Robinson and had, in the supporting cast, Richard Jaeckel, who had worked with Aldrich on an episode of *Four Star Playhouse* and who would become a regular in Aldrich's films. *The Big Leaguer* was meant to be a "companion" film, a B-movie to accompany a more important release. As Jaeckel remembered, the shooting was done quickly: "Aldrich couldn't emphasize quality. He had to do as many set-ups as possible." Still, Jaeckel was impressed by the young director's complete professionalism. "You could be the star or have one line, even then he showed great respect for you," Jaeckel said. "I really learned my professionalism from him. You soon began to feel that you were making a contribution to the film."[49]

Edward G. Robinson's role as the chief baseball scout was the pivotal one in the picture, but the film was a difficult experience for the distinguished actor who was once accustomed to more prestigious work. Robinson had been a victim of the political "graylisting" which accompanied the Communist scare in Hollywood at the time. As Aldrich explained, "Graylisting was when you may or may not have been a Communist. You probably were, but you never had a card . . . . You couldn't say you were sorry for anything, because you didn't belong, but nobody would give you any jobs. It was more serious than blacklisting."[50] The role in *The Big Leaguer*, however insignificant in comparison to his earlier screen roles, marked the end of Robinson's political exile from films. But the actor was also not in good physical condition, and Aldrich had to take great care in filming many of his scenes to hide that fact and make him believable.

The Big Leaguer is about boys and baseball and the American Dream. Invited one spring to the New York Giants training camp in Florida for two weeks of try-outs, a group of amateur ballplayers competes, under the watchful scrutiny of veteran major league scouts, for a limited number of $150-a-month contracts with the Giants' farm club organization. Practice sessions are grueling, and only the most talented players survive the final cut. Aldrich focuses the narrative on the lives of five individuals who represent, by means of nationality and/or personality, a vision of America in cross-section: Adam Polachuk (Jeff Richards), the raw-boned, rugged kid from an Eastern mining town who arrives in camp without his immigrant father's knowledge or approval; Julie Davis (William Campbell), an abrasive, jaunty, street-tough New York City boy; Bobby Bronson (Richard Jaeckel), an aggressively confident, highly regarded pitcher from Massillon, Ohio; Tippy Mitchell (Bill Crandall), the son of a former big league star who yearns to follow in his famous father's footsteps; and Chuy Aguilar (Lalo Rios), the affable, broken-English-speaking Cuban emigré. Presiding over this quintet is the gruff but paternal mentor, chief scout John Lobert (Edward G. Robinson), who, with unshakable faith in America's youth, implores his charges to do their best and "give it all you got!" The presence of Carl Hubbell and other professional ball players in cameo roles lends the film an aura of authenticity and a semi-documentary flavor.

The protagonist Polachuk meanders through the predictable plot to a fairy-tale finale, winning the girl (Vera-Ellen) and the game (with a resounding, climactic ninth-inning homerun), and getting the go-ahead (from his father, a recent convert to the national pastime) to pursue a career in baseball rather than academia. Despite its flaws, *The Big Leaguer* is of interest, for it introduces, if only superficially, a number of themes with which Aldrich would be preoccupied throughout his career. Foremost is the idea of a man attempting to regain his lost self-esteem and discovering, in the process, the true value of personal integrity. Polachuk learns, for instance, that, regardless of his father's wishes and expectations of him, he must follow his own dreams (an idea Aldrich must have appreciated). In addition, Aldrich studies here the perversely powerful influence which fathers often exercise over their children's lives. The elder Polachuk dreams of his son's college education; Tippy Mitchell's father pressures his son into competition despite the boy's obvious shortcomings. These meddling parents prompt Lobert to grouse, late in the film, that "this camp is lousy with fathers." Finally, key characters realize that, occasionally, they must compromise their personal principles to fit specific moral and emotional situations. Aldrich explores in this first film the nature of group solidarity and the behavior of men under pressure, a theme to which he would return fre-

Carl Hubbell and Edward G. Robinson discuss baseball in *The Big Leaguer*. Used by permission of the Museum of Modern Art/Film Stills Archive, courtesy of MGM.

quently in years to come in such works as *The Flight of the Phoenix*, *The Dirty Dozen*, and *The Longest Yard*.

At one point in the film, a veteran scout offers sage advice to an aspiring third baseman: "Don't try to make a big impression your first time out." It was advice Aldrich himself followed in making the movie. "I feel the film was good," he later said, "but not indicative of what I wanted to express in the motion picture medium."[51]

After completing *The Big Leaguer*, Aldrich returned to New York to resume directing television episodes of *The Doctor*. He then came back to California to work on the *China Smith* series. During a four-week break in the shooting schedule, he thought of expanding a version of a *China Smith* episode into a feature-length film for theatrical release.

He approached Bernie Tabakin, the series' producer, with his idea. Tabakin, an excellent promoter with a gambler's instinct, agreed to the project and raised about three-quarters of the money needed. The film, *World For Ransom* (1954), was co-produced by Aldrich and Tabakin and written by Aldrich, Lindsay Hardy, and (uncredited) Hugo Butler. It marked the beginning of a very successful collaboration: assembled for the first time was a team of technicians and craftsmen with whom Aldrich would work regularly during the next twenty-seven years. Among them were photographer Joseph Biroc, whom he knew from the *China Smith* series; film editor Michael Luciano, who had worked at Enterprise; art director William Glasgow; and music director Frank DeVol. When the money ran out before shooting was completed, Aldrich and his crew made several beer and razor commercials to secure the remaining funds. Aldrich believed that the finished product, released by Allied Artists, "looked like it was done in thirty or forty [days]" rather than the ten in which it was shot,[52] thanks to the skill and expertise of Biroc, who created "reflections in water where there was no water and all kinds of silly things."[53] Clearly, Aldrich already understood the principles of marketing a film like this one. He knew it "had to have bizarre, outlandish kinds of situations to even be noticeable. So you made a potboiler and you try to make it as outrageous as possible so it has some marketable value."[54] It was a fun and exciting picture to do, working with friends on a shoestring budget but having the freedom to let the imagination run wild. "I've always looked back on that film with a wistful kind of happy feeling," Aldrich later admitted.[55]

World For Ransom was meant to be, at least in part, "a parody on the usual exotic espionage adventure films,"[56] Aldrich later said, a fact noted by French critics several years later, who favorably compared it to John Huston's *Beat the Devil* (1954), a film Aldrich himself did not like.[57] Words like "bizarre," "outlandish," and "outrageous" perfectly describe the plot of *World For Ransom*. Singapore private detective Mike Callahan (Dan Duryea) is hired by an old wartime girlfriend named Frennessey (Marian Carr) to investigate the suspicious behavior of her husband Julian March (Patric Knowles). March, as Callahan soon learns, is involved in a scheme masterminded by international gangster Alexis Pederas (Gene Lockhart) to kidnap noted nuclear physicist Sean O'Connor (Arthur Shields) and auction him to the highest bidder, American or Communist. After successfully evading an attempted frame-up arranged by Pederas, Callahan discovers that O'Connor is being held captive in a remote jungle hideout. Aided by a British intelligence agent, Major Bone (Reginald Den-

Dan Duryea in *World For Ransom*. Used by permission of the Museum of Modern Art/Film Stills Archive, courtesy of Allied Artists.

ny), Callahan finally locates the kidnappers and kills them. Only he and O'Connor—who is safely ensconced in an adjoining room during the attack—escape alive. When Callahan returns to woo the newly-widowed Frennessey, she accuses him of murdering her husband (an unjust allegation, since Callahan had given March ample opportunity to escape), rejects his amorous advances, and berates him for misunderstanding her motives and intentions. Callahan is left alone to puzzle out for himself the manifold mysteries of mankind and womanhood.

The fallen, intractable locale of *World For Ransom* is a far cry from the placid, Florida-fantasyland of *The Big Leaguer*; and Mike Callahan, private eye and anti-hero, romantic and cynic, is a stark reflection of the seamy Singapore setting. What Aldrich began to discover here was a more personal tone and milieu: *World For Ransom* marked the first presentation of certain character types and relationships which would reappear in his later work. Indeed, film critic Richard Combs calls *World For Ransom* "the seminal film of this period" in Aldrich's career,[58] a film which draws attention to the complex relationship between the idealist and the pragmatist, both of whom behave imperfectly under morally gray circumstances. Aldrich himself wrote of the picture:

> The first film towards which I have a personal feeling is *World For Ransom* .... I think my general film themes were crystallized in this. The hero, Mike Callahan, is a sort of anti-hero in his cynicism and general attitude towards humanity, but he has a code he follows unwaveringly, and is romantic towards women, which was given a satirical connotation in the film. But it was mainly about two men with good and bad points, but one standing for a firmer order of individual liberty and respect for humanity, while the other's liberty did not include this respect. I feel that the enemy has to be known, and its good points even admired, before it can be fought intelligently and with dignity.[59]

Because March and Callahan once were friends, because they love the same woman, and because they adhere to disparate codes, the two men are locked together in a fatal struggle in which each jostles for advantage over the other. Thus, *World For Ransom* explores the problematical themes of brotherhood, partnership, and alliance; at the same time, it probes some difficult questions about power and authority in a paranoid world, the atomic world. The film is not without its larger political implications.

World For Ransom also marked Aldrich's first brush with censorship. Originally, Aldrich wanted to show that Callahan's love, Frennessey, was a lesbian. He shot an opening scene which revealed her dressed as a man, kissing another woman. Aldrich took his inspiration for this scene from Josef von Sternberg's *Morocco*, in which Marlene Dietrich played a similar scene. Aldrich justified this characterization in terms of its effect on Callahan. "Callahan does not hold the girl's past, loose life with men against her," Aldrich said, "but the thing he cannot fight is her preferring women to him. This destroys his code of manliness."[60] Not surprisingly, the scene was subsequently cut, and Aldrich had to settle for a few oblique references to Frennessey's life of prostitution during the war.

At the time of its release, *World For Ransom* was poorly received. Typical was Bosley Crowther's uncomprehending review (the first of many such critical appraisals of Aldrich films) in the *New York Times*: "Robert Aldrich produced and directed. He was trying. Some day he may learn how."[61] Others were more impressed, however. The film caught the eye of Hecht-Lancaster Productions. Formed in 1947 by Burt Lancaster and his agent Harold Hecht, the production company already had four films to its credit, but, in Aldrich's words, was "still kind of sprawling and struggling." Aldrich had worked on two of these films—*Ten Tall Men* (1951) and *The First Time* (1952)—as "assistant to the producer [Hecht], which was really just a glorified way of paying me more money so that I could be their production manager."[62] Immediately following *World For Ransom*, Hecht-Lancaster offered the young director the chance to do *Apache*, the film that formally launched Robert Aldrich's career.

2. "Le Gros Robert"

Apache (1954)

With thirteen years of eclectic Hollywood experience behind him, Aldrich was more than ready in 1954 for the proverbial big break to occur. Aldrich joked that he got the job to direct *Apache* for Hecht-Lancaster Productions because "they wanted a 'bright young man' they didn't have to pay much money to."[1] Burt Lancaster remembered Aldrich's hiring in somewhat more positive terms. "Hecht knew of Aldrich as an assistant director. He had a great reputation for running a picture. We were anxious to make the picture for $90,000. He shot the film in around thirty days, and it grossed over $6 million. It was very clear that he was a fine technician, that he knew everything there was to know about the business." Moreover, Lancaster indicated, they were impressed that he had been associated with Chaplin.[2]

Although *Apache* was ostensibly a Hecht-Lancaster project, a starring vehicle for Lancaster, it became a distinctly personal film for Aldrich that brought the thirty-six-year-old director immediate international acclaim, especially among influential French critics when it and other Aldrich films were first shown in France in 1955. André Bazin, for example, in his seminal essay "The Evolution of the Western," identified a new generation of western filmmakers in the 1950s, directors whose work, he felt, was "sincere" (they were careful to "play fair" with the genre even when they were conscious of "making a western") and "novelistic" (without departing from traditional themes, they enriched the western from within by the "originality of their characters, their psychological flavor, and an engaging individuality which is what we expect from the hero of a novel"). Of the many films noted, Bazin singled out *Apache* as the "most recent and brilliant example" of the "delight in the western that is both classic and novelistic."[3]

Apache was also an impressive example of the "pro-Indian" western which became popular in the 1950s, along with *Broken Arrow* (1950), *Devil's Doorway* (1950), *Drum Beat* (1954), *White Feather* (1955), and *Run of the Arrow* (1957). These films were unique in that they made the attempt to present the Indian as something more than a one-dimensional or stereotypical figure, good for local color or easy villainy. They acknowledged the Indian's "otherness" but questioned the white man's superiority and posited the moral dilemma inherent in the supplanting of one culture with another. Underscoring these films was a sense of tragedy as well as guilt.[4] Also, given the far-reaching social changes that were taking place in the United States at the time, focused primarily on the *Brown* vs. *Board of Education* Supreme Court decision in 1954 that called for racial integration of the schools, these films, with their emphasis on racial conflict of another kind, inevitably took on an even greater social significance. Burt Lancaster, for example, said of *Apache* that while the film told of the "genocide of the Indian," it was meant by all involved to make a broader statement on the injustice of racism.

In *Apache*, Lancaster plays the role of Massai, the last Apache warrior (based on an historical figure), an isolated, alienated character. Written by James R. Webb, his screenplay based on Paul Wellman's novel *Bronco Apache*, the film relates the struggle of Massai to survive—with dignity and self-respect—the cataclysmic historical upheavals of the late nineteenth century which have left him exiled and outcast, not only from the white community but from his own people as well. A fiercely proud individual, Massai is a man unwilling to accommodate to the grim realities of life on a reservation and determined to reject the corruptive blandishments of life in a "civilized" society. Dispossessed of his heritage, deprived of human contact, and betrayed, finally, by a fellow Apache, Massai becomes for a time a one-man army, a renegade ravaging the countryside and waging a merciless war of attrition against his sworn enemies, both red and white. Only after considerable carnage do the wisdom of a Cherokee farmer and the love of an Apache maiden finally persuade Massai that a life of compromise and acculturation may be preferable to one of bloodshed and brutality. His life spared in a final violent encounter with the U.S. Cavalry, Massai returns to his wife and child and—apparently—a life of stolid domesticity.

But this was not the ending Aldrich wanted, and he was openly critical of the change imposed on him:

> The original script ended with the hero, Massai, going back up to a shack to be shot needlessly in the back by Federal troops. That was the script I'd been given, that was the script I'd approved, and that was the script I'd shot.
>
> Two or three days before shooting on the picture was due to finish, United Artists prevailed upon Hecht to shoot two endings. . . . I refused to shoot the alternate ending, and for about two days Burt agreed that the original ending was what this picture was all about.

Then, for reasons best known to himself, he changed his mind. Now once Burt had changed his mind it made little difference if I refused to direct the other ending because the next day they could have got someone who would. The point was lost because a $500-a-week director had no hope of prevailing against Hecht-Lancaster and United Artists.

If Burt had stood firm, I think the picture would have been more—"significant" is a pompous word—but I think it would have been more important. It was seriously compromised. You make a picture about one thing, the inevitability of Massai's death. His courage is measured against the inevitable. The whole preceding two hours become redundant if at the end he can just walk away.[5]

Lancaster's memory of the altered ending largely coincides with Aldrich's:

United Artists said, "You can't kill Burt." Everybody came to me, even my own partner, and talked to me. I regret to this day that I didn't do what I wanted. It would have been—who knows what would have happened if we had made it that way at that time? It was my opinion that we would have had something of a classic. The ending prevented the picture from taking the position it could have held.

This tampering with the content of *Apache* was the kind of meddling and interference on the part of studio executives which would prompt Aldrich to strive for independent status as a filmmaker. But the damage to *Apache* is less traumatic than Aldrich and Lancaster might have supposed. In its portrait of the Indian and the consequences of his clash with white culture, *Apache* is both a disturbing indictment of racism and a circumspect analysis of the nature of heroism, idealism, and compromise.

Aldrich explores the theme of the passing of a way of life essentially through the experiences of Massai, who is denied the fame and glory of a warrior's death when he is captured alive and placed in chains by the army (the first of many captures and escapes which structure the film). His failure to find meaning in *death* is soon replaced by an equally fervid desire to find meaning in *life*, not life as he would like it to be, but life as it is, life as he finds it. After escaping from the Florida-bound train on which he is held captive, Massai begins his real "education" that awakens him to the realities of heretofore unknown worlds and shakes to their very foundations many of his most deeply-felt convictions. On the first leg of his homeward journey, a stowaway in a wagon, he finds himself abruptly deposited one evening in the streets of downtown St. Louis. It is his first glimpse of urban civilization and *Apache's* most cleverly-edited and humorous sequence of shots. In a montage of vivid images juxtaposed in jump-cut fashion, Aldrich and cameraman Ernest Laszlo convey the nightmarish, alien, unintelligible quality of big-city life as seen through the eyes of the outsider. The sights and sounds of a Chinese laundry, a player piano, a fancy restaurant, a shoeshine boy, fire trucks, streetcars, and throngs of pedestrians combine to exacerbate Massai's horrible sense of dislocation. An angry mob and their barking dogs finally run the terrified Indian out of town.

As his westward odyssey continues, Massai becomes progressively more disenchanted with the human community, the most severe blows to his sense of cultural identity coming, ironically, from members of his own race. Massai is accustomed to the spectacle of domesticated whites, but the thought of a domesticated Indian is practically inconceivable—until he meets a farmer named Dawson, an Oklahoma Cherokee in whose barn Massai seeks shelter one night. Dawson preaches a doctrine of reconciliation to the ways of the white man. He advocates the ownership of private property—"This is *my* house," he proudly announces—and espouses the cause of peaceful co-existence between the races. At first Massai is incredulous, remonstrating with Dawson that "Apaches are warriors, not farmers." But before he departs—his exit through a window nicely suggestive of his temporary escape from constraint and confinement—Massai accepts from Dawson a gift, a sack of seed corn for planting. He is, however, more convinced, for the moment, of its usefulness as a provision for an arduous journey than its potential to guarantee the survival of his people.

What does convince Massai of the value of seed corn is the deplorable condition of his peoples' lives, a condition he witnesses immediately upon his return to his village, having (as did the historical Massai) traversed the country alone. The men are employed as slave laborers by the Indian agent Weddle (John Dehner); Massai's woman, Nalinle (Jean Peters), is being courted by an Indian soldier-scout (Charles Bronson [Buchinsky]) who demands her affection in exchange for whiskey to support her father's habit; the once-proud, now piteous Chief Santos himself exists in the final throes of alcoholic consumption. The tribe awaits its redeemer, and Massai finds himself, in the welcome spaciousness of an Indian tepee (a sharp contrast to the cramped quarters of Dawson's home), cast suddenly in the role of prophet, preaching the gospel of Dawson. In the spirit of compromise, he alludes to "a warrior's peace between equals," and to the corn as "the seed of a new life for our tribe." Aldrich's masterful low-angle shot reveals Massai as a towering figure, larger than life, his status as savior punctuated by Nalinle's hopeful acclamation: "Our people are dead; Massai will make them live again."

This hope, however, is short-lived. Massai is betrayed by Santos to the soldiers, who reward the debauched chief with whiskey. Thus delivered by his own people into the hands of his enemies, Massai vows revenge. His estrangement from both white and Indian society is now complete; the "education" which began in St. Louis and which culminated in New Mexico has made of Massai a bitter and relentless avenger, dedicated to the annihilation of his tormentors. The crusade begins when Massai, together with other prisoners, escapes from a trap laid by Weddle as he escorts them to prison. Massai kills one guard, rejects the offer of fellow captives to fight beside him, and spares Weddle's life "long enough [for him] to tell them who they fight." The whites are the first to feel the fury of Massai's wrath: soldiers are slaughtered, a supply room set ablaze, telegraph lines severed, horses stampeded, and, in the film's most brutally ironic shot, Weddle, framed in the doorway of Army Headquarters, is killed by a bullet which passes through his body and shatters a peace pipe hanging from the wall inside. Nor are the Indians spared Massai's retribution. In retaliation for Santos's traitorousness, Massai kidnaps Nalinle, the chief's daughter, whom he mistakenly assumes to have been a co-conspirator in the plot to betray him. He subjects her to torture and indignity, binding her hand and foot and depriving her of food and water. Untouched by Nalinle's suffering, blinded by revenge, cruel and dispassionate, the erstwhile redeemer is now the candidate for redemption.

The agent of Massai's conversion is Nalinle, who berates the warrior for his callousness and inhumanity: "My father wronged you. Many men wronged you. But now you make yourself worse than they are. Now there is nothing in you but hate." In the disconcerting scene which follows, Massai attempts to abandon her in the mountains, beating her brutally with a stick and throwing away her moccasins to prevent her from following him. The subsequent sight of Nalinle, however, bloodied and supine in the dust behind him, reawakens in Massai, for the first time since the beginning of his one-man revolution, the spirit of genuine human sympathy. The two embrace, and though Massai believes that there is "no place in my life for love" and that "all men are my enemies who will someday kill me," he accepts the logic of Nalinle's consolation that the two, then, "will live until someday." The structure of *Apache* is thus predicated on the pattern of Massai's redemption, or, more precisely, his humanization. Although he still regards himself as the last fighting Apache, Massai recognizes the folly of continued guerrilla warfare against an invincible enemy. He eschews the romantic ideal of detachment and accepts the more fallible and vulnerable life of an ordinary mortal—marriage to Nalinle and fatherhood to the "little Massai." What began as a saga of resistance, rebellion, and death becomes, in effect, a tale of corn and compromise.

The corn for their mountain home is Nalinle's, stolen from a settlement supply store; the compromise is Massai's. Wearing white man's clothing, harnessed in a primitive plow and cutting long furrows in the sloping hillside, Massai becomes the farmer who can only dream of the warrior's death. The life of domestication Massai has chosen is certainly less glamorous—and perhaps less satisfying—than the business of killing U.S. cavalrymen, but it is, nonetheless, appealing and attractive in its own way. Until the "someday" of his death arrives, Massai appears to be content and serene with the accommodation and acclimation to life required of him by his self-proclaimed marriage to Nalinle and the imminent birth of their first child. Their life together is hardly ideal and surely not the realization of an agrarian dream, but Aldrich's attention to the positive elements therein indicates that he finds Massai's compromise at least momentarily acceptable, since it allows the warrior to retain his sense of personal dignity and self-esteem within the context of his marriage. In his willingness to accept responsibility for his own actions and for the lives of other human beings, Massai demonstrates a maturity and wisdom which differ substantially from the romanticized, solipsistic, almost childlike impulses which guided his earlier vendetta. This growth and maturation is admirable, and it confirms the validity of the *life* Massai has elected to lead, his longing to die a warrior's death notwithstanding.

Massai's day of reckoning with the white man—*Apache*'s final scene—arrives when the Indian scout Sieber (John McIntire) and his soldiers discover the location of the remote mountain hideaway. Acknowledging to Nalinle that "someday has come," Massai initially reacts with diffidence: "Only a warrior chooses his place to die. I am no longer a warrior." It is Nalinle, already in advanced stages of childbirth, speaking without regard for her future well-being, who reminds Massai of the imperishability of his dream: "Die the warrior's death you've always wanted. Don't let Sieber cheat you out of it again." In a shot reminiscent of *Apache*'s first scene, a shot which neatly completes the film's symmetrical structure, Massai, stripped of the white man's apparel, charges his enemies head-on, bounding and leaping as if free at last of all constraints, even those of gravity. But it is an illusion. The warrior fights his way to the protective cover of the cornfield, now tightly en-

John McIntire and Burt Lancaster have their final confrontation in *Apache*.
Used by permission of the Museum of Modern Art/Film Stills Archive,
courtesy of United Artists.

circled by dozens of heavily-armed soldiers, the futility of his attack and
the impossibility of his escape underscored by Aldrich's long shot of the
scene. The trap once more closes. Ironically, the corn which "spoke"
to Massai of life has furnished, ostensibly, the setting for his death. But
at that instant when Massai and Sieber, his long-time adversary, come
together in final hand-to-hand combat, a sound is heard—the unmistakable wail of a baby. Massai stands suddenly erect; Sieber orders
his men to hold their fire. And as Massai walks slowly to the shack hiding
his wife and newborn child, Sieber engages in some wishful—and

wistful—thinking: "He planted corn and made it grow. I wish the Bucks on the reservation could see this." But his thoughts are nostalgic as well, for the end of the battle marks the end of an era, the cessation of hostilities which have given his life meaning: "It's the only war we had and we ain't likely to find another." In an extreme long, high-angle aerial shot, Aldrich withdraws the camera from the final scene of *Apache*. Massai is apparently left to live out his life with Nalinle, but at what price?

In his review of the film, *Time's* critic wrote mockingly of this unlikely resolution: "When the Army scouts find them, Massai, Nalinle and their brand-new papoose prove too homey a family to break up, so Massai goes free. How the scouts straighten out this arbitrary law enforcement with headquarters will have to wait for the sequel, to be titled, no doubt, *Son of Apache*."[6] Aldrich himself, as indicated earlier, shared the doubts expressed by the critic. "I felt he could not possibly be re-accepted or survive, for progress had passed him by. I respected his audacity, courage and dedication, but the world no longer had a place for his kind."[7] But even with the altered ending, *Apache* is still quite honest in its tragic account of the Indian's dilemma: the disgusting racist attitudes that would suppress or exterminate him, the tough compromises demanded of him for cultural assimilation, the painful education and the growth toward maturity which cause him to regard a life of responsible fatherhood as preferable to the brave but ultimately pointless death called for by tribal tradition. By returning alive to his wife and child, Massai expresses an integrity which, though different in kind from that practiced by his ancestors, is conditioned and guided by its own new principles of honor, courage, and heroism. And yet, even with these changes, Massai is probably doomed. The French critic Roger Tailleur has pointed out that in those scenes in which Massai is "free," there is a pervading sense of claustrophobia caused by Aldrich's structuring of the scenes. Massai is often physically enclosed or overshadowed by his surroundings. For Tailleur, the film illustrates the death of liberty; even Massai's marriage is finally seen as a form of imprisonment.[8] This pessimism was shared by Burt Lancaster. "Here was an Indian who tried to get along but couldn't. We wanted to show that there was no hope for him. The white man didn't want him. 'Let him drink and stay by himself,' they said. There was no hope for him."

Apache may not have meant what Aldrich intended it to mean (indeed, eighteen years later, Aldrich would return to these same problems and offer very different conclusions in *Ulzana's Raid*), but it remains a tough, serious, and important film nonetheless.

Vera Cruz (1954)

"We immediately went from *Apache* into *Vera Cruz*," Burt Lancaster remembered. *Vera Cruz* was a high-spirited western which teamed Lancaster with Gary Cooper. Made in Superscope (a technique Aldrich hated) and Technicolor, set at a budget of $3 million, and filmed at the relatively leisurely pace of two and a half months, it was Aldrich's first big film, an adventure-drama done on a grand scale. The film proved to be a good test of the director's organizational abilities. It was shot on location in Cuernavaca, near Mexico City, the weather in Vera Cruz itself being judged too unpredictable. With James Hill as producer and Ernest Laszlo as cameraman, Aldrich brought a cast and crew of 100 people, a stable of 50 horses, and equipment including 25,000 rounds of live ammunition (to supplement the inadequate supply of blanks) into the heat and dust of the Mexican valley. There they hired another 200 locals to work on the set. The weather was oppressive, and some of the crew came down with sun poisoning. The Spanish actress Sarita Montiel, who played one of the chief roles, had to learn enough English to deliver her lines and had to adapt her acting style to the demands of the American filmmaker. As she told a reporter from the *New York Times* who was visiting the set, "We are used to being very dramatic. You act quietly. Mr. Aldrich says smile, so I smile. 'Not so much,' he cries at me, 'they'll see you in the back row. Easy.' "[9] There were also rumors of an actual bandit on the loose in the area, and one of the film bandits, Charles Horvath, was mistaken for the desperado and arrested by the local militia.

In addition to these annoyances was a much larger problem. Borden Chase had written a first draft of the script, which was then reworked by James R. Webb and Roland Kibbee, but as Lancaster recalled, "We had half a script to go on. The writing was still going on during the shooting." Aldrich also remembered that the making of the film was as loose and spontaneous as the action it narrates: "*Vera Cruz* was total improvisation because the script was always finished about five minutes before we shot it, and we'd sit right down and work it out and then shoot it as we went along. I'm not sure that that's the right way to work."[10] Indeed, the experience was very trying to Aldrich, who much preferred to plan his films rigorously before shooting ever began, who needed rehearsals to work through a scene or to develop a sense of character. The freewheeling manner in which the film was made, however, actually contributed to its success. The pervasive sense of spontaneity, together with the playful, ironic mood which associates with it, was more an asset than a liability, accounting in large part for *Vera Cruz*'s lasting appeal and making it, in the mid-to-late 1950s, one of the top grossing films of all times. Andrew Sarris, for example, has praised the film's "elegant escapism,"[11] and Richard Combs has noted Aldrich's "general delight in taking the [western] genre into new territory."[12] The film was yet another example of Aldrich's ability to take an unconventional and un-formulaic approach to the formula film, to use the dictates of the filming to enhance the film.

Vera Cruz is the story of two American mercenaries, Ben Trane (Gary Cooper) and Joe Erin (Burt Lancaster), seeking their fortunes in Mex-ico in 1866. Trane is a loner, a taciturn, expatriated, ex-Confederate soldier made cynical by the war. Erin is an unmannered, garrulous thug, leader of one of the nastiest bunch of outlaws put on the screen, among them Ernest Borgnine, Charles Bronson [Buchinsky], and Jack Elam.[13] Together Trane and Erin form an unlikely alliance in their attempt to transport (and eventually obtain) $50,000 in gold belonging to the Emperor Max-imillian, gold which is also wanted by the peasant revolutionaries who are fighting against the emperor (George Macready). Accompanying them on their journey to the port of Vera Cruz is Erin's gang, a French mar-quis (Cesar Romero), and a mysterious and duplicitous French woman (Denise Darcel). Along the way they are constantly attacked or harrassed by the Juarestes and their sympathizers, including Niña (Sarita Mon-tiel), a lovely but dangerous rebel. Trane and Erin prove to be strange partners in this project, and much of the film's comic appeal derives from the irreconcilable and irremediable differences in their personalities.

On the one hand, then, *Vera Cruz* is a wonderful big-screen adven-ture, a consistently exciting film, which anticipates, both in story and characters, Sam Peckinpah's more serious, violent, and elegiac western *The Wild Bunch* (1969), as Aldrich himself later recognized.[14] At the same time, however, Aldrich plays so fast and loose with the themes of duplici-ty and doublecross that the cumulative effect is one almost of parody: the film becomes an endlessly inventive game of one-upmanship. There are exaggerations, improbabilities, implausibilities, reversals, and varia-tions throughout. In the process, the motif of the double-cross occurs with such mind-boggling regularity that Francois Truffaut discussed the structure of the film in terms of the double-cross theme, pointing out that numerous scenes duplicate previous ones, but always with a twist.[15] As Pierre Sauvage has written of the film, "Historically, it is one of the very first Westerns to substitute a largely cynical, amoral

Ernest Borgnine, Burt Lancaster, and Gary Cooper reach the city gates in *Vera Cruz*. Used by permission of the Museum of Modern Art/Film Stills Archive, courtesy of United Artists.

attitude for the Manichaean moralism that had characterized the genre. The film has two heroes, neither of them a 'good' guy, or even a 'good/bad guy' in the traditional sense of the phrase. Both are larcenous and different only in the extremes to which they are prepared to go get what they want."[16]

Although Sauvage's basic thesis is correct, he overstates the case in terms of what the film actually shows us. In the end, it *is* Ben Trane who wins the girl and the gold, which he, as a former rebel himself, gives to the revolutionary cause. But letting the decent Gary Cooper character emerge triumphant from his final confrontation with the villainous Burt Lancaster character is perhaps the only convention Aldrich does not deliberately violate. According to Lancaster, this sticking to the code of the western was largely due to Gary Cooper's insistence. As Lancaster remembered, Cooper was uneasy during much of the filming. "Cooper prided himself on representing certain values. He was very decent, a man of high morality. He represented the hero—all-American. He didn't want his character to be identified with the heavy. If his character appeared to be a man of evil, he would object, and we would have to rewrite the script." Nevertheless, Aldrich treats the final gunfight itself in an unconventional manner, typical of *Vera Cruz*'s tongue-in-cheek approach to iconography. After facing off for their showdown, Trane and Erin draw and fire simultaneously. Erin twirls and reholsters his pistol, still cocky, apparently unwounded. For a moment, in fact, both men stand stiff and immobile, neither appearing to have been hit, until Erin suddenly falls dead to the ground, flat on his smiling face. Thus, though the resolution of conflict is predictable, Aldrich's style and methodology in the film remain playfully unorthodox to the very end.

Beneath all the play, however, *Vera Cruz* tells us a great deal about Aldrich's developing concerns. Truffaut spoke of the film as an "intellectual" western.[17] Ben Trane and Joe Erin are two characters who represent and embody radically different philosophies of life which, despite the film's spirited nonsense, lend themselves to serious thematic investigation. It was this relationship which Aldrich himself cited when explaining his own personal fondness for the film: "I liked this one, and it again had a hero and an anti-hero, with the hero surviving only after choosing a rightful battle and destroying the anti-hero, whom he admired in spite of their disparate credos."[18] Joe Erin is a solitary. He trusts no one; although he is leader of a gang, he has no friends. In this way, as Roger Tailleur has noted, Erin resembles the warrior Massai, although Massai lives according to a code of honor and Erin is directed only by self-interest.

Nonetheless, Erin, like Massai, should die: he cannot adapt to the changing world. Ben Trane, on the other hand, *can* be converted, within the limits of his healthy skepticism. He is brought back to a sense of duty and responsibility by his love for Niña (again like Massai). There is for him the possibility of change. Or it may be that Trane never really lost this honor, that he has simply taken on a false cynicism which hides his essential hopefulness. It is, in Tailleur's words, not so much a question of choosing a partner as choosing an ethic—either "rougery and duplicity" or "sincerity and love."[19] Trane chooses (within his limits) the latter.

But *Vera Cruz* takes the idea of respect and affection between opposing figures one step further: the film becomes, in effect, an extended meditation on the risks of "liking people." Joe Erin's attitudes toward life are shaped primarily by his mentor, a surrogate father named Ace Hannah, who, though dead before the action of the film begins, continues to exert a profound influence on Erin's behavior. After killing Erin's father during a poker game, Ace adopts the young orphan, presumably the only gesture of kindness and compassion in his life. It was, Erin explains, a fatal error in judgment: "Ace used to say, 'Don't take any chances you don't hafta take, don't trust anybody you don't hafta trust, and don't do no favors you don't hafta do.' Ace lived long enough to know he was right—he lived thirty seconds after I shot him." Joe Erin kills his surrogate father, Ace Hannah, not out of understandable revenge for his real father's murder—indeed, Erin remembers Ace with real fondness—but apparently for some quasi-Oedipal need to remove a rival, to take his place as leader of the gang. When the older Ben Trane (another version of Ace Hannah) becomes Erin's partner, it is only a matter of time before Erin must likewise try to kill him, despite the fact that each, on different occasions, has saved the other's life. Erin senses a "softness" in Ben Trane that he also found in Ace: "Colonel Ben is a real Southern Gentleman. He likes people, and you can't count on a man like that." And Trane does like people—the Mexican rebels, the corrupt Countess, dangerous Joe Erin— in spite of himself. He kills Joe out of a sense of duty, complicated by the fact that he has affection for the younger man. He has come once more to think that "a man needs something to believe in . . . something more than money." He kills Joe, the rebellious child, to restore order, the father chastising the son. It is the kind of combative relationship between "parent" and "child" that Aldrich would explore in greater detail in later films.

Trane thus fights and wins the "rightful battle" (to use Aldrich's phrase), and there is, at the end of *Vera Cruz*, a fleeting sense of goodness having prevailed, of the right ethic followed. But the lingering impression from the film is somewhat different, for, despite the overall humor of the work, what remains is a disturbing awareness of the pervasiveness of evil and deceit in the world. *Vera Cruz* makes so convincing a case for the ubiquitousness of villainy that its final resolution rings hollow, and one is left rather more skeptical than convinced by the film's outcome, the final joke in Aldrich's bag of tricks.[20]

Vera Cruz ended Aldrich's relationship with Hecht-Lancaster. He wanted more control over his work in the future, which he could not have with the Hecht-Lancaster company. Moreover, although he had enjoyed working with Lancaster on *Apache*, he felt that in making the second film they had had "a less amicable relationship than we anticipated. This was because Burt, until he directed *The Kentuckian*, thought he was going to be a director, and when you're directing your first great big picture you don't welcome somebody else on hand with directorial notions."[21] In Lancaster's words, "We had our arguments. He was very, very stubborn in many ways. It was hard to dissuade him. In a way that was very good when he tried to do things outside of the conventional. An Aldrich film had to be an Aldrich film." Lancaster and Aldrich would not work together for another eighteen years, but they remained good, though not close, friends, each admiring the other for his strengths, passions, and beliefs.

Kiss Me Deadly (1955)

Following the filming of *Vera Cruz*, Aldrich was contacted by Victor Saville, who owned the film rights to the works of Mickey Spillane. Saville wanted Aldrich to direct a film version of Spillane's 1952 novel *Kiss Me, Deadly*, the seventh in his series of Mike Hammer detective books. Two movies had already been made of other Spillane-Hammer thrillers, but neither Saville nor Aldrich thought much of them. As Aldrich recalled, he agreed to do the job for Saville "provided he would let me make the kind of movie I wanted and provided I could produce it."[22] Saville consented and, according to Aldrich, gave him the freedom he had demanded. Although Saville was listed as executive producer in the credits, Aldrich, as both producer and director, had ultimate control of the project.

In comparison to *Apache* and *Vera Cruz*, *Kiss Me Deadly* might have seemed something of a comedown for Aldrich. It was filmed in twenty-one days on a limited budget of $425,000 and used no "name" actors at all. Moreover, although Spillane was at that time one of the best-selling authors in the world, his work was judged, at best, as sensationalistic. The exploits of his private investigator Mike Hammer were notorious for their extreme violence and sexual explicitness. Because of his profession, Hammer could, of course, be seen in the tradition of the hard-boiled detective hero, the solitary crusaders of Dashiell Hammett and Raymond Chandler. But Hammer lacked the razor-sharp, unsentimental morality of Hammett's characters and the quixotic romanticism of Philip Marlow. Spillane's Hammer was, instead, a violent, brutal avenger, the hero as psychotic, who employed a very personal brand of justice to excuse his essentially sadistic nature. Indeed, as Hammer smashed his way through the mysteries, his tactics were often more appalling, his kill ratio much higher, than those of the so-called villains.

Aldrich had no sympathy for either the book or its hero. Hammer he saw as a "cynical and fascistic private eye" and viewed him with "utter contempt and loathing."[23] He told Francois Truffaut that both Hammer and Spillane represented an "anti-democratic spirit."[24] What did attract him, besides the chance to shape his own work, to act as an independent, was his recognition that Mike Hammer, in his self-righteousness and brutal pragmatism, acted as a paradigm for the witch-hunting America of the 1950s. Hammer was McCarthyism carried to its logical and not-so-far removed extreme. Without overemphasizing the point, Aldrich meant the film to make a political statement: "It did have a basic significance in *our* political framework that we thought rather important in those McCarthy times: that the ends did not justify the means."[25] As he argued before the Motion Picture Association of America (MPAA) Code Administration, he intended Hammer to be seen as an anti-hero and for the film to imply that "justice is not to be found in a self-anointed, one-man vigilante."[26] Years later, Aldrich said of the film's reception that "most people in America put it down as a Spillane movie done with a little more energy, a little more compression . . . they didn't understand at all the political implications."[27]

And yet Aldrich seemed to court the controversy that surrounded the film and caused it to be seen as another exploitation of violence and sex. In the February 20, 1955 edition of the *New York Herald Tribune*, for example, an article by Aldrich appeared entitled "You Can't Hang Up the Meat Hook." In this article Aldrich defended the portrayal of violence in his films. (*Vera Cruz* had been attacked by Bosley Crowther in his *New York Times* review as "a pretty atrocious film, loaded with meaningless violence and standard horse opera clichés. There are not many ways of hurting people that are missed in this sadistic show . . . As a matter of fact, the whole picture appears to be designed as a mere exhibition of how wicked and vicious men can be."[28] Aldrich argued that violence was an essential element of all literature and art, and that "such phases of human behavior can be neither ignored nor removed from any true pictorial account of the emotions of two-legged animals." He went on to describe a specific scene in *Kiss Me Deadly* in which a girl is tortured to death. He wrote of it in terms that would later be used to describe Alfred Hitchcock's shower scene in *Psycho*:

> The camera focuses first on the helpless girl and her antagonists. The situation leading up to this moment of torture is well established and is a logical development of the plot. Hands are then laid on the victim, and from that moment on the suspense is maintained, the violence high-keyed and the horror spotlighted through the sound effects, focusing the camera in a series of close shots, on her feet, her hands, shadows on the wall and similar devices.[29]

He concluded that "60 per cent" of what people perceived in this scene "will be the product of their own thinking." Nonetheless (although Aldrich's description of the scene is accurate), such a statement, headed by such a provocative title, was a direct challenge to all arbiters of public taste and morality, and he was quickly answered by the editors of *America: The National Catholic Weekly Review*, who observed that Aldrich's argument "springs . . . from subhuman thinking. It defends depravity, tries to justify morbidity and totally misrepresents the record of human violence as portrayed, without being glamorized, in great literature."[30]

Aldrich certainly never confused Spillane's story with great literature. "The original book . . . had nothing," he claimed. "We just took the title and threw the book away."[31] This boast was not absolutely true. Some of the film's central images and situations can be found in Spillane's work, and most of the names are retained, although the characters to whom they are given usually have little in common with the book's originals. But certainly the screenplay by A.I. Bezzerides (with contributions by Aldrich) made no effort to follow the book's convoluted plot. Both book and film are structured around Hammer's search for a mysterious box. His quest is further inspired by a desire for personal revenge. The film begins as Hammer (Ralph Meeker), driving his sporty Jaguar toward Los Angeles (a shift from the book's New York setting for financial as well as artistic reasons: Aldrich wanted to do location work for realism, and many of the scenes were filmed at night in Los Angeles, including scenes at the Club Regalle[32]) almost runs over a near-hysterical woman (Cloris Leachman) standing in the middle of the highway, her arms held out in a crucified position in a desperate effort to flag him down.[33] Although Hammer is angry, he agrees to give her a ride, more out of curiosity than gallantry, for the woman is barefoot and wears nothing under her trench-coat. She tells him that her name is Christina (another change from the book but an important one, for it links her with Christina Rossetti, as she carefully points out to Hammer, and sets up a clue to the mystery of the box). Despite her obvious fear, Christina is a gutsy woman. She answers Hammer's questions obliquely but with spunk and finally tells him that, should anything happen, he must "remember me." Shortly thereafter, they are waylaid and Hammer is beaten unconscious, although he does come to long enough to witness Christina's last moments as she is tortured to death and to hear the melodious but unfeeling voice of her murderer. Hammer is later placed in his car and pushed over a cliff but is thrown free before the Jaguar bursts into flames. After remaining unconscious for three days (another of several references to death and resurrection in the film), he is welcomed back "among the living" by his secretary Velda (Maxine Cooper) and a police detective Pat Murphy (Wesley Addy).

After this introduction, which more or less follows the first chapter of the book, Bezzerides and Aldrich play fast and loose with Spillane. The film evidences a masterful inventiveness, an adventurous creativity, which uses the book as its springboard. One essential difference between the book and film is in the film's sly reinterpretation of Mike Hammer. As portrayed by Ralph Meeker, Hammer seems an arrogant, sneering brute, an overbearing bully. Meeker's slight chubbiness, his softness around the face and belly, play against our romantic image of the private investigator: his Hammer is a sleazy second-rater. What the conversation between Hammer and Christina in the opening scene does is to establish Hammer's self-image and to undercut it at the same time. When she apologizes for almost wrecking his Jaguar, she refers to it as his "pretty little car," emphasizing the importance of appearance to Hammer while also mocking it. Later she says to him, "You're one of those males who thinks about nothing but his clothes, his car, himself. . . . You're the kind who never gives in a relationship, who only takes."

This unfavorable view of Hammer is reinforced after Hammer is released from the hospital. We learn that he specializes in divorce cases

Ralph Meeker captured by gunmen Jack Lambert and Jack Elam in *Kiss Me Deadly*. Used by permission of the Museum of Modern Art/Film Stills Archive, courtesy of United Artists.

(again unlike Spillane's hero) and uses his secretary Velda in the process: she sets up the husband, he romances the wife, and they play both against the middle. "I'm a real stinker," Hammer sarcastically admits when confronted with these and other accusations, and we have to acknowledge the truth of the statement. Aldrich later expressed how much pleasure he took in subverting the standard image of Hammer. "Spillane, you know, never understood that this was the greatest Spillane put-down in a long time. He just thought that it was a marvelous picture."[34]

And yet, for all this, and against Aldrich's intentions, Hammer does become a somewhat sympathetic figure, due, in part, to his being such an obvious fraud. In Spillane's book, Hammer is found impossibly attractive by every woman he meets, but he coolly puts them off with a kiss, a wink, or a promise: his chastity becomes evidence of his male superiority—the women will be there when *he* wants *them*. In the film, Aldrich suggests that Hammer is avoiding rather than delaying the sexual encounters, that indeed he is either uninterested in women and sex or he fears them. For Aldrich and Bezzerides, Hammer's sexual escapes become a running joke. When he first meets Christina's roommate Lily Carver (Gaby Rogers), the camera angle makes her gun appear aimed directly at his crotch. They also underscore Christina's initial appraisal of Hammer by emphasizing his essential isolation. His apartment is plastic, womb-like. He avoids windows and channels his phone calls through an automatic answering machine which allows him to talk only when he so chooses. As others have noted, Hammer rarely looks *at* people and tends instead to stare off into space or at blank walls. One of the triumphs of Ralph Meeker's performance is that he shows the emptiness inside Hammer, his dead soul. One of the film's sharpest ironies thus is its emphasis on resurrection: Hammer comes "back from the grave" at least three times, but he is never really alive in any emotional sense. The only time he expresses any real feelings is when he inflicts pain on others.

To Aldrich, Hammer is simply a loser. For all of his surface arrogance, he is clearly in over his head. Still, in the film we are encouraged to think that Hammer is one step ahead of the police in his search for the box. After all, he does have Christina's clue: "Remember me." This clue is a reference to the Christina Rossetti sonnet "Remember," with its lines:

Remember me when I am gone away,
  Gone far away into the silent land;
  When you can no more hold me by the hand,
Nor I half turn to go yet turning stay.
  . . . .
Yet if you should forget me for a while
  And afterwards remember, do not grieve:
  For if the darkness and corruption leave
A vestige of the thoughts that once I had,
Better by far you should forget and smile
Than that you should remember and be sad.[35]

These lines lead Hammer, in a bizarre and unlikely manner, to the morgue holding Christina's body, in whose stomach the coroner has found a key. This key opens a locker at a local health club, in which Hammer discovers the box itself. Thus the film is predicated on a series of boxes within boxes (or bodies), with the last containing the biggest surprise of all, the greatest corruption of all. Hammer's misunderstanding of what the box contains ultimately brings about catastrophe. "You penny-ante gumshoe," Pat tells Hammer in disgust. "You thought you were so bright. You saw something big and tried to horn in." "I didn't know," Mike alibies. "You didn't know," Pat sneers. "Do you think you'd have done any different if you had known?" The unspoken answer is clear.

In Spillane's book, the black box holds rather prosaic contents: Mafia drugs. Bezzerides and Aldrich impart a symbolic and mythic depth to the box until it becomes the central image—almost an icon—in the film.[36] What the authorities already know—and what Hammer slowly discovers—is that this box contains some undefined radioactive substance, some power which, once released, will escalate in destructiveness. Pat Murphy relates its contents to the "Manhattan Project—Los Alamos—Trinity"; the villain Dr. Soborin (Albert Dekker) puts it in a more metaphysical perspective: it is the box of Pandora, it holds the "head of Medusa," it contains *evil* itself. When Hammer first finds the box, it burns his hands, a clear warning of its destructive powers. When the girl known as Lily Carver (by now revealed to be Carver's mentally-unstable roommate Gabrielle, who has, in fact, killed the real Carver) opens the box despite Soborin's dying warnings, she lets loose all the forces of hell. Her real name thus becomes all the more appropriate—she is Gabriel, wreaking final destruction. But she is also Pandora, controlled by curiosity and greed. The film ends abruptly as the box's fury continues to grow; the conflagration rises as the beach house where all this action occurs is engulfed by flames. Moreover, the film indicates that this destruction is only the beginning. As *The End* appears over the multiplying explosions, the words take on a prophetic double-meaning. It is, in every sense, an apocalyptic conclusion.[37]

When Aldrich was interviewed in 1956 by Francois Truffaut, he expressed some reservations about *Kiss Me Deadly*, saying that he should have refused to do the film.[38] This defensive manner was partly in reaction to what he saw as excessive French praise over the film. "I'd like to say that I thought of all the things the French say are in the picture," he later commented, "but it's not true. It was the first year of *Cahiers* and those guys jumped on that picture like it was the Second Coming." And yet, as he also recognized, "I had a career due to the European reaction to *Kiss Me Deadly*."[39] In fact, *Kiss Me Deadly* became a milestone in Aldrich's career. "I was very proud of the film," Aldrich remembered. "I think it represented a whole breakthrough for me. In terms of style, in terms of the way we tried to make it, it provided a marvellous showcase to display my own ideas of movie-making. In that sense it was an enor-

mous 'first' for me."[40] The style was that of a B movie made with an A
sensibility. Its black-and-white, small-screen images were in marked
contrast to the scope and sweep of *Vera Cruz*, but they were exactly appropriate for this tale of corruption. "We tried to have a very obvious
stylised impact of energy," Aldrich said. ". . . you had a chance to
establish a very graphic, hard-hitting, short-cut, staccato kind of style. . . .
That wasn't brand new but it was new for that kind of film."[41] Aldrich
credited Michael Luciano's editing for achieving much of this impact:
"Basically that picture was a refinement of Mike's assembly," he later
said.[42] Luciano recalled that they "fought like hell" but went for a "rough
and tough rhythm" and "fast sequencing."[43] In the end, *Kiss Me Deadly*
becomes *film noir* at its most paranoid. The camera shifts, cranes, hides,
and scurries—a creature of the night peering into and out of shadows
in a world which, the film suggests, perhaps *deserves* the cleansing purga-
tion of the Bomb.

Of course neither the film's seriousness nor wit was noticed at the
time of its release. When *Kiss Me Deadly* was finished and presented
to the Code Administration of the MPAA, the administration felt that
the film was justifying Hammer's actions. After Aldrich argued that he
intended no such meaning, the film did receive the administration's Seal
of Approval. Shortly before the film's release, however, Aldrich encountered opposition from the Catholic Church's Legion of Decency,
which proposed a "Condemned" rating for the film. Aldrich protested
that "there certainly could not be this wide divergence between the opinion of the Legion and that of the Code Administration. The Legion has
even failed to recognize any voice of moral righteousness."[44] When the
Legion still rejected Aldrich's argument, United Artists, the distributors,
made the cuts demanded by the Legion against Aldrich's wishes. Even
then the film received only a "B" rating, which meant that it was "morally objectionable in part for all."

Upon its release *Kiss Me Deadly* was paid almost no critical attention in America, but it quickly developed a reputation among French
film enthusiasts. Writing in *Cahiers du Cinema*, Charles Bitsch called the work "one of the most striking American films of the last ten
years" and compared it favorably to Orson Welles's *The Lady From
Shanghai*.[45] Claude Chabrol praised the way Aldrich had taken "the worst
material he was able to find," maintained all the traditional elements
and devices of the detective novel, and still, beneath the surface, confronted the serious questions of the Atomic Age.[46] The young Francois
Truffaut more or less summed up their attitude:

Gaby Rogers opens Pandora's Box in *Kiss Me Deadly*. Used by permission of the Museum of Modern Art/Film Stills Archive, courtesy of United Artists.

To appreciate *Kiss Me Deadly*, you have to love movies passionately. In Aldrich's films, it is not unusual to encounter a new idea with each shot. In his movie the inventiveness is so rich that we don't know what to look at—the images are almost too full, too fertile. Watching a film like this is such an intense experience that we want it to last for hours. It is easy to picture its author as a man overflowing with vitality, as much at ease behind a camera as Henry Miller facing a blank page. This is the film of a young director who is not yet worrying about restraint.[47]

Over the years, the film has done more than delight its viewers; it has gained a solid reputation as one of the finest American films of the 1950s. Paul Schrader, in his 1972 article "Notes on *Film Noir*," calls *Kiss Me Deadly* the "masterpiece" of that genre and observes that Aldrich "carries *noir* to its sleaziest and most perversely erotic."[48] Pierre Sauvage compares it to Welles's *Touch of Evil* in its willingness to confront the corruption of the world.[49] Indeed, some critics are inclined to see it as Aldrich's finest work, although to do so one must overlook the more mature, and, ultimately, more demanding films of the 1970s.

Kiss Me Deadly is still an influential film. One might compare Aldrich's Hammer to J.J. Gittes (Jack Nicholson) in Roman Polanski's *Chinatown* (1974). Gittes is also a divorce specialist who is never as smart as he thinks and whose ignorance results in final tragedy. The mysterious and deadly box was resurrected in Steven Speilberg's *Raiders of the Lost Ark* (1981). Although the special effects employed when the ark is opened are more sophisticated, they are not necessarily more frightening than the sight and sound of Lily Carver/Gabrielle screaming as she is consumed by the hissing and shrieking flames which shoot out of the box. (Aldrich explained that the sound was created through a combination of an airplane exhaust, loud breathing, and a blow torch, which resulted in a kind of unearthly chanting. The ghosts from the ark make much the same sound.) The film's apocalyptic ending, which is both funny and horrifying, anticipates the similar shock one feels at the end of Stanley Kubrick's *Dr. Strangelove* (1964), another meditation on the end of the world. There are echoes of the film in Aldrich's later works as well: the final destruction in *Sodom and Gomorrah*, for example, or the overall sense of moral perversity found in *The Grissom Gang* and *Hustle*. *Kiss Me Deadly* remains a film which does not date—after twenty-five years it is still a richly imaginative, quirky, and darkly funny work.

The Big Knife (1955)

The commercial success of *Kiss Me Deadly*, although modest, allowed Aldrich the means and power to form his own production company, The Associates and Aldrich, in 1955. Aldrich planned for the company to produce ideally five films a year, two at an average budget which Aldrich would direct, and three at a smaller budget which he would give to new, upcoming directors in whom he had confidence.[50] Over the next seventeen years, however, The Associates and Aldrich would produce only twelve films, made independently of the major studios although distributed by them. The choice for the company's first film was, in some ways, a declaration of its independence. It was a film adaptation of Clifford Odets' 1949 play *The Big Knife*, which had run on Broadway starring John Garfield in the role of a once-gifted actor now turned a disillusioned, alcoholic Hollywood star (a role which Odets apparently based, in part, on Garfield himself). The play was an indictment of the film industry, a tearing down of the glitter and glamour which still surrounded the movie business in the 1950s. *The Big Knife* was not a film likely to be made by the studios and studio heads which it attacked, both directly and by implication, but it provided just the sort of challenge—and just the kind of controversy—which Aldrich relished. It was, in fact, a film Aldrich had wanted to do for some time. He originally pictured Burt Lancaster in the role of Charlie Castle, but Lancaster was not interested, and Aldrich, remembering his disagreements with the actor on the set of *Vera Cruz*, declined to press the matter.[51] Thus, the role went to Jack Palance, who would be the leading man in three Aldrich films.

Odets' play was adapted to the screen by James Poe, and his screenplay followed Odets' work rather closely. Both play and film tell of the last two days in the life of Charlie Castle, nee Cass (Jack Palance), a film star who has tired of making "lousy, lousy films" and is now resisting signing a new seven-year contract with Stanley Hoff (Rod Steiger), the dictatorial studio chief. Charlie has come to recognize the artificiality of his life, the disgrace of his betrayed talents, and his urgent need for spiritual and artistic redemption. In this desire he is encouraged by his wife Marion (Ida Lupino), who has, in effect, delivered an ultimatum to him: to sign a new contract is to lose her forever. Charlie is determined to resist Hoff's enticements, but when Hoff's pleadings and histrionics fail, the studio chief threatens Charlie with scandal and ruin. Several years earlier Hoff had covered up for Charlie when, drunk and accompanied by a young starlet Dixie Evans (Shelley Winters), Charlie had killed a child in a hit-and-run accident. Hoff arranged, through his aide Smiley Coy (Wendell Corey), for Charlie's friend and associate Buddy Bliss (Paul Langton) to take the blame, even though it involved a prison term. Faced with the possibility of this revelation, Charlie capitulates and signs, while recognizing the complete ignominy of his action.

When Charlie admits to Marion that he has once again failed, she feels betrayed and plans to leave town with Hank Teagle (Wesley Addy), a writer and old friend of both Castles. Charlie, now drinking heavily, continues his self-abasement by engaging in an almost sado-masochistic liaison with Connie Bliss (Jean Hagen), Buddy's wife, a vamp who toys with a backscratcher throughout the film and who believes in "secret sins and locked doors and doing the wildest things that come into my mind." But Charlie still retains some vestiges of honor. Smiley Coy tries to enlist his help in handling Dixie Evans, who is fed up with Hoff and the studio and is now threatening to tell all she knows about Charlie and the accident. Coy suggests, apparently without Hoff's knowledge, that murder is the answer. At this point, Charlie balks, turns to Marion for support, and confronts Hoff, Coy, and the whole system. "You threw away your kingdom today," a furiously sputtering Hoff shouts, and for a moment Charlie is allowed a sense of victory. But it is all too late, and Castle's kingdom does indeed collapse about his head: Dixie, drunk, is killed by a city bus, a parallel to the earlier accident in which she was involved; Buddy discovers that Charlie has betrayed him with his wife and spits in his face; and Charlie finally knows that he has fallen too far, has waited too long, to rid himself of the corruption which has eaten at him. "Marion," he says to his wife as he walks up a set of spiraling stairs, "I pledge you a better future." He then commits suicide, leaving Marion alone, crying for Charlie and for herself, as Smiley Coy issues a press release stating that Castle, world-famous star, has died of a heart attack.

Over the years *The Big Knife* has developed a cult following. Some admire the film for the courage it displays as an anti-Hollywood film; others take an almost campish delight in the melodrama of the story and the extravagance of the acting. More serious Aldrich critics see the film, along with *Kiss Me Deadly* and *Attack!*, as Aldrich's early trilogy in which he firmly established the themes and concerns heretofore only suggested. *The Big Knife* is one of the most effective and biting satires yet made on Hollywood, more so than Odets' play, which today seems too serious and self-satisfied. Aldrich adds the necessary anger and outrageousness to bring the satire off. Odets approved of Aldrich's work. He called it the best film version of any of his plays and declared that it showed "that Hollywood is finally ready to take a responsible place in the community of arts. . . . It represents a milestone . . . in the affairs of a community that has always maintained a clannishness and secrecy about itself and which, despite intramural conflict, has presented generally unified opposition to projects it considered detrimental."[52] As a satire, the film is generally unswerving in its vehemence against Hollywood. Although the film does acknowledge that "this industry is capable of bringing out good pictures—pictures with guts and meaning," the overall view of the business is disparaging. As Aldrich's camera tilts and cranes down from above at the beginning of the film, a voiceover (by Richard Boone) pointedly explains, "This is Bel Air. Lush, luxurious retreat of the wealthy and powerful. If you work in the motion picture industry and are successful, this is where you will probably make your home. Failure is not permitted here." This idea is quickly reinforced by the gossip columnist Patty Benedict (Ilka Chase), who tells Charlie, "I'm in the movie business, darling. I can't afford your acute attacks of integrity." Hollywood names are sprinkled throughout the screenplay (Aldrich wanted Hedda Hopper to play Patty Benedict), and Rod Steiger's performance as Stanley Hoff contains clear allusions to studio boss Harry Cohn (Charlie's agent Nat Danziger [Everett Sloane] says at one point that Hoff gave him "Hail Columbia" in his office, a reference to Cohn's Columbia Studios).

Aldrich, however, had more in mind than an attack on the Hollywood studio system. "I do not feel it is exactly anti-Hollywood, for that would make it too sectional," he said in 1958. "To me it can apply to any sphere of business, or the arts, where man's natural liberty or expression is squelched by unworthy, incompetent, tyrannical leaders or bosses, many of whom are not deserving of their powers."[53] Aldrich later said that Hoff "is [Senator Joseph] McCarthy";[54] but whether Hoff is linked with McCarthy or Cohn or Louis B. Mayer or Jack Warner, he is still a disturbing figure of destructive authority. He is constantly presented in terms of militarism and gangsterism. A drum roll accompanies him on screen: when he finally forces Charlie to sign a new contract, he gives him a pen "used by Douglas MacArthur." Charlie kneels before him to write his name and ruefully says, "I'll keep the pen. It's my only proof the war is over—or ever fought." Moreover, Hoff looks like a Mafia chieftain, a precursor of Brando's Godfather. Steiger masterfully uses his dark glasses as a prop, removing them to express sincerity, replacing them to deliver ultimatums. Through his aide and henchman Smiley Coy, he is capable of—or at least willing to abide—murder to preserve the studio. "I need your body, not your good will," Hoff tells Charlie. It's all business.

It is easy to see why Odets' play—and specifically its hero—attracted Aldrich, for Charlie is yet another variation of the Aldrichian protagonist. Roger Tailleur links him to Ben Trane, caught between the gold and the revolution, but without Trane's maturity or strength of character.[55] But he is also like Joe Erin. Charlie is the child who has failed to grow up, to accept responsibility for his careless actions, as well as the idealist who has betrayed his early dreams and is now wracked by the results of that betrayal. Smiley Coy calls Charlie "the warrior-minstrel of the forelorn hope," and later Hank Teagle refers to him as "half an idealist" and opines, "There's nothing more tortured on the face of this earth." Charlie's old idealism is also linked with liberal politics—he used to believe in the "New Deal, the Fair Deal, or some Deal," according to Patty Benedict, before he became the pawn of the fascism of Hoff and Company.

Aldrich's view of Charlie and his suicide changed over the years, or at least he spoke of the character's gesture from different vantage points. In his 1956 interview with Aldrich, Truffaut suggested that Aldrich's films illustrated the ultimate destruction of basic human values in the "atomic" world (a theme which would run throughout French criticism of Aldrich's films of the 1950s). Aldrich answered that that was but half the problem: "I show heroic characters," he said. "I am against the idea of tragic destiny. Each man must fight even if he is broken. My characters have that 'suicidal' attitude because the voluntary sacrifice of their lives is the height of their moral integrity. Suicide is a gesture of revolt."[56] Yet in 1958 he spoke of Charlie as a "false realist [who] had to be shown up as a guilty, tormented victim for he had made half-concessions." Aldrich went on to explain, "I feel I can think only in whole terms when it comes to the moral climate of my films. The characters have to be completely dedicated to their code of life, be they good or bad. That is why my unswerving heroes usually are killed by a system that is not ready for change, and the half-convinced may die by their own hand."[57] Later, in 1973, Aldrich said that in his opinion Charlie had lost at the end through his suicide:

There's a line in *The Big Knife* where the agent tell[s] the star, "Struggle, Charlie, you may still win a blessing." Well, that's really true. Now the Antonioni school would have you believe that the struggle isn't worth it. Since you are going to lose anyway, why don't you relax and enjoy it? Well, I don't think you can relax and enjoy it. To relax is to say, well, I'm dead already. Why not struggle and maximize the victories. They may not come, probably *won't* come, but they might come, and if they come you're one victory ahead of total defeat.[58]

Whatever our final reading of the film, Charlie is clearly one more Aldrich study of man scrambling for grace.

The Big Knife was Aldrich's first attempt to transfer a stage play to the screen, although he would do so again with *Attack!* and *The Killing of Sister George*. The film retained the basic three-act structure, each act ending with Charlie's going up the spiral staircase—once with Connie Bliss, once with Marion, and finally alone, to commit suicide. With the exception of the opening shot and a later shot on the beach, the entire film takes place indoors, largely in Charlie's house. (As Michael Luciano remembered, much of the film was shot inside an actual house, which caused many problems in filming and editing.[59]) Rather than attempt to open up the play, Aldrich tended to close it up, to emphasize the claustrophobic nature of Charlie's situation.[60] The film is marked by long takes, which Aldrich attributed to the slow, careful work of cameraman Ernest Laszlo and the pressure of a tight, sixteen-day shooting schedule. Aldrich had to forego certain set-ups and make do with relatively little cutting.[61] He managed, however, to use this aspect of the filming to his advantage by moving the camera within a given take and by using creative editing.

Indeed, the film is one of the tightest of Aldrich's works, partly because of its theatrical origin but also because of the limitations under which he had to film. One is repeatedly struck by his effective use of transition from one scene to the next. In *The Big Knife*, Aldrich employs the use of the slow fade, resulting in superimpositions which underline visually—and often more emphatically—what the words have been telling us. In one scene, for example, we see Charlie admit over the phone to Marion that he has signed the contract. She hangs up on him, and as Charlie stands there, the dead phone in one hand, the MacArthur pen in the other, there is a fade to the next scene, which is shot through sliding glass doors. As the two scenes mix, the doors form a bar-like effect over Charlie's face, emphasizing his entrapment. Aldrich also makes his transitions through sound. The type of music playing on the record player or radio alerts us to Charlie's emotional state. As Charlie goes up the stairs with Connie Bliss, raucous jazz music is playing, becoming louder and louder before turning into the roar of the sea as we move to the more idyllic beach shot. This release is only temporary, however, for soon the sound of the waves blends into the shouts of a crowd and the scene jumps jarringly to a shot of Charlie's being knocked bleeding to the mat in a boxing match. It takes us a moment to realize that we are back in Charlie's house and that what we are seeing is an old film, a "good" film (like *Body and Soul*?), made before Charlie sold out, but which accurately reflects Charlie's present situation. Other visual metaphors exist. When Charlie leaps away from threat and cowers behind a lamp, placing himself next to a painting of a clown by Rouault, we are silently struck by the resemblance, the visual link, between the two. Moreover, the clown, as Tailleur has noted, is also Christ—"the Christ behind the Clown"[62]—so that Charlie's own passion is underscored. But when Charlie looks at the painting and speaks—"He broods. Old clown waiting in the wings, waiting to go on. But he's done it a million times. It doesn't mean anything any more"—we are exasperated by the obviousness of the lines: the visual metaphors are much more effective than the ponderous dialogue. Frequent references to the Rouault picture, the phone, the lamp, and doors give the film a continuity. At no time does Aldrich allow the film to become visually static, quite a feat given the limitations of the set. Indeed, there is, in the words of Jean-José Richer, an "acceleration of events" in the film, a quickening of pace, leading to the final stasis of death.[63]

The film ends with a remarkable closing shot, a reverse of the opening dolly into Charlie's self-enclosed world. Marion now knows of Charlie's suicide and its implications (he has slashed himself in *three* places). Hank has made a fatuous and totally false farewell speech: "He killed himself. Out of the pain and anguished love he had for others. He gave up his salvation. But no man had a greater reverence for life, a greater zest for living." And on and on. But these thoughts are quickly forgotten as Marion begins to cry to the dead Charlie for help. Her anguished words say all that Hank's pontificating missed. Her voice echoes as the camera retreats. Lights begin to shut off, emphasizing the theatricality of the set, leaving Marion alone surrounded by darkness. The camera then abandons her, the lens irising in until she is swallowed by the black. Aldrich would use this shot again at the end of *The Killing of Sister George*, and a variation of it in *Attack!*, and in neither case does it lose its effectiveness.

Although *The Big Knife* won the 1955 Golden Lion Directorial Award for Aldrich at the Venice Film Festival, it was not initially a success and would, in fact, lose money (despite the fact that it took in $1,250,000)

Ida Lupino and Jack Palance in *The Big Knife*. Used by permission of the Museum of Modern Art/Film Stills Archive, courtesy of United Artists.

as Aldrich's "first completely independent production": "It seems that just being one's own producer is not enough nowadays," Aldrich wrote, "one may also have to begin to release one's own films. It is not to be avoided: film-making is also a business besides an art."[64] One possible reason for the film's lack of success was the casting of Jack Palance in the role of Charlie Castle. While Aldrich praised him as a "wonderful, wonderful actor" who had "that kind of intensity and burning integrity that I thought the part required," he felt that most viewers could not see him as "a guy who could or could not decide to take $5000 per week. We failed to communicate to the mass audience . . . that it was not primarily a monetary problem; it was a problem of internal integrity such as you or I or the guy at the gas station might have." Aldrich even quoted his own father on the film: "If a guy has to take or not to take $5000 per week, what the hell is the problem?"[65] This misunderstanding of the film's intentions was also evident in reviews of the film. Bosley Crowther, for example, felt that the film was "asking the audience to have sympathy for a dunce."[64]

With *The Big Knife* Aldrich embarked on his turbulent career as an independent. "It seemed almost too pat that I should be shooting a theme of major-studio wickedness on Hollywood's smallest lot," he later wrote. "But I liked the atmosphere of the place. I determined that some day I would own this studio, or one like it."[67] The rest of Aldrich's career would be built around this need to be free of the major studios and to make his films uniquely his own. It was to be a roller-coaster of a ride, marked by both exhilarating success and painful failure. As he indicated in the title of his 1958 article, there would indeed be a "high price" to be paid for independence.

Autumn Leaves (1956)

Autumn Leaves, Aldrich's second independent production, seemed at the time an abrupt shift from his previous work. Even today it appears on the surface as an anomaly, what Andrew Sarris has described as an "inexplicable digression into so-called women's pictures."[68] Aldrich himself discussed it in terms of a change, a new direction. "I guess self-survival made me do *Autumn Leaves*," he said in 1969. "People were getting collective in their criticism of the violence and anger and wrath in my pictures, although these things weren't intentional, and I thought it was about time I made a soap-opera—firstly, because I wanted to do one anyway, and secondly, because this seemed a pretty good one."[69] The Associates and Aldrich bought the rights to a story written by Jean Rouverol titled "The Way We Are" in July 1954. The title change was made to take advantage of a French song, called in translation "Autumn Leaves" and sung by Nat "King" Cole, which went on to become a popular hit. In September 1954, Joan Crawford, who was at this time the reigning queen of the "weepies," signed to star. The film was a joint venture between Aldrich and Bill Goetz, the "nominal producer" of the film, although Aldrich later noted that he and Goetz had "certain built-in guarantees of non-interference."[70] The film was distributed, ironically enough, by Columbia, the studio headed by Harry Cohn, one of the targets in *The Big Knife*. Shot in forty days and handsomely produced, *Autumn Leaves* was Aldrich's most "commercial"-looking film so far. He told Francois Truffaut at the time that "of all my films it's probably the best acted."[71] It would win him the Best Directorial Award at the Berlin Film Festival in 1956.

Taking all of these elements—star, story, title song, director's stated intentions, superior production—into account, it is at first a shock to find *Autumn Leaves* described as "the most grotesque of Aldrich's films"[72] or the "sickest"[73] of his work. And yet, both estimations are, in a manner of speaking, absolutely accurate. Indeed, one might add that it is also the most sexually suggestive of any Aldrich film before *The Killing of Sister George* (1968) and his most horrific up to (and perhaps including) *What Ever Happened to Baby Jane?* (1962).

Autumn Leaves is the story of Millicent Weatherby (Joan Crawford), a middle-aged spinster who makes her living as a professional typist. She has no social life or love interests and attempts to lose herself in her work. As a younger woman (shown in a flashback, with Crawford's face hidden by shadows), she refuses dates because of her invalid father, but now older, her father dead, she finds that no one asks her out, in part because they assume that she is "tied up."[74]

Into Milly's life comes a young man, Burt Hanson (Cliff Robertson), who cajoles her into letting him sit with her in a restaurant on one of her rare nights out. He strikes her as both offensively forward and oddly shy, but he is, above all, perceptive and caring. "You know something. You're lonely," he tells her that first night. "It's no disgrace to be lonely." A whirlwind romance follows, one which pleases Milly—she is flattered by Burt's attention—but which also disturbs her—she cannot ignore the difference in their ages and Burt's growing dependence on her. Finally, she tries to dismiss Burt, telling him to find a girl his own age. Like a child, Burt calls to her through the closed front door, begging her to reconsider, but Milly stands firm and Burt eventually leaves.

Milly now attempts to forget Burt and to renew her acquaintanceship with loneliness. But after a month Burt returns, flowers in hand. "I stole this from your garden," he tells her. She allows Burt to reenter her life, and soon he is bringing her gifts much too expensive for his department store salary. He asks her to marry him, and, after the usual arguments ("People don't—well, they shouldn't go around getting married simply because they're lonely, simply because they need each other"), Milly agrees. Their first weeks of married life are happy ones. Milly is fulfilled as woman and wife, and Burt enacts his role as middle-class husband. Soon, however, the gifts become outrageous, and Milly begins to notice discrepancies in Burt's stories about himself. Finally the truth comes out. While Burt is at work, Milly receives a visit from a young woman, Virginia Hanson (Vera Miles), who identifies herself as Burt's former wife, divorced only one month earlier. She further informs Milly that Burt has a history of shoplifting and that Burt's father, who Burt had said was dead, is indeed alive and in town. "You can't believe a word he says. . . . He just lies," Virginia concludes.

Highly distraught, Milly decides to meet Burt's father without telling Burt. Mr. Hanson (Lorne Greene) is a manly, slightly threatening figure. "My son is no good," he tells her. "He was, he still might be, a lost soul. If he is, no one is going to save him." He suggests putting Burt in a psychiatric hospital and, before Milly leaves, even makes a subtle pass at her. That night, Milly confronts Burt with all she has learned. "I have no past," he tells her. "My life began the day I met you." "How can you go around in that kind of dream world, remembering what you want to remember?" she asks. "The present is built up of little bits of the past. You can't just pick and choose." The irony of Milly's statement—and its applicability to her own life—is lost on her, but following this confrontation, a shift occurs in her relationship with Burt. Whereas up until this point he has largely been the motivating force, prodding, joking, pulling her out of her shell, enticing her into life and love, now she finds that she must become the strong character, she must direct and demand and control their future. Thus, she insists that Burt see his father, although Burt is clearly terrified at the prospect. Like a child facing punishment, Burt arrives at the hotel the following day; and, like a mother protecting her child, Milly secretly goes also. There, before Burt's arrival, she sees what she had missed the day before: that Burt's father and Virginia, Burt's ex-wife, are lovers, that this most basic betrayal is at

Joan Crawford, Ruth Donnelly and Cliff Robertson in *Autumn Leaves*. Used by permission of the Museum of Modern Art/Film Stills Archive, courtesy of Columbia Studios.

the heart of Burt's illness, and that she—Milly—has forced her child/husband back into a situation whose incestuous reality he has frantically sought to deny. In bringing about this meeting, Milly has driven Burt to the brink of collapse. Indeed, from this point forward, Burt begins a rapid disintegration, becoming more depressed and more violent until finally he begins to brutalize Milly, alternating between acute withdrawal and physical violence.

Soon, Burt is, as his father has suggested, quite crazy: "No more lies. . . . You're all against me," he tells Milly. In the film's most shocking scene (and one of Aldrich's most powerful anywhere), he picks up Milly's prized typewriter, raises it over his head, and (shot from below) hurls it at his wife, whom he has knocked to the ground, crushing her hand as she rolls desperately away. Later, he cries for forgiveness, but that night she finds him beating at the the linen closet (the scene shot expressionistically *through* the closed door), shouting, "Virginia—Dad—you left the door open. You left the door open. . . . Somebody help me!" Milly now realizes that Burt needs more than she alone, with all her love, can give him. She consults a doctor and tells him, "He's like a child." "Yes, like a child with his mother," the doctor replies. "But a child has to grow up." Milly makes the necessary sacrifice, and Burt is dragged away to the hospital, screaming, "I didn't do anything wrong" as the siren grows louder and louder on the soundtrack. After a series of shock treatments, Burt improves enough to see Milly again. She gives him the opportunity to leave her—"You're free, Burt. Completely free to make any choice you wish. . . . People have to grow up"—but Burt's choice is already made. Taking Milly's hand in his—"The scars are almost gone," he says—he kisses it, and together they walk away among the flowers on the hospital grounds.

This film warrants such a detailed plot synopsis because it is, as a final product, so different from what it appears to be. Unlike the melodramas of Douglas Sirk, whose films consciously (some would say) draw attention to their artificiality in order to comment on the artificiality of the society which demands them, *Autumn Leaves* only *pretends* to be a soap opera and, in fact, uses the mask of a "woman's picture" to present much deeper and darker ideas and emotions. There is actually relatively little "romance" in this film, and there is much horror. As R. Lachenay wrote in *Cahiers du Cinema*, this is a film built not on sentimental romanticism but on a kind of insane, delirious obsession.[75] The more obvious Freudian nightmare which haunts crazy Burt Hanson is ultimately less disturbing than the aggressive repression we find in "normal" Millicent

Weatherby. Burt's miracle cure—a result of long-suffering patience, motherly love, and high-voltage encounter sessions—is not, as others have noted, particularly convincing, but that may be the point, for Aldrich is not one given to simple, happy endings.

Although it is a constant theme in Aldrich's pictures, in no other film does he detail so explicitly the destruction which results when people fail to assume responsibility for their actions, when they fail to "grow up." When Milly asks Burt about his earlier marriage to Virginia, he answers defensively, "Maybe we did get married, but we were just kids, playing grownup, see." Burt is "playing grownup" throughout, and his childishness is more than disturbing: it is offensive. As his father recognizes, and as we recognize, Burt *is* a weakling, "only half a man." Indeed, he is, in some ways, more acceptable to us as an enraged psychotic than as a whining child. There are obvious similarities between Burt and such destructive characters as Captain Cooney in *Attack!* or (a more complicated case) Slim Grissom in *The Grissom Gang*.[76] Perhaps Burt has been "cured" by the end of the film, but Aldrich's direction—and Cliff Robertson's performance—do not give us a great deal to go on. What Aldrich does make clear is that although Mr. Hanson must be held responsible for Burt's condition, his accountability reaches back before the traumatic moment when Burt, as a grown, married man, spies his father with his wife. This is a shocking discovery, to be sure, but not in itself enough to knock a stable man around the bend. We can assume that, as with Captain Cooney and his father, the Judge, the parent-child relationship in *Autumn Leaves* represents another example of father-as-terrorist in Aldrich's films. And once again we must be reminded of Aldrich's relationship with his own father, a man he tried to please (within his own self-imposed limits) but one who never approved of or understood his son's accomplishments.

But what of Milly herself? Consumed in her work, fingering away with masturbatory delight at her typewriter (it is certainly appropriate that Burt should smash her hand with that machine, his rival), she is also the twisted result of a bizarre parent-child relationship, although one more of her own making. Because of perceived responsibilities to an invalid father (who encourages her to go out), she foregoes—avoids—the companionship of men her own age. Burt, coming later in her life, is a problem. She is attracted to his boyishness, his apparent harmlessness, yet there is a suppressed sexuality beneath this facade. On their first real date, Burt takes her to the beach. She is concerned about her appearance in a bathing suit and wears a robe as she leaves the bathhouse. Burt removes it, an innocent yet portentous undressing. In the ocean, he swims far out, but she struggles in the waves. "Are you all right?" he asks, swimming back. "Why don't you breathe?" "That's the coward's way," she gasps. "Can't breathe and swim at the same time." "I'm not going to bring you back here until you learn to swim," Burt says between kisses as the waves wash over them.[77]

This linking of sea and sexual release is reemphasized after Milly has made her break with Burt. Alone, she walks the halls of her apartment (shot from an extremely low angle, weirdly lighted) and then goes back to the beach. In a disorienting shot, Aldrich positions Milly to the right of the screen, watching the waves as they sweep toward her. But the camera is tilted so that the waves come at her from left and above; like a waterfall they threaten to engulf her completely. Interestingly enough, Aldrich again uses these tilt shots when he shows the montage of Burt's shock treatments, so that Burt, hose between teeth, electrodes fastened to the skull, is also held at impossible angles as the electric waves course through his body. That Burt is apparently being exorcised of the same emotions which so rack Milly at the beach is perhaps the point, for after his "cure" Burt is a calm but passionless man, almost an automation. At the end of the film, Burt doesn't want his freedom, for he has found real security in Milly, a mother and wife in one. And Milly has found in Burt another invalid-child to take care of. If one chooses to see the film in this way (and one may not so choose), *Autumn Leaves* is an amazing send-up of the usual Hollywood romance.

It is ultimately easier—and safer—to classify the film as the first of Aldrich's psychological horror shows. Richard Combs has astutely remarked on its similarity to Alfred Hitchcock's 1960 masterpiece *Psycho*.[78] The opening shot, in which the camera tracks down and in to Cedar Court, the apartment complex where Milly lives, anticipates Hitchcock's use of the peeping camera four years later (and recalls Aldrich's opening to *The Big Knife*). Aldrich repeatedly contrasts the bright sunlight of the California outdoors with the murky interiors of Milly's apartment, in which Burt slowly goes mad. Yet even the outdoors can be treacherous, as Milly discovers at the beach, for example, or when she faces Mr. Hanson and Virginia in the hot, dazzling courtyard. As Combs says, "Instead of setting the proper soap opera limits to the subject, the domestic milieu is turned into an anarchically unpredictable environment,"[79] a world in which people are forced to open doors which should perhaps remain closed, or which should never have been shut.

While it would be possible to suggest numerous other parallels between *Autumn Leaves* and *Psycho*—the similar characters of Burt Hanson and Norman Bates, the crippling effect of parents on children, the facile use of psychological "explanations" and cures, the explosive sexual violence which lurks, skull-like, under the skin of the most normal people—it is more to our point to see the film in terms of Aldrich's other work. For this "digression" in Aldrich's career is no digression at all. It restates themes and characters found in earlier films and anticipates many to come, specifically in the brilliant black comedies of *What Ever Happened to Baby Jane?* and *The Grissom Gang*, and in the less successful *Hush . . . Hush, Sweet Charlotte* and *The Killing of Sister George.* Of Aldrich's films of the fifties, *Autumn Leaves* is too often ignored or dismissed. Even his French admirers did not consider it as one of his best, although Truffaut liked it and Lachenay noted that "Aldrich continues to fascinate the viewer."[80] Still, it very much belongs in the same company with his acknowledged successes and prepares the way for his achievement in *Attack!*.

Attack! (1956)

"It must have been very difficult to have been told you were a genius by the French and to be ignored at home," Lukas Heller said of Robert Aldrich. Certainly the adulation received from film critics such as Truffaut, Chabrol, Bazin, and Tallieur must have been a heady experience for the young director, although he treated much of it with amusement and skepticism. Still, it was true that the European reviewers better understood the philosophy beneath the entertainment surface of his work in a way American critics did not. To the Americans, Aldrich made violent, overwrought movies, distinctive to a degree, perhaps, but basically studio stuff. To the French, he was an *auteur*, making each film his own, shaping each to reflect his own views.

In one way, the Europeans were better able to see the threads which linked together Aldrich's films—the developing philosophy, the standard character types, the visual style—because (with the exception of *The Big Leaguer*) all of these films were shown in France over a period of several months rather than over the three-year span they had been released in America. And Aldrich was, of course, one of several young

American directors who had captured the imagination of the French critics at this time. Jacques Rivette, in his *Cahiers* article "Notes Sur Une Révolution," praised the films of Nicholas Ray, Richard Brooks, and Anthony Mann in addition to those of Aldrich. These men, he felt, represented the new masters of American film, the "future of the cinema." Their works not only challenged existing conventions and standards, they indeed *destroyed* them through violence, creating a "vacancy," a "state of grace," in which their heroes, thus freed from "arbitrary obstacles," were able to question themselves, their beliefs, and finally to master their destinies. "The violence," Rivette wrote, "is justified through the meditation. . . ." Aldrich in particular, he felt, achieved "accord" through "dissonance." His films—especially *Kiss Me Deadly*—were fables of the destruction of the artificial world, saved from absolute nihilism by their sense of play, of excitement, which infused the violence and made it creative.[81] *Cahiers* called Aldrich the "revelation of the year." He was "le gros Robert," a big man full of life, of energy, of creativity, the one in whom they found "more love of the cinema," more pleasure in making films, than in any other. Each film was different—a spy thriller, a western, a detective novel, a Broadway play, a soap opera. He often used common or inferior material, but all of his films were inspired by a "poetic" sensibility which lifted them above their respective genres. He was compared again and again to Orson Welles, another "big" man, filled with artistic vitality, who was difficult to label. He was *the* director of the Atomic Age. "We know now," wrote Truffaut after viewing the director's works, "that the year 1955 will be the year of Aldrich."[82]

In America, however, Aldrich was still struggling for survival as an independent filmmaker. His next film was *Attack!*, which Aldrich once more both produced and directed. *Attack!* was adapted from Norman Brooks's unsuccessful stage play *Fragile Fox* by screenwriter James Poe. The film was made as part of a deal with United Artists. It was budgeted at $750,000, most of which Aldrich borrowed from the banks, but some of which UA advanced to The Associates and Aldrich. Thus, the financial burden rested on Aldrich rather than the studio. Aldrich took a percentage of the film in place of a large salary, so his personal finances were wrapped up in the film as well.

Both play and film presented an extended and explicit study of the corruption of authority and the failure of courage in the U.S. Army during the Battle of the Bulge in World War II. Because the film dealt seriously and realistically with these issues and because it ended with the killing of an American officer by his own men, it was bound to raise some eyebrows, particularly in the sensitive Cold War political climate of the mid-1950s. Indeed, among the top-grossing films of the past few years had been such "positive" war movies as *Strategic Air Command, To Hell and Back, Mr. Roberts,* and *Battle Cry.* Aldrich wanted to make an "angry" war film. He had tried to buy both Irwin Shaw's *The Young Lions* and Norman Mailer's *The Naked and the Dead. Fragile Fox,* he assured, would not be "the usual dose of movie heroics."[83]

Not unexpectedly, the Defense Department refused to cooperate with the making of the film. "The Army saw the script and promptly laid down a policy of no co-operation," Aldrich told Arthur Knight. "Which not only meant that I couldn't borrow troops and tanks for my picture—I couldn't even get a look at Signal Corps combat footage."[84] The controversy over this refusal eventually led into the U.S. Congress when Rep. Melvin Price, a member of the House Armed Services Committee, charged that the Pentagon was practicing censorship, that it would have allowed an enlisted man to be portrayed as a coward, but not an officer.[85] Nevertheless, all the equipment used in the film was either bought or rented, including the two tanks with which Aldrich had to make do. (Truffaut suggested that this need for economy perhaps benefited the film, giving it a "stylized and poetic" look which set it apart from the ordinary, big-studio war film. Aldrich agreed, but noted that more money would still have helped.[86]) The movie was shot in thirty-two days on the back lot of RKO Studios, the same lot on which Aldrich had worked as an assistant director on *The Story of G.I. Joe.*[87]

For this film Aldrich brought together one of his best ensemble casts, an all-male crew that included Jack Palance, Eddie Albert, Lee Marvin, William Smithers, Richard Jaeckel, Buddy Ebsen, and Robert Strauss. Some of the casting was off-beat. Albert, for example, who had the role of the psychotic captain, was still making the change from a song-and-dance man to a dramatic actor; this was one of the roles which proved Albert's acting ability. Lee Marvin remembers that Aldrich first wanted him to play the role of Sgt. Tolliver (eventually played by Buddy Ebsen) rather than the corrupt Colonel Bartlett, the role he preferred: "Having been a P.F.C. in the Marine Corps, I was aware of officers that didn't come up to the standards and respect of the common man—the dogface. I did know this colonel who had that attitude, browbeating the guys at poker games to win, just covering his own tracks, and I just looked forward to playing that kind of little bastard."[88] Jack Palance again played the Aldrich lead, the emotionally demanding role of Lt. Costa, the man tragically pitted against an incompetent and cowardly officer.

As had now become standard practice on an Aldrich film, the cast began work with rehearsals. Marvin recalled:

> He always rehearsed a film, which not many directors do because the time element is so costly. But we'd sit around a table for days, sometimes even weeks, and we'd read a script over and over again. And, of course, when you're sitting there, reading it, if he had any doubts prior to the reading, he would suggest changes, cuts. You would iron out the rough spots at those readings. The actors would contribute and he would listen to any comments the actors had and consider them.

The rehearsals had become essential for Aldrich. Richard Jaeckel, who was one of Aldrich's most trusted actors and friends, explained, "If a line was changed, it had to be then. He didn't like surprises on the set. 'Don't change it without me,' he'd say. He was special. He *did* give you the time. He *did* give you the allowance." He also, however, expected his actors and crew to be as prepared as he was. Albert recalled one actor who was late to rehearsals on two successive days. "We had been waiting around, and Aldrich was keyed up, waiting to do the scene. He didn't say anything when the actor came in. But after the scene, he called everyone together. 'If somebody comes in late one day,' he said, 'that's understandable—traffic and everything. But if he comes in late the next day—*horse shit!*' And he exploded."[89]

Attack! was Eddie Albert's first film with Aldrich. He had, with Aldrich's approval, prepared for the role by studying with Stella Adler. When he arrived on the set, he was immediately impressed with Aldrich's professionalism. "Aldrich was a great example of responsibility," Albert said. "I knew that when we began to shoot at seven o'clock, he had been up since three, preparing the script. It was all very controlled. Filming is highly collaborative anyway. In Aldrich's case, he blended all of us together very, very well, to work toward a common end." "It was more or less like a stock company," Jaeckel observed. "It was an easy set if you paid attention. If you didn't pay attention, then you were off." In Lee Marvin's words, "Robert was a very tough man. He was definitely a man you listened to, and you had to weigh your answers. He was enamored of discipline. After all, it is the discipline of life that flows over into your work."

Aldrich, however, was not above inspired manipulation to get the kind of performance he wanted, especially in the case of Jack Palance, a much more emotional actor than Marvin or Albert. "Jack Palance always liked to shout and scream," Joseph Biroc, the cameraman, remembered. "Aldrich said it was good, it would help the part."[90] As Richard Jaeckel put it, "Palance was quite a scary guy. You never knew where he was coming from. He could stand there one minute and then he could jump thirty feet in the air. There was just a very scary side." Aldrich used this "scary side" to intensify the antagonism between Palance's Costa and Albert's Captain Cooney. As Albert recalled, "That was Aldrich's greatest virtue, his love for conflict, which is the essence of all drama and comedy. He would build an antagonism, even while the scene was rolling. During one scene with Palance and Marvin at the table, Aldrich had goaded Palance to such an extent that I felt he might take a punch at me. I even moved my foot under the table so that I could duck if he did." Certainly, that sense of imminent violence added to the overall feeling of the film. "There were scenes of incredible tension," Jaeckel said. "Palance coming down the stairs to get Albert—we were all impressed, even in rehearsals. It was a heavy project."

There was a difference, however, between Aldrich the director and Aldrich the man. "*Attack!* was a very pleasurable film to work on," Marvin said, "for Bob had an affinity for a male cast. He liked to sit around in between scenes and joke with the boys, and, of course, in that film there was a pretty good hard group." Marvin recalled one example of the interplay between cast and director: "There were some good storytellers in there, and Bob would come in and laugh at the jokes, and then *he'd* set up a joke or a story, and we'd all straight him—we wouldn't laugh at all. We drove him crazy because we'd just kind of tolerate his telling a story until eventually he'd get into an absolute tizzy. And we wouldn't let up on him. But then *he'd* get us back in the scene. Which is a good way to direct anyway."

It was Aldrich's practice throughout his career to have a party for cast and crew on each Friday or Saturday night of shooting (depending on whether the film was being shot on location or not). "Then," in Marvin's words, "he would become one of the boys. But on the set he was *Robert Aldrich.* Except for when he set the conversation, you didn't interfere with that film. He set the mode of the set, and you followed it."

Attack! was a very personal film for Aldrich. "My main anti-war argument was not the usual 'war is hell,' " he said, "but the terribly corrupting influence that war can have on the most normal, average human beings, and what terrible things it makes them capable of that they wouldn't be capable of otherwise."[91] It was meant, he said, to be a "sincere plea for peace."[92] Thematically, the film focuses on the notion of solidarity, on the essential plight of a group of men drawn together by desperate circumstances, whose very existence is threatened by sinister and irrational forces over which they have little or no control, and on the possibilities of honorable and heroic behavior among the individual members of that group. These are concerns to which Aldrich would return in later films of the sixties and seventies, films like *The Flight of the Phoenix* (1965), *The Dirty Dozen* (1967), and *The Longest Yard* (1974), which Aldrich would group together as his "patrol" pictures. Technically, *Attack!* bears the indelible stamp of Aldrich's emerging personal style, a visual technique emphasizing a carefully constructed *mise-en-scene* and highly subjective camera shots and angles. Indeed, a close analysis of the film reveals a tight interconnection between theme and technique.

    Attack! begins explosively. Shell bursts from an artillery barrage rock the landscape before us: the setting, as an opening title indicates, is "Europe, 1944." Separated from their platoon, a squad of American soldiers—Ingersoll's squad—is pinned down by withering machine gun fire from a German bunker near the small town of Aächen. Ingersoll volunteers to attack the bunker, having received assurances from Lt. Joe Costa (Jack Palance), his platoon leader, that Captain Erskine Cooney (Eddie Albert), the company commander, will support the attack with reinforcements. But Costa's men, overhearing Cooney's promise of support, are openly skeptical, fearful that the "glory guys and heroes" of Ingersoll's squad are doomed, for Cooney's cowardice under fire and failure of nerve are by now well known to the men of "Fragile Fox" company.

    By means of a hand gesture, Cooney signals to Costa his readiness to provide support for Ingersoll's assault on the pill box, and the attack commences. The placement of the camera precludes our seeing Cooney's face: instead we see him from behind, sitting stiffly in a jeep, his men looking on disrespectfully from a distance. Close-up shots reveal that Cooney's hands, which gave the signal to attack, are now alternately clasped tightly together and wrung in fretful agitation. Immobilized by fear, Cooney ignores Costa's subsequent anguished appeals for help. Shots of Cooney's trembling hands are interspersed with shots of Ingersoll's squad being cut to pieces, defenseless in the hail of German bullets. The scene closes with a disturbingly prolonged shot of a dead American soldier's helmet, jostled by machine gun fire, coming to rest beside a single daisy growing on the desolate and barren battleground. Upon this stark, still-life scene of delicate flower and punctured helmet, the credits announce a film "Directed by Robert Aldrich."

The brisk and vigorous pace, the *in medias res* approach to narrative exposition, the attentiveness to key visual images—these are the elements one typically discovers in the prologue to an Aldrich picture, and their use in *Attack!* is particularly effective. In the next sequence of shots, Aldrich slows the pace considerably, shifting the setting abruptly from the ubiquitous dangers of a combat zone to the relative safety of company headquarters. But the "safety" of the men of "Fragile Fox" company is a fleeting delusion, for we are plunged suddenly into the dark world of Captain Cooney, whose political corruption and psychological debility present to his men a threat more insidious than that of the Germans themselves. Aldrich carefully orchestrates our entrance into Cooney's world, beginning with a close-up of a loudspeaker dispersing big band music courtesy of the Armed Forces Radio Network. Through the spokes of a motorcycle wheel, the camera views a column of men in a chow line, the image evocative of men behind bars, entrapped, as indeed they are, by the incompetence of their superior officer. The camera follows an adjutant officer, Lt. Woodruff (William Smithers), as he returns from the line with coffee to Cooney's quarters, where the film's first interior shot occurs: the room is dimly lit, heavily shadowed, and Cooney is viewed initially through the pigeonholes of a letterbox, his face darkened and obscured by the checkered bars of criss-crossing shelves. Cooney, too, as the image suggests, is a man imprisoned, trapped by the inexorable deterioration of his own mind, teetering on the brink of a complete nervous breakdown. In his office, awaiting the arrival of Col. Clyde Bartlett (Lee Marvin) for a poker game and some political maneuverings, Cooney issues orders for the requisition of winter underwear, a confident bureaucratic banter sharply in contrast with his fatal indecisiveness in battle. Clearly, the office is Cooney's domain, a refuge from the pressures and perplexities of command in the field.

The skillful use of cross cutting and the emphasis of striking visual images enable Aldrich further to dramatize the vast differences between the heroes and villains of *Attack!*. Bartlett arrives and his glib conversation with Cooney soon reveals the opportunistic nature of their relationship. Bartlett's post-war political ambitions depend heavily on the patronage of Cooney's father, a powerful judge back home. To curry favor with the judge, Bartlett will arrange a phony citation for Cooney, and Cooney, thus decorated, will become the kind of son the judge has always wanted. Such ruthless schemes, which place the private gains of the individual above the larger interests of the group, and which are often achieved at the expense of the group (in this case, the lives of good soldiers) represent, in Aldrich's view, an unconscionable evil, the most contemptible kind of compromise. Characters are often called upon to negotiate their fates in an Aldrich film, but it is the kind and the terms of the bargain they strike which determine their worth in Aldrich's moral universe. Although Cooney and Bartlett's "arrangement" is morally reprehensible, there will arise, for other characters in *Attack!*, situations where compromise is morally desirable, situations where, in fact, an absolute sense of integrity may prove a distinct liability.

On Cooney's orders, Woodruff is sent to find Costa, the designated fourth player in the CO's poker game. As Woodruff walks toward his destination, the camera frames him through the jagged shards of a stained glass window. The visual effect is one of entrapment: Woodruff appears to be surrounded, enclosed. And in many ways Woodruff's trap is the most excruciating of all, for he is caught between the conflicting claims of friendship to Costa and fidelity to the "system"—the inviolable claim of military command. As his walk across the yard and his immediate orders indicate, Woodruff functions as a kind of intermediary between two extremes: his eventual attempt to reconcile the dictates of personal conscience with the mandates of military law will form the moral crux of Aldrich's drama. Woodruff locates Costa, the other "extremist," in a near-by blacksmith's shop, a setting which readily reveals the true nature of Costa's character. Tending the bellows, speaking in quiet and dignified fashion of this honorable "500-year-old profession," Costa is identified as a craftsman, a man of incorruptible and uncompromising integrity. (To underscore Costa's role as artist, Aldrich shows him, a few scenes later, thoughtfully carving and whittling a new wooden handgrip for his bazooka, a fitting image of his creative/destructive nature.) And to accentuate the vast differences between these pairs of characters, Aldrich intercuts shots of Costa at the blacksmith's forge, explaining to Woodruff the necessity to rid "Fragile Fox" company of Cooney, with shots of Cooney and Bartlett at the poker table, still concocting their cynical stratagems of self-interest. The sharp antagonism between Costa and Cooney erupts into near violence a short while later, during the card game itself, when the Aächen debacle is dropped idly into the conversation. Costa threatens retribution should Cooney blunder again. In a single, striking bird's-eye shot, Aldrich makes visibly and spatially clear the tensions and oppositions which divide these players, each man pitted against the other in this most dangerous game of chance. For the poker game *is* an apt metaphor for the fate of the men of "Fragile Fox" whose lives are at stake in Cooney's and Bartlett's ruthless gamble to advance their careers.

Aldrich's precise placement and positioning of characters within the frame is particularly evident in the next scene of *Attack!*, when the company is ordered back to the front, despite earlier assurances from Col. Bartlett that their odds of seeing combat again were "one hundred to one" (again the language of gambling). Once more, Cooney is seen "behind bars" as the camera views him through the window panes of his quarters. As the camera dollies forward, Cooney can be seen clasping his nervous, sweaty hands, now emblematic of his gradually deteriorating mental condition. Cooney's plan is to send Costa's platoon unprotected into enemy territory, a reconnaisance mission to detect the presence and test the strength of the German forces. If attacked, Costa's men are to secure a farmhouse and hold out until relieved by company reinforcements. When Costa and Woodruff are advised of the risky plan, they are foregrounded in the frame, while Cooney can be seen, slightly out of focus, positioned exactly between the men. Having convinced Woodruff, but not Costa, of the tactical merits of his plan, Cooney has literally become a divisive wedge between the two friends. The lighting is ominous and suspenseful: the upper and lower portions of the screen are darkened, leaving only the men's faces, and particularly their eyes, sufficiently illuminated. It is a somber and disquieting mood befitting Costa's final warning to Cooney: "If you double-cross me once more, if you play the gutless wonder, I'll get you. I'll shove a grenade down your throat."

The attempt to take the farmhouse is an appalling, unmitigated disaster. In their effort to cross hundreds of yards of open terrain, Costa's men present easy targets to well-camouflaged German machine gunners. Once again, Aldrich makes full use of the frame to underline the futility of their attack: an extreme long shot reveals the soldiers advancing from the top left-hand corner of the screen; the farmhouse, their destination, is situated to the right toward mid-screen; foregrounded is the German gun emplacement, its position offering the gunners a clear, unobstructed field of fire. Only six soldiers survive the murderous dash to the farmhouse (a number are killed; others are held back on Costa's orders). These six are caught in an insidious trap: beseiged from the front by heavy German armor and betrayed from behind by the cowardly Cooney, who has, predictably, reneged on his promise to provide reinforcements. To achieve maximum dramatic effect, Aldrich once again employs the three-shot in which characters are strategically, almost thematically, positioned. When Costa's impassioned plea for help finally reaches headquarters, the message is received by Woodruff and his radio operator, who are foregrounded and sharply in focus; behind and between them, blurred and diminished in stature in a narrowed depth of field, Cooney shouts hysterically his refusal to risk the whole company for "one lousy platoon." Bound by his word of honor to Costa but bound even more firmly to military rules which insist that he carry out the orders of a superior officer, Woodruff finds himself the unwitting agent of his friend's betrayal. It is an unholy compromise and an unholy alliance, one which Woodruff must ultimately reject if he is to be redeemed in Aldrich's morality play.

Who *is* the enemy? This is the most disturbing question put forward in *Attack!*. The ambiguous nature of *enemy* is made evident at this point in the film. "Cruddy Krauts," one of the soldiers in the farmhouse mutters contemptuously at the Germans firing at them. "I'm not the enemy; I'm an *American!*" Although this is a comic line, it emphasizes the tragic irony of the film, for the American command in the form of Cooney is as deadly an enemy as the Germans to these trapped men. Indeed, the film suggests, it is *authority* in general, whether German or American, which most threatens. Thus, when Costa's men discover two Germans, one of whom is a colonel, hiding in the cellar of the farmhouse, it is the officer who is most haughty and despicable. Costa's hatred toward Cooney—and toward all figures of corrupt authority—explodes when the German colonel refuses to answer the questions asked him. Despite the officer's shouts about the "rules of war," Costa throws him out of the farmhouse to be shot down by his own men. By doing so, Costa has in fact broken the "rules" of war, and the parallel to Cooney's fate is unmistakable. This idea is further expressed in the next scene, one of the film's most agonizing moments. Costa, realizing that they have been abandoned by Cooney—and Woodruff—orders his men to retreat. One man is hit. As Costa stops to help the mortally wounded soldier, he looks at first to the right of the screen, in the direction of the Germans who have shot the man. Then he turns slowly to the left, in the direction of the American lines, in the direction of Cooney, who must finally be held accountable. As this shot fades out, another fades in: that of Cooney back at headquarters. The lingering fades effect a memorable superimposition, with Costa's anguished and vengeful gaze (slowly dissolving) falling

The interrogation in the farm house: Jack Palance, Steven Geray, Peter Van Eyck, and Richard Jaeckel in *Attack!*. Used by permission of the Museum of Modern Art/Film Stills Archive, courtesy of United Artists.

directly on Cooney (now gradually coming into focus at the left of the screen). The point is clear—Costa has killed the German colonel, but Cooney is the real enemy and now Costa must kill him.

Thematically, the final scenes of *Attack!* explore the consequences and implications of the behavior of the film's major antagonists—Costa and Cooney—and the significance of Woodruff's intervention in and, to some degree, resolution of their conflict. With the Germans mounting a furious counterattack, Colonel Bartlett arrives at "Fragile Fox" company headquarters with orders for Cooney to hold the town at all costs. Before Bartlett leaves, the two men quarrel violently; to Woodruff, an astonished observer of the altercation, Cooney confesses that he hasn't "the guts to live or die." Aldrich conveys his crack-up in a series of unsettling images: pathetically clutching his slippers, reenacting a brutal childhood beating at the hands of his father, Cooney finally curls up in the fetal position on his bed, his regressive withdrawal from reality nearly complete. For his role in a callous conspiracy to salvage his career, Cooney pays with his sanity and, ultimately, his life. *Attack!* acts as an indictment both of the man whose incompetence precipitates disaster and of the "system" whose corruption places him in a position of power.

Aldrich locates the broad moral questions of *Attack!* within the context of what can best be described as utilitarian ethics. To secure the greatest good for the greatest number of soldiers, a certain end—the removal of Cooney from command—must be achieved. But the question of how he is to be removed provokes a heated exchange between Costa and Woodruff. Costa, presumed dead, reappears from the grave brandishing a .45 pistol, determined to kill Cooney and avenge the death of his men. Woodruff, mindful of Cooney's derangement, blocks Costa's way, arguing instead for a militarily-sanctioned solution. The showdown between Costa and Woodruff is averted only by the news that Costa's squad is under attack by German tanks. Costa's decision to help his squad is thematically significant: by setting aside his personal vendetta against Cooney and acting in behalf of the group, whose safety is his responsibility, Costa affirms the importance of community and solidarity. In this assertion, he is, of course, the antithesis of Cooney and Bartlett, for whom selfishness and self-indulgence are the customary motives for living. Costa's heroism, and, conversely, Cooney's and Bartlett's villainy, are largely determined by each man's capacity to subordinate self-interest to the common good. Costa's rescue attempt, which costs him his life, is thus the epitome of self-sacrifice. Aldrich establishes the sacrificial quality of Costa's gesture in the sequence of shots which follow. To escape the German tanks, Costa's squad has taken refuge in the basement of a demolished building. On one wall can be seen a portrait of the Sacred Heart of Jesus. A quick cut reveals Costa in the streets outside, disabling one tank (with a bazooka) before being crushed beneath another, crucified, his left arm mangled under the tread. The editing and imagery link Costa to Christ, the archetypal savior and sacrificial victim. One critic has called this aspect of the film a "slightly demented Christ parable,"[93] and there is a fundamental and dark irony in this Costa-Christ, for Costa's death wish is not one of forgiveness but one of vengeance. When, fatally wounded, he confronts Cooney for the last time in the cellar where his squad is gathered (in a crazed and drunken state Cooney has managed to locate them there), Costa implores God to give him just enough strength to kill his enemy. But his prayers are unanswered, and he dies in Woodruff's arms.

Costa's devotion to the cause of revenge has been absolute to the point of fanaticism, an approach which we have come to expect from this uncompromising man. With his death, the problem of Cooney's behavior is inherited by Woodruff, who has, all along, preferred a more moderate and temperate solution. But extreme circumstances call for extreme responses, and Woodruff understands finally that there is no solution to this problem short of murder. Cooney has certainly gone mad: laughing fiendishly at the sight of Costa's corpse, he orders the squad, at gunpoint, to surrender to the SS troops above, unmindful of the risks to all the men and insensible, in particular, to the fate of Pvt. Bernstein (Robert Strauss). Acting in violation of personal conscience, in violation of the codes of military law which have thus far governed his actions, Woodruff shoots Cooney and places himself immediately under arrest, at the mercy of the system whose laws he has chosen to disobey. A spokesman for the group, Sgt. Tolliver (nicely played by Buddy Ebsen), points at Cooney and offers a justification for the shooting phrased in the picturesque vernacular of the common soldier: "If ever a man needed killing, it's that no-good, putrid piece of trash lying there." Despite the enormity of the crime, the men insist on a ritualized participation in the event: one by one, they fire their weapons into Cooney's body. They have affirmed their membership in the group for whose sake Costa has given his life and in whose behalf Woodruff has compromised his personal and professional ethics. It is a positive gesture of solidarity and communion.

Only one threat now remains to the squad's integrity—the invidious Col. Bartlett; he appears on the scene only moments after Cooney's death to herald the arrival of American troops who have retaken the town. Always the opportunist, Bartlett is quick to size up the situation and to calculate the possibilities for personal gain. The real truth, he suspects, can never be told without disastrous consequences to the participants. By distorting the truth, however, by reporting "officially" that Cooney died heroically, everyone could profit from this "unfortunate" turn of events. Woodruff can be promoted to captain; Cooney and Costa can be awarded posthumous citations; and Bartlett himself can win political favor with the Judge back home. But Woodruff, like Costa a man of integrity and principle, balks at the prospect of further compromise. Once more Aldrich positions his camera and his characters so that the essence of the moral drama is revealed: between Woodruff to the left of the screen and Bartlett to the right, the bodies of Cooney and Costa are arranged in tandem, effectively dividing the two sides of the issue. To Bartlett, the bodies are merely indistinguishable cadavers, useful only insofar as they prove advantageous to his career. To Woodruff, they are unique, even in death, emblematic of a moral order and a sense of moral purpose to which he himself subscribes. If the meaning of Costa's heroism is to be publicly proclaimed, so too must the meaning of Cooney's cowardice. In the dialogue which follows, Woodruff accuses Bartlett of complicity in the affair: "I may have pulled the trigger, but you aimed the gun. You set the whole thing up so it could happen." Bartlett's reply is couched in the metaphor of the game: "You got the high hand, son; you'll play it right. . . . I know you, Harry. You got too much to lose." What Woodruff stands to lose, of course, is not his career or his freedom but his self-respect, the most dreadful loss of all for an Aldrich character.

To retain that self-respect, to uphold the values of courage, decency, integrity, and self-sacrifice—those values which give meaning to men's lives and which bind them to the community—Woodruff decides on a full disclosure of the facts. In the film's final scene, Woodruff passes the jeep where the two bodies now lie: the camera pauses to view Cooney's face, reposeful at last in death, and Costa's, horribly anguished, his mouth gaping in grotesque rigor mortis, raging still.[94] Woodruff speaks to his dead friend: "You know what I got to do, Joe. You'd do the same thing." As he places a call to division headquarters, he is bathed in the light radiating from a nearby lantern, the only brightly-lit interior shot in this otherwise *militaire film noir*. Aldrich's camera cranes up and away, leaving Woodruff a lonely and isolated figure about to engage in the most difficult battle of his life.

The ending is an ambiguous one. Aldrich told Truffaut in 1956 that he found the ending too conventional, that he would have preferred that Woodruff (like Charlie Castle in *The Big Knife*) capitulate, accept Bartlett's orders and sign the declaration that Cooney died a hero. Or, he suggested, the film should have ended when Woodruff sees the two corpses, leaving the viewers with the *suggestion* that Woodruff would then make the call rather than immediately showing them the lieutenant's about-face, a decision Aldrich felt came too quickly.[95] Still, according to Aldrich's own definition, the gestures—both Costa's and Woodruff's—are victories of sorts, for these characters "find their own integrity in doing what they do the way they do it, even if it causes their own deaths. . . . Considering what the odds are, what's involved, it becomes very expensive to have opinions that strong. . . . These guys thought they had a chance to win outside the system or against the system. And didn't. Or only did temporarily."[96]

As for Captain Cooney, Aldrich had hoped to show him as more than a contemptible coward. He pointed out to Truffaut that Cooney had been raised very harshly by his father, who wanted "to make a great man of him," and that this psychological explanation was not necessarily facile or artificial. "It is less a question of finding excuses than explanations," he said.[97] Aldrich later wrote, "In my war film, *Attack!*, the hero went all the way against incompetent authority in trying to kill a cowardly captain reponsible for the death of his men. This is why I wanted to depict my utter contempt and loathing for this captain in making him do sadistic things that probably smacked of 'guignol'. . . . The captain was a neurotic weakling, made so by a harsh father, but this did not excuse his failure as an officer and a man."[98] Aldrich's extreme language, matched by the hysteria and madness of Cooney's last scenes, would certainly indicate the personal investment the director had in this character whose father, like Aldrich's own, was a powerful and manipulative politician who tried to direct his son's life.

Eddie Albert remembered trying to work out the nuances of Cooney's character with Aldrich during filming:

> I had been in combat as a naval officer. I was commended for bravery in battle. Two or three days later I wondered, "Was I brave, or was I a coward just trying to get out of action?" Is there such a thing as a coward? During action, the coward rationalizes his actions. James Poe showed in the script that the coward does not exist at the moment. It's only the outsiders who say this later, who put this view on it.
>
> Aldrich approved of my approach. He had sympathy for Cooney. He made Cooney *understandable*. He wasn't just a cheap villain. That was the moral base. Bob brought it out with a sense of compassion, of pity. But he's got to be killed; he's a danger. He rationalized himself out of responsibility.

Albert later added, "The more I think about it, the more I come to admire Bob and his psychiatric understanding of villains."

Attack! earned Aldrich some of his best reviews yet in America. Even the normally antagonistic Bosley Crowther wrote in the *New York Times*: ". . . Mr. Aldrich . . . has put some withering battle action on the screen. The attack on the town is breathtaking. The brief holding of the position is intense. And the return of the lieutenant to take his vengeance on the cowardly captain is sheer agony." He concluded, however, that "the completion of the drama is so charged with personal anger and hate that the whole situation collapses in a flood of hysteria."[99] Today, *Attack!* has achieved a remarkable status among war films. As Norman Kagan observed in his book *The War Film*:

In the history of U.S. war films, *Attack!* is a great watershed: the Cold War themes of the brutality of war, command levels, social responsibility, the nature of the enemy in a shifting moral world are all transformed and transfigured. *Attack!* is the first postwar film to connect the new brutality of war with confusion, corruption, and incompetence of American leadership and American motives—in this sense it is the first Cold War anti-war film.[100]

In retrospect, it is clear that "the system" and the individual's stand against it is the major theme of Aldrich's films during the fifties. But these films offer no pat solutions, no easy victories, indeed, little hope of victory at all. In *Apache*, Massai opts for an honorable death when he realizes (at the *beginning* of the film) that the government cannot be defeated; he is forced, however, to accept a compromise. Charlie Castle is already corrupted by his compromise when *The Big Knife* begins, and his suicide is a weak, ineffective try for redemption. Joe Costa refuses to compromise and is crushed by the system, but again it is unclear just how ultimately purposeful his sacrifice has been. Mike Hammer works outside the system as a loner, but, like Joe Erin, he lacks the fundamental decency to make his individualism anything more than self-interest. Burt Hanson's mental aberrance sets him apart, but he is forced back into the system through shock treatment and made to act as a responsible member of society, under the guidance of his protective wife. Only Ben Trane seems to find a balance in his life between compromise and revolution.

Linking all these films is the moral and political context in which they were made. Aldrich had known and worked with men who had defied, or compromised with, or caved in to the powers unleashed during the McCarthy era. All had been hurt, and many destroyed. Even those like Robert Rossen, who had tried to cooperate within self-prescribed moral limits, found that they had betrayed the best in themselves. Aldrich's films, although packaged as entertainments, were nonetheless moral studies of individual integrity, often infused and confused by romantic idealism, in conflict with the collective power of authority. If you stand against the system, you will be crushed. If you compromise with the system, you will pay with your self-respect. If you step outside the system, you forfeit your self-determination by default. Thus the conundrum posed by Robert Aldrich.

3. Aldrich in Exile

So far, Aldrich himself had yet to test conclusively his philosophy of the individual against the system. In his quest for independence, he had managed to work within the system while still making more or less his own films. His works had commanded attention, especially in Europe— even if they were usually accompanied by controversy. *The Big Knife* had won the Golden Lion Directorial Award at the 1955 Venice Film Festival; *Autumn Leaves* won the Silver Bear Award for Best Direction at the 1956 Berlin Film Festival; and *Attack!* was a winner at the 1956 Venice Film Festival (with the American ambassador walking out of the screening in protest). *Autumn Leaves*, made at Columbia, was the first of a three-picture deal Aldrich had signed with studio head Harry Cohn. Aldrich had accepted the two-year contract knowing that, in order to make his own projects, he would have to deal with the major studios for distribution. His pact with Cohn would nevertheless prove to be the beginning of one of the most difficult periods of his career.

The second film he agreed to make at Columbia was *The Garment Jungle*. The script was written by Harry Kleiner based on a series of *Reader's Digest* articles by Lester Velie entitled "Gangsters in the Dress Business."[1] The script by Kleiner (who would be listed as producer of the film) was, in Aldrich's words, a "terribly tough, controversial" one.[2] He referred to the film as the "first pro-labor picture"[3] to come out of Hollywood, although Kleiner's script took both sides of the union issue into account. Within this larger picture, Aldrich again hoped to show the plight of one man, the loner, who attempts to stand up to the corruption which surrounds him.

Soon, however, life began to copy art, and it was Aldrich who was having to make his stand. The filming was plagued by problems from the beginning. Although there were seasoned actors in the picture—Lee J. Cobb, Joseph Wiseman—Aldrich also had several "new faces"—Kerwin Mathews, Robert Loggia, Gia Scala—imposed on him by the studio. More threatening problems arose. Aldrich explained that "halfway through [filming] Cohn became frightened of how tough [the film] was. It had some very strong things to say about the unions and about the mobs, and he wanted to soften the picture."[4] Cohn's concern seems to have come in part from pressures brought on him by interested parties in labor and rackets. Aldrich refused to make the "boy meets girl in a dress factory"[5] story Cohn now seemed to want. Another conflict came from Lee J. Cobb, who wanted to change the focus of his character, to make him "more heroic and not as tough."[6] When Aldrich became ill with the flu and missed one day of filming, Cohn took advantage of the situation and replaced him with Vincent Sherman, although there were only a few days left of shooting. Sherman reshot some of Aldrich's scenes and added new ones of his own, but the finished film contained, in Aldrich's estimation (although he never saw the film), from one-half to two-thirds of his original work.[7] Still, Aldrich never considered the film as one of his own, and it is impossible today to determine just how different the picture would have been if Aldrich had been allowed to finish it.

Aldrich had told Francois Truffaut, before filming began, that he intended *The Garment Jungle*, with its exposé of gangsterism and corruption, to be a film like *On the Waterfront*,[8] and, the Cohn-ordered softening notwithstanding, it does retain a similar toughness of spirit, probably attributable to Aldrich. The violent murders of two union sympathizers by the henchmen of gangster boss Artie Ravidge (effectively played by Richard Boone) are graphic and terrifying. But it was the Lee J. Cobb character—Walter Mitchell, owner of Roxton Fashions—that caught Aldrich's fancy. "On the surface," Aldrich noted, "it was about hoodlumism in the unions of the garment trade in New York. But I got interested in one of the . . . characters. He [Walter Mitchell] was an immigrant who had created a thriving business, but now, at 45, found himself being squeezed out by both big business and excessive labor demands and gangsterism."[9] The film is structured, typically, around a father-son relationship: Mitchell is a father whose prodigal son Alan (Kerwin Mathews) has returned home to join him in the trade. Alan, who believes in the necessity of moral choices, is appalled by his father's ostensible amorality ("Right or wrong—there's no such thing in the garment business!" Walter snaps) and by his partnership with Ravidge, whom Walter has hired to keep the unions out. When Walter can no longer ignore the brutality of Ravidge's methods ("I should have known—I just closed my eyes to it," he confesses), he breaks with Ravidge and resolves to go to the district attorney. Alan is justifiably proud, and their reconciliation makes for one of the film's most dramatic moments. "That's all I ever wanted—to have a father!" Alan exclaims. Shortly thereafter Walter Mitchell is murdered, the price he pays for his moral courage.

Father and son: Lee J. Cobb and Kerwin Mathews in *The Garment Jungle*. Used by permission of the Museum of Modern Art/Film Stills Archive, courtesy of Columbia Studios.

Thus, in addition to its social and political significance, *The Garment Jungle* is also a characteristic Aldrich study of individual integrity, the struggle for self-esteem, and the painfully difficult relationship between a father and his son.

Because Aldrich was under contract to Columbia, Cohn had to pay his salary, but Aldrich was prevented from starting other projects in Hollywood. It seems likely that Cohn was, in part, taking revenge on Aldrich for the satiric portrayal of the studio boss in *The Big Knife* (Cohn finally understood that he was a model for the Stanley Hoff character), but both Aldrich and Cohn accepted the fact that, in the long run, business and not retaliation was the primary reason for Aldrich's dismissal. "I had a great fondness for Cohn," Aldrich admitted. "Naturally I think he was wrong in firing me but that's beside the point. I think he ran a marvellous studio . . . . He wasn't in the money business, he was in the movie business. I had a chance to have a reconciliation with him later—a reconciliation in terms of doing other work—and I didn't go. I've always regretted it."[10] Nevertheless, for the first time since he had arrived in Hollywood in 1941, Aldrich, with a string of critical and commercial hits to his name and an ever-growing reputation at home and abroad, was out of work.

Ten Seconds to Hell (1959)

Although he sued Harry Cohn to break his contract, the case dragged on, and for eighteen months Aldrich "sat home"[11] after being fired from the set of *The Garment Jungle*. During that time, his production company, The Associates and Aldrich, produced a psychological western with Anthony Quinn, *The Ride Back* (1957), the first of several planned productions, and it was rumored that Aldrich took a hand at directing this film, although the credit went to Alan Miner. But the film lost money, doing little to revive Aldrich's sagging fortunes in Hollywood. For all practical purposes, Aldrich's directorial career had come to a halt, and he was open to almost any project. "It goes back to staying at the table," he said. "Anybody that stays away for awhile, voluntarily or involuntarily, risks never coming back."[12] Finally, he was offered a film to be made in Europe through a deal United Artists had made with the German UFA Studios. It was to be a co-production between the English Hammer and the American Seven Arts companies, the film to be shot in the German studios and distributed by United Artists.

The Phoenix, as the project was then called, was based on a novel of the same name by Laurence Bachmann. It dealt with the post-war experiences of six German soldiers, all demolition experts, who are given the job of defusing unexploded bombs scattered throughout the devastated city of Berlin. It sounded like an ideal Aldrich project, concentrating as it did on a group of men in a life-and-death situation, a variation of what he had done in *Attack!.* "I figured I might as well get out of town,"[13] Aldrich said, so he wrote the screenplay with co-writer Teddi Sherman, gathered together some of his standard group—actors Jack Palance, Wesley Addy, Dave Willock; cameraman Ernest Laszlo—and went to Germany. After two weeks of rehearsal, filming began in February 1958 at the UFA Studios in West Berlin.

Working in Europe soon presented advantages and disadvantages. His major awards had been presented by Europeans, and his reputation among them as an auteur, a man whose films expressed a coherent and personal view of the world, encouraged him to think he could continue his work there without undue interference. Moreover, the deal United Artists had made with UFA was a good one, and Aldrich was able to make his film at a reasonably low cost and with excellent production values.[14] Still, Aldrich had to work with German crews, and, though he found some of their methods to be more efficient than his own, there remained continuing minor irritations which arose when Aldrich's style of shooting came into conflict with that of the Germans. More serious, however, were the problems soon evident with the script and with lead actor Jack Palance. As Aldrich recalled, "The scenario was too long, too superficially philosophical, and far too talky."[15] As for his relationship with Palance, who had now worked with Aldrich in two of his finest films—*The Big Knife* and *Attack!*—Aldrich admitted that "we both ran out of the ability . . . to continue our professional rapport . . . . [In] *Ten Seconds to Hell,* Palance's was the pivotal part, and when I lost control of him, and he lost confidence in me, the resulting damage to the final film was catastrophic."[16] Indeed, this film would prove to be the final collaboration between the two men, a rupture Aldrich regretted.

Still other problems plagued the film. United Artists apparently had expected of Aldrich a typical adventure movie; what they got was a slower, more thoughtful, and—to use Aldrich's word—"talky" film than they wanted. "I don't think anyone ever read the script before we started the picture," Aldrich said. "The area of disappointment between the distributor and myself was that they had expected one kind of film, a dramatisation of the Bachmann novel. Well, the script was never changed from the day it was submitted, budgeted and agreed and cast and started, until we finished. So when they came on the scene in Berlin and saw this picture, which was pretty melancholy, they were terribly shocked . . . . So they overreacted to what they saw. They chopped it to pieces. I think everybody had a hand in the re-editing."[17] Aldrich's version of the film ràn 131 minutes, but the released version was shortened by over 40 minutes.

The plot and structure of *Ten Seconds to Hell* is simple. Six German soldiers, in disfavor with the Nazi regime during the war, have now after the war been sent back to the Allied sector of Berlin to dismantle unexploded bombs. All six realize that theirs is a very dangerous business— there were ten of them six months ago—and they agree to set half their salary aside for a common fund which will go to whatever survivors are left at the end of three months. In alphabetical order, they will tackle the bombs, and no man can pass up a turn without the permission of the others. Of the six, two men stand out. Karl Wirtz (Jeff Chandler) is, as the voiceover at the beginning of the film sententiously tells us, "The big man . . . with one big idea in mind—his own survival—and one way to assure it—play for high stakes and deal from the bottom of the deck." Eric Koertner (Jack Palance) is "another big man . . . a man whom other men followed instinctively. A strange, brooding mixture of passion and compassion. Passion for the promise of words like 'right' and 'justice'; compassion for other confused and lost souls." Koertner and Wirtz, obviously, make up the center of the film—the other four men work more as *types* rather than as individuals—and the film quickly narrows its focus to the antagonism between these two men who represent, in Aldrich's dichotomy, the "fascist" and "democratic" ideals. Wirtz, for example, argues that he should lead the group because he is not as "emotional" as Koertner, but Koertner is the one elected by the other men. Still, both men are presented as lost souls. Thus Koertner makes Wirtz his assistant because, "next to me, you have the least to live for."

Eric Koertner is another of Aldrich's hurt heroes, a man who has suffered disillusionment and now is trying to cope with a shattered life. As we learn later in the film, Koertner was before the war an architect; indeed, he had designed a number of the buildings which now lie in rubble around him. In what is a central irony of the film, he understands that by getting rid of the bombs, he is helping to rebuild his country: he is creating by destroying. However, he has been hurt too much by life; he has withdrawn into himself, unwilling to make himself vulnerable to emotional demands. When he meets Margot Hofer (Martine Carol), the landlady of the house where he and Wirtz live, she recognizes his spiritual exhaustion, his fear of love. "What you want, you deny yourself," she tells him. "But why? Tell me, does it make you feel pure and superior to walk away from something you want?" "I don't know," Eric answers. "I've never seen anything I wanted that badly." Later, however, after several of the men under his command have died, Eric does turn to Margot. "Don't let me stand alone," he pleads. "Nobody can, Eric," she says. "And the greatness comes in not pretending to be able to." Eric, then, is finally able to reach out, to admit fear and weakness and doubt, and because he is able to, he becomes one of Aldrich's few self-realized heroes.

But there is also Karl Wirtz to consider in this film, a man who, as played by Jeff Chandler, is strangely likeable and appealing despite his selfishness and cruelty. As Aldrich stated in an article he wrote for *Cahiers du Cinema* in 1959, he wanted to look at both sides, both personalities, involved in this conflict; he wanted to recognize that the "anti-hero" could in fact appear admirable in some ways, which perhaps makes him all the more dangerous.[18] Aldrich had earlier studied this type of character in such films as *Vera Cruz* and *Kiss Me Deadly*, in which Joe Erin's and Mike Hammer's childish arrogance held a certain uneasy charm. Karl Wirtz is of their type. He is attracted to Margot Hofer because she is physically appealing, yet he sees nothing of the emotional strength to which Eric Koertner is drawn. When Karl tries to make love to her, she tells him that he "has no right to do that." "Of course I do," he answers. "I am a man and you are a woman. It's as simple as that." When he finally realizes that Margot prefers Eric to him, however, he steps aside with a certain gallantry. "A good man doesn't try to follow an act he can't top," he says, refers to himself ironically as a "shining knight" and departs. At one point, Karl echoes the tale told by Joe Erin about Ace Hannah when he recalls for Eric the story of his "Uncle Oscar," who taught him, "Only a fool doesn't look out for himself first." Years later, during a bombing raid, young Karl shuts the shelter door in his uncle's face. "Take care of yourself first," Karl preaches.

"This is a battle for survival between the Karls of the world and the me's of the world," Eric finally declares, but what Aldrich makes us realize is that the battle is never as clear-cut and precise as Eric would have it. As the introduction points out, both Eric and Karl are "big" men: neither can be easily dismissed. Moreover, what Eric sees and fears in Karl is really a reflection of what he sees and fears in himself. Certainly his self-pitying withdrawal is simply a variation of Karl's more hedonistic

Jeff Chandler and Jack Palance and the double-fused bomb in *Ten Seconds To Hell*. Used by permission of the Museum of Modern Art/Film Stills Archive, courtesy of United Artists.

egocentrism. Just as there are flashes of honor, even of pity, in Karl, so are there shadows of hatred and cruelty in Eric. Karl is called a child by Margot, but his seeming irresponsibility is a protest against a crazed world, just as is Eric's crippled stoicism; Karl can play by the rules when he so chooses. Indeed, his rebellion against this world is in some ways more easily accepted than Eric's sulking withdrawal.

Karl and Eric's essential twinship is emphasized in the final scenes of the film. In the picture some members of the team have been killed when supposedly-defused bombs have nevertheless exploded, leading the survivors to question the possibility that they were double-fused weapons. By the time this suspicion is confirmed, only Karl and Eric remain of the original group. The next bomb found is Karl's, and it is of the double-fused variety. Eric says that he will look at it with Karl—"It's the least I can do"—but acknowledges that Karl must take it as his lot.

In a series of long shots, Aldrich establishes the scene of these two men, small figures surrounded by devastation, working over the deadly cylinder. Eric finally thinks he understands the mechanics of the weapon and gives his advice to Karl; then he shakes Karl's hand and retreats to the safety point while Karl undertakes his task. Karl, however, fails to follow Eric's advice, and, suddenly, he is in trouble. Eric's basic sense of humanity compels him to return. "Still acting like a child," he accuses Karl; "Still noble till the bitter end!" Karl retorts. Then, when Eric sends Karl to retrieve some necessary wrenches, Karl attempts to set off the bomb—and thus kill Eric—from a distance. It is a foolish and unlikely thing for him to do, and when it fails, he is prepared to accept his fate. "Guess it's still my bomb," he says. "Still your bomb," Eric agrees, knowing full well that Karl will not be able to defuse it alone. As Eric walks away, the smaller figure of Karl descends into the pit, to his death. Two fuses require two men. In the inevitable explosion which follows, Eric has, in a sense, vanquished his doppëlganger, but the look on his face indicates that he has done so at a price. He has shut his own shelter door on Karl, and he must now live with that knowledge.

Ten Seconds to Hell begins with stock footage of airplanes dropping bombs; it ends with shots of new buildings going up amid the destruction and with images of the dead five superimposed over them. This ending has been read in two different ways. Harry Ringel feels that it shows that "a man more broken than Costa and Castle put together *can* act: an out-of-the-ashes view of salvation . . . ."[19] Alain Silver, however, thinks that it merely recapitulates the fact that "many have miscalculated and perished."[20] Certainly *Ten Seconds to Hell* is a bleak film. It is appropriate that the first of the six to die is Blobke, "the boy, who somehow had held on to fragments of his youth and innocence." The world of this film has been blasted of its innocence long before; it lies in scattered ruin. In this world, men may join in groups, but each must ultimately face his destiny alone. "You musn't count too much on [the future]," Eric tells Margot. "Nothing is certain." "I don't ask for that," she says. "I don't ask for certainty from Fate. . . . Certainty is for children." But even given this view, it is difficult to agree completely with Silver's pessimism. Karl, the fascist, loses his nerve, breaks his own rules, and (albeit with courage and resignation) dies. Eric, the humanist, survives. He abandons his solipsistic posture; he reaches out to another, faces his own fears, and accepts them. He is not made whole, but he has found qualified hope, a reason to go on.

Despite his closeness to the film, Aldrich did not remember it with affection. It was, he said, "a bad picture. . . . No matter if I did [it] tomorrow I wouldn't know how to make it any better."[21] Given the mutilated state of the film as we have it, it is impossible to assess how well it could have lived up to Aldrich's original concept of it. Certainly, the film suffers from the weaknesses Aldrich noted: it is talky, sometimes slow, and often didactic. Still, those moments in which man faces the bomb are gripping. Each episode is varied so that the suspense is always fresh—one bomb is in a collapsing building, one is under water—and there is always the hazard of the double-fuse. To create further tension, Aldrich typically dispenses with background music during these moments. At times he amplifies the physical sounds of breathing or the mechanical sounds of wrenches on bolts; at other time he allows silence itself to work for him, until it is broken by the dooming tick of the bomb's detonating device. He uses close-ups to focus on the intensity of the individual facing death, but he also pulls back to long shots to remind us of each man's relative helplessness in this huge, ruined landscape. Moreover, although *Ten Seconds to Hell* drew rather mixed reviews in the United States, some critics admired what Aldrich was attempting in the film: Richard Nason, writing in the *New York Times*, found it "a strange and unconventional bit of entertainment that unfortunately falls between the genres of an art film and a suspense drama. . . ." Nonetheless, he felt that in the "rather patent story," Aldrich had bracketed "a profound set of ideas involving moral responsibility in a world dedicated to violence and destruction." Aldrich, he concluded, "persuasively reasserts his claim to being one of America's distinctive film makers. . . ."[22]

The Angry Hills (1959)

Ten Seconds to Hell was, for Aldrich, a film irreparably flawed. About *The Angry Hills*, the second film of his European exile, he was considerably more sanguine. This film, he thought, seemed always to have "a potential that was never even remotely realised." Thus, Aldrich was disappointed with *The Angry Hills* not because he believed it was a bad film, but because "it *could* have been good. . . . I'd know [now] how to make [it] better in a thousand ways."[23] In fact, Aldrich faced many of the same obstacles in this film that he encountered in *Ten Seconds to Hell*. Like its predecessor, *The Angry Hills* was cut by more than a half hour before its theatrical release.[24] In addition, the film's producer, Raymond Stross, and its distributor, MGM, relied on a poor marketing strategy. Its chief star was Robert Mitchum. "[Stross] understood,"

Aldrich noted, "that Metro was buying film by the yard then, and Mitchum was reasonably hot. So they thought that as long as it was an hour and a half with Mitchum and some Greek scenery, it would work. Obviously, it didn't."[25] Then there were impracticable contractual obligations to be honored: Stross and MGM had signed star Robert Mitchum to an agreement specifying a definite starting date and a fabulous salary. Unfortunately, they neglected to give similar assurances that a script would *also* be ready by that date. Principal photography thus had to commence before the screenplay was complete, a situation Aldrich detested.[26]

The script itself presented perhaps the most serious problems of all. Based on the novel of the same name by Leon Uris, *The Angry Hills* concerned the activities of the Greek resistance movement during the first chaotic months of the German occupation in World War II. Oddly enough, neither Uris nor the MGM producers of the film had ever traveled in Greece, and Aldrich, after arriving on location, considered the first draft of Uris' screenplay to be incompatible with the setting. Not even a producers-subsidized, six-day, all-expenses-paid tour of Greece could inspire novelist Uris to produce a more plausible draft. Thus filming and rehearsals were already under way but without an overall sense of direction because no one—not even Aldrich—knew exactly where the film was headed.[27] To bail out the troubled project, Aldrich summoned to the scene an old associate, A.I. Bezzerides, whose screenplay for *Kiss Me Deadly* had proved so successful. But Bezzerides was unaccustomed to playing the kind of catch-up game demanded of him by Stross and Metro; uncomfortable from the start, Bezzerides found the situation at odds with his creative habits: "That turned [Bezzerides] right off," Aldrich recalled, "and what could have been a rather extraordinary piece of material became just another story."[28]

Thus began a film that simply was not ready to begin, a film which, Aldrich readily admitted, showed a "loose wandering quality that doesn't enhance it at all and needn't have been there if we'd had another couple of months."[29] A seriously flawed film, particularly with respect to its "loose," rambling plot, *The Angry Hills* remains one of Adlrich's less well-known and less important works. Nevertheless, Aldrich's exploration of the issues of heroism, personal integrity, and compromise, as well as his presentation of character and relationships, sets the film apart from the run-of-the-mill World War II espionage thriller.

The plot concerns the adventures of Mike Morrison (Robert Mitchum), an American journalist trapped in Athens during the sudden Nazi advance into Greece in 1941 Morrison has in his possession a list of the names of sixteen partisans who will organize the Greek underground resistance to the Nazi invasion. For obvious security reasons, this list is as valuable to British intelligence as it is to the Gestapo. Heading the Gestapo's efforts to acquire the list is Konrad Heisler (Stanley Baker), who enlists the aid of fifth columnist Tassos (Theodore Bikel) to ensure the success of their mission. After Tassos makes an unsuccessful attempt on Morrison's life, Morrison escapes to an outlying village where his wounds are dressed by Greek patriot Eleftheria (Gia Scala, who had worked with Aldrich in *The Garment Jungle*), a beautiful woman who falls in love with him. After his recovery, Morrison is asked to lead a raid on a German armory, but he and his comrades are betrayed and ambushed by Heisler's alerted soldiers. Morrison survives and hides in a nearby convent; when the local Greek villagers refuse to divulge Morrison's whereabouts to the Gestapo, Heisler orders the execution of ten men. Meanwhile, Morrison, still hoping to deliver the list to British authorities, returns to Athens where he makes contact with Lisa (Elizabeth Mueller), a patriot who once was Heisler's lover. Heisler threatens to kill her children unless she hands Morrison over to the Gestapo, but Lisa cannot betray her country. Luckily, another agent, Chesney (Sebastian Cabot), assassinates Tassos and arranges a safe passage for Morrison and the children. In the film's final shot, Heisler and Lisa are left to face their undisclosed fates while the boat bearing its precious cargo leaves the harbor for the refuge of the open sea.

Aldrich said that what primarily interested him about *The Angry Hills* was "its story of an easy-going American coming of political age, and assuming commitment and responsibility, during the early days of the last war in Greece."[30] As Aldrich's remarks imply, Morrison is not by nature the heroic type; at first he prefers to remain neutral in the affair, electing to sell the valuable list of names to an unscrupulous black marketeer, a Dr. Thackery, who has promised to pay handsomely for it. But Tassos kills Thackery before the transaction can be completed, and Morrison, injured in the ensuing chase, is befriended and protected by Eleftheria and her friends. Inspired by their courage, Morrison now begins to accept responsibility for—and commit himself to—the struggle for Greek freedom. Only then does he take part in the decisive, though abortive, action against the German munitions depot. Morrison's conversion is similar to that of Ben Trane in *Vera Cruz*; like him Morrison is led to choose the good cause through the love of a woman. He becomes

Robert Mitchum and Elizabeth Mueller in *The Angry Hills*. Used by permission of the Museum of Modern Art/Film Stills Archive, courtesy of MGM.

a reluctant hero: a man who finds himself the unwitting victim of circumstances far beyond his purview and control but who discovers within himself the strength and resourcefulness to wrestle heroically with adversity.

The war-torn world Morrison contends with in *The Angry Hills* is one in which subterfuge and terrorism are standard procedures, in which the torture and slaughter of innocent civilians are commonplace occurrences. When he learns that Eleftheria has chosen to die under Gestapo interrogation rather than reveal his hiding place, Morrison bitterly announces to Lisa that "there's not much left to believe in." Morrison's cynical attitudes are certainly understandable: he is double-crossed twice, once by the British and once by the Greeks. But Morrison attains his "political coming of age"—to use Aldrich's phrase—through his recognition, gradual and painful, that the cause of political liberty is worth risking his life for. Like Ben Trane, Morrison discovers that to believe in something is to give meaning to life, and, though the odds of his prevailing against the Gestapo and the Nazis are great, the rewards—his self-esteem and his personal redemption—are greater still.

But in many ways, the predicament of Lisa, Heisler's former mistress, is even more painful and precarious than Morrison's, for she *has* something to believe in all along—her children—and they are being used by Heisler as pawns in this ruthless chess game of espionage. Although she is compelled to choose between motherhood and country, her choice—to spare Morrison and risk her children—is a calculated gamble, rooted in an intimate awareness of Heisler's nature. As his former lover, Lisa instinctively feels that "there's a point beyond which Heisler won't go," and her hunch proves to be correct: when a local priest escorts the children to safety, Heisler fails to intervene. His conscience will not permit it.

Heisler, then, emerges as a curiously sympathetic character, faring considerably better than most Nazi Gestapo chiefs in conventional World War II spy thrillers. Once again, Aldrich avoids a stereotypical antagonist. Heisler is a complexly divided figure; and in his role as reluctant villain, he acts as an ironic double to Morrison, the reluctant hero. Although Heisler orders the execution of innocent people, he does so with misgivings, and his threat to shoot Lisa's children is, finally, an empty one, mere posturing. His attachment to her is stronger than his attachment to the party. In a scene near the end of the film, Heisler, suspecting that Lisa has become fond of Morrison, sternly reminds her that "love is one thing, duty another." Ironically, Heisler is, however, too human to follow his own advice. As the boat carrying Morrison and the children to safety leaves the harbor, Lisa embraces Heisler and departs, undetained, despite a desperate phone call from Nazi headquarters which Heisler chooses to ignore.

Neither Robert Mitchum's nor Robert Aldrich's careers were helped much by *The Angry Hills*. Aldrich accepted full responsibility for Mitchum's rather lackluster performance, admitting that he had failed to get sufficiently close to Mitchum to bring Morrison's character adequately to life.[31] Although Aldrich's relationship with Mitchum went back to their RKO days in the mid-forties, when Aldrich had worked with Mitchum on *The Story of G.I. Joe* (the film that started Mitchum's career) and *The Red Pony*, the two men had never been good friends, and their ability to work together deteriorated during the filming of *The Angry*

Hills. The film's failure can be traced, moreover, to each man's fundamentally different perception of the *kind* of film they were making. Aldrich explained:

> We were about a week into the film, living in a sensational place outside Athens. The picture was going terribly. So one evening after dinner I walked down to Mitchum's cabaña at the other end of the beach. I told him, "We're making a lousy movie. I'm trying the best I can, and I sense you are, but it's not working and I don't know what to do." "Don't you understand what we're making?" he asked. "We're making a gorilla picture." What was a gorilla picture, I asked. "A gorilla picture is when you get 250,000 dollars for doing all the wrong things for ten reels and in the last shot you get the girl and fade into the sunset. That's a gorilla picture. I don't care how well you make it, it's still going to be a gorilla picture. Now if you understand that, you'll be very happy. If you don't, you'll be very unhappy." "I don't understand that," I said. "So I'm going to be very unhappy. I don't want to make a gorilla picture."[32]

Despite Aldrich's intentions, Mitchum's description of *The Angry Hills* as a "gorilla picture" is an adequate one.

Aldrich had now made two disappointing films working in Europe. He had less control over their final form than he had had in the United States. They were doing little for his reputation (except among select critics), and he was no closer to regaining the direction of his career than when he first left America. Thus, when he began work on his third foreign-made film, Aldrich was both depressed and concerned.

The Last Sunset (1961)

After completing *The Angry Hills* in Greece, Aldrich went to Mexico to shoot his third western, *The Last Sunset.* Once again, it was not a pleasant experience, as he vividly recalled: "The whole thing started badly, went on badly, ended up badly. Dalton Trumbo had done a screenplay. This was just towards the end of the McCarthy period and he had yet to be given a screen credit, though Preminger had promised him one for *Exodus.* He quit his concentration on *The Last Sunset* to concentrate on the Preminger picture and by the time he came back to our film it was too late to save it."[33] Then too there was trouble with co-star Kirk Douglas: Lukas Heller and two other writers had accompanied Aldrich to Mexico to work on their own respective projects—not on *The Last Sunset* script—but, as Aldrich remembered, when Douglas spotted them on the set, he "went berserk."[34] Lukas Heller described the situation in greater detail:

> I arrived in Mexico with a tiny, startlingly ugly, but thoroughly amiable German writer, who was to translate my screenplay, and another writer who was a West Indian, extremely black and about six foot six. The three of us—this gigantic black man, this little German, and me with my Beatles' haircut—came onto the set the first day, and I saw Kirk Douglas sitting under a tree with his hat over his eyes like a cowboy. When he noticed us, I saw that the hat went up, Kirk Douglas looked, and then looked away again. But the next morning we were on the train back to Mexico City, because Kirk Douglas had thrown a fit and said how *dare* Aldrich distract himself in any way by having not one, nor even two, but *three* writers working on other projects when he was supposed to be directing him in a movie.

Such on-location antagonisms—and lapses in creative concentration—made for less than ideal working conditions, and once more Aldrich found himself with a difficult film on his hands. The problems—with the script, with Douglas's performance—were apparent to most critics when the film was released in 1961 (although subsequent reconsiderations have been more positive and insightful).[35] Whatever its weaknesses, *The Last Sunset* is certainly a provocative film, an adult, psychological western.

The basic plot of *The Last Sunset* is taken from Howard Rigsby's novel *Sundown at Crazy Horse*. U.S. lawman Dana Stribling (Rock Hudson) crosses into Mexican territory in pursuit of Brendon O'Malley (Kirk Douglas), accused murderer of Jimmy Graham, the husband of Stribling's sister. Eventually both men arrive at the Breckenridge ranch in Mexico, home of Belle Breckenridge (Dorothy Malone), O'Malley's long-ago lover; her alcoholic husband John Breckenridge (Joseph Cotton); and their nubile daughter Missy (Carol Lynley). The Breckenridge outfit is about to embark on a cattle drive to Crazy Horse, Texas, and O'Malley and Stribling, being good gunslingers, are invited along. The Sheriff and the outlaw agree to put aside personal differences until they reach Texas. Meanwhile, John Breckenridge is killed in a bar fight, and the full responsibility for the safe passage of both cattle and women falls on the shoulders of Stribling and O'Malley, who grapple with outlaws, Indians, sand storms, stampedes, and quicksand in route to Crazy Horse. By journey's end, Stribling has fallen in love with Belle, and O'Malley—spurned by Belle—has fallen in love with Missy. When the entourage reaches Texas, Stribling guns down O'Malley in the climactic sundown shoot-out, the defenseless O'Malley having previously unloaded his revolver after learning that Missy, his lover, is, in actuality, Missy, his *daughter*. O'Malley's

Kirk Douglas and Rock Hudson square off in *The Last Sunset*. Used by permission of the Museum of Modern Art/Film Stills Archive, courtesy of Universal-International Studios.

discovery of his incestuous relationship with his daughter—an idea whose emphasis Aldrich credits to author Dalton Trumbo—is a real shocker, and it makes of *The Last Sunset* a sustained study of sexual perverseness and neuroses, what Richard Combs has described as Aldrich's "most poeticised treatment of a sexual pathology."[36]

Initially, the sexual motifs in *The Last Sunset* are presented in a lightly titillating, even playful manner. When O'Malley first arrives at the Breckenridge ranch, for example, he is quizzed by Missy about why he prefers to carry his pistol in his belt rather than in a holster. "So," answers O'Malley, "I always know where it is, so I can feel it close to me all the time." O'Malley is a fellow whose "gun" regularly gets him into trouble, and it most certainly would have made life miserable for pathetic John

Breckenridge, had Breckenridge survived. When the intoxicated Breckenridge offers O'Malley the job of hired gun on the cattle drive, O'Malley accepts, but he demands outrageous terms: "I want," he brazenly announces to Breckenridge, "one-fifth of the herd, and I want your wife. I mean to take your wife." At first nonplussed, Breckenridge abruptly agrees to the terms, his body trembling with nervous laughter. But Breckenridge does not live long enough to keep his end of the bargain: in one of the film's most harrowing scenes, Breckenridge is sexually harrassed and humiliated, his tormentors taunting him to display the dishonorable wound he received in his backside at the Battle of Fredricksburg. His assailants then shoot Breckenridge in the back, as if to seal his reputation as a coward. From that point, the sexual motifs in *The Last Sunset* become progressively more grim and serious.

By far, the most profoundly disturbing sexual perversion in *The Last Sunset* is the incest motif. The disclosure of the awful truth about Missy's and O'Malley's incestuous relationship comes on the morning after the party celebrating the end of the cattle drive. Missy appears at the dance that night in her mother's pretty yellow dress, the very same yellow dress Belle had worn on that fateful night years earlier when she was seduced by O'Malley. This, too, is a fateful night for Missy. Irresistible in her gown (she has heretofore worn only jeans), Missy joins O'Malley for a rendezvous beneath the stars: "I love you," she implores, "I'm not young . . . I'm a woman . . . I don't want a boy . . . I want you." Captivated by her youthful, innocent charms, O'Malley succumbs; the two passionately embrace and make love. The next morning, O'Malley approaches Belle with his plan to take Missy away with him: "Nothing bad will ever happen while I'm with her . . . . She loves me in a way that she'll never love any other man." Stunned by the terrible, tragic irony of O'Malley's words, Belle utters the horrible truth: "She's your daughter!" O'Malley, at first incredulous, reacts violently: he accuses Belle of lying, slaps her face, and storms off, staggered by the enormity of her revelation. But the truth is undeniable. Resigned to it, O'Malley spends the remainder of the time before his sunset showdown attending solicitously—one might say paternally—to Missy's comfort and happiness, speaking to her of angels, starry skies, and romance. These scenes—one on a pier jutting out into the river, another in a grassy, flowery meadow—are among the most tender and sensitive in the film.

O'Malley has turned to Missy, then, because he sees in her a surrogate for Belle (who has rejected him for Stribling), a youthful carbon copy in whom he can fix his memory of an idealized past. To have Missy is to have the little girl of his dreams, not, ironically, the *woman* Missy wants to be to him. This is the Oedipal stuff of which *The Last Sunset* is made, the theme of "sexual pathology" to which Combs has referred. T.J. Ross, writing perceptively about the film, sums up the matter nicely:

> ... Lynley [Missy] latches on to Douglas [O'Malley] who, entranced by nostalgia, draws Lynley into the embrace which marks the ultimate flight of his unwitting demonism: the scorned poet fails to recognize in the symbol he makes love to, his own child. He is blinded by his obsessive notion that innocence is reclaimable, like some item in a Lost and Found department. And his obsessiveness keeps him continually on edge, makes him increasingly brutal in his present time. Perhaps in no film of his, has Aldrich developed a more ruthless and more brilliant critique of the lust for innocence ... than in this Western.[37]

If *The Last Sunset* is a critique of the lust for Innocence, it is no less a critique of the lust for Experience. Corrupt and decadent, characters in the film resort to extreme forms of destructive behavior: John Breckenridge is driven to alcoholism and personal disgrace; Stribling's sister to whoredom and self-destruction; the Julesberg Kid and company to kidnap and attempted rape; the Rebel soldiers to sadism and murder; O'Malley to incest and suicide. To account for this generally dim view of human nature, Aldrich stages this conversation, early in the film, between Missy and O'Malley: "Are you a killer?" Missy inquires of the gunfighter. "When you come right down to it," replies O'Malley, "all men in their hearts are killers." Significantly, this elucidation of the heart-of-darkness theme takes place just after a most shocking moment in the film, a scene in which O'Malley leaves the cabin and confronts a dog growling in the yard. He seizes the dog by the throat and begins to choke it to death. After several agonizing seconds—man and beast locked head-to-head in close-up profile, mirror images of one another— O'Malley's rage subsides, and he releases his grip on the cowering animal. And although the film ends on a somewhat more positive note—Belle and Stribling and Missy survive to comprise a happy, if chastened, family—we are left, finally, to ponder the darker, more sinister implications of *The Last Sunset*, whose very title, Andrew Sarris notes, "suggest[s] a mood befitting the Decline of the West."[38]

Before returning to Hollywood, Aldrich made one more film on locations outside the United States. It was a film on a grand scale. In fact, the difficulties Aldrich faced on the set of *The Angry Hills* and *The Last*

Sunset would seem puny in contrast to the massive production and post-production morasses engendered by his one, and only, Biblical epic, the expansive and expensive *Sodom and Gomorrah*.

Sodom and Gomorrah (1963)

Sodom and Gomorrah, which Aldrich called a "terrible" film, was made in Italy and Morocco in early 1961 (it was released in America in 1963). On this project, Aldrich joined forces with Joseph E. Levine, although their relationship quickly soured after an initial honeymoon period. Aldrich was attracted to this story, taken loosely from the book of Genesis, for several reasons. First, he had never directed this kind of film before. "I think every director wants to make one biblical spectacle," he said. "I think he's probably unwise if he wants to make more than one, but I think it's something that you should do . . . to see if you can make a picture that is not repetitive or so cliché or imitative." He also felt that, because the story came from the Old Testament, he could con-centrate on the historical scope of the story and not be overly restricted by religious implications or interpretations. Moreover, he noted parallels between the "social-moral decay of Sodom" and that in the modern world, although in the film, "we tried to do it without being too obvious."[39]

Because of the Italian subsidy system under which Aldrich was work-ing, it was necessary to employ Italian counterparts for major production positions. Thus there had to be a "director" for the "Italian version," an Italian screenwriter, assistant director, and so on, although, according to Aldrich, these men actually added little or nothing to the filming. The second unit director for *Sodom and Gomorrah* was, interesting-ly, Sergio Leone, who lasted about four days on the job before Aldrich fired him for not doing things "quite the way I envisaged."[40] One day when he visited the second unit set, Aldrich saw that Leone was giv-ing thousands of extras three-and four-hour lunch breaks and was do-ing very little work in general. "I called him and I said, 'Get your ticket and go back to Rome; you're through.' He went back to Rome, and they had no director for the first Clint Eastwood picture [*A Fistful of Dollars*] and that's why he's a zillionaire and I'm broke."[41]

For the first time Aldrich shot with multiple cameras (a method he would use on all subsequent films[42]), and he ended up with a very long picture, over four hours in length, which he then cut to a little under three hours. Because of the Italian subsidy system, Aldrich, as "author," had legal control of its final shape, a prerogative he was denied on his other two European-based films over whose final versions he had no control whatsoever. When the Italian producer insisted on further cuts, Aldrich threatened litigation. He explained the legal complexities and ironies to Charles Champlin:

> . . . what the court finally said was that if the producer could cut it, then it wasn't being made under Italian copyright law, and therefore it wasn't an Italian production and therefore it wasn't entitled to the Italian government subsidy. That finding had a very sobering effect on everybody.
>
> We got our injunction but we compromised and the film came out 15 minutes shorter, which didn't make a hell of a lot of difference one way or the other. I realized that it was ludicrous to have had that fight over an Italian sex-and-sand epic. It's the court's decision that is interesting now.[43]

Because he had produced his own films in the fifties and because he had worked for major studios both at home and abroad, Aldrich could fully appreciate, perhaps even more than the average Hollywood director, the significance of the Italian court's decision. Aldrich understood the advantages of independence and control, the power and authority of studios, the importance of the director's right to his cut, the value of artistic integrity. Early in the sixties, in this Italian court, Aldrich was already preparing himself, legally and tactically, for the many tough battles he would fight years later on behalf of his colleagues as president of the Directors Guild of America.

It is unclear how well this final version, which ran two hours and 34 minutes, reflects Aldrich's original intentions, but *Sodom and Gomorrah* is a disjointed and uninspired film. Although Lot (Stewart Granger) occasionally nods in God's direction—"We believe that only God knows our future. And that belief gives us the faith to move mountains"—the film is among the least religious of biblical epics. It concentrates rather on politics and commerce. The Sodomites, led by Queen Bera (Anouk Aimee), are at odds with the neighboring Helamites. When Lot and his band of Hebrews wander into the region, Bera allows them to stay because they act as a buffer between Sodom and her enemy. To solidify the relationship, Bera also gives Lot the beautiful Ildith (Pier Angeli) as bride and (secretly) as spy. Lot is a widower with two grown daughters, one of whom, Sheeah (Rossana Podestra), falls in love with Bera's evil, treacherous brother Astaroth (Stanley Baker), who is in league with the Helamites so that he might displace his sister as ruler of Sodom. When, halfway through the film, the Helamites finally attack the Hebrews, they are drowned when Lot orders the dam built for irrigation to be destroyed. The waters also wash away the Hebrew village, but in the process a great supply of valuable salt is discovered on the Hebrew land. This salt gives the Hebrews the commercial power they need to establish themselves. It also leads to their corruption, since it brings them into Sodom as tradesmen. Soon, they are taking part in Sodom's social life, despite Lot's pleas. When Lot learns that Astaroth has taken his daughter Sheeah as a concubine, he kills the royal brother and is put in jail. He is released by two angels, however, and leads those who will listen away from the doomed city just before it is obliterated by holocaustal earthquakes and a rain of fire. Ildith, who has come to love Lot but cannot accept his belief in the Hebrew God, looks back at the destruction despite Lot's orders and is turned into a mound of salt. Lot, a grieving, broken man, is then helped away by his daughters.

The film has less structure and makes less sense than this synopsis would suggest. Because in 1961 Aldrich could not be explicit about Sodom's sexual proclivities, he placed his emphasis on sadism and torture instead, but these scenes are more ludicrous than horrifying. There are suggestions of lesbianism (Bera and Ildith) and incest (Bera and Astaroth), and even Lot is tempted by the ways of the flesh. He wants Ildith to think of him as "Lot the man," and his relationship with Sheeah is tinged with sexual jealousy. There are also references to some of Aldrich's major themes, although they are never explored or developed. Astaroth is another of his childish villains, who hurt and destroy out of spite. Lot, as tribal leader and as a father, can be both overdemanding and wrongheaded in his judgments. It is his decision that brings the Hebrews into Sodom, a decision which he comes to repent. There are also parallels between Sodom and modern civilization, and the destruction of the city is accompanied by a mushroom cloud, although it lacks the ominousness and suggestiveness of the end of *Kiss Me Deadly*. Indeed all of this is at best superficial to the film, which remains, for the most part, unfortunately dull. One exception: in the fight between the Hebrews and the Helamites, Aldrich and the film seem to wake up. The battle does not make a great deal of sense, but it is an exciting episode in an otherwise unsuccessful film.

One of Aldrich's major disappointments during these years abroad was his failure to make the blockbuster film that would revive his career and provide that measure of independence as a filmmaker he so desperately desired. Throughout this period, he had spent considerable time and money on a script based on the life of Taras Bulba, the 16th century Cossack leader. Aldrich believed this film biography might prove to be the hit he needed. He also identified personally with the figure of Taras Bulba during these years of exile. His efforts to make the film were finally unsuccessful, however, when he and Burt Lancaster, whom he wanted for the title role, were unable to come to terms. Aldrich explained: "Burt Lancaster never refused to play the lead in *Taras Bulba*. His oldest son had been recently stricken with polio and Burt wanted to postpone doing the picture for one year. Unfortunately and stupidly, I refused his reasonable request (much to my regret) and the company who duped me into selling the property (*Taras Bulba*) to them was acting as an agent for Hecht-Lancaster."[44] Although unable to make this film, Aldrich would soon get his blockbuster hit and would begin the most successful and adventurous period of his career. The film was *What Ever Happened to Baby Jane?*. In it Aldrich would explore what co-star Joan Crawford called "evil, horrendous, vile things";[45] and it would prove to be Aldrich's first significant commercial success since *Vera Cruz*. Once again, he would be in charge, in control of his own destiny—an idea as important to Aldrich the man as to Aldrich the director. The years of exile, unkind but terribly instructive, were finally over. But for Aldrich, as for his heroes, it was the struggle that had mattered.

4. Cannibal Time

What Ever Happened to Baby Jane? (1962)

Aldrich was still wrapping up *Sodom and Gomorrah* when he received a letter from Geraldine Hersey, who had worked as his secretary on *Ten Seconds to Hell* and *The Angry Hills*. In effect, Hersey's letter was an enthusiastic review of a novel written by Henry Farrell entitled *What Ever Happened to Baby Jane?*. Hersey was convinced that the book would make a superb movie, and, as she expected, Aldrich thought so too. In his own words, he "flipped for it."[1] Hersey's present employer held the film option on the book, but this option had only another forty days to run, and the price for the movie rights was just $10,000, a price Aldrich could easily afford. The present owner seemed unlikely to exercise his option. While waiting for the forty days to pass (a bit of biblical irony which Aldrich, finishing *Sodom and Gomorrah*, might have appreciated), he sent a copy of Farrell's novel to Joan Crawford, who had long wanted to do a film with Bette Davis and had also wanted to work again with Aldrich. Clearly, Aldrich felt, this was the opportunity they had been waiting for.

During this time, however, other problems arose. Word leaked out that Aldrich was interested in the film rights, and when the forty days were up, he found the price had risen to $61,000, well beyond his financial reach. But Joseph E. Levine, Aldrich's co-producer on *Sodom and Gomorrah*, did have the money, and, largely as a result of Aldrich's work on the biblical epic, decided to join with Aldrich in purchasing the novel and making the picture. Soon, however, relations between the two men deteriorated. Levine took his share of the profits from *Sodom and Gomorrah* and left Aldrich to contend alone with the Italians concerning the massive legal and financial problems created by the film. Thus, in order to make *Baby Jane*, Aldrich had to buy back Levine's share of the film (which now included Lukas Heller's screenplay) for $85,000. Finally, The Associates and Aldrich, after having been turned down by the major studios (who wanted younger actresses in the roles), made an agreement with Seven Arts to distribute the film and were able to come up with the money needed to make the picture. Aldrich had approximately six weeks in which to film.[2]

To write the screenplay for *Baby Jane,* Aldrich had hired Lukas Heller, the young German-born screenwriter with whose work in British and American films and television Aldrich was already familiar. (Aldrich had, in fact, bought the rights to an original story of Heller's called *Cross of Iron,* a U-Boat yarn which Aldrich never filmed because of legal problems with the German government; it was this script Heller had planned to revise in Mexico when his presence caused such a furor on the set of *The Last Sunset*). *Baby Jane* was Heller's first Hollywood movie and the first of six successful collaborations between him and Aldrich. Heller was proud of his work with Aldrich on *Baby Jane*: "It was shot almost exactly as written: you can look at the screenplay and see it shot for shot. Mind you, I had great opportunity there because we were able to spend six months writing the screenplay [Aldrich worked with Heller in Rome while editing his "sex and sand" epic]. And after I wrote a scene or shot or whatever, he might say, 'Wouldn't it be better if we . . . ?' I'm certain it was as much *his* movie as much as any movie is a director's movie."

What Ever Happened to Baby Jane? is another Aldrich film about Hollywood and Hollywood people, cast in the form of a psychological horror picture. It is also a grotesquely comic work, one of Aldrich's best in the genre. Aldrich's hunch in casting Bette Davis and Joan Crawford as the leads proved to be a stroke of genius and was, perhaps, the one decision most responsible for the success of the film. They had never before worked together, despite their many years making movies, and their personal dislike for each other was legendary. But the two women had all along been Aldrich's first choices, and his faith in them as professionals who could rise above personal antagonisms was solidly confirmed on the set. "People couldn't see the chemical combustibility of these two ladies who were so different. . . . They act differently and they think differently. Their attitudes are so different, you'd put them in a room and you know that they've got to—in terms of theater—explode. They just can't inhabit the same area together without having a friction situation," Aldrich said.[3] But while filming, "There was never an abrasive word in public, and not once did they try to upstage each other. Nor did Miss Davis allow her enmity with Miss Crawford to colour her playing of the scenes in which she was supposed to torment her. People who loved the violence of it read that into it and thought it was inherent, but it wasn't."[4]

Although Aldrich had been confident about getting Crawford for the part of Blanche—they had worked together on *Autumn Leaves* (a film whose psychological horror clearly anticipates *Baby Jane*) and he en-

Robert Aldrich directing *What Ever Happened to Baby Jane?*. Used by permission of Adell Aldrich.

joyed a good relationship with her—he was less certain of signing Davis for the part of Jane. Aldrich knew that Davis was selective about the parts she played and that she had never before done a film quite like this one. It would take some convincing on his part:

> So I took a lot of time composing a letter that was arrogant but I thought necessarily so, saying that if this isn't the best screenplay you've ever read, don't do the picture, but if it is, I'd like an appointment and I'll come to New York to see you. About a month went by and then I got a very long, very polite, but very aloof letter from Miss Davis saying that no, it wasn't the best screenplay she had ever read, but that it came close. She'd be delighted to meet with me, but didn't know if she'd want to make the picture or not. So I came to New York two or three weeks after that and met with Davis and her lawyer. They were terribly hospitable and friendly, and Davis asked only professional questions. At the end of the three or four hour conversation she said: "Fine, if the economics can be resolved, I'd like to do it."[5]

Aldrich resolved the economics by offering Davis, and Crawford, a percentage of the picture in addition to their salaries.

Aldrich was particularly impressed by Davis's performance and by her substantial contributions to the part. He credited her, for example, with originating Jane's ugly, chalky mask of makeup, and proclaimed that "Bette Davis knows more about the technical end of the business than any actor" he had worked with.[6] Still, directing her was not always an easy task. "I couldn't get her to slow down enough to make a [cut]," Aldrich remembered.[7] Gradually, however, Aldrich earned her trust and respect: he noted that when he showed Davis the final version of *Baby Jane,* "she was smart enough to realize the erosion of the editing process and managed to accommodate her style to leave room for a 'cut' in *Charlotte* [their next film together]."[8] The final result, as Aldrich said, was "such a bravura, all-out Gothic eye-catcher that everybody thought it superior."[9] At Cannes in May 1963 Davis was hounded so mercilessly by fans and photographers that she frequently required police protection, and *Baby Jane* was easily the most talked-about film at the festival. About Davis, Aldrich remarked, "I think the highest compliment I've ever been paid as a director was to have Davis say, 'I know what you mean.' "[10] About Aldrich, Davis has said, "Bob Aldrich is a genius."[11]

Certainly, there is a strong camp appeal to *What Ever Happened to Baby Jane?*, a point underscored by the casting of Davis and Crawford. "In *Baby Jane*, we thought that if you made a movie about the periphery of Hollywood which had something to do with the ancient Hollywood, and you put in two stars who were getting old, people would read in-

Robert Aldrich, with his wife Harriet and daughters Adell and Alida on the set of *Baby Jane*. Used by permission of Adell Aldrich.

to that picture a secret show-biz mythology, almost a nostalgia," Aldrich explained. "The audience feels that they are privy to real life secrets about Crawford and Davis."[12] But elsewhere Aldrich played down this aspect of the film, calling it a "quite intense and very personal" story about "two sisters who live in an active hate for each other," about the demise of a child prodigy "who just didn't mature emotionally or intellectually."[13] And, to be sure, it is the horror of "active hate" and the grim, although often darkly comic, consequences of regression and arrested development that make the film more than a nasty exploitation of fading beauty and forgotten fame.

The two sisters in the film are spinsters Blanche (Joan Crawford) and Baby Jane Hudson (Bette Davis). Blanche is a once-famous actress whose career was abruptly halted by an automobile accident which left her crippled and confined to a wheelchair. Jane is a has-been child vaudeville star who, finding her own fame eclipsed and surpassed by her sister later in life, becomes insanely jealous and precipitates (presumably) her sister's

debilitating accident. Now in their fifties, Blanche and Jane find themselves caught in a perversely symbiotic relationship—Blanche dependent
upon Jane for her daily necessities; Jane dependent upon Blanch for
economic security—from which each woman seeks to extricate herself.
Blanche considers sending her deranged sister to an asylum, and Jane
desires to dispatch her disabled sister to a nursing home. Jane bitterly
resents her role as her sister's keeper (a role she grudgingly accepts, in
part, because of her apparent responsibility for Blanche's condition), and
her resentment expresses itself in acts of deliberate and premeditated
cruelty. Jane bars the windows and locks the door to Blanche's room,
severs all ties and communication with the outside world by dismissing
the maid Elvira (Blanche's only visitor), by ripping out the telephone
and call button, and by intercepting all letters and gifts from friends and
admirers. She eventually binds and gags her, making the helpless cripple
a prisoner in her own home. Jane practices other forms of torture and
torment as well: in a systematic effort to starve and terrorize her sister,
Jane serves Blanche disgusting dishes of dead parakeet and rat. The rodent
repast, in particular, sends Blanche wildly spinning and screaming in
her wheelchair, arms flailing, her horror caught nicely from above by
a fine bird's eye shot—a scene Heller himself invented. Blanche is finally
reduced to devouring stale chocolates which she discovers by accident
in her dresser drawer.

In addition to Jane's psychological intimidation and harassment of
Blanche, there are moments of sheer physical terror as well. When Elvira
(Maidie Norman) discovers Blanche bound and gagged in bed, the unfortunate maid is bludgeoned to death by the hammer-wielding Jane.
And in the film's most brutally shocking scene (played without stunts
or doubles), Jane kicks Blanche repeatedly and drags her sister up the
stairs to her room after discovering that Blanche has made a telephone
call designed to secure her freedom.

But perhaps the most frightening and disturbing aspect of the film's
horrors is the ghastly destructive effects of a too possessive, too demanding parent-child relationship. The smothering, stifling results of such
a relationship are particularly evident in the case of Jane herself and in
that of Edwin Flagg (played superbly by Victor Buono), a hypochondriacal
and effeminate pianist who answers Jane's ad—"Established Star Seeks
Accompaniest"—in the local paper. Of the two, Jane is the more seriously
wounded victim. Because of her father's profound influence over her
during their vaudeville years and because she associates success and self-
esteem solely with childhood and her father's approval of her perfor-

mance on stage, Jane lives literally in, and for, the past, rummaging often through dated clippings from *Variety* and fondling "Baby Jane" dolls symbolic of her faded stardom. Caught up in the glories of the past, Jane plans a return to her former profession; she wants to revive her act, and wishes only that her daddy could be there to see it. Significantly, the two pieces of music she asks Flagg to practice for her comeback are entitled "I've Written a Letter to Daddy" and "I Wouldn't Trade My Daddy." Although, as Jane explains to Flagg, she lost her daddy when she was young, he continues to exercise, even in death, a powerful and abnormal control over her life, stunting her growth, leaving her hopelessly unable to make the transition to responsible adulthood. Pathetically, she rehearses her "Baby Jane" routine in rented costume and finger curls, dancing before a mirror whose footlights illuminate the shattered remains of a child-woman loved not wisely, but too well, by a domineering daddy. Writing in *Positif*, Jean Boreil rightly calls this scene "one of the most heart-rending and cruel in the history of cinema."[14]

To a lesser extent, Edwin Flagg too is an instance of arrested development. Overweight, unemployed and middleaged, his surname evocative of declining powers, Flagg lives at home with his nagging mother, an overbearing woman who "manages everything" for her son, including his appointment with Jane. Flagg owes his affected accent and mannerisms to his British father, a "classical Shakespearean actor who never got a chance in Hollywood." But Mrs. Flagg never understood her thespian husband (who presumably has died or drifted off), and the young Flagg has not forgiven her. His utter contempt for his mother is revealed in a sharp exchange late in the film: after Mrs. Flagg explains the mysterious circumstances surrounding the evening of Blanche's accident, noting that Jane had at first disappeared but was located three days later in a hotel room with a man she had never seen before, Edwin snaps sarcastically in reply, "Is that how I was conceived?" Although he finds Jane obviously unbalanced, Flagg needs the $100-a-week salary she promises for his services; thus he cynically encourages Jane's warped and distorted view of herself and her revival, pretends to befriend her. In one bizarre scene near the end of the film, the two take a wild ride—Jane on Edwin's lap—in Blanche's wheelchair. In this compelling and disconcerting shot, Aldrich joins together inextricably the film's two aging Oedipal misfits, illustrating the devastating consequences of their psychological paralysis.

Baby Jane ends with the disclosure of a startling truth. Blanche confesses, for the first time, that it was *she*, not Jane, who orchestrated her

Joan Crawford and Bette Davis on the beach in *Baby Jane*. Used by permission of the Museum of Modern Art/Film Stills Archive, courtesy of Warner Brothers.

own accident: "You weren't driving that night. I made you open the gates because I wanted to run you down to crush you. I hit the gates and snapped my spine. You ran away and I crawled out of the car and up to the gates where they found me. They assumed it was your fault." By this time, Jane has made a final, irrevocable return to childhood. Afraid that she will be punished for Elvira's murder, Jane has taken Blanche, now in a seriously weakened condition, to the beach. Barely comprehending the substance of Blanche's confession, Jane offers to buy dessert, some conciliatory strawberry ice cream. And there on the beach, clutching the two cones in a bizarre parody of childhood, she reenacts her "Baby Jane" routine for a crowd of puzzled, bemused bystanders gathered around her. The camera cranes up and away to reveal a long shot of Jane encircled by the amazed spectators, while Blanche lies alone, and probably dying, in the sand in the distance. After the horror, the perversity, and the creepy comedy of the earlier scenes, this ending is unexpectedly beautiful and touching. In the gawking, laughing, pointing spectators we see ourselves, the audience, who have also gawked, laughed, and pointed at the misfits on the screen. Thus it is also a moment of reevaluation, for now we understand Jane and Blanche and Edwin and feel sympathy for their plight. The final horror of *Baby Jane*, then, is the horror of loss— lost youth, lost identity, lost love. "All this time we could have been friends," Jane says sadly after Blanche confesses, and there is real regret for their wasted lives.

Baby Jane is a notable instance of what Charles Derry has named the "horror of personality" film. In this type of film, peculiar to the sixties, the horror itself is neither the product of atomic mutation (a "something" from beneath the sea) nor is it a quality abstracted from man and symbolic of his animal desires (a Kong), his baser instincts (a vampire), or his worst fears (a zombie). Rather, the horror is very specific: the monster is man himself. The horror of this kind of film is psychological. What Aldrich achieved in *Baby Jane*, Derry notes, was to combine the major ideas of *Diabolique* and *Psycho* (in addition to his own *Autumn Leaves*) into a "psychological study of two women whose relationship was based on some past crime, yet a study which dealt very overtly with the ambiguity of insanity." Moreover, Aldrich invented his own conventions for the film (his use of the audience's foreknowledge of and preconceptions about his actors and actresses, and the distance in time Aldrich interposes between the crime itself and the story proper), conventions he would use again in *Charlotte*. "The contribution of Robert Aldrich to the horror of personality films," Derry concludes, "cannot be overestimated."[15]

Although substantially different in tone and subject from his previous work, Aldrich continued to explore in *Baby Jane* a certain type of character relationship and a specific kind of psychological conflict. The French critic Jean Boreil noted that in *Baby Jane* we once again have two people who are antagonists and yet are "absolutely necessary to each other."[16] Other examples would be Erin and Trane in *Vera Cruz*, Hoff and Castle in *The Big Knife*, Stribling and O'Malley in *The Last Sunset*. In this film Aldrich gives us for the first time two *women* acting out the conflict which has heretofore been reserved for men only. And here, the Jekyll-Hyde quality of the relationship is most clearly illustrated: Blanche and Jane are two sides of the same personality. Jane is infantile, without discipline; Blanche is adult, responsible, but also paralyzed and ineffectual. In this sense, Jane's (and Edwin's) revolt is that of the child against the tyranny of the parent, against the injustice imposed

Bette Davis, Jack Warner, Joan Crawford, and Robert Aldrich celebrate the success of *Baby Jane*. Used by permission of Adell Aldrich.

upon them by cold authority. But it is also a revolt without a moral base and therefore ultimately useless. Indeed, nowhere has Aldrich so confused the issue of Good and Evil as in *Baby Jane*. A variation of the "who is the enemy" theme found in his war films, the question of "who is the monster" mocks us throughout this horror show. Despite appearances, despite unexpected revelations, we can never take absolute sides with either Blanche or Jane. They are both villains, and they are both victims. By the film's end, to condemn either would be an act of supreme hypocrisy.

As a story of illusion and impersonation, *Baby Jane* can certainly be seen as a comment on Hollywood and the film industry and the very nature of stardom. As a horror film, as a "horror of personality" film, it is expertly done, its shocks effective and its terror sustained. In the words of Arthur Knight, *Baby Jane* "achieves its goals with something breathlessly close to perfection."[17] But for all its sadism and masochism and macabre comedy, it is ultimately the human tragedy which most affects us. As Lukas Heller explained, "It sounds far-fetched to say that *Baby Jane* is about real people, but I always had the feeling that it was very much more than a horror movie. I think it really did reflect something about Hollywood and growing old and all sorts of other things." It is this portrayal of the human tragedy, the human waste and loss, that is surely Aldrich's finest achievement in the film.

4 For Texas (1963)

Baby Jane was Aldrich's biggest success since *Vera Cruz* and reestablished his position as a major force in Hollywood. It cost $825,000 to make but grossed an incredible $2 million in rental fees within the first fourteen days of its American release; it would eventually earn more than $12 million.[18] Aldrich's career was again off and running. His next film, however, was a brief misstep. He wanted *4 For Texas* to be a " 'fun' picture, a satire on Westerns, a kind of high-style comedy."[19] Using the power gained from the success of *Baby Jane*, Aldrich produced, directed, and wrote (with Teddi Sherman, his co-writer on *Ten Seconds to Hell*) the screenplay. The film starred Frank Sinatra, Dean Martin, Anita Ekberg, and Ursula Andress, none of whom Aldrich had directed before. In supporting roles, however, were a number of Aldrich regulars: Victor Buono, Nick Dennis, Richard Jaeckel, Wesley Addy. He had Ernest Laszlo and Joseph Biroc as cinematographers, Nelson Riddle writing the score, and Oscar Rudolph (who had replaced Leone on *Sodom and Gomorrah*) directing the second unit. Moreover, in a transitional role marking his movement toward stardom was Charles Bronson, who had appeared in *Apache* and *Vera Cruz* and who would later work with Aldrich in *The Dirty Dozen*. Despite the possibilities inherent in the idea and in the cast and crew, *4 For Texas* turned out to be, as Aldrich admitted, a dismal film. The beginning sequence, which involves a stagecoach chase, a robbery, and a series of one-upmanships between Sinatra and Martin, is not without charm, but it lacks the spontaneity and surprise which marked the similar sequence in *Vera Cruz*, on which it is clearly modeled. And after this introduction, the film becomes slower, more predictable, and finally dull.

As in *Vera Cruz*, we have two good-bad men (Sinatra and Martin) who are compelled to join forces against a common enemy (Victor Buono and his henchman Bronson). But in *Vera Cruz*, Cooper and Lancaster played original, interesting characters, whose rivalry was real and whose final showdown had an inevitability about it which overshadowed their occasional joking. In *4 For Texas*, the principal actors are less interested in the story than in embellishing their personas as laid-back ladies' men. Indeed, the story is often halted, held in abeyance, so that Sinatra or Martin (or even the Three Stooges or Arthur Godfrey, who make guest appearances) can run through a routine which has little or nothing to do with the plot. Sinatra is especially annoying in this film: Aldrich confessed that he failed to control the singer and that Sinatra never put forth the kind of effort that was needed. Aldrich found Martin, however, a complete professional in every respect.

Still, Aldrich was simply not at his best with this kind of broad comedy; he needed the intensity and absurdity that is so much a part of his apocalyptic black humor, as found in *Kiss Me Deadly* or *The Grissom Gang*. Sinatra and Martin are so self-centered in this film, so busy mugging for the camera or eyeing women, that we not only don't care what happens to them, we end up rooting for Charles Bronson, who is just about the only source of vitality in the film. Andress and Ekberg come off no better than Sinatra and Martin. Women in general are presented as servants and handmaidens to the men. Andress and Ekberg want to get married; Martin and Sinatra want to avoid it at all costs. "A man as an equal partner I don't understand," Maxine (Andress) tells Joe Jarrett (Martin), "but a man as a master I can handle." Despite its irony, her statement reveals the basic assumptions of the film.

Daniel Bates, writing in *Film Quarterly*, observed that "what began as a serious 'fun' picture ends up more fun in the making than the viewing: a 'throw-away' movie, as it were."[20] Reflecting on his own experience in the film, Richard Jaeckel made a similar point: "It was an entertainment, nothing serious. In fact, people came from all over Hollywood to watch the filming of the final fight scene. You could see that, at some point, Aldrich just wanted to cut his losses—just wanted to get in and get out." *4 For Texas* is one of the few Aldrich films which fails to deliver, which betrays our expectations. On the whole, it is a clumsy, slack, and ultimately depressing film.

4 For Texas marked the end of Aldrich's working relationship with his director of photography Ernest Laszlo. Laszlo was a slow, deliberate worker who had his own ideas as to how a scene should look. Although

Aldrich appreciated suggestions from his cameraman, he insisted that the final decision be his alone. As Aldrich explained: "I want to have [my cameraman] understand the way I would like [a scene] to look, so I often explain my ideas to him in terms of artistry or craft. I don't want him to tell me anything about what lens to use or where the camera should be. I like him to make as many set-ups a day that reasonably capture what we are trying to get."[21] Laszlo, wanting more responsibility than Aldrich was willing to give, had finally been unable to work this way and was replaced by Joseph Biroc, who would be Aldrich's principal photographer for the rest of his career. Biroc's style was much more compatible with Aldrich's. "He gave me a set-up and I would agree. He was very receptive as to how a scene should look, but I never told him, always suggested. Aldrich was always the boss," Biroc remembered. He would talk with Aldrich in rehearsals during the breaks, and they would discuss possible shots. Once filming began, everyone would be encouraged to watch the rushes, and Biroc would be responsible for his crew; but Aldrich would take ultimate responsibility for the film. "He wanted to be the heavy," Biroc said. " 'If something goes wrong, blame it on me,' he'd say."

Hush . . . Hush, Sweet Charlotte (1965)

After the failure of 4 For Texas, the prospect of a follow-up to Baby Jane became more appealing than ever to The Associates and Aldrich. The "sequel" (in spirit more than in subject) was called Hush . . . Hush, Sweet Charlotte (originally, What Ever Happened to Cousin Charlotte? to cash in on Baby Jane's success, but fortunately changed). It, too, grew out of an idea developed initially by Henry Farrell, author of the Baby Jane novel. Aldrich found the story line and concept "very exciting,"[22] and although he had employed Farrell to write the script, Aldrich and Heller actually ended up doing much of the screenplay themselves. Heller explained:

> It had to do with Aldrich's irascibility, for in Farrell he met someone who was equally irascible. Farrell had written the first draft of this thing and had an appointment to meet Aldrich to discuss the changes that Aldrich required or that Aldrich thought were necessary. And he turned up at this meeting which was for, say, 2 o'clock, and the secretary said that Mr. Aldrich was tied up and may be a bit late. And apparently after twenty minutes had gone by, Farrell walked out and said, "I'm not going to be treated this way." So after that we rewrote it fairly extensively.

Aldrich speculated that a replay of the material he had explored in *Baby Jane* would still prove marketable.[23] But the reteaming of Davis and Crawford, whose *Baby Jane* roles he planned to reverse in *Charlotte*, was more problematical than Aldrich expected. Unlike the spirit of professional cooperation and propriety which had marked the filming of *Baby Jane*, a "terribly hostile atmosphere,"[24] as Aldrich recollected, prevailed on the set of *Charlotte* from the very beginning. Tensions subsided only when Joan Crawford became ill and could no longer continue with her part. With production half-completed, finding a replacement for Crawford was no easy task, since Davis, 20th Century Fox, and The Associates and Aldrich all had final cast approval. After much discussion, the only choice acceptable to all parties was Bette Davis's friend, Olivia de Havilland. Despite Davis's assurances, de Havilland was understandably reluctant to take the part since, as Aldrich reasoned, "obviously she was going to finish second to Davis" in what was clearly a "one vehicle picture."[25] Aldrich set out to convince de Havilland to take the part, no easy task in that she lived in a "remote corner of Switzerland." Aldrich described the undertaking:

> It took plane, train, boat and goat trail to get to the village where she was staying, and I arrived exhausted but certain I would simply say "please" and we'd head back to Hollywood. I gave her the script and when we met for breakfast the next morning she raved about it; how wonderful it was, what a great picture it would make and how Bette would win the award and "no, thank you, I don't play heavies." It took me four days of my most persuasive manner and being underfoot wherever she turned to convince her. By then it was easier for her to do the part than to face me anymore.[26]

Like *Baby Jane, Hush . . . Hush, Sweet Charlotte* is about the strangely perverse relationship between two women. Charlotte Hollis (Bette Davis), a suspect in the murder of her illicit lover John Mayhew (Bruce Dern) some thirty-seven years earlier, now faces eviction from the Louisiana plantation where she has lived alone since the death of her father. In desperation, she begs assistance from Miriam Deering (Olivia de Havilland), her cousin and childhood companion, currently a public relations expert in Baton Rouge. But there are vicious, ulterior motives behind cousin Miriam's return home: still jealous of Charlotte for being daddy's "pure, darling little girl," still smarting from the slights and snubs she received while living in the Sam Hollis household as a "poor relation," Miriam now conspires with Drew Bayliss (Joseph Cotton), local physician and her former beau, to inherit the Hollis estate. Their plan (which bears

Olivia DeHavilland torments Bette Davis in *Hush . . . Hush, Sweet Charlotte*. Used by permission of the Museum of Modern Art/Film Stills Archive, courtesy of 20th Century-Fox.

a strong resemblance to the one found in *Diabolique,* Clouzot's 1955 classic thriller) is to drive Charlotte (the rightful heir) mad by inducing her to remember the gruesome details of the murder she is alleged to have committed and further to convince her that, in her madness, she has also killed Drew Bayliss, who then comes back from the grave to haunt her. Charlotte knows she is innocent of John Mayhew's death. In fact, she strongly suspects that her father was the murderer. But her susceptibility and excitability make her easy prey to her tormentors' schemes and contrivances. Soon, she is hallucinating to their hearts' content. Ultimately, Charlotte comprehends the conspiracy against her, discovering (as she eavesdrops on a conversation between Miriam and Drew) that it was Jewel Mayhew who murdered and dismembered her unfaithful husband. Only then does Charlotte commit the one truly violent act of her life, crushing the two conspirators beneath a huge earthen planter she has aimed at them from her perch on the balcony overhead.

Even this skimpy synopsis reveals the basic plot similarities between *Charlotte* and *Baby Jane.* Both films begin in the past with violent actions done in ambiguous circumstances, actions whose destructive effects relentlessly haunt the lives of tormented people. In both films, the central characters are made to suffer intolerably for crimes they never committed, with the surprising and liberating truth being revealed only at the end. In both films, intense rivalry between two young girls for the approval and affection of a father figure produces, in those adult females, serious identity problems and warped value systems. In both, a father's too-possessive love for his daughter leaves her with permanent psychic damage. And in both films, the central horror, the "horror of personality," is the psychological terrorism practiced on an unsuspecting victim which, in its ruthlessly calculating fashion, is more repulsive than the physical violence itself.

Of the two films, *Charlotte* is considerably more brutal. Not counting Drew's terrifying staging of his own death, there are four violent murders which occur at regular intervals in the film. Of these, the pre-credit opening sequence—devised by Heller, who confessed to a "talent for very nasty things"—is by far the most grisly. Seated in a darkened room, his arm resting on an adjacent table, John Mayhew is assaulted by an axe-wielding assailant who remains unseen. As the axe falls and falls again, Mayhew loses first his arm, and then his head, to the onslaught, and in a touch of macabre comedy, a nearby marble sculpture of Cupid is bespattered by the dead man's blood. The camera then cuts quickly to

Charlotte's debutante party inside and to the rhythmic echo of a band leader's directive to his orchestra ("Now, one more time . . ."), the refrain providing both much-needed comic relief from, and an ironic counterpoint to, the just-consummated carnage.

It is arguable whether the Mayhew mayhem was, as publicists and advertisers at the time declared, "the most shocking scene ever filmed," but it does retain a visceral power even today. And in *Charlotte*, Aldrich does indeed trot out for display all manner of Gothic machinery: the eerie haunted house with its dark, winding stairs and its heavy air of gloom and fatality; doors that creak and floors that squeak, curtains that billow and shutters that rattle in savage evening thunderstorms; dogs that bark ominously in cemeteries and a dead body that rises (apparently) from its muddy, watery grave. There are many such moments in *Charlotte*, but what holds the picture together is Bette Davis's fine performance. It was not an easy part to play, as she recalled:

> The role is a cheat. To begin with, it's the sort of film where you can't give anything away because everything depends on keeping the audience guessing. The part of Charlotte really has to be played dishonestly, because though she didn't do the murder and knows that she didn't, she has to keep doing things in such a way that you think she might have, though there is no reason inherent in her situation in the story why she should. I tell you, it was one of the most difficult parts I have ever played; I just had to try to construct some sort of reality for the character in my own mind so that I could do it all.[27]

Davis's observations on her role give ample evidence as to why the film is ultimately not as satisfying as *Baby Jane*: much of *Charlotte* is simply dishonest, a "cheat." It does not play fair with the audience. In one key scene, for example, as Charlotte and Miriam are attempting to hide Drew Bayliss's apparently dead body, it almost topples into view of a policeman who has happened on them. Neither Miriam nor Charlotte see the body in this precarious state; only the audience holds its breath until the policeman leaves. It would obviously ruin Miriam and Drew's plan, however, if such a thing were to happen. The scene is inserted for the thrill, to convince us that Drew is really dead and thus to set us up for his later reappearance. But it is a fraud. Indeed there is a series of such manipulations throughout the film which ultimately override the human tragedy. The machinery simply creaks.

Hush . . . Hush, Sweet Charlotte rarely rises above this level of horror, and although it is effective, one expects more from Aldrich after the success of *Baby Jane*. Aldrich described Charlotte as "cannibal time in Dix-ie,"[28] and while he adequately contrasts the surface Southern charm and gentility with the gruesome goings-on underneath, his Gothic South fails to exude the sense of loss and perversity found in his Gothic Hollywood of *Baby Jane*. Also, as in the earlier picture, Aldrich drew on some of Hollywood's most prominent actors of yesteryear. In addition to Davis and de Havilland and Cotton, he included Mary Astor as Jewell Mayhew, wife and killer of John; Cecil Kellaway as Harry Willis, the kindly insurance investigator who finally discovers the truth; and (in an outrageously overacted role), Agnes Moorehead as Velma Cruther, Charlotte's housemaid who suspects Miriam and who meets her own spectacular end. But the echoes reverberating in *Baby Jane* are not sound-ed here, for there is no correspondence between actor and role. "It was a pot-boiler," Heller remarked, "a sort of schlock horror film. It isn't about *real* people." Thus, *Charlotte* often becomes the freak show that *Baby Jane* avoided.

Still, there are moments of beauty in *Charlotte*—Aldrich can be as delicate as brutal—and by the end of the film we do feel sorry for this woman whose life has been stolen away from her. As she leaves her home to enter an asylum, with the wistful theme music playing in the background,[29] Bette Davis gives Charlotte a dignity and a calmness denied her throughout the rest of the film. An exorcism has occurred, but she has little left to live for. It is a fine moment in an otherwise all-too-conventional work.

Again, Aldrich had only the highest praise for Davis's performance. In an article he wrote for *Cahiers du Cinema* in May 1965 he paid tribute to her professionalism, her integrity, and her unselfishness as an actress:

> When Bette Davis and Olivia de Havilland wept and panted and hauled the heavy mannequin on the stage of *Hush . . . Hush, Sweet Charlotte*, I could not help but think of a similar scene in *Baby Jane*. But in that film the body was flesh and bone, and Bette had insisted on dragging Joan Crawford in person rather than following my idea of using a dummy. "The best way to do that scene realistically," said Davis with insistence, "is to let me handle it all the way with a real body." At the end of the scene, Bette collapsed, exhausted, and we all hurried over, fearing the worst, when she caught her breath, raised her eyes to me, and simply asked, "How was *that* for you?"
>
> In our second film I was thus aware—I knew—that this was one of the last actresses who considered realism as one of the duties of her profession.[30]

Lured by its promise of gore and terror, film goers found *Charlotte* enormously attractive; it became one of The Associates and Aldrich's most lucrative enterprises to date, earning more than $3,300,000 in the first year of its release.[31] Between them, *Charlotte* and *Baby Jane* garnered twelve Academy Award nominations and considerable profit. Their success made possible Aldrich's next project, a more serious and ambitious film which would prove one of his best works.

The Flight of the Phoenix (1966)

As he had demonstrated so expertly in earlier films like *Attack!*, *Kiss Me Deadly, What Ever Happened to Baby Jane?* and *Hush . . . Hush, Sweet Charlotte,* Aldrich constructed the pre-credits sequence of his films with the skill and dexterity of a craftsman carefully shaping his art. "I don't know why certain directors follow certain patterns," Aldrich explained. "But I always have a scene at the beginning of the picture where everybody has to sit down because there is too much story to tell. After you get that out of the way, then you can go on."[32] In *The Flight of the Phoenix*, he created perhaps the most perfect of these prologues. The film opens with a telephoto shot of the blazing sun and an obsolete Arabco cargo plane lumbering toward take-off. As the craft slowly becomes airborne, it casts a long shadow on the desert floor below— a disturbing portent of things to come. Inside the cockpit, the pilot and navigator discuss the plane's deteriorating condition (both radio and regulator are malfunctioning) as the passengers, a motley mix of soldiers and oil company employees, while away the time mocking the army or the corporation, strumming a guitar, or reading *Playboy* magazine (the "reader," killed in the ensuing crash, is Aldrich's son, William). The mood in the cabin is comfortable and relaxed until the captain, Frank Towns (James Stewart), notes the presence of a violent sand storm directly ahead. Towns seizes upon the occasion to reminisce nostalgically about the good-ole-days when "flying used to be fun" and "when you took real pride in just getting there." As the storm increases in intensity, Towns and navigator Lew Moran (Richard Attenborough), cognizant of the danger of their present course, consider heading for an alternate landing site while, in the rear of the cabin, passenger Heinrick Dorfmann (Hardy Kruger) complains loudly of what he perceives to be the crew's incompetence. Suddenly, one engine fails; then the other. The cabin lights sputter and short out, and the heavy cargo loaded in the rear of the plane begins to break loose from its lashings. High winds buffet the plane about; blowing sand makes for zero visibility. As Towns prepares for a desperate wheels-down emergency crash landing, a succession of freeze-frames captures the expression on the face of each man just prior to the moment of impact. Upon these individual freezes appear the credits for *The Flight of the Phoenix.*

If Aldrich has galloped apace in the prologue, he settles back to an easy canter for the remaining 130 minutes of his film, judiciously studying the reactions of the survivors to the terrible, near-hopeless reality of their circumstances. The prospects for their deliverance are not favorable, stranded as they are in the barren, alien wastes of the Sahara without adequate provisions, without serious hope of rescue, and without a viable means of escape. It is the kind of film situation Aldrich most delighted in, this story of men striving to survive against impossible odds, and it is the type of film Aldrich did best. Aldrich himself called it a "patrol picture: It's X number of men trying to get from here to there and back, or from here to there and survive. So there are a number of built-in, inescapable similarities which you try to camouflage, but they're set. They're standard. You can camouflage them, but you can't escape them."[33]

Formula film or not (and Lukas Heller has said that it was "the last example of that kind of film"), *The Flight of the Phoenix*, despite its rather long running time, won almost universal acclaim from contemporary reviewers and remains one of Aldrich's most critically successful films. "Measured against the ordinary run of adventure epics," the reviewer in *Time* wrote, "*Phoenix* is a bonanza." He concluded: "Most of the time, *Phoenix* flexes its muscles as the sort of virile enthralling entertainment moviegoers too seldom see."[34] What most reviewers admired was Aldrich's skill in transcending the conventions of the genre. "What it deserves to be especially commended for," wrote Brendan Gill in the *New Yorker*, "is that it succeeds in seeming so fresh and ingenious."[35]

The main surprise in *The Flight of the Phoenix* issues from the imagination of Heinrick Dorfmann, the supremely self-assured and arrogantly self-righteous German aircraft designer who proposes that the men construct, from the undamaged parts of their wrecked plane, a *new* vehicle, a smaller single-engine craft capable of carrying them to safety. Based on his painstaking calculations, Dorfmann speculates that "an entirely new and aero-dynamically sound structure" can be fashioned by affixing the starboard wing to the port fuselage and by re-rigging all essential control cables. Dorfmann's haughty German manner and icy efficiency have already alienated him from the group, who reject his scheme as ludicrous and unworkable. Frank Towns, the group's titular leader and the voice

of incredulity, sarcastically asks the humorless Dorfmann if he's "trying
to be funny?" "Precisely the reaction I expected from a man of your obvious limitations," replies Dorfmann. Soon, however, Dorfmann's con-
traption is built—the group has no other recourse—but before it can be
tested, the plot twist is revealed: Dorfmann is not a designer of *real* aircraft; he is, rather, a designer of *model* aircraft. "He builds *toy* airplanes,"
Towns shouts in disbelief. "The principles are the same, basically," the
unflappable German insists. Dorfmann's theories are vindicated at last
when the "Phoenix," named after the mythical bird of rebirth, finally
glides aloft, the men clinging fast to its wings and the redoutable Towns
at the controls, and ferries the remnants of this mini-society to safety.

Dorfmann's observations about Towns's "limitations" bring us to
the thematic heart of the film. For people here are shown to have limitations: to be fallible and fickle, to collapse under pressure, to make fatal
mistakes. Although shot in the vast deserts near Yuma, Arizona, the
film is remarkably claustrophobic, marked by frequent images of
enclosure in which the survivors appear dominated by the wreckage,
weighed down by it, entrapped by it. A tough oil rigger, Trucker Cobb
(Ernest Borgnine), suffering from mental exhaustion, goes mad and makes
a futile effort to walk home; a young husband, Gabriele (Gabriele Tinti),
injured in the crash and mordantly depressed by his separation from his
sick and pregnant wife, commits suicide by slashing his wrists; a cowardly
British soldier, Sgt. Watson (Ronald Fraser), fakes an injury and willfully
disobeys his commander's orders to undertake dangerous missions; the
commanding officer himself, Captain Harris (Peter Finch), is murdered
when his courageous but ill-conceived plan to make contact with a
Bedouin raiding party goes awry.

But the specific weaknesses and limitations of human nature to which
Aldrich gives his most careful consideration are those of the central antagonists, Dorfmann and Towns. What these two men have in common
is a fierce, stubborn pride in their respective positions. For most of the
film, Dorfmann is as thoroughly convinced that the "Phoenix" *will* fly
as Towns is convinced that it will *not*. Each parades his credentials proudly: Dorfmann is a technologist, a modern engineer, a theorist to whom
the future of flight has been entrusted; Towns is a fallen romantic, a
veteran pilot with a flair for the dramatic and that instinctive feeling
in his guts, a graduate of the flyer's school of hard knocks in whom the
glories of the aviational past have been enshrined but who now
reminisces a little too often. At one point, Towns writes regretfully in
his captain's log that "the little men with slide rules and computers will

inherit the earth," an inevitability which, Towns allows, Dorfmann already knows to be true. If Dorfmann is the bookish student of flight, Towns is its seasoned practitioner, and the distance which divides them seems vast indeed.

Thus once again we find in an Aldrich film two antagonists who illustrate opposing principles: what Aldrich labeled the "democratic" and the "fascist." Towns feels a responsibility for all the men "under his command," as it were. Dorfmann is much colder, more practical. He realizes, for example, that Gabriele (the injured man) will not survive and simply does not include him in his calculations. When the infantile Trucker Cobb wanders off into the desert, Towns insists on going after him, but Dorfmann is appalled by his "romantic quest for Mr. Cobb" for two reasons: not only is Towns, as pilot, completely necessary to his plans, but Cobb is "of absolutely no use to us." Towns carefully rations out the water supply although he has no real hope of ultimate survival. Dorfmann takes more than his share because he "works harder" than the rest and needs it in order to complete his plans. Whereas in his earlier films like *Vera Cruz* or *Ten Seconds to Hell* the choice between the antagonists was relatively clear—we may have liked Joe Erin or Karl Wirtz, but we *knew* Ben Trane and Eric Koertner were right—*The Flight of the Phoenix*, like *Baby Jane*, offers us a less obvious selection. We admire the individualist Frank Towns; we are put off by the calculating Heinrick Dorfmann. But Towns, with his reliance on instinct and judgment, has ignored some very basic procedures—he has taken off with a broken radio, for example—and he is in good part responsible for the crash (he attributes the accident to "pilot error" in his log). To him death is the necessary punishment, and he *does* sometimes behave in a romantic, quixotic manner. Dorfmann, in his cold objectivity and discipline, gives these men a chance at survival. He may be petty and conceited, but he is also the initial means of salvation.

Still, the group's very survival requires that the two adversaries reach some kind of agreement by which the theoretical skills of Dorfmann can be felicitously combined with the instinctive expertise of Towns. Although opposite in such basic ways, both men need each other. A compromise is clearly called for. Each man insists on holding the power of authority, however, and it is up to the navigator Lew Moran to mediate effectively between the extremes (the role taken by Sieber, the Indian scout, in *Apache*, or Woodruff in *Attack!*, for example). Moran works first on Towns, selling him on the advisability of the "Phoenix" project through a very practical argument: "If there's just one chance in a thousand that he has got something, I'd rather take it than just sit around here waiting to die." At the same time, Moran works on Dorfmann, berating him for refusing to let Towns shoulder more responsibility in the construction project. "Well, for God's sake, man, you're not a child, are you?" he says. "You told Towns he was behaving as if stupidity were a virtue. If he's making it into a virtue, then you're making it into a bloody science."

As a result of Moran's intervention, Towns bends a lot, even to the point of relinquishing his authority in the matter. "I guess old Frank Towns could never stand to be told what to do," Towns admits. He apologizes to Dorfmann, who has stopped work on the project in retaliation against Towns. Having gathered the men together, Dorfmann demands, "Mr. Towns, who is in authority here?" "You are," Towns says. "Very well, then," Dorfmann concludes. "Since I am in authority, I have decided to finish this plane and make it fly. We shall now go back to work." But once the plane is actually built, the power naturally shifts back to Towns, the pilot. There are seven cartridges with which Towns must start the engine: if these fail, there is no other hope. Towns tries four without success. Then, relying on his instincts, he announces that he will fire the fifth cartridge with the engine off in order to clean out the cylinders. To Dorfmann, this is a foolish waste, not at all a part of his calculations. "Stop! I forbid you!" he shouts, clambering up the wing toward Towns. "Do you hear me? I forbid you!" But Towns ignores him, blows out the cylinders, and then fires the sixth cartridge. The engine catches, Towns nurses it with all the knowledge and talent of his experience, and the plane is ready to fly. "All right, Mr. Dorfmann," he announces from his seat high above the other men. "Start pulling!"

In an exhilarating shot, the "Phoenix" does fly, the survivors strapped to its wings, and Towns pilots it to safety.[36] In the film's closing scene, Dorfmann and Towns stride shoulder to shoulder across the desert sands, a hint of a smile breaking across the German's face. In exchange for their compromise, each man has come to a better understanding of the other, and perhaps of himself.

In terms of character and theme, the film is another Aldrich study of the ambiguity of courage and of the possibility for redemption. There are no "villains" in this film. There are men who behave foolishly and men who behave badly and men who behave bravely, but we can never easily classify their actions. For example, it is obviously insane for Trucker Cobb to strike off into the desert, for he goes without water or sense of destination. But, as Dorfmann points out, does it really make any more sense for Towns to go after him? And why does Towns go after him—to save Cobb's life or to assuage his own guilt? Furthermore, what about Captain Harris, who intends to march out of the desert? "I know it's a gamble," he tells Towns in private, "but it'll increase your chances of being picked up." Is he brave or crazy, or both? There are no easy answers.

Still, the "Phoenix" itself is an obvious symbol of regeneration—wreckage is rebuilt and made to fly; men are reborn and regain self-respect. "That's the yardstick whereby effort, whether it's heroic or imaginative, is really measured," Aldrich said. "I'm concerned with man's efforts to prevail against impossible odds."[37] Certainly, both Towns and Dorfmann do "prevail" in this particular instance. By rejecting, finally, their childish jealousies and by combining their imagination and courage, they bring the lost group out of the barren desert. Because all the men in this group band together, they survive. In this sense, *The Flight of the Phoenix* is one of Aldrich's most hopeful and affirming films.

The Flight of the Phoenix is a fine work, one of Aldrich's best. The script by Lukas Heller is first-rate, an intelligent adaptation of Elleston Trevor's novel. (When Trevor saw the picture, he admired it, and remarked to Michael Luciano, Aldrich's editor, that "you write with film." "Yes," replied Luciano, "but I get great material from a fine director.") Aldrich had learned about the book from Lukas Heller and had acquired the rights; he then discovered that Jimmy Stewart was also interested in the property. The two came to terms, and Stewart gave one of his finest performances, induced partly, perhaps, by the highly professional ensemble cast Aldrich had assembled. William Aldrich, who was on the set, told a funny and revealing story about the first day of rehearsals:

> Jimmy sat down at this table and looked up and down and there was Dickie Attenborough and Peter Finch and Ian Bannon and Hardy Kruger and a lot of good actors. So he sits down and all of these guys close their scripts and knew their lines, had them memorized. And Jimmy was looking at the script and flipping his pages, trying to figure out where the hell they were. And Stewart, I think, was very much embarrassed by that: the first day, everyone knew his lines and Jimmy didn't. It was the English training, the stage training. And Dad didn't say anything because he wasn't used to actors knowing all their stuff—and these guys knew everything. And the next day we all came to the table, and Jimmy sat there, with his script open, and when we start, everybody closes his script again and Jimmy looks around—and closes *his* script and knew all *his* lines for the rest of rehearsal. He must have stayed up all night long.

Other performances were also outstanding. Richard Attenborough and Hardy Kruger were especially good in the main roles. Peter Finch, Ronald Fraser, Dan Duryea (from *China Smith*), Ernest Borgnine, and George Kennedy gave impressive support, and Ian Bannon was nominated for an Academy Award for best supporting actor for his role as Crow, the wisecracking Irishman. And yet despite these performances, rave reviews from the critics, a sensational preview, and an expensive promotional campaign, the film proved to be a commercial disaster, one Aldrich could never fully account for. "There are different kinds of failures," he said. "There are failures you never think are right or justifiable or understandable. For example, I put *Too Late the Hero, Flight of the Phoenix*, and *The Grissom Gang* in a category that says these are all fine movies, very well made films. People understood what they were about, what they aimed to say. They were entertaining and exciting and should have been a success. . . . I'll never understand the failure of [these films] because they were marvelous movies."[38]

The Dirty Dozen (1967)

The Dirty Dozen was Aldrich's seventeenth film and would prove to be one of the most significant. Based on the novel by E.M. Nathanson, it was another of Aldrich's "patrol pictures." Like *The Flight of the Phoenix*, it detailed the adventures of a disparate group of unlikely men who are involved in a seemingly impossible task and who, through their efforts, achieve a kind of personal salvation. Although *The Flight of the Phoenix* had failed at the box office, Aldrich had a hunch about *The Dirty Dozen*. He first tried to buy the rights to the work even before Nathanson had finished writing it, while, Aldrich claims, the book was still in step outline.[39] Although it was in structure a rather conventional commando war story, Aldrich was attracted both to the action-adventure elements inherent in the plot—he regarded himself as the best action picture director in the business—and to its central irony: the "heroes" of this tale were unreconstructed criminals—murderers, rapists, psychopaths; the "villains" were those in authority—not only the German generals the Dozen are sent to destroy but also, by strong implication, the Allied commanders who are willing to commit the Dozen to certain death in an almost aristocratic game of war. It was precisely the kind of subversive twist Aldrich delighted in.

Despite Aldrich's early interest in the property, it was first bought by MGM.[40] After they had made several unsuccessful attempts to write a suitable screenplay, Aldrich was brought in on the project. What he inherited was an "old-fashioned" script written by Nunnally Johnson, the seasoned and experienced screenwriter. "This would have made a very good, very acceptable 1945 war picture," Aldrich stated. "But I don't think that a 1945 war picture is necessarily a good 1967 war picture."[41] Metro was thinking of *The Dirty Dozen* as a film with a long running time—a road show with two parts and an intermission—an idea perfectly suited to Aldrich's style of film making.[42]

Aldrich sought the help of Lukas Heller, who had now worked with him on *What Ever Happened to Baby Jane?, Hush . . . Hush, Sweet Charlotte,* and *The Flight of the Phoenix*. Heller remembered the script he was given and the problems caused by his arrival on the scene:

> What Nunnally Johnson had written was a straight war drama which was to be taken perfectly seriously; it even had another long sub-plot from the original book, which was about some aristocratic English lady on whose estate all this training was taking place, and Lee Marvin was thinking of embarking on an affair with her, and then it turned out that she had a lover who was a General in the SS or something ridiculous. Aldrich was offered the movie to direct, and he said he would do it on the condition that I rewrite it, which the producer objected to violently—not so much because at that time he objected to me but because he felt I was being shoved down his throat.
>
> There was a great deal of dissension about that movie. Ken Hyman was mad at me, partly because he couldn't quite stand up to Aldrich, couldn't deal with Aldrich, and I was a good scapegoat, and he claims that I said that any pages I gave to Aldrich I would give to him. I thought I did; maybe I didn't. And when it came time for him to announce the credits on the film, he simply said, "Screenplay by Nunnally Johnson." And when my British agent said, "Could we see the script that was finally shot?" he said, "No. There is nothing in the agreement that says I have to show you the script. I have to submit one to the Writers Guild. If you want one, ask the Writers Guild." In fact, the one at the Writers Guild contained a lot of what I'd done, but by no means all that I had done. And even so, the Writers Guild finally adjudicated that it would be a co-credit.

Heller's revision of Johnson's script underscored the anti-authoritarian, anti-establishment, practically anarchic tone of the story and introduced much of the cynical humor and many of the comic touches. (Heller was particularly fond of two scenes: one with Donald Sutherland inspecting the troops and another with Charles Bronson taking the free-association tests, both of which he felt Aldrich had brilliantly directed.) As Aldrich summed up the final script, "The first two-thirds were Mr. Heller's contribution towards making it a 1967 picture and not a 1947 picture, and the last third was a pretty high-class, well-done war adventure."[43] Aldrich was proud of the final script.

Further problems arose with regard to casting the lead roles in *The Dirty Dozen*. Aldrich had cast approval, but without his knowledge or consent Hyman and Metro offered John Wayne the part of Major Reisman (commander of the Dozen), a part Aldrich wanted Lee Marvin to play. Aldrich was distressed: "I'm a Wayne fan. His politics don't bother me, that's his mother's problem. But not Wayne for a Marvin part."[44] Fortunately, Wayne withdrew from the film to concentrate on making *The Green Berets*. Jack Palance, whom Aldrich originally wanted for the part of Maggott, the deranged Southerner, also withdrew because he "thought [the role] made an unserious comment on bigotry."[45] Palance was replaced by Telly Savalas. Its cast and script problems resolved, *The Dirty Dozen* was at last ready to roll.[46]

The Dirty Dozen—book and film—is built on a rather preposterous but nevertheless intriguing idea: that during World War II a group of misfit soldiers, all convicted criminals facing either execution or long prison terms, are offered a chance to escape their punishments by forming a commando unit, undergoing intensified training, and infiltrating the German lines. There they are to seek out a chateau which important German officers use as a retreat and destroy both it and as many of the officers as possible. Then they are to make it back across the lines as best they can. If they survive, their sentences will be commuted; if they die, at least it won't be at the end of a rope. The plan goes by the code name of Project Amnesty, the bitter irony of which is quickly made evident, for this is a mad scheme with almost no chance of success, nor do the officers who conceived it really care if these men return or not. The Dozen are being sacrificed, not forgiven. Indeed, the generals in charge are shown as a particularly brutal and repellent lot, smarter (perhaps) and more powerful than the Dozen, but certainly not morally superior.

The dilemma Aldrich faced in making this film was to convince his audience that, on the one hand, these men *were* dangerous and outside the pale of society but, at the same time, make us want to see them succeed at their bloody business. He needed to enlist the audience on the side of morons and psychopaths. He did so by selling the criminals as underdogs against the power of the establishment—the enlisted men against the officers, the little men against the big. We are encouraged to see authority—be it American or German—as essentially corrupt and

Lee Marvin inspects his charges in *The Dirty Dozen*. Used by permission of the Museum of Modern Art/Film Stills Archive, courtesy of MGM.

unfeeling. The American officers who devise the plan command from an ornate, decadent mansion in England, one which is visually linked with the French chateau which houses the Germans. By destroying this chateau and killing the German officer within, the Dozen are metaphorically killing the Allied officers as well (an idea already express-ed in *Attack!*, wherein Costa throws the German officer out to be shot by his own men, foreshadowing Cooney's subsequent death by *his* own men). Indeed, the practice mission, held as part of war games just before the actual raid (and these games are surely a paradigm for the real "game" being played with the lives of the Dozen), is directed against the American general in ultimate command of the Dozen, who holds their fate in his hands. When one of the Dozen says, "This killing generals could get to be a habit," we are likely to find ourselves nodding in silent approval, our own sense of rage and impotence having been touched.

It is this apparent spirit of anarchy that gives the film much of its power and momentum. In 1967–1968, the film tapped the violent, rebellious mood of the country, especially among the young and disadvantaged. It was this audience reaction that so disturbed many of the establishment critics. Bosley Crowther, in his *New York Times* review, called it a "brazenly antisocial" film.[47] And Penelope Gilliatt in the *New Yorker* haughtily condemned it for pandering to the unworthy and disreputable class of people who so responded to it. "The moronic muggings of the title characters were hailed by colleague thugs in the audience with gales of comradely laughter," she wrote, horrified.[48] But the point Crowther and Gilliatt—and others like them—missed was that the film does not advocate an overthrow of *all* authority, nor does it deny the need for discipline and cooperation. As Major Reisman (Lee Marvin), the officer given the task of training the Dozen, explains, if any *one* of these men fails, then *all* will be sent back to their punishments. Reisman's training, vicious as it sometimes is, emphasizes that these men must work as a unit, that they must control their individual rages and hates and direct them toward the object of the raid itself. Moreover, the *purpose* of the raid is a worthwhile one: by killing the German officers, the Dozen will weaken and confuse the enemy on the eve of the Normandy invasion, thus strengthening the chances for Allied success and hastening the end of the war. The generals' plan, for all its unsavoriness, still remains only a slightly exaggerated version of the basic brutality of war itself. The raid does become a "turkey shoot," as Reisman calls it, but it differs from other acts of war only in degree, not kind. Marvin was certain Aldrich intended to make such a point in the film. "Life is a violent situation," Marvin replied when asked about the violence in *The Dirty Dozen.* "Let's not kid ourselves about that. It's not just the men in the chalet who were Nazis; the women were part of it too. I liked the idea of the final scene because it was their job to destroy the *whole* group and maybe in some way speed up the demise of the Third Reich. We glorify the 8th Air Force for bombing cities when they killed 100,000 people in one night, but remember, there were a lot of women and children burned up in those raids."

Although tame by today's stands, *The Dirty Dozen* upon its release soon developed a reputation as a graphically violent film, provoking the usual round of discussions about the need for censorship in the cinema. Aldrich adamantly opposed censorship in any form on the grounds that it was up to the viewer to decide what he wanted, or didn't want, to see, and he viewed industry efforts to curb violence in films to be the outgrowth of some curiously confused moral priorities. When Bernardo Bertolucci asked Aldrich if he had had problems with the violence in *The Dirty Dozen,* Aldrich offered his personal theory of the history of censorship:

> We had problems with violence because there wasn't an alphabetical rating system. When *The Dirty Dozen* came out, there was a code that you agreed with or didn't agree with. They disagreed with some of the violence in the picture. But you see the Catholics did a strange thing. In their thirty years of tenure in running the Breen Office, they substituted permissive violence for sex. So they would say, "Look to violence for excitement, but leave sex and marriage sacrosanct." So you could be as violent as you wanted for many, many years. It has only been in the last ten years that violence has been a problem. So our history of film has been that if we can't show people in bed, at least we can show them killing each other.[49]

Lots of people *do* get killed in *The Dirty Dozen,* but Aldrich argued that his use of violence in the film was justifiable: "Now, what I was trying to do was say that under the circumstances, it's not only the Germans who do unkind and hideous, horrible things in the name of war, but that the Americans do it and anybody does it. The whole nature of war is dehumanising. There's no such thing as a nice war."[50] When Aldrich made statements like this about *The Dirty Dozen,* some critics accused him of pontificating, of attempting to ennoble a blood-and-guts adventure with deep thoughts and high-sounding words. They did so by ignoring his earlier works, however: he had made the point in other films and there is no reason to doubt him here. While the attack on the chateau is exciting, it is also frequently ugly. The method by which Reisman and his men kill the German officers—and a number of innocent civilians—is appalling. The Dozen lock these people in an underground shelter, pour gasoline on them through the ventilator shafts, and then drop grenades to set off the conflagration while the victims scramble and scream in horror. The parallels to Nazi gas chambers in one war and to American use of napalm in another are surely evident. (Aldrich admitted that "the gas and the bombs are probably the only symbols in the picture."[51]) There is also a frenzy in these final battle scenes, a crazed, frightening release of energy, and a cruelty which should make it hard for us to relate completely with the Dozen. Even Major Reisman, who is the character we can most easily identify with in the film, being neither as emotionally detached as his superiors nor as unbalanced as most of his charges, displays a surprising callousness at the chateau. When one of his men asks what to do with the servants captured at the retreat, he answers, "Feed the French and kill the Germans." Although the line insures a shock laugh, it is also an upsetting reminder of the brutalizing effect of war.

Still, we *do* cheer for these men in this final battle, and here Aldrich's skill as an action director may have worked against him. We become so caught up in the excitement that we miss the central irony of the situation: that these men are now being praised for doing the very thing that most of them were imprisoned and condemned for in the first place. It is only in retrospect that we may be tempted to question their motivation and the rightness of their acts. "I do think that war brings out both the best and worst in men," Aldrich said,[52] but in *The Dirty Dozen* it is sometimes difficult to determine which is meant to be which. Thus we come back to the problem of the ambiguity of heroism in war, which Aldrich had addressed in *Attack!* and *The Angry Hills* and would return to in *Too Late the Hero*. Because *The Dirty Dozen* is packaged more as an entertainment than these other films, the idea is less clearly stated, but it is there, nonetheless.

The fact remains, however, that Aldrich does not play entirely fair with us in this film. He wanted, he said, "to show the necessity for collective courage in circumstances that would make collective cowardice more likely, and to show that almost anybody can be redeemed if certain circumstances and pressures are sufficient."[53] The theme of redemption would be more valid if the Dozen were really as "dirty" as is suggested at the beginning of the film. We soon come to see that there are "good" and "bad" criminals among the Dozen, however, and they are treated with differing amounts of respect, allowed differing degrees of redemption. Wladislaw (Charles Bronson), for example, is condemned for killing a man in combat, but we learn that the man was trying to make off with needed medical supplies at the time. Jefferson (Jim Brown) killed some "cracker bastards" who were trying to castrate him, and Posey (Clint Walker), a simple-minded giant, "sure didn't mean to kill that feller": he is a victim of his own strength. Wladislaw, appropriately, is one of the three survivors of the raid (along with Reisman and Sgt. Bowren [Richard Jaeckel], Reisman's assistant). Jefferson is given a spectacular and heroic death, cheered on by the other men as he makes a desperate run setting off the explosives which destroy the chateau. Only Posey is not shown in the battle, his scene apparently edited from the final cut.

This is unfortunate, for Posey deserves a Herculean demise. The truly sick Maggott (Telly Savalas), however, who is the most—and, in fact, the only—completely repulsive member of the group, dies a traitor's death, killed by his own men, and Franko (John Cassavetes), the former Mafia hit-man who has largely refused to join in the group, is killed at the last minute while exulting in the slaughter surrounding him. Others of the Dozen are simply too likable (Pinkley [Donald Sutherland]) or too bland (Jiminez [Trini Lopez]), for us to accept as among the nastiest renegades in the U.S. Army.

Indeed, although the film never sentimentalizes this group, it does romanticize them, and turns their aberrations into virtues. We are encouraged to see these men as martyrs, almost in religious terms. Reisman is the leader, the savior who takes them to—at least—a better death; they are his disciples. There is one traitor (Maggott) and one doubter (Franko) among them. They eat a Last Supper together in a setting replete with icons, a scene devised by Aldrich himself.[54] They die not as criminals but as heroes. Aldrich does not push this view, as, for instance, happens with Randall McMurphy and his fellow inmates in *One Flew Over the Cuckoo's Nest* (both book and film), which resembles *The Dirty Dozen* in structure and theme. Unlike McMurphy, Reisman is never deified, and Aldrich played down further religious parallels: "I am not as aware as I should be that I am a salesman for Christ. I don't think that I am."[55] But the film does make it easy for us to accept these men, even to like them. This is due, in part, to the casting of the Dozen. Bronson and Cassavetes are magnetic actors who convey, respectively, the power and the madness of violence. Brown's and Walker's sheer size, strength, and physical grace command respect. Marvin and Jaeckel achieve the necessary balance between hardness and humanity.

Marvin was especially impressed by the casting of *The Dirty Doze* and believed that it contributed significantly to the film's success: "Everyone was ideally cast, and even when they ad-libbed a scene, invariably it was in character, so all it could do was to help the film." And Marvin, who had been on an Aldrich set before as Colonel Bartlett in *Attack!,* knew what to expect from his boss: "He was a tremendous man to work with. You knew when you went to work with him you were both going for the same object—a good final print." Marvin recalled two episodes in particular from *The Dirty Dozen* which revealed Aldrich's style and tone as a director and which illustrated the methods he used to get what he wanted from his performers:

Over in England we read for a week or so—again the rehearsal table—so one day he said, "OK, boys, tomorrow when you come in, I want you all to have your haircuts" (because everybody had their mod haircuts then). So I went out that afternoon and got a crew cut that was very tight—military style, 1944—and came back in, skin around my ears and all that. And some of these guys had kind of a nice creative hair clipping; they just knocked the edges off. And so he looked at them all and he said, "All right, I'm gonna tell you again: I want you to go out and get your hair cut." Well, the same thing the next day. So he says, "I'll tell you what: don't come in tomorrow without that hair cut, or else call your attorneys." And that's how he dealt with it. And sure enough, John Cassavetes was the first one—he came in with a skin head! And it just broke Aldrich up, and he laughed, and everybody could see what he was driving at. So they all went out and did the job properly.

He had that kind of way. He'd play with you and tease you and put you in a personal jeopardy with the other actors, which I thought was good. So all these guys were fighting for their lives in the film. I remember the first day that he said, "All right, let's put it on its feet. First of all, let's line up for the first inspection when Reisman comes in to check the men." So he's calling off names and positions. And you know Charlie Bronson would wear boxing shoes on the sound stage for rehearsals—I guess it gave him a better grip on his feet or something. But what I mean is he was *ready to go*. And so Aldrich is calling off the list of the men in the order they should be standing in line, so he said, "Clint Walker," who is about 6'7" or something, and then he said, "Charlie, you're next." Then he got Donald Sutherland, who's about 6'4" or 6'5", on the other side of Charlie. So Charlie's standing there, looking straight forward; and then he looks up to his left and he sees Sutherland about a *foot* over his head and then he looks over to his right and there's Walker about a *foot and a half* over his head. So he just stepped out of line and walked towards Bob and said, "Fuck this!" Well, the whole joint fell down because that's a funny bit. Of course, it took Aldrich about ten minutes to quit laughing. He was just hysterical over this.

Because this was the type of test that he put guys through, which I found to be very advantageous to the film. It's people taking advantage of each other at playing THE GAME. He knew, at least by that exercise, that if there was ever a scene with Charlie standing up next to these guys that it'd be in Charlie's favor, that something was going to happen. These are the kinds of nice, little in-house games that you like to watch.

Marvin *is* good in the film—Aldrich thought he was "marvelous . . . he was and could not be better"[56]—but other aspects of characterization are less successful. Telly Savalas's portrayal of Maggott is a glaring weakness: his "Southerness" is never convincing, and his instability, rendered ludicrous by overacting, should have logically precluded him from any carefully planned mission. Trini Lopez is also miscast: with his sweet, smiling face, he would surely have been strangled with his own guitar strings before he finished the first stanza of "Don't Sit Under the Apple Tree." (Thankfully, Jiminez is the first to die, his neck broken when his parachute is caught, appropriately enough, in a tree. Jiminez's death was determined by more than the script. Lopez's agent, having agreed to contractual terms, suddenly demanded more money and threatened to pull Trini out of the picture. Aldrich, never one to be bullied by his actors, promptly wrote Lopez out of the film.[57]) Finally, both Robert Ryan and Ernest Borgnine seem awkward in their authoritative roles of Colonel Breed and General Worden (the originator of the plan), although the fact that either could have easily and convincingly portrayed any one of the Dozen is perhaps a subtle comment on the relative morality of the officers and the criminals.

Aldrich was hard-pressed to explain the appeal of *The Dirty Dozen:* "I'd love to say we sat back and calculated it, that we anticipated that there was going to be a rash of anti-Establishment feeling, and it was going to be captured in a semi-humorous, semi-cynical picture. I think we knew part of that, but . . . a ground swell that went way beyond being anti-military . . . caught up with the timing of that movie and took it way over to what we had no right to expect, an astronomical success."[58]

The Legend of Lylah Clare (1968)

Like *The Big Knife* and *What Ever Happened to Baby Jane?* before it, and *The Killing of Sister George* and (to an extent) . . . *All the Marbles* after, Aldrich's *The Legend of Lylah Clare* is a film about show business. Taken together, these films comprise a genre all their own—the Hollywood Exposé Film—a genre which enabled Aldrich to explore his own tumultuous relationship with, and to project his own bitter indictment of, the Hollywood film industry. On the whole, this group of films is sometimes less successful and less compelling than the work Aldrich has done in his other genre films, partly because they *are* so personal and self-reflexive. Of this group, *Lylah Clare* is perhaps the most personal and self-conscious of Aldrich's efforts. The film combines his scathing criticism of the Hollywood studio system with his most boldly experimental visual style since *Kiss Me Deadly* thirteen years earlier, and, while the combination does not always work, *Lylah Clare* remains a challenging, provocative film.

The original idea for the plot of the film came from a television episode of the Dupont "Play of the Month" series, with Alfred Drake and Tuesday Weld in the parts played in the movie version by Peter Finch and Kim Novak. Only Novak, Aldrich contended, could convey the kind of sensuousness the role demanded: "What . . . made Kim a star is the American male dream that there be innocence and beauty in the eyes, and one millimeter below the surface, an extraordinary sensuality. She has that rare mixture: ice and fire."[59] Aldrich, in fact, had the screenplay written expressly for Novak and undertook some "very, very adroit Machiavellian maneuvering to get her into the picture."[60] It was thus Novak whom writers Jean Rouverol and Hugo Butler had in mind when they took the story concept—about a film director attempting a screen biography of the famous actress he once had loved—and developed it finally into a script.[61] As a favor to his friend Butler, Aldrich veteran Lukas Heller also worked on the script but without acknowledgment: "This was going to be his [Butler's] first opportunity to get his name back on the screen after being blacklisted for about ten years or more. I agreed from the outset that I would work on it without asking for credit, whether it was merited or warranted or not."

The nightmare world of *Lylah Clare* is so callous and unfeeling, so crass and perverse, that virtually everyone who makes contact with it is either corrupted or destroyed. The plot concerns the attempted comeback of reclusive Lewis Zarkan (Peter Finch), a Hollywood director coaxed from a lengthy, self-imposed retirement by Bart Langner (Milton Selzer). Langner is a talent scout whose discovery of the gorgeous Elsa Brinkman (Kim Novak) prompts him to suggest to Zarkan a risky and ambitious film project: the life story of the legendary starlet Lylah Clare, Zarkan's wife and a well-known actress whose tragic death twenty years earlier has left Zarkan artistically impotent. Langner argues that Elsa, an uncanny Lylah look-alike, is perfect for the part. Although initially reluctant, Zarkan eventually consents to direct this film biography but must first procure the help of Barney Sheean, a loud, crass studio boss, to finance the project. Intrigued by the extraordinary resemblance between Elsa and Lylah, and convinced of the profitableness of such a venture, Sheean (Ernest Borgnine) agrees to produce on the condition that stringent penalties be imposed should Zarkan fail to complete the film on schedule. For much of the film, shooting goes badly, each scene calling for countless re-takes. With the deadline drawing near, Zarkan, dissatisfied with his original ending, proposes another, despite protests from cast and crew that the additional stunt work required on such short notice could

Kim Novak and Peter Finch discuss the image of the starlet in *The Legend of Lylah Clare*. Used by permission of the Museum of Modern Art/Film Stills Archive, courtesy of MGM.

endanger Elsa's life. Zarkan's stubborn and incautious persistence precipitates her death, but the film opens to rave reviews and appears to be the sensational hit Sheean envisioned.

The Hollywood of *Lylah Clare* is a wonder-wasteland, a world in which "reality" runs second to the magic and deceit of the camera. As Zarkan explains to Elsa, "You're an illusion. Without me you don't exist." To Zarkan, then, Elsa is merely raw material to be molded and shaped to his specifications, an object to be displayed for public consumption. Shortly after their first meeting, Zarkan cooly announces his intentions to her: "I'll rummage through your soul like a pickpocket through a stolen purse," indicating the predatory nature of their partnership. Elsewhere, he describes Elsa as "Cinderella," or as a fantasy/magical trick that only he is capable of performing. This idea of Zarkan as the master illusionist is underscored when we learn that the director's real name was (appropriately enough) "Flack," and that it was changed by Barney Sheean to the more flamboyant "Zarkan" at the beginning of his career, that name being taken from—what else?—a magician. Thus Zarkan is himself a kind of illusion.

Elsa's metamorphosis from *her* former self—preacher's daughter and college student—to her present self—remodeled Hollywood star—is, of course, a destructive one, a kind of perverse Pygmalion; for the transformation wrought by Zarkan and company is an undoing rather than a remaking. Assisting in Elsa's deconstruction are other "benefactors" who have their own, rather than Elsa's best interests in mind. Bart Langner had originally discovered Lylah in a Berlin brothel which specialized in "some pretty unusual fantasies"; when he offers Elsa as the "new" Lylah, he leads her into the same world of corruption. Moreover, Langner is now dying of cancer, and he is primarily concerned with having "something [worthwhile] to leave behind" after his death. The film serves as a potential living monument to his memory. Producer Sheean, always the tough-minded pragmatist, views the project mainly in terms of dollar signs, yet he also sees the chance to get his own son Mark (Michael Murphy) started in the film business and an opportunity to demonstrate his theory of "winning," which, according to his shrewd businessman's mentality, "keeps me in the business . . . keeps us all alive." And even Zarkan himself really needs Elsa in a way he can never admit. As Bart Langner suggests, the main reason Zarkan has done nothing for the past twenty years is that he is afraid to direct without Lylah, his greatest creation. Elsa gives him the opportunity to recapture his former success.

Elsa, then, is at first nothing more than a pawn in the hands of the Hollywood Establishment, but as the shooting progresses, she fashions an identity of her own, sometimes quite unconsciously. She begins to adopt Lylah's mannerisms, speaks in Lylah's guttural German voice, and, in essence, *becomes* Lylah. We know that Elsa has long been obsessed with the dead actress—her apartment is filled with news clippings and photos of Lylah—but her identity change often goes beyond the rational or the plausible. The crippled gossip columnist Molly Luther (Coral Browne), whose opinion makes or breaks aspiring young actors and actresses, asks Zarkan in Elsa's presence, "She's tame enough now, Lewis, but will she turn into a slut like the last one?" Elsa turns on her maliciously and calls her a "freak." The morning after, *Variety's* headlines report the news: STARLET TAKES SWITCHBLADE TO MOLLY LUTHER. But it is Lylah talking, not Elsa—Lylah speaking through Elsa—who has humiliated the vicious critic. As Zarkan's drug-addicted, lesbian housekeeper Rosella (Rosella Falk) says, "Elsa—Lylah? What's the difference?" When Elsa makes love to Zarkan in a room filled with Lylah memorabilia, she taunts him to "see if you can tell the difference between the woman and the actress." Portraits of the two women displayed in Zarkan's home are indistinguishable. Elsa's dress measurements are identical with Lylah's; her footprints match the impressions made years ago by the actress at Grauman's Chinese Theater; both take on Italian gardeners as lovers. The lines of demarcation blur. Elsa comes to know things that only Lylah herself could reasonably know: that Zarkan, for example, had insisted that Lylah abort the child they had conceived.

It is soon clear that *Lylah Clare* is two movies in one, as is perhaps befitting such a schizophrenic subject. It is, on the one hand, a satire on both Hollywood and Hollywood films about Hollywood (a film about a film about an illusion). And it is also a popular film with art-film pretensions, compounding the schizophrenia. Although by his own admission Aldrich "tried to avoid making it *Marienbad Revisited*," some self-conscious "arty-crafty" elements crept into the film anyway.[62] Because these moments often seem serious within the context of the film, they tend to undercut the more obvious satire. If they were intended as part of the satire itself, the point is not made clear.

Part of the blame for this confusion among the various levels of the tale Aldrich attributed to Michael Luciano's editing, though Aldrich, characteristically, assumed much of the blame himself. The collaboration between Aldrich and Luciano dated back to *Kiss Me Deadly*, and *Lylah Clare* was the eleventh of nineteen films they would do together. Aldrich liked Luciano and considered him a member of his professional family: "Mike and I have an extraordinarily good relationship. . . . He knows what I like and I know what he is particularly good at."[63] But Aldrich felt that Luciano had failed to grasp the complexities of this film: "He lost *Lylah Clare*. . . . He knew Lylah Clare was two people. He knew that there was a time slip. But what he knew had no relation to what was on film."[64] Luciano, who loved and respected Aldrich and who regarded his old friend as a "god-damned genius," acknowledged his own bewilderment with the film. "Yeah, the final scene was symbolic, but of what?" he wondered and suspected that the film's problems had more to do with the *kind* of narrative structure Aldrich was attempting to impose on it. "Aldrich was terrific when he tried to tell a story in a simple way," Luciano explained. "When he tried otherwise, he got into trouble." Luciano may be right: perhaps Aldrich *was* out of his element with *Lylah Clare* (though it is just as likely that Luciano simply was not up to the material). At any rate, Aldrich took the rap, as he always did, for the film's structural weaknesses: "I don't think it worked. I think Robert Aldrich the Director did a marvelous job, but Robert Aldrich the Producer failed to make the parallel stories sufficiently coherent so that the guy who pays the three dollars can go home and figure it out."[65] Despite Aldrich's best efforts, Fellini-Antonioni-arty-crafty elements *had* crept into *Lylah Clare.*

Still, the art film elements in *Lylah Clare* are ultimately rooted in the illusion-reality theme which is the film's central narrative strategy. Nowhere is this more clearly shown than in the series of three dream-reverie flashbacks, each one color-coded, by which the "true" facts surrounding Lylah's death are revealed. The first flashback is Rosella's, who envisions Lylah being attacked by a male assailant brandishing a knife. As she defends herself, her attacker falls to his death from the balcony staircase of Zarkan's mansion, and Lylah follows suit. The second flashback is Zarkan's: in his version, Lylah's attacker is a woman dressed as a man who, after struggling with Lylah, tumbles to her death, again followed by Lylah. But in the third episode, which belongs to Elsa as Lylah, it is *Zarkan* who engineers the disaster: after seeing his bride fend off the advances of the woman in disguise (but jealous of what may once have been an illicit union), Zarkan urges Lylah—who suffers from vertigo—to look down at the sprawled corpse of her attacker, whereupon Lylah plunges to her death. Elsa experiences this last vision while filming the new ending to Zarkan's film. In the film, Elsa re-enacts Lylah's former life as a circus performer and dies in a fall not from the balcony but from her trapeze. At precisely the instant when Elsa "remembers" Lylah's balcony death (with Zarkan's help)—and Aldrich uses a superimposition shot to make his point—Zarkan the director urges Elsa the actress to "look down" from her precarious perch on the trapeze. She does so and topples to her death while the cameras roll. Elsa's death thus becomes the new ending, the final revision, of Lylah's life, as related in Zarkan's finished film, *The Legend of Lylah Clare.* As Zarkan says, "We make the legend. The legend becomes the truth."

If all this sounds more than a little confusing, it is: layers of reality and unreality are piled on so thickly here that disbelief is difficult to suspend. But the film's most disorienting and surreal moment is still to come. In the final scene, Aldrich orchestrates a bizarre ending in which three events—the film's opening, a dog food commercial, and Rosella's loading of Zarkan's pistol—are cross-cut in montage fashion. Typically, a TV reporter hypes the film as a celebration of the indomitable Hollywood spirit carrying on in the face of tragedy: "the unfortunate, untimely death of that shining meteor, Miss Elsa Campbell" (whose name even has been changed from the original). But the intrepid reporter must interrupt for a station break and an important message from his sponsor, Barkwell's vitamin-enriched dogfood. Cut to opening night audience responding to the film. Cut to Rosella loading a pistol—to kill Zarkan, presumably, as she once threatened. Cut to Molly Luther raving about the brilliant director Lewis Zarkan. Cut to TV reporter interviewing Zarkan, asking the director, "How much fact and how much fiction is there in the film?" And then, before the obviously distraught director can answer (he is now impossibly lost in his love/hate/fear/guilt relationship with Lylah/Elsa), a final and savage cut to the dog food commercial. It begins innocuously enough with a voice-over narrator extolling Barkwell-fed dogs as a pretty young woman fills the dish of a cute fluffy poodle. Then a bizarre and terrifying twist occurs: the poodle is joined by a pack of growling, meanacing mongrels. The girl is visibly shaken by the rabid pack and its feeding frenzy, but the voice-over continues uninterrupted, as if all were normal and well. The film's final image is a close-up freeze frame of one of the dogs, its teeth bared in a vicious snarl. Earlier it was suggested that Elsa was an object formed and shaped by ruthless creators, packaged like a product for public consumption in a cutthroat, dog-eat-dog world. In this final image, Aldrich crystallizes his vision of the condition and quality of life in Hollywood, where not tinsel and glitter prevail, but grotesqueness, predation, and madness.[66] Aldrich claimed he intended for the ending to be taken seriously, not as a joke: "It [said] . . . that it's all dog meat, and you're all going to be destroyed. If you haven't figured that out by now, here's the commercial that's going to let you know that."[67]

Lylah Clare has powerful moments, the ambiguous final scene among them. But it does suffer from incohesiveness—the various strata of the plot remain disjointed—and a lack of credibility, particularly in terms of Kim Novak's portrayal of Elsa/Lylah. Although Aldrich thought Novak was "marvelous" in the picture and never publicly faulted her performance, it was nevertheless obvious to him that audiences did not find her believable, and "because people won't take her seriously, the picture gets evaluated on that level."[68] Cinematographer Joseph Biroc, another

Aldrich regular, offered a blunter assessment: "Novak failed him. After rehearsals, long after she should have been *in* character, she was still unsure of her motivation; she kept asking questions like 'What is my attitude?' Aldrich disliked that kind of uncertainty. It just burned him up." The finished product, apparently, burned up MGM too. Because MGM disapproved of the film, they simply refused to promote it, and without distribution, the film was doomed to financial failure. It was a critical disappointment as well. Richard Schickel, reviewing the film for *Life*, was almost as vicious as the Barkwell dogs: "*The Legend of Lylah Clare* is an awful movie. But it is not merely awful: it is grandly, toweringly, amazingly so. . . . I laughed myself silly at *Lylah Clare*, and if you're in just the right mood you may too."[69] Renata Adler was kinder: "*The Legend of Lylah Clare* . . . is a take-off on some of the highly serious tragic movies Hollywood has made about itself—a take-off so faithful in spirit that it is almost indistinguishable from its model. . . . "[70] Faithful to his own spirit, Aldrich took the heat for the film's failure: "*Lylah Clare* was a failure and if it's a failure, then you have to say that either the subject or the way you handled the subject matter didn't communicate itself to the people. And if it did, they didn't care about it."[71]

5. "A Better Mousetrap"

The Aldrich Studios

The Legend of Lylah Clare was completed in November 1967, five months after the release of *The Dirty Dozen*. With *Lylah Clare*, Aldrich fulfilled his contractual obligation to MGM. During that five-month period, *The Dirty Dozen* had proved to be a phenomenal success and was well on its way to becoming one of the biggest money-makers in MGM's history, grossing $7,500,000 in only the first five weeks of its U.S. release and earning $18,200,000 in its first year, making it the No. 1 box office hit of 1967.[1] On the basis of the film, Aldrich was named Director of the Year by the National Association of Theatre Owners. The film received four Academy Award nominations, including John Cassavetes for supporting actor and Michael Luciano for editing. Many had expected Aldrich to receive a nomination as best director, although Aldrich himself did not. He felt that both he and the film were too controversial to receive such awards.

Nevertheless, the success of the film allowed Aldrich to fulfill a longstanding dream: the purchase of his own private studio. He sold his interest in *The Dirty Dozen* (which Aldrich usually put at 15 percent) to MGM for approximately $1,500,000. With this money he then bought, in January 1968, the John Sutherland Productions Studio at 201 North Occidental Boulevard in Los Angeles. He also purchased land surrounding or near the studio for proposed expansion. The Sutherland Studio had originally been built in 1913 for Mary Pickford Productions. By 1919 it was owned by Famous Players-Lasky Corporation, and in 1946 it became the property of John Sutherland Productions, Inc., which was the largest producer of government, educational, industrial, and documentary films in Hollywood. Sutherland, however, also rented the lot to some of the major studios for stage work, and Aldrich had worked there on portions of both *Kiss Me Deadly* and *The Big Knife*.[2]

Aldrich quickly began a two-step program on the studio. First he renovated the one existing sound stage, which measured 65 by 130 feet, and the adjoining complex, which included offices, dressing rooms, a projection room, editing room, and scene docks. Then he built a new

stage, 80 by 120 feet, which was specially soundproofed and set up as
Hollywood's "most modern film-making facility."[3] The initial cost for
purchase and remodeling ran over $1 million.

Aldrich had great hopes for his studio. He felt that by owning his own
independent operation, being in charge of all aspects of the filmmaking procedure, he could make better pictures at a cheaper price and, from
both an artistic and financial viewpoint, compete with the major studios.
Aldrich believed that the Hollywood Studio System was doomed, that
within fifteen to twenty years there would be no pictures made in
Hollywood because of runaway production costs. His kind of studio
would be the only possible way to survive, and even then the chances
were slim. As he argued, "If a producer in Italy can make a film exactly
as well for one half the money, nothing that I or anybody else in the world
can do is going to change that. . . . There is a self-destructive lemming-like
irresistible urge on the part of Hollywood unions, creative crafts (and
yes, this certainly includes Producers/Directors) . . . . All of them—and/or
us—are simply pricing ourselves out of the market. It's called: 'Killing
The Golden Goose' Syndrome."[4]

Aldrich saw his studio as a fifteen-to-twenty year investment. He intended to keep the overhead down by avoiding unnecessary expenses
such as a commissary or elaborate dressing rooms or specialized sets
which could be rented from the major studios. If the studio proved successful, he also hoped to add two additional sound stages that he could
himself rent to other filmmakers at no more than seven cents on the
dollar, as he projected. "If, as I suspect, we're entering the last chapter
of movie-making in Hollywood itself, I like to think that the Aldrich
Studios will be there at the finish," he wrote.[5]

In one sense, Aldrich had been working toward the kind of control
he felt he could have with his own studio since his days at Enterprise.
He noted the "unique atmosphere" at the Aldrich Studios, "one of teamwork and relaxation in the midst of a hard day's work," a description
which could have also applied to Enterprise. "Maybe it's because I'm
relaxed. I feel freer to schedule cast rehearsals before and during principal photography. We have a payroll to meet, of course, but no landlord
is breathing down my neck."[6] He was, however, intending to avoid the
mismanagement and artistic extravagance which had finally destroyed
Enterprise.

On another, more personal level, the studio allowed him to practice
the kind of paternalism he was most comfortable with, to gather together
in a "family" that group of artists and craftsmen he had worked with

The dedication of the Aldrich Studios in Los Angeles on August 8, 1968. Used by permission of Adell Aldrich.

over the years. "It didn't make any difference, really, if it was the prop man or the character actor; he wanted the *same* person each time," William Aldrich remembered. This sometimes meant using people who were not first-rate: their dependability was more important to him than their talent. But it also meant working with people who had proved themselves, people who could be trusted to do the jobs assigned. Among the key studio personnel were his old friend Walter Blake, who would serve as associate producer, cameraman Joseph Biroc, and art director William Glasgow. William Aldrich was named studio manager, the role Aldrich had filled at Enterprise.

He was, then, with the studio both challenging Hollywood and insulating himself from it. He had worked within the vagaries of the system; now he was attempting to create an ordered system of his own. And, just as surely, he was building, within the business, the kind of secure family structure he had not had as a child. In this system, he could not only *belong*, he could control, through his benevolent paternalism, those around him. The studio was, in its clearest form, "us against them." As Lukas Heller put it: "It was certainly part of his character that he was obsessively loyal to anyone who was in any way dependent on him, and paranoically aggressive toward anybody who might be considered in a position to tell him what to do. He was a very combative-type character and . . . in dealing with the people who were, at least theoretically, more powerful than he, he would always say, 'Fuck 'em.' "

The Killing of Sister George (1968)

This complex mixture of apparent practicality and aggressive arrogance was evident both in his plans for the studio and in his first choice of projects. When the Aldrich Studios was officially opened on August 8, 1968 (the same month *Lylah Clare* was released by MGM), Aldrich announced that they would produce between eight and sixteen films over the next five years.[7] The Associates and Aldrich had signed a four-picture deal with Palomar Pictures, the film distributing branch of ABC, as a means of getting started. Aldrich planned to do his own distribution at a later date, and even at one point hoped to own three "flagship" theaters in different cities as a "minimum guaranteed outlet" for his films.[8] The four films he promised to Palomar were *The Killing of Sister George, Whatever Happened to Aunt Alice?, The Greatest Mother of 'Em All,* and *Too Late the Hero.* A fifth film mentioned was *The Crowded Bed,* to be written and directed by Theodore Flicker.[9]

The first of the Aldrich Studios films was *The Killing of Sister George,* which Aldrich chose for a number of reasons. First of all, Frank Marcus' play of the same title had been a popular success in both England and the United States, partly because it dealt with the subject of lesbianism in a tragi-comical manner. Aldrich had bought the rights to the work in April 1967 and was fully aware that it would make a controversial film. "It's going to give a lot of self-styled critics a field day," he boasted.[10]

Aldrich also wanted a project which would show off his new studio and prove its viability. He was proud of the fact that, although the film was set in present-day London, he was able to do much of the work in the studio, on his own turf. "If ever a picture was a natural to make abroad, it's *Sister George*," he wrote. "But instead of shooting the works in Britain, we merely filmed exteriors in and near London and only those interiors . . . that couldn't be duplicated anywhere, regardless of cost. For the rest, we transported chunks of an English pub, pieces of an English Ford truck and BBC-TV cameras and control panels—to say nothing of costly stars and co-stars—to Hollywood."[11] One of the few scenes filmed on location was shot in Chelsea at the Gateways Club, an internationally-known lesbian nightspot which had never before allowed cameras inside. Aldrich convinced its owners that the picture would present lesbianism in a manner "neither approving nor disapproving—but with honesty."[12] He even used regular patrons as extras in this scene, which was probably the first of its kind in a major American film. But despite such bits of authenticity, the film was, for better or worse, clearly meant to be a showcase fo the studio itself. As Lukas Heller, who wrote the screenplay, noted, "It could have been made anywhere. It's a studio film. There was a tremendous sense of unreality about the whole thing to me. That was the peculiar thing about Aldrich. There were certain sorts of details that he simply didn't seem to be concerned about. I suppose you could say he created his own reality."

Although Bette Davis and Angela Lansbury were considered for the lead role, Aldrich finally chose Beryl Reid, who had createed the part on the stage, to repeat her performance. "I knew that Beryl Reid was great in it on the stage and that was enough for me," Aldrich said.[13] Other English actors and actresses—Susannah York, Coral Browne, Ronald Fraser—were also brought to Hollywood to make the film. Shooting began in May 1968 and ended the following October. The film was released in December, in time for the holiday crowd.

The Killing of Sister George was, however, not a "holiday" film. June Buckridge (Beryl Reid) is a BBC actress, beloved by the public for her portrayal of "Sister George," a kind, philosophical village nurse in a television soap opera. In reality, George (as she is most often called) is an alcoholic, often spiteful, and very frightened woman who lives with her younger, rather simple-minded lover "Childie" McNaught (Susannah York). George is teetering on the edge of disaster: her forthright and often outlandish behavior has brought her unpleasant publicity, her show is losing ratings, and she is becoming increasingly jealous of Childie. George's situation is neatly portrayed by Aldrich during the opening credits, as George walks out of a bar and down various walled-in paths on her way home: she is trapped from the very beginning, but she has also planted the seeds of her own destruction.

Beryl Reid and Susannah York in *The Killing of Sister George*. Used by permission of the Museum of Modern Art/Film Stills Archive, courtesy of the Aldrich Studios.

The film (and play) center on George's disintegration and her desperate attempts to avoid it. She is most obviously threatened by a BBC assistant head, ironically named Mercy Croft (Coral Browne, who played the role of film critic Molly Luther in *The Legend of Lylah Clare*). When she comes to George's apartment to discuss George's latest outrage (she has attacked two young nuns in a taxi during a drunken spree), George fears the worst. After some uncertainty, she learns that her character is, indeed, to be eliminated, wiped out by a ten-ton truck. "Why kill her?" she asks in despair. "Because that's life," Mercy answers.

Although George must die, June Buckridge will be allowed to work on in a new program: she will become the lead character in "The World of Clarabell Cow," a "flawed, credible cow," she is assured. It is all a question of ratings. But by the end of the film, the more lacerating and graphic truth has come out: "You were fired because you are a fat, boring actress, and people are sick to death of you," Mercy tells her. "Look at yourself, you pathetic old dyke!" Added to this disgrace is Croft's seduction of Childie, whom she takes home with her. Despite the fact that George has adamantly refused the Clarabell Cow role, she begins to practice her moos as the film ends. With each low, the camera pulls back a bit further, leaving her isolated in the dark of the abandoned studio (a reprisal of the ending shots of both *Attack!* and *The Big Knife*). The final moos become moans, horrible cries of anguish, as June is swallowed by the blackness into the void.

The film version of *Sister George* was fairly close to Frank Marcus' play. Lukas Heller did switch the background from BBC radio to television. "It was not a hard film to write," he recalled. "I thought I wrote some relatively funny scenes that never existed in the original. In the stage play there were no actual scenes that take place in the studio, when she gradually realizes that she's being written out—all that was mine." Still, Aldrich was obviously taking quite a chance on this material, for homosexuality was—and still is—very much a taboo subject for American films to treat with honesty and compassion. Moreover, Aldrich intended to include in the film a very explicit seduction scene between Coral Browne and Susannah York. He realized that with such a scene he would be open to charges of exploitation and sensationalism (as, indeed, he was), but he felt that it was essential to the picture. He insisted that "unlike the stage version, the picture had to play out the betrayal, and the story itself is so genteel, it's possible you could be sitting in Sheboygan and the film could be so 'well done' that nobody would know what the hell you were talking about."[14] At the same time, he wanted "to bring off the most erotic, provocative English-language sex scene that anyone has photographed."[15] It proved to be a very difficult scene to shoot, one with numerous ramifications.

First of all, Susannah York had to be practically forced into doing the scene. "The English Rose," as Aldrich derisively called her, "was difficult . . . but not intentionally. She didn't come in and say, 'I want to make your life tough today.' She came in very embarrassed and very filled with inhibitions, and it was very, very hard for her to do it." Coral Browne took a more detached, professional attitude toward the scene, regarding it as a necessary part of the role. In Aldrich's words, she "put it in the female perspective so that Susannah didn't feel dirty. . . . What [Susannah] needed to sustain her through those embarrassing moments couldn't have come from a man. . . . Susannah was a bitch to her. But in this particular sequence, Coral really, really helped her and therefore helped the movie through a very tough time."[16] Joseph Biroc remembered that Aldrich was quite tense during the shooting of the scene. In all their years of working together, it was the first time Aldrich lost his temper with his cameraman. "He got on me for not going fast enough, and it wasn't my fault. The girls kept changing, and I had to relight over and over." Biroc knew that Aldrich was, in effect, using him as a scapegoat.

But perhaps the worst result of the pressures Aldrich felt was manifested in his relationship with Frank DeVol, who had written the music for his films since 1954. When they were screening the picture for scoring, DeVol was outraged by the scene and asked to be relieved from the picture. Aldrich agreed but several weeks later told him, "We'll always be friends, but I'll never use you again." DeVol understood that Aldrich considered his refusal to be a betrayal of trust: "Like a John Ford, he had his own company," DeVol said. "He wanted to know that when he moved, everybody would move with him. And I could understand that he couldn't have a composer to whom he had to say, 'Do you like this picture? Would you like to do it?' " Three years later Aldrich called him back—"Friendship won out," as DeVol put it—and they renewed their working relationship.[17]

Aldrich was courting controversy when he made the film with the Big Scene, but he was also a victim of events beyond his control. When he began the film, the movie industry operated under the old Seal of Approval system: a film either got the Seal or it didn't, and a film without a Seal could still be released without the kiss of death on its brow. However, during filming the industry moved to the new Ratings System—P, PG, R, and X. *Sister George* received its X rating on December

11, 1968, the day before its general release. Aldrich objected, and the film became the first test case to come before the ratings board. Aldrich argued that, in the public's mind, an X automatically meant an obscene picture rather than an adult film, and he demanded that clarifications be made in the ratings system. Largely as a result of the X rating, Aldrich also had problems with the film's advertising. Both the *Los Angeles Times* and KMPC, a Los Angeles radio station, refused to accept advertisements, and Aldrich sued.[18] He felt that the case involved more than his right to make and distribute *Sister George*, that, in fact, these actions were violations of the First Amendment. As William Aldrich put it, "He just thought that it was ridiculous for any monopoly not to allow you to advertise your product." Aldrich asked for support in his suit from ABC-Palomar (the distributors) and the Motion Picture Association of America, but they refused to take part. The major studios stayed out of the fight as well because they felt that X-rated films would never make money, and they were more than willing for Aldrich—the independent—to take the heat. Finally, at one point, Aldrich agreed to a compromise: he would cut the offending seduction scene in exchange for an R rating. He was told, however, that the film would keep the X, no matter what he did. "The X was based on subject matter alone," Aldrich explained to Vito Russo, author of *The Celluloid Closet*, a study of homosexuality in film. "So there was a curtain in front of that picture. No matter how good it was, it was dirty because it was an X film. *The Pom Pom Girls* was an X, and *The Killing of Sister George* was an X. No difference."[19]

In May 1969 Aldrich's suits were dismissed. He had spent $75,000 of his own money in legal fees, the film kept the X rating, and because of (or despite) the controversy, *Sister George* never attracted the audience Aldrich had expected. "I thought the picture would really cross over that market, that it wouldn't just be a freak-sex picture, that people wouldn't have to be terribly liberated to understand and feel sorry for those people caught up in that thing [homosexuality]. And it just didn't work."[20]

After a decade and more of R- and X-rated films, the scene in *The Killing of Sister George* still retains an unmistakably erotic power. Filmed largely in one take, it has a different, cruder *look* than the rest of the film, almost as if it were an insert from another, cheaper, less "respectable" picture. It seems tacked on, not as essential to the film as Aldrich insisted.[21] Lukas Heller still considers it a "horrendous scene." But on a more subliminal level, its obvious difference—its "cheapness"—may be exactly the point. Certainly one of the attractions of a film on a "forbidden" subject is to see how far it will go, what degree of vicarious experience it will permit us. There is a certain dishonesty in films which treat such subjects with respect and delicacy and thus render them sterile. Aldrich does not cheat.

Aldrich insisted that he was not trying to make a "freak-sex picture." Although he never underestimated the importance of publicity or ducked controversy, neither did he indulge in rank sensationalism. Even with the Big Scene, *Sister George* remains a sympathetic study first of the human condition and then of homosexuality. Indeed, Aldrich's view of Sister George is ultimately more caring, more understanding, than that of Frank Marcus, the playwright. (According to Lukas Heller, Marcus told Aldrich after the premiere that the film was better than the play. "I think he revised his opinion later," Heller added.) Aldrich does not ignore George's offensiveness as a person, but as he explained to Vito Russo, "Sister George's loud behavior and individuality . . . are encompassed in her character, they're not a product of her lesbianism."[22] She is vulgar and abrasive, but she is also a woman whose life is falling apart. Aldrich, unlike Marcus, allows her a few quiet moments. When she is finally overwhelmed by the betrayals around her, she visits her friend Betty Thaxter (Patricia Medina), a prostitute into "Corrective Therapy," but a kind and considerate lady nonetheless. "I'm sorry," George says. "I don't want to. But I think I need somewhere to cry." As Russo has written, "Though generally maligned as an offensive and nasty character, Sister George is in fact the only multifaceted woman in the film. The honesty and openness of her character, when set beside the cartoon treachery of the sleek and sophisticated Mercy Croft or the loveless opportunism of Susannah York's Childie, make George the more complete human being."[23]

The Killing of Sister George will never be ranked among Aldrich's major films (although it remained one of Aldrich's favorites), but neither is it a work to be ashamed of. Certainly it deserves serious reconsideration. As the first film made at the Aldrich Studios, however, it proved a disturbing portent of what was to come in that venture's rough and rocky history.

Aunt Alice and The Greatest Mother (1969)

Following *Sister George*, Aldrich turned his attention to two new projects. First there was *Whatever Happened to Aunt Alice?*, a black comedy starring Geraldine Page, Ruth Gordon, Rosemary Forsyth, Mildred Dunnock, and Robert Fuller. Aldrich produced the film, which was directed by Lee H. Katzin, at the Aldrich Studios. It was the second of the films promised ABC-Palomar. Theodore Apstein wrote the screenplay; Aldrich regulars Joseph Biroc and William Glasgow also worked on it. The film was based on a novel, *The Forbidden Garden*, written by Ursula Curtiss. The title was changed to play off the success of *What Ever Happened to Baby Jane?* There were numerous similarities. Again, the lead roles were played by aging actresses who ran through a series of macabre and darkly comic situations. Mrs. Marrable (Geraldine Page), an alcoholic widow of pretensions, maintains her lifestyle by hiring and then killing off a number of housekeepers after she has convinced them to entrust their savings with her. Mrs. Dimmock (Ruth Gordon) comes in to solve the mystery, and what results is an intriguing battle of wills not unlike that between Jane and Blanche. The film was moderately successful and earned appreciative reviews, but it had nothing like the blockbuster popularity of *Baby Jane* or *Charlotte*, both of which it clearly emulated.

Aldrich's second project was more interesting. *The Greatest Mother of 'Em All* was an experiment in filmmaking and film selling which Aldrich's ownership of his own studio made possible. It was also an unmitigated disaster, one of several examples of bad luck and poor judgment on Aldrich's part that would lead to the eventual loss of the studio. The idea was to make a "mini-movie," a twenty-minute promotion for a full-length film which Aldrich would complete if he could find the financial backing for it. He could run the preview reel for potential investors; they could better see from this film just what Aldrich had in mind. The ploy was certainly more effective than handing them a script or telling them the story, but it was also much more expensive and risky. Nevertheless, Aldrich worked from July 28 to August 8, 1969, at his studio filming the preview, at a cost of $140,000.

The original script for the film had been written in 1965 by A.I. Bezzerides (who had written *Kiss Me Deadly* and *The Angry Hills*). Aldrich shot a revised version by Bezzerides and Leon Griffiths (who would script *The Grissom Gang*).[24] The story was similar to *The Legend of Lylah Clare* since it dealt with a washed-up director, again played by Peter Finch, who becomes obsessed with a young starlet. Greater emphasis, however, seems to have been intended for the character of the girl's mother, the "greatest mother" of the title in both senses of the term. Although Tricia Murdock (Alexandra Hay) is only fifteen, her mother, Dolly (Ann Southern), has her working as a stripper while she tries to promote her into the movie business. Tricia is spotted by a TV producer, Gene Frazer (Barry Russo), and is taken to bed by him and his wife. Later Tricia meets Sean Howard (Finch), who works for Frazer. Dolly pushes Tricia on Howard and later attempts to blackmail him because Tricia is underage. But Howard loves Tricia and even proposes marriage. When he dies of a heart attack, Dolly tries to sell her daughter's "diary" which supposedly details their affair. Tricia is finally driven to suicide.

Quite clearly, Aldrich intended the film as another attack on the Hollywood system, with the child Tricia as victim of her mother's ambition and the industry's callousness. The story of the wasted director and the underaged actress contained allusions to the Errol Flynn-Beverly Aadland scandal, and the finished film would probably have caused Aldrich even more censorship problems, dealing as it does with a *Lolita*-like obsession. But Aldrich was never able to raise enough interest in the project to acquire the necessary backing. He blamed this, in part, on the inadequacies of Alexandra Hay's performance as Tricia, although, as usual, he shouldered most of the responsibility himself: "If I had been bright enough, I would have known that the cycle had passed. Whereas a year before that picture would have sold like hotcakes. So . . . no more 'Hollywood' pictures for a while. I'm a sucker for them. I can't find any; and I'm trying not to look."[25]

Too Late the Hero (1970)

Thus, despite Aldrich's aspirations, his studio was in big trouble very shortly after it had opened for business. So far ABC-Palomar had not had a hit in their association with Aldrich, and they were becoming unhappy with his choice of projects. Aldrich later explained, "ABC wanted another *Dirty Dozen*. The only other 'Dirty Dozen' I had in the drawer was one I wrote in 1959 with Bob Sherman. So we pulled out *Too Late the Hero*, and they thought it was sensational."[26] By all rights, it should have been. It was precisely the kind of "patrol picture," the kind of action-packed, adventure-filled drama at which Aldrich had proved so adept in his other war films. Instead, it proved to be a disastrous effort critically and commercially, what Harry Ringel tagged "one of the hugest flops in ABC's history."[27] One problem was with the script, which Aldrich and Sherman had originally developed as a possible television series. Aldrich saw it as another study of the ambiguous nature of individual courage: "South

Pacific warfare was almost exclusively hand-to-hand with small forces engaged in a death struggle," he said. "The dramatic effect we're aiming for is more intense than if thousands were in personal battle."[28] But Lukas Heller, who rewrote the script, saw it from another viewpoint. "That film was an illustration of his enormous failings as a writer, and to some extent as a director. It was *terribly* elaborate. To get to the dramatic conflict that he wanted to establish, there had to be so many convolutions of plot, so many situations that had to be explained. It seemed to me a tremendously self-conscious examination of heroism."

There were other problems as well. ABC insisted that one of the leads be given to Cliff Robertson, who had been nominated for (and would win) an Academy Award for *Charly* (1968). Aldrich, on the other hand, wanted Robert Culp for the role and was openly dissatisfied with Robertson. Joseph Biroc remembered that "Cliff Robertson was not cooperative, and Aldrich kept giving the picture to Michael Caine, who was very cooperative and would do whatever you asked." Some on the set, however, felt that the fault was more Aldrich's than Robertson's. Although Aldrich was always professional in his dealings with the actor, his unhappiness at being forced to use Robertson ultimately hurt the film.

Finally, the film proved to be a difficult location shot. Much of the film was made at Subic Bay in the Philippines and in the nearby jungles. Joan Bennett, who was Aldrich's secretary, recalled the primitive conditions. "We all lived in a converted whorehouse. I don't know what they did with the former inhabitants. But when we got there, Mr. Aldrich gave everybody a radio and a bottle of booze. And there we were." Later, as she remembered, "we all took a vote to shoot seventeen days in a row so we could take four days off. It was like R&R."[29] In the years that followed, whenever Aldrich heard that a film was to be shot in the Philippines or under similar conditions, he would call the director and give suggestions as to how to avoid problems he had encountered while shooting *Too Late the Hero*.

Too Late the Hero is set in the Southwest Pacific during the Spring of 1942. An American officer, Lt. Sam Lawson (Cliff Robertson), finds the brief respite of his R&R abruptly interrupted when his commanding officer, Capt. John Nolan (Henry Fonda), orders him to report immediately to a British outpost located on an island still occupied by Japanese forces. Lawson is told that his knowledge of Japanese language and codes is exactly the expertise required for a secret Allied operation headed by the British Camp Commander, Lt. Col. Thompson (Harry Andrews). The plan calls for Lawson to accompany a team of British soldiers whose mission is to infiltrate the Japanese-held portion of the island, destroy the enemy's communication equipment, and broadcast—using their own portable radio transmitter and Lawson's special competencies—false information about the whereabouts of the soon-to-sail American fleet, thus guaranteeing its safety from Japanese naval forces in the area. The British patrol is commanded by Capt. Hornsby (Denholm Elliott), whom the troops neither respect nor trust. The group's medic is Pvt. Tosh Hearne (Michael Caine), self-appointed cynic-in-residence, who takes an instant dislike to Lawson and badgers him incessantly.

From the start, things go badly. The troops encounter an enemy patrol and take heavy casualties, largely because of Hornsby's errant judgment in positioning his men. Along the way, their *own* radio transmitter is smashed, prompting Hornsby to concoct a daring change in plans—an attempt to capture the Japanese transmitter intact and use it instead. But this effort to salvage the operation also goes awry: Hornsby is killed and the transmitter blown to bits. Their mission apparently aborted, the remnants of Hornsby's band retreat, but they have stumbled upon some vital and startling information—the presence of Japanese warplanes on the island, a piece of military intelligence heretofore unknown either to British or American authorities. If the American convoy sails, it will be struck a lethal blow by Japanese dive bombers.

The Japanese forces, commanded by Major Yamaguchi (Ken Takakura), know what Hearne, Lawson, and the others know—that without proper radio gear this information about enemy aircraft on the island can be communicated *only* if the survivors can return safely to camp. Yamaguchi, utilizing an intricate system of loudspeakers fastened to the tops of palm trees, offers the raiders a deal: if they will surrender and remain in captivity for three days (by which time the aerial bombardment of the fleet will have taken place), they will then be free to return to base. Three men accept Yamaguchi's terms, but Hearne and Lawson remain hidden in the bush, debating not whether they should surrender, but whether they have an obligation to save the lives of American sailors sure to be killed in the impending air raid. Hearne, unsympathetic to the Yank plight, opts to hide out until after the attack has occurred. Lawson, the patriot, decides otherwise. His pistol drawn, he orders Hearne at gunpoint to return with him to the British base. Hearne grudgingly consents but proposes, first, a diversionary tactic—that they kill the Japanese leader Yamaguchi to throw the enemy momentarily into confusion and thus enhance their chances of a safe return. Lawson agrees to the plan and shoots Yamaguchi, and the two begin their mad dash across the open ground between the jungle and the British compound. Only Hearne survives the withering fire, presumably to deliver the top-secret message that will save hundreds of American lives.

The final scene of *Too Late the Hero*—the suicide run of Hearne and Lawson across the no-man's land—is perhaps the film's most suspenseful, certainly its most visually powerful, moment. As the men begin their sprint, zig-zagging erratically to avoid the hail of Japanese bullets, Aldrich positions his camera at eye-level, revealing Hearne and Lawson in full and medium shots. We witness, close up, the agony and terror of their ordeal. But as the two approach the compound, the camera's rendering of the men's personal and immediate crisis gives way to a kind of impersonal detachment: extreme long shots and high camera angles obscure even the identities of the two runners, so that, when one falls mortally wounded, short of the camp perimeter, and the other reaches camp safely, warmly embraced by cheering soldiers, we don't know who is alive and who is dead. Ever so cautiously, the camera circles the converging throng and angles down to disclose that Hearne has survived and Lawson has perished. Hearne greets his astonished comrades with a parody of the hero's oration: "Out there," he raves, pointing to the crumpled body of Lawson, "is a hero . . . killed fifteen bloody Japs single-handed . . . thirty if you like." Delivered in a bitterly ironic and mocking tone, these exaggerations, this instant inflation of the body count, serve to undercut the traditional myth-making process by which the exploits of heroes are made known and made legendary.

Indeed, the ironies of character and situation are pervasive, and they call into question conventional notions of heroism. Lawson and Hearne become heroes in spite of themselves. In an early exchange with Hornsby, for example, Lawson, who never wanted to undertake the mission in the first place, gives "8 to 5 odds" *against* the prospects of his own heroism, rejecting Hornsby's characterization of him as a "real fire eater . . . one of the first over the top." And Lawson's blunt refusal to obey Hornsby's order to charge the Japanese radio shack contributes directly to Hornsby's death. In a chilling shot, Lawson's abject eyes make contact with the vacant eyes of the dead Hornsby, who has been killed in the attack; his stare foreshadows Hearne's similar gaze at Lawson's corpse at the film's end. Hearne is even more radically, more vehemently outspoken in his criticism of the hero's code, becoming, in effect, an advocate for the anti-heroic point of view. After the group's initial contact with the enemy, Hearne argues that the entire "bloody suicide mission" exists solely for the sake of the United States Navy and is, therefore, "pointless to us [British]." He proposes that the men turn back: ". . . in six months we and the Japs will still be in our parts of the jungle and none of this will have made any difference." Later, after Yamaguchi's ultimatum to surrender or die, Hearne suggests that he and Lawson hide out for a few days: "Getting ourselves killed doesn't mean anything except to us. . . . You're worried about letting Hornsby down—he's your problem and so are the Yank sailors." Even the Japanese commander himself—in some ways the most cultured and humane character of the bunch—speaks to the issue of heroically-ineffectual behavior. After giving water to two of the soldiers who have surrendered, rather than executing them as he had threatened, Major Yamaguchi lauds Hearne's and Lawson's stubborn refusal to yield as a "remarkable effort, but to very little purpose . . . medals given to dead heroes only add weight to their coffins." Yamaguchi may be right: the tragic irony of the final scene would appear to confirm his thesis. But Lawson, unlike Hearne, has expressed a belief in a "certain responsibility to those around you." By so doing, he acknowledges a moral imperative that transcends the obligation to preserve one's own personal existence at any cost; he acknowledges, that is, the larger obligation to preserve the lives of others, those comrades-in-arms to whom the individual soldier swears loyalty and allegiance. Lawson dies and his death would appear to be rendered meaningless by Hearne's sarcastic ravings. But many men will live because of Lawson's sacrifice and devotion to duty. Interestingly, Aldrich himself preferred the more positive and affirmative reading: "I would think that . . . the Cliff Robertson character in *Too Late the Hero*, had it been played as I wanted it, would have won, even though he is killed and Michael Caine lives."[30]

As Aldrich stressed elsewhere, one can still preserve his self-esteem, still retain his dignity and integrity, still "win" even in a losing cause. But except for Lawson's singular, if belated, heroics, much of the action of *Too Late the Hero* evokes a sense of unmitigated, irredeemable loss. To underscore this condition, Aldrich fills the screen with images of decadence, futility, and corruption—images which bespeak a cynicism about humanity surpassing even that of *The Dirty Dozen*. An early shot of cattle wandering aimlessly about an airport runway suggests the prospect of men being led to the slaughter. Sweating soldiers rolling enormous petrol drums through the British camp re-enact Sisyphean rather than Herculean labors. A cockroach race orchestrated by the impious

Hearne aptly foreshadows the desperate race for their lives that men must run to reach the refuge of the compound. If Hornsby's stupid misdeployment of his troops—which causes his men inadvertently to shoot one another—is a paradigm for the absurdity of war, Pvt. Campbell's (Ronald Fraser) scavenging of corpses for jewelry, his abominable strangulation of one of his own buddies, his grisly death by disembowelment at the hands of his Japanese captors are all compelling proof of the barbarous dehumanization of war. Sand crabs scuttling about the abandoned ruins of a Chinese railway station in the heart of the jungle delineate the stark landscape of the Wasteland and symbolize the inexorable disintegration of what once was an outpost of progress. In these and other ways, *Too Late the Hero* takes us into Aldrich's own "heart of darkness."

The failure of *Too Late the Hero* was yet another disappointment for Aldrich and his studio. As usual, Aldrich tried to understand what had gone wrong. The film, he later noted, "came out at exactly the wrong moment, after the student revolution had begun; the country was polarized, and Vietnam was the most unpopular war in history."[31] The ambiguous ending, indeed, the spirit of the entire film, gave the audience no one to identify with. The film was simply too bleak, or too unresolved, for the audience of the 1970s.

The Grissom Gang (1971)

Aldrich's next film, a venture into the gangster genre, has been called his "most authentically Aldrichian film since *Kiss Me Deadly*."[32] This arresting statement begs closer attention, for *The Grissom Gang* has been ranked more often among Aldrich's failures, both in artistic achievement and simple good taste. Upon its release, the film was savagely attacked for its violence, cruelty, and even sadism.[33] Vincent Canby, however, in a more thoughtful review, saw something else in the film. Although he ultimately found it a "very mixed-up movie," he nonetheless noted, "There is . . . lurking around the edges of the film, if not actually on the screen, the suspicion that Aldrich is such an uncompromising (maybe even revolutionary) moralist that he can only make his points in terms of action so grotesque that it challenges easy, safe compassion, sympathy and credibility."[34] Canby's review, hesitant though it is, indicates the complexities of this film. Like *Kiss Me Deadly*, it defies obvious judgment and classification. It is a work which must be taken on its own terms, and those terms can be very demanding indeed.

The Grissom Gang was based on James Hadley Chase's *No Orchids For Miss Blandish* (1939), a popular British gangster novel which, like Mickey Spillane's *Kiss Me, Deadly*, achieved much of its success from its willingness to test the limits of brutality in fiction. George Orwell made it the subject of an essay in which he compared it to E.W. Horung's *Raffles* books, more respectable works concerning a gentleman thief. Although he found *No Orchids For Miss Blandish* to be totally without moral value, Orwell confessed that it was a "brilliant'" piece of writing, however objectionable its subject and tone.[35] Aldrich was aware of the controversy surrounding the book when he decided to make the film. Indeed, he essentially agreed with Orwell's opinion of the work.[36] But as with *Kiss Me Deadly*, Aldrich was after something more than a simple translation from page to screen. He had transcended the trashiness of Mickey Spillane; he would do the same with James Hadley Chase. Although he hoped the film would benefit from the "nostalgia cycle" set off by *Bonnie and Clyde* (1967), Aldrich would, within the broad framework of the gangster genre, create a very bleak and black comedy of manners which commented on and attacked many of our more sacrosanct institutions and beliefs. All in all, it would represent the satirist Aldrich at his iconoclastic and moralistic best.

The Grissom Gang follows the plot of *No Orchids For Miss Blandish* rather closely. It is set in Kansas of the 1930s. Barbara Blandish (Kim Darby) is a spoiled, rich debutante. Three small-time crooks learn that she will be wearing a valuable necklace to a party at a local roadhouse. Although they realize that she is bigger game than they are accustomed to, they decide to waylay her and take the jewelry. The job is botched, however, when Barbara's drunken date fights back and one of the gang kills him. In a panic, the bumbling gangsters take Barbara with them to hide out until they can work out their next step. On the way, they run into several members of a rival faction known as the Grissom Gang, who quickly realize what has happened. The next day, this gang, led by Slim Grissom (Scott Wilson), appears at the hideout, kills the three crooks, and takes Barbara as its own captive.

The true head of the Grissom Gang is "Ma" Grissom (Irene Daily); the rest of the gang comprise a kind of family, made up of the "sons" Slim, Eddie Hagen (Tony Musante), Mace (Ralph Waite), and Woppy (Joey Faye), and her "man," Doc (Don Keefer). Barbara proves an intrusion into the family, and Ma plans to kill her after they collect a ransom of

$1 million from her father. Ma intends to take the money, clean it through middlemen, and then go into a "respectable" nightclub business. Complications arise, however, when Slim, her simple, murderous son, falls in love with Barbara and claims her as his own. Ma is faced with a real domestic dilemma: she cannot cross Slim and risk his deadly wrath, but neither can she tolerate the outsider Barbara as an actual member of the family. Her temporary solution is to force Barbara to submit to Slim's desires and hope that Slim will outgrow his infatuation with her.

When Barbara is not returned after the ransom payment, the police assume that she is dead, but her father (Wesley Addy) refuses to accept this possibility. He hires a down-and-out private detective, Dave Fenner (Robert Lansing), to continue the investigation. Fenner tracks Barbara through Anna Borg (Connie Stevens), a former girlfriend of one of the three crooks who first kidnap Barbara and the present mistress of Eddie Hagen. When Eddie realizes that Fenner—and the police—are closing in, he kills Anna, betrays the family, and steals Barbara from the club, hoping to make a deal with her father. Slim discovers them, however, as Eddie is about to rape Barbara, and he kills Eddie as Barbara watches. Returning to the club, he finds it under heavy attack by the police. He and Barbara are spotted and barely escape in a wild and often funny chase, the absurdity of which is underscored by the strains of "Pop Goes the Weasel." Slim and Barbara take final refuge in a barn, but they are again seen. The next day, realizing that the police have surrounded them and that Barbara could be killed in a shoot-out, Slim knowingly and calmly walks out to his death. John Blandish, outraged by Barbara's behavior as she mourns the dead Slim and infuriated by his imaginative reconstruction of the life she has led, turns coldly away from his distraught daughter and leaves her to Fenner as the reporters close in for the sensational details of her captivity.

This plot summary makes clear the more lurid aspects of the story. If Aldrich wanted simply to make a trendy, exploitative picture, he certainly had the material here to do it. Yet, despite the fact that he stayed fairly close to the novel in terms of plot, Aldrich made some very distinct changes in his manner of telling the story. Whereas *Miss Blandish*, with its constant amorality, allowed its readers the freedom to remain detached from all its despicable characters, *The Grissom Gang* humanizes its two protagonists, Slim Grissom and Barbara Blandish, causing us to become uncomfortably close to them, even to sympathize with them. This sympathy forces us, eventually, to make difficult moral choices, decisions which the book neatly excuses. Aldrich, however, does not go so far as to romanticize his characters as does Arthur Penn in *Bonnie and Clyde*: they merit no mythology, no gauzy views. Aldrich will not make it easy for us on either count. "I thought it would make that rare connection that you make, say with a James Cagney picture," Aldrich later commented. "In that kind of picture you like the bad guy for all the wrong reasons, but you like and understand him. You sympathize if not identify with him."[37]

Moreover, Aldrich keeps us emotionally off guard with the tone of the film. Although the movie is filled with violence, the style he employs is basically comic, bordering on the burlesque or slapstick in the action scenes. There is also a strong element of satire running throughout the film which gives it significance and strength. Most of the humor—and spleen—is aimed at the stereotype of the typical American family. As noted earlier, the Grissom Gang does make up a family, and Ma treats her boys, especially Slim, as children. Although a grown man and experienced killer, Slim depends on Ma for guidance and protection, as well as for cookies and pies, which she bakes every week. Ma has raised her boys with certain middle-class values. When they first arrive at Johnny's hideout to take Barbara from her original captors, Slim is shocked by their denials of Barbara's being in the house. "Why you want to lie like that?" Slim asks. "Didn't your folks teach you no better?" Slim's reproach is a prelude to their deaths.

A clearer picture of the Grissom's home life is shown when they take Barbara as hostage back to Ma, who tells Slim to put her in the "guest room." Later, when Barbara calls Slim "a dirty, half-wit cretin," he runs in tears to his mother for comfort. "Ma, Ma," he cries. "She's calling me names, Ma. You told me you'd make her my friend. You promised. And now all she's doing is saying bad things. . . . What are you going to do?" Ma sets things right by first drying Slim's tears and then beating Barbara into playing with Slim. Later Ma counsels Slim to forget Barbara: "We've kept ourselves out of trouble for a long time because everybody figured Ma knows best," she says in a nice satiric shot at one of America's more stereotyped family television shows. "Do you think I'd let a boy of mine lose his head over a fool girl?" Ma, for all her viciousness, is loyal to the family, but she clearly prefers to keep Slim a child in their relationship, yet another restating of one of Aldrich's most common themes. When Slim hears of his mother's death in the shootout, he cries pathetically, "They killed Ma. . . . That's real sad. I love my Ma."

The central comic irony of the film is that Ma and Slim—murderers and thieves though they be—are more capable of love than the more respectable, wealthier, powerful Blandish family. It is through her capture and captivity that Barbara comes to an understanding of love for the first time. Aldrich uses the song "I Can't Give You Anything But Love, Baby" to begin and end the film. Not only does it set the historical period, it also alerts us to the thematic center, for this is ultimately a film about the importance of love. When we first meet Slim, he is presented to us as a creature of great cruelty, one who takes perverse delight in violence. Killing with a knife is a rather obvious substitute for sex, which both bewilders and frightens him. His emotional attachments have been centered on his mother. But when he first sees Barbara at Johnny's hideout, he is dumbstruck at her beauty, and as Slim begins to mature in his feelings toward Barbara, Aldrich manipulates our sympathies toward him. Although he is still capable of violence, from this point on he kills only in her defense.

Slim has a cheaply sentimental view of romantic love, but he is sincere in his efforts to fulfill what he assumes are Barbara's expectations of any suitor, for he is acutely aware of the social barriers and distinctions which separate them. As a part of his romantic barrage, he tries to develop a new image. Thus he begins to bathe, buys new clothes, attempts to sharpen his wit, brings all manner of presents, and personally helps decorate the new apartment in which he will keep her. "Yes, sir," he tells her proudly, "it's really elegant. All this furniture is imported from out of state." Our emotional responses are soon divided: we know that Slim is a moronic murderer, but there is something touching in his single-minded devotion to Barbara. It is, of course, the King Kong syndrome, the tale of Beauty and the Beast. Beauty's disgust, and her haughtiness, however appropriate, still tend to align us with the creature. "I'm not going to let these others do anything to you," Slim tells her. "Not seeing as how I love you."

Barbara quite naturally despises Slim, whom she sees as a "creepy, crawly slug." She is repulsed by his touch and sickened by his desire. But she soon realizes that his love for her gives her control over him, a method of manipulation which she then uses with a perverse satisfaction. Slim's discovery of love leads to an unexpected maturation on his part: he wants to be "worthy" of Barbara. But finding herself in an untenable situation, Barbara undergoes a slow degeneration, turning into a drunken, shrewish woman. Her change is much like that of Temple Drake in William Faulkner's *Sanctuary* (1931), a book to which *No Orchids For Miss Blandish* owes considerable debt. As a result of her captivity and humiliation, she discovers heretofore unsuspected depths of cruelty and hatred within herself. The captive becomes in a sense the captor, and we are back, for a time, within the world of *Baby Jane*.

What Barbara cannot comprehend is the utter simplicity of Slim's love, for she comes from a world in which nothing is freely given. And yet it is only through this realization that her redemption can take place. Aldrich uses two key scenes to illustrate this growing awareness. Early in her captivity, Barbara appeals to Eddie to rescue her from Slim, but when Eddie does take her away, she discovers how dangerous a "grown-up" man can be. When Slim finds Eddie attacking Barbara, he and Eddie fight, and in the struggle Eddie falls to the floor with Slim atop him, knife in hand, in a perversely sexual embrace. With each thrust of Slim's knife into Eddie's prone body, Barbara convulses in orgasm. In the novel, it is Eddie who climaxes as the knife enters. The switch to Barbara in the film is significant, since for her the act represents a kind of liberation. (Barbara's orgasm is not clearly indicated in Leon Griffiths' screenplay, which has her profoundly horrified by the murder.) From this point on, she sees Slim as something other than the "slug" she had earlier called him. He has risked his life for her, reasserted his claim to her, and once again become her rescuer and savior. But more importantly she has for the first time responded to him in a sexual sense, with Eddie as surrogate and with sex and death impossibly mixed. She faces her own capacity for evil, for violence, and, indeed, recognizes the basic kinship she shares with these people she has so hated.

The second scene takes place in the hayloft where Slim and Barbara have taken refuge from the police. Their dialogue illustrates the extent of Slim's development and Barbara's self-awareness. Slim tells her that he is not afraid to die, but now Barbara insists that she is "not worth dying for. Nobody's worth that." Slim answers, "If I ain't got you, I don't care what happens. . . . Haven't you ever loved nobody?" And Barbara must admit, "Not like that. Nobody's ever loved me like that either." After he tells her to "get some sleep. Don't you worry about me," she initiates the act of lovemaking, reaching out for him. Aldrich commented that at this point Barbara bestows the "supreme gift" on Slim, the final proof of his manhood,[38] although the discrete fadeout leaves much of this to our imagination. But certainly in his own mind Slim has been transformed, both physically and emotionally. He is now a man. The next morning he quietly walks out of the barn to his death without firing a shot.

There is little reason to argue whether or not Barbara comes to "love" Slim at the end. Given the bizarre situation in which she finds herself,

Wesley Addy, Kim Darby, and Scott Wilson after the shoot-out in *The Grissom Gang*. Used by permission of the Museum of Modern Art/Film Stills Archive, courtesy of Aldrich studios.

such a question may be beside the point. But she has come to have sympathy for him and to appreciate his devotion for her. At the same time, she has confronted her own unworthiness, and this is an important insight for her. When the game has been played out, Slim really can't give her anything but love, but that is exactly what she has never had. When Slim is shot down and Barbara holds his bloody hand in mourning, Aldrich places the camera below Slim's body, below ground level, so that it looks up past Slim to the kneeling Barbara. Aldrich reserved this particular *mise en scene*, with its Pieta-like effect, for moments of greatest emotional intensity in his films, and such is the case here. Barbara's father approaches his daughter and the dead Slim. "Get away from him," he hisses, but when Barbara drops Slim's hand and reaches for her father's own, he refuses to touch her. "He wouldn't let me go," she cries to Blandish. "He loved me. Don't you understand?" But Blandish cannot understand. He is incapable of appreciating—or expressing—the love shown by Slim. His rejection is the cruelest action in the film.

Aldrich discussed the deliberation surrounding the ending of the film. Originally, he said, they shot "a much sexier scene in the barn" between Slim and Barbara, but "we elected to go with the more gentle, tender one. I think it was right . . . it seemed to be much more effective."[39] The "sexier" scene would have been more in keeping with the novel, in which Slim savagely rapes Barbara in the barn and then runs hysterically at the police, firing his gun, cursing and screaming. Indeed the screenplay has Slim die in much the same manner. But Aldrich gives us a different Slim and a different Barbara. He has let them both develop and grow. The courage and dignity of Slim's death—his suicide—is befitting his new character. Barbara's case is more complicated. In the book, realizing the extent of her degradation and her growing taste for it, Barbara throws herself from a window rather than face her father. Aldrich considered such an ending and even shot a scene in which Barbara drowns herself in a river, with Fenner's complicity. But the ending Aldrich finally chose is even more devastating: a freeze-frame of Barbara looking helplessly over her shoulder as Fenner spirits her away from the clamoring reporters. Again the musical theme of "I Can't Give You Anything But Love, Baby" swells, but this time in full symphonic orchestration, slow, emphatic, funereal. She has been freed, released into the real world, and, without the love offered by Slim, she finds it empty. It is the final irony of a tough, penetrating film.

But, once again, it was a film which failed to work at the box office, and ABC-Palomar pulled out of its association with the Aldrich Studios, an act which effectively spelled its doom. Their relationship was, in Aldrich's words, "terminated after four pictures, with much mutual acrimony."[40] Aldrich admitted defeat and sold the studios to Video Cassette Industries at a considerable loss. "Everybody has a dream," Aldrich said. "It was a sensational operation. We only needed around sixty-five production days a year to break even. Then I followed that classy act by making four dogs in a row. Nobody is going to finance you after four dogs. It makes no difference that you can prove that in your own studio you can make a picture literally two-thirds cheaper. So the sheriff came and took the studio. But it was an experience I would go through again. I enjoyed every minute of it."[41] He concluded, "Well, we built a better mousetrap, but the mice went out of business."[42]

William Aldrich felt that another reason for the Studio's failure was his father's loyalty to the people under him. "One of the reasons the Studio went broke was because he carried and carried and carried these people forever when there was nothing to do. And I was saying to him, as studio manager, 'You can't do this. You've got to cut them off. It's not being cruel to them to do that. *We're* not working; what are we paying *them* for?' But he felt an obligation to these fellows. It was a family kind of thing. It was an extended family of people who liked to make movies."

6. At the Table

Ulzana's Raid (1972)

Following the loss of his studio, Aldrich was pragmatic as usual about his situation. "You jump on a bottle of whiskey for about six months, and then you've got to go back to work. How? You cut your price, and you take pictures you wouldn't have taken before."[1] Aldrich maintained his office at the Aldrich Studios (which were not sold until 1973), but no films were made there after *The Grissom Gang*. His next project was *Ulzana's Raid*, a freelance job for Universal Studios. *Ulzana's Raid* clearly indicated Aldrich's loss of power and prestige. During his successful days, he had been one of the highest paid directors in Hollywood, making as much as $750,000 per picture. He agreed to do *Ulzana's Raid* for $150,000. As William Aldrich said, "He *had* to go back to work. When he didn't work, he was hard to live with. He just came down on everybody." Still, Aldrich refused to become simply a hired man. William Aldrich recalled:

> When this picture came along, it was a script he liked, and Universal thought that he could attract Burt Lancaster to the picture, which was true. It had to be made at a certain budget, to which he agreed, and he said, "We have a deal." During the closing-up points of the deal, they came back and said, "Look, you're only going to Tucson; we're not paying you your usual contractual living allowance," which was about $1,500 a week for the six weeks they would be on location. He said, "I'm not doing the movie." I said, "Ah, come on, Dad. Your *living allowance* is a deal breaker? You just dropped $600,000 off the salary of the last picture, and you're saying no deal?" They were offering $1,000 a week—$500 less than usual—so that for $500 a week, $3,000 all together, he wouldn't do the picture. It was the principle of the thing. Until they came up with the extra $500 a week, he wouldn't do it.

Once agreements were made, Aldrich went to work. He was able to get Burt Lancaster into the film, and others of his people as well. Richard Jaeckel, for example, told the director, "Aldrich, anything you want, anytime, whatever, just let me know"; Jaeckel took a substantial pay cut to work on the film. Westerns were not particularly successful with the viewing public in the early 1970s, but in this case Aldrich had a first-rate script by a fine writer, Alan Sharp, who, in Lancaster's words, "had done an enormous amount of research on the subject." Moreover, this was a film which could both entertain and challenge the audience, a combination Aldrich appreciated. Despite the circumstances in which it was made, *Ulzana's Raid* showed Aldrich working at his best, at the very top of his form.

As the film begins, a small band of Apaches led by the warrior Ulzana escapes the San Carlos Indian Reservation and begins a series of outrages in the surrounding countryside. A detachment of cavalry at nearby Fort Lowell is assigned the task of tracking them down. The command is given to Lt. Garnett DeBuin (Bruce Davison), a young officer only six months out of the military academy, when Captain Gates (Lloyd Bochner), frightened of Ulzana, begs off. "I thought, Sir," he tells the major (Douglass Watts), "that this detail might be an excellent opportunity to initiate young DeBuin." Because Gates has influence in Washington (his uncle is an undersecretary, perhaps an in-house reference to Aldrich's own relatives), he is relieved of the duty. The chief scout to accompany DeBuin is McIntosh (Burt Lancaster), a quiet, sardonic man who serves in a purely advisory capacity to the lieutenant. Assisting McIntosh is a young Apache, Ke-ni-tay (Jorge Luke), who, because he has "signed the army's papers," accepts this assignment although Ulzana is his brother-in-law. Rounding out the main characters is the sergeant (Richard Jaeckel), a seasoned veteran who harbors no illusions concerning his duty, his enemy, or his chances.

The plot of the film is a simple and direct one, structured on the concept of the chase, with each side endeavoring to outwit the other, with each achieving momentary advantages soon erased in the continuation of the over-riding pursuit. "Remember the rules, Lieutenant," McIntosh says. "The first one to make a mistake gets to burying some people." This, of course, is familiar ground for any filmgoer. We soon feel that we know these characters; that we can anticipate their actions, reactions, and development; that indeed we can foresee the inevitable confrontations and conclusions. But Aldrich confounds our expectations early in one expert and horrifying scene.

A soldier has been dispatched to warn the settlers of Ulzana's escape. The first group he meets heeds his advice, but the next, an immigrant family named Rukeyser, is unwilling to leave its farm. Finally the mother and young son accompany the soldier while the father remains behind to defend their home. As the three ride toward the safety of the fort—the soldier on horseback, the mother and son in a wagon—they are surprised by Ulzana and his men. The soldier takes one look at the Indians, establishes the odds, and rides furiously away, abandoning the defenseless pair in the wagon. "Don't leave us here!" the woman screams. The soldier reins his horse, hesitates. Making up his mind, he draws his pistol, rides back into the attack, takes careful aim, and kills not an Indian but the woman herself with a shocking blast between the eyes. Reaching the wagon, he grabs the stunned child, wheels the horse, and again attempts escape. But now the Indians are too close, the boy is an extra burden, and the horse is easily shot down. Both riders are thrown sprawling on the ground. The soldier, shaking off the fall, searches frantically for his pistol, which has been flung several feet away. As the Indians run toward him, he rolls to it, inserts the barrel into his mouth, and blows out his brains. The boy is left surrounded by death as the Indians approach. This is a shocking scene, not only because of its explicit violence, but because it so suddenly defies—even mocks—our smug preconceptions. We simply do not expect this to happen, and when it does, we realize that *anything* can follow. We can no longer rely on the comfortable formulas which dictate how such films should develop; our sense of security is shattered.

Although the desire to avoid the unexpected is typical of Aldrich's best work, in *Ulzana's Raid* the resulting sense of uncertainty helps establish the basic mood of the film. In an article on the picture, Alan Sharp wrote that, to him, the American Southwest from 1860 to 1886 represented one of the most terrifying periods in all of recorded history. He specifically used this period and setting because the film was "an attempt to express allegorically the malevolence of the world and the terror mortals feel in the face of it."[2] How do men act in a situation without order or reason, in which the worst can and surely will occur? It is a question which runs throughout Aldrich's work, but rarely does he confront it as starkly and uncompromisingly as he does here. "I just don't like to think of people unprotected," DeBuin says at the beginning of their search. "Yes," McIntosh answers. "Well, it's best not to." What McIntosh knows is that most of us are "unprotected" in this world.

Thus, *Ulzana's Raid* is perhaps best seen as an initiation story (as Captain Gates suggests), albeit a bleak and severe one, with Garnett DeBuin as the idealistic, naive initiate. At the beginning of the film, he is introduced umpiring a baseball game at the fort, and his calls of balls and strikes are questioned by the players, anticipating DeBuin's later judgment on more important matters. Despite his military training, DeBuin tends to defer to the philosophy of his father, a Philadelphia preacher, when discussing the situation he faces. His father believes that the

Indians' greatest fault is a "lack of Christian love," and he has impressed upon his son that "it is possible to be both a Christian and a soldier." "You may have an opportunity to test some of your father's theories out there," the skeptical major responds, but "out there" will obviously be a testing ground for more than theories and conventional beliefs.

DeBuin's attempts to comprehend the situation, rooted as they are in his father's Christian teaching, are quickly shown to be inadequate in this land. These convictions, based on a sense of cultural superiority, assume that there are universal standards of right and wrong, the acceptable and the unacceptable. But DeBuin is forced to see that such is not the case. In several scenes, the film specifically debunks this self-satisfied reliance on a Christian God. Ulzana escapes from the reservation on a Sunday, a mock resurrection. When DeBuin, on that same Sunday, describes his father's beliefs about the Indian, the major replies, "I doubt that the Apache Indian would consider Jesus Christ an inspiring leader." Later, when the immigrant Rukeyser is beseiged by the Indians, he takes refuge in his cabin and bravely fights until suddenly the attackers disperse. In the distance he hears the approaching call of a bugle, which he takes as a sign of his salvation, but which is, in fact, an Apache trick. He looks up through the hole that has been burned in his roof, at the sunlight pouring in as if a benediction. "God, You take all the praise and all the glory," he shouts joyously over and over as he puts down his pistol and leaves his cabin, walking unknowingly to his torture and death. When DeBuin sees the remains of Rukeyser's body, he is horrified. "Why do they do these terrible things?" he asks the more experienced sergeant. "After all, they are men, made in God's image, like ourselves." The sergeant explains that the teachings of Christ do not hold in this land. "Christ never fetched no infant child out of a cactus tree and then waited around for two hours until it died so he could bury it, did he, Sir," the sergeant says. "Ain't nobody going to tell me to turn the other cheek to an Apache, Sir." At the end of the film, when McIntosh wants to be left alone to die in the desert, DeBuin protests, "It's not Christian!" McIntosh slowly answers, "You're right, Lieutenant, it's not." DeBuin's philosophical and religious teachings simply do not apply in Ulzana's world.

But it is to DeBuin's credit that he wants to understand the Apache, and much of the film is devoted to his groping toward that understanding. What most horrifies DeBuin about the Indians is the butchery and torture they inflict on their victims. Rukeyser is killed very slowly by his captors, mouth stuffed with the tail of his dog, arms tied to a post, chest mutilated, legs spread, feet and genitals burned by smoldering coals. The body of

the young soldier who kills himself is ripped open and his heart toss-
ed from Indian to Indian in a grotesque parody of the earlier baseball game.
When DeBuin questions Ke-ni-tay about these actions, the Indian first
gives a simple non-answer: "It's how they are. They always be like that."
When DeBuin demands more, Ke-ni-tay tries to explain: "Each man that
die, the man that kill him take his power. Man give up power when he
die. . . . Here in this land, man must have power." Because Ulzana has
been kept on the reservation, with the "old smell" of white civilization
in his nostrils, he too has become "old." He needs the smell of death,
of bullets, of courage; he will have to kill many men to regain his power.
And they must die slowly: the fire that burns the longest gives off the
greatest heat. But Ke-ni-tay finally concludes, "You not know about
power. . . . You no understand."

Indeed, one of the main points of the film is that no white man can
understand the Apache's mind; the cultural gap is simply too great, and
the resulting confusion serves only to reinforce the tragedy. As Aldrich
explained it, "Through ignorance of other peoples' cultures, behaviours,
deities, customs, you do more damage to them than by intention."[3] De-
Buin's ignorance leads him to a temporary unreasoning hatred of the
Apache. When this hatred affects his ability to command, McIntosh tells
him, "You'd be advised to stop hating and start thinking, Lieutenant.
Because you ain't been doing too well up until now." Certainly the
greatest difference between DeBuin and McIntosh is that McIntosh accepts the fact that he cannot comprehend the Apache. He knows that
the escaped Indians intend to "burn, maim, torture, rape, and murder"
until they are caught or killed. But he doesn't hate the Indian. As he explains, "It's like hating the desert because there ain't no water on it. I
can get by just by being plenty scared of them."

What McIntosh represents is a kind of balance in this film. Captain
Gates calls him "a willful, opinionated man with a contempt for all
discipline, either moral or military," but such is not the case. He has
long known that no race has a monopoly on good, and that all men too
often share a real propensity for evil. Yet, he does not view the Indians'
actions in terms of right and wrong. A key explication of this idea is found
in a scene near the middle of the film. Ulzana and most of his warriors
have abandoned their horses and doubled back behind the soldiers. When
McIntosh realizes the plan, he tracks the two Apaches who have the
horses, killing one and wounding the other, leaving Ulzana on foot. When
the soldiers arrive, they take their revenge by hacking the dead body (actually that of Ulzana's son) with knives, an action parallel to that of the

Burt Lancaster, Bruce Davison, and Jorge Luke in *Ulzana's Raid*. Used by permission of the Museum of Modern Art/Film Stills Archive, courtesy of Universal.

Indians in the earlier scene. When DeBuin discovers them and orders them to stop, he is both baffled and outraged. The soldiers try to explain: "The Apaches don't like it when you do this to their dead. It spooks them." This reasoning is perhaps as valid as that offered by Ke-ni-tay, but DeBuin cannot condone either one. It is McIntosh who puts it all in perspective, for DeBuin and for us. "What bothers you, Lieutenant, is that you don't like to think of white men behaving like Indians. Kind of confuses the issue, don't it?"

It is indeed a confusing issue that the film presents, and one of the many strengths of *Ulzana's Raid* is its refusal to resort to easy resolutions. McIntosh insists on a rather bleak view of man, but, again, it is not a totally negative view, for it encompasses the need for acceptance as well as the need for action. In describing McIntosh's character, Alan Sharp compared him to Ethan Edwards, the hero of John Ford's classic western *The Searchers*. (Sharp intended *Ulzana's Raid* to be "my sincere homage to Ford.") Of the two men, Sharp thought McIntosh "a more stoical, more pessimistic, yet more humane figure, whose rage against the gods has cooled into a weary antagonism. He has seen the worst and expects to see more and yet he will not judge, not presume to be right. Yet he is still a man who can act, can make choices. His is the spirit of the liberal but not yet reduced to impotence by introspection. In many ways, McIntosh is my ideal historical hero."[4]

McIntosh, seen in this way, is certainly the man of balance, of thought and action, and it is therefore appropriate that he becomes DeBuin's adviser and teacher, that he replaces DeBuin's real father as authority figure. The significance of the child-father relationship in Aldrich's films is nowhere more important than in *Ulzana's Raid*, and there are numerous father-son configurations to deal with. At first DeBuin follows the Christian teachings of his minister father, but from McIntosh he learns to temper his basic sympathies with the realization that hard choices must often be made. When the inexperienced DeBuin sends two soldiers after the Indian that McIntosh has wounded, his concerns are largely humanitarian: the Indian should not be left to die in misery. The larger, more practical concerns which DeBuin overlooks are underscored when one of the soldiers is killed by the Indian, a needless loss. Later, when the soldiers find more victims of Ulzana's attacks—a man tortured to death, his wife raped but alive—DeBuin's initial impulse is to spare the woman any further horrors. "If they come back, promise me you won't let them take me," she begs, and DeBuin so promises. But when McIntosh explains that Ulzana left the woman alive knowing that DeBuin would split his forces to see her safely to the fort, DeBuin, hardened by experience, agrees to use the woman as bait in an attempt to trick Ulzana at his own game.

DeBuin is now determined to kill Ulzana—it is "no more than justice," he says—and he is willing to take whatever risk is necessary, even if the innocent must suffer. "Don't be confused, Lieutenant," McIntosh replies. "We're not in the Justice business." McIntosh knows that Ulzana must kill the soldiers to get their horses. The plan is to allow Ulzana to attack the small force led by McIntosh and then, when Ke-ni-tay gives the signal by flashing sunlight off his binoculars, to counterattack with De-Buin and his men. The sergeant discusses the plan with McIntosh: "Lieutenant DeBuin is *supposed* to ride up and save us when we're down to our last bullet, ain't that right?" And, of course, the plan does not work. DeBuin mistakes an accidental flash from the binoculars of a hostile Indian for Ke-ni-tay's signal and rides off, bugle blaring, toward the canyon' where McIntosh and his men have been ambushed. The bugle warns Ulzana of their approach and gives him time to escape. When DeBuin arrives, he finds all the men dead and McIntosh critically wounded. As he lies dying, McIntosh directs his last words to DeBuin. "Don't start 'if'-ing, man. You made your pick—live with it. Hell, man, there ain't none of us right." DeBuin has earned McIntosh's respect despite his error. "You'll learn," McIntosh says.

Parallel to the McIntosh-DeBuin relationship is that between McIntosh and Ke-ni-tay. Ke-ni-tay is more knowledgable than DeBuin and has already learned what DeBuin has yet to face, but he also treats McIntosh as a figure of authority. Anticipating DeBuin, Ke-ni-tay has already shifted his loyalties to McIntosh from another "father," Ulzana himself, who is a relative by marriage and, more importantly, represents a way of life Ke-ni-tay has left behind. It is symbolically appropriate that McIntosh kills Ulzana's real son, leaving him without a child to continue the family and, by implication, the conflict. But it is also right that it is Ke-ni-tay who finally kills Ulzana, tracking him into the hills after his escape. He first shows Ulzana the bugle which his son had worn, to indicate his death. Ulzana now knows that with this death, the revolt is finished. Thus Ulzana himself chooses to die in a ritualistic fashion, kneeling, chanting, passively accepting his fate. There is no hope for Ulzana, for his time has passed. But both DeBuin and Ke-ni-tay have moved from their cultural fathers to McIntosh, and thus, although the film does not end in actual resolution, it does at least suggest its possibility.[5]

Despite the richness and suggestiveness of this three-way relationship in the script, Aldrich was finally displeased with the way it was transferred to the screen. "Your problem there is a marvellous story plotted around a big major star. The focus of that picture should have been between the Indian scout [Ke-ni-tay] . . . and the young lieutenant. . . . Then you would have a very clear picture . . . that should have been the principal conflict. Now, you couldn't do that because (a) you couldn't get the picture financed, and (b) you couldn't get the picture made without a Burt Lancaster."[6] In a later interview Aldrich elaborated on this problem: "In *Ulzana*, I hoped that by having Lancaster speak for the Indians you got an educated and experienced point of view on their culture and what they meant. It worked, but not for the audience. They sat there and knew what he was saying but didn't emotionally relate to it. They don't know whether he's the good guy or the bad guy. They're sorry to see him die but they don't really understand whether he represents good or evil."[7]

Although in retrospect Aldrich's criticism seems overstated, the apparent ambiguity may have been one reason for the film's failure. Some critics accused the film of pretentiousness; others were appalled by the violence and charged it with exploitation and insensitivity. On this last point, however, it should be noted that the film actually becomes *less* graphically violent as the story continues. The more brutal scenes occur at the beginning, for the reasons already discussed. Thereafter, what we usually see is the *aftermath* of violence. The shootout which ends the film is not explicit; Ulzana is killed offscreen; and McIntosh "dies" after the film is ended, frozen in a still frame as the credits roll.

Other critics recognized the film's considerable merits. Martin Levine, in *Newsday*, found it "probably the year's best western—but only if you're willing to talk and think about it afterward and work out its implications."[8] Andrew Sarris saw it as an allegory of the Vietnam War, an idea Aldrich fully intended.[9] And Vincent Canby, who continued to struggle with the paradox he found in Aldrich, wrote: "In almost every Aldrich film there are more people who behave badly than well, but not, I think, because he has an especially bleak view of mankind. Rather it's his way of entertaining us while shaking a warning finger."[10]

At one point in the film, McIntosh observes, "Apache war parties come in all sizes. There's the kind with a hundred braves. And there's the kind with one." In *Apache*, Aldrich had shown the revolt of one brave, the warrior Massai (also played by Burt Lancaster), and he made it clear that *Ulzana's Raid* represented a reworking of that material. McIntosh, he said, was "an 1870 guy who had seen *Apache*. This was his frame of reference: he respected the Indians, because he knew more about them than the soldiers did."[11] Later he said, *"Ulzana's Raid* is a remake of *Apache,* told from the scout's point of view. It's terribly un-dramatic, un-flamboyant. . . . The story had to do with the Indians growing out of time."[12] Burt Lancaster also thought of it as a "remake of *Apache."*

Numerous echoes exist between the two films. *Apache* begins with Massai's capture and subsequent escape; *Ulzana's Raid* opens with the escape from the reservation. Massai, like Ulzana, is unable and unwilling to exist in the white man's civilization, as shown by his bewildering experiences in St. Louis after his escape. When Massai shoots the corrupt Indian agent Weddle, the bullet passes through his body and smashes a peace pipe hanging on the wall; when McIntosh shoots Ulzana's son, the bullet first punctures the bugle (the symbol of false hope throughout the film) hanging around his neck. Massai's revolt is ended when he hears the first cries of "Little Massai," his newly-born son, a symbol of a new way of life. McIntosh, however, kills Ulzana's real son and "adopts" Ke-ni-tay, indicating that the Apache's way of life is at an end. In more general terms, *Ulzana's Raid* is less sentimental about the Indians' plight but ultimately much more effective. Ulzana is not romanticized as was Massai, but he is allowed the death Massai is denied, and the dignity that goes with that death. Ulzana demands our respect along with our fear, for he is true to his beliefs. He is in every way a most worthy adversary.

Today, *Ulzana's Raid* has become one of Aldrich's films most respected by his serious critics. It is a tight, focused, philosophical work, reminiscent of his early films. The acting is uniformly good, but Burt Lancaster's understated performance is especially impressive in its strength and assuredness, virtues which extend to Aldrich's direction as well. All in all, it is hard to refute Tom Milne's assertion that *Ulzana's Raid* is Aldrich's masterpiece.[13]

Emperor of the North (1973)

Aldrich's second film after the loss of the studios was *Emperor of the North,* which he had actually begun work on before the studios were sold. The film was made for 20th Century-Fox. Originally called *The Emperor of the North Pole* (which star Lee Marvin preferred, "because if you're *Emperor of the North Pole,* that means you're an 'emperor' of nothing, and *Emperor of the North* doesn't say that to me"), the title was changed shortly after its release in May 1973 because of audience confusion over what the title meant. Although the second title was not much clearer, the decision to change indicated that Aldrich was trying for a more commercially viable work than his films since *The Dirty Dozen* had proved to be. In an attempt to regain his audience and his bargaining power, Aldrich turned to a subject and actors who should have guaranteed success. Based on an original script by Christopher Knopf, *Emperor of the North* was another all-male, action-oriented adventure film but one closer in tone and style to *The Dirty Dozen* than to *Too Late the Hero* or *The Flight of the Phoenix*. Indeed its two leading actors—Lee Marvin and Ernest Borgnine—had worked with Aldrich on several occasions, most notably in *The Dirty Dozen*. They were actors he felt comfortable with and knew he could trust. To this experienced pair he added Keith Carradine, a talented young actor who had gained critical recognition as part of Robert Altman's stock company. Carradine had caught Aldrich's eye when he read for the part of Lt. DeBuin in *Ulzana's Raid*, and, though he was not quite right for that role, he had made a favorable impression on Aldrich: "So when I came to do *Emperor*, I called him and he did a *sensational* test. And those . . . who sit in judgment about who should be in those pictures wanted a much less tough-minded kid. They wanted someone more routinely handsome—pretty is being unfair—they wanted a less unique individual guy, and there was a lot of bloodshed. But he did a superb job."[14]

The film centers on a prolonged duel between two larger-than-life combatants: A No. 1 (Marvin), the supreme hobo, and Shack (Borgnine), the deadliest railroad man on the line, whose train A No. 1 has boasted he will ride. The setting is the Depression years of the 1930s, the same period as in *The Grissom Gang*. After the stark realism of *Ulzana's Raid*, Aldrich was moving in the direction of the tall tale, and the film is imbued with a sense of the past, a nostalgia which contains overtones of the legendary. Both Shack and A No. 1 are clearly folk "types"—Shack is equated with the Devil, and A No. 1, as one hobo puts it, with the "road" itself—and each is apparently quite antithetical to the other. But into this clear-cut confrontation intrudes a third character, a young, inexperienced vagrant named Cigaret (Keith Carradine), who tries to share in the making of legend through mere proximity and pretense. His unworthiness is made clear by Shack when they first collide. "You ain't no 'bo," Shack snarls. "You're a tenderfoot. . . . There's only one 'bo that's got the stuff to try me. You ain't even on the list." A No. 1 also quickly recognizes Cigaret as a "punk" and a "deadbeat" rather than a "good bum."

Thus what we have expected (and what the film has encouraged us to expect) as a two-man conflict loses its simple symmetry but in doing so becomes much more typical of the mature Aldrich in its complexity. Indeed *Emperor of the North* soon reflects the same situation found in *Ulzana's Raid*, with the young initiate being introduced to the realities—and the responsibilities—of the world by the older, more experienced father/teacher. For despite A No. 1's early proclamation that he "don't give lessons" and "don't take partners," this is exactly what he does with Cigaret. "You can be a meateater, kid. I mean people, not their garbage. I want to see you rough as a jungle cat," A No. 1 tells him. "You tighten your belt, turn up your collar, do everything you're told, you can be Emperor of the North Pole. You don't, you're out—o u t."

Ulzana's Raid and *Emperor of the North* mark a change in Aldrich's philosophy toward the child-parent relationship. In past films, whenever he dealt with this situation, it was usually shown in destructive terms. Both *The Flight of the Phoenix* and *The Dirty Dozen*, however, show that some form of authority can be acceptable and even necessary. And now in *Ulzana's Raid* and *Emperor of the North*, Aldrich shows how valuable the knowledge and wisdom held by the experienced can be for the young. McIntosh, as "father" to DeBuin and Ke-ni-tay, leads them both to a greater understanding of themselves and the world around them. A No. 1 offers the same opportunity to Cigaret, although it is refused. He does not accept the lessons offered: he never matures, never recognizes the responsibilities that go even with being a hobo. He remains a "kid" throughout, never a "meateater." When he attempts a boast, it has a hollow ring. "I can fight like a house afire. I'm ready," he tells A No. 1, but has to add, "Hey, I'm talking straight. You better listen." He carries no sense of authority, as do both A No.1 and Shack.

That Aldrich thought of these characters not so much as individuals but as symbols is made clear from his discussion of the film. "It never occurred to me that the audience would miss the relationship—that Borgnine was the Establishment, that Marvin was the anti-Establishment individualistic character, and that Keith Carradine was the opportunistic youth who would sell out for whatever was most convenient." Aldrich went so far as to label the Carradine character as representative of the "post-Vietnam era, when everyone went back to sleep and said, 'I don't care. It's over. I'm gonna play melody.' "[15]

On this highly schematic level, the film simply does not work; the allegory does not hold, nor does it seem very relevant. The characters do not represent what Aldrich and screenwriter Knopf intended. Because both A No. 1 and Shack are cast in the tall tale mold, they are imbued with that boisterous comic essence, that outrageous vitality which we find in all heroes and villains of legend and myth. And there is also a kind of insane self-destructiveness in their nature which we again find in these same types of characters. To attempt to categorize either of these two men as "Establishment" or "Individualist" seems beside the point. Although he works for the railroad, Shack stands apart from the other railroad men, who fear him as much as do the hobos. In fact, Shack is another instance of the good/bad man found so often in Aldrich's films, an ambiguity Aldrich himself noted: "There's an ambivalence about the train conductor that Borgnine plays. The railroad guys hate him too, because he's too cruel for them, too single-minded, too dedicated. So that, you can't say, oh well all the railroad guys are against all the hobos. It's not that clear. The fact that a hobo might beat him, ride on his train for free, delights some of the railroad men. It would be much easier movie-making if all the good guys are over here and all the bad guys are over there."[16] Shack's is a purely personal ideal—to run *his* train on time and without freeloading vagrants. In his own way, he is as much of an individual as A No. 1. And A No. 1, as personification of the "road," must be as single-minded as Shack in order to prove the validity, not of *tramp-dom* in general, but of his own personal honor as the best 'bo.

"This ain't no game," A No. 1 tells Cigaret at one point. "The hell it ain't," Cigaret answers, and for once he may be correct. The train ride, the challenge, is a game of the highest sort, both deadly and highly invigorating, both serious and supremely comic. In such a situation, Cigaret proves both intrusive and, finally, reductive. He is not the stuff of myth. Thus, although we have been primed to pull for A No. 1 and against Shack, we find ourselves reserving our hatred and our contempt for Cigaret. It is impossible to condemn Shack without doing the same to A No. 1, for they are in one sense cut from the same cloth. As Aldrich has expressed it, Shack has "total integrity towards his corruption. Therefore, the Marvin character has extraordinary respect for him—in that arena."[17] And Shack feels the same respect for A No. 1, as indicated in his earlier remark to Cigaret. Thus, when they meet in combat, they each play by an unspoken understanding, rules which they would follow in no other situation. Even after A No. 1 has defeated Shack, Shack's yell of undiminished defiance can be heard as the train continues on its way: "You ain't seen the last of me," he shouts, and it is surely no idle threat.

As befits their stature as titans of the railway, the clash between A No. 1 and Shack is one of epic proportions. They meet as gladiators in

the arena. To heighten verisimilitude, both Marvin and Borgnine agreed
to shoot the scene without stunt men or doubles: a strenuous, dangerous
bit of acting. It was, as well, a complicated, difficult bit of directing, calling
upon all of Aldrich's technical skill and expertise. Marvin vividly recalled
the scene:

> We shot that flat car scene for a total of 13 days, not all consecutively because
> we couldn't do it. I mean, it was just physically impossible. But whenever
> we got stuck in another sequence, we could always go back to the end of an
> airfield where Aldrich had the railroad cars on trucks in an Indian circle. And
> they would go one way and the camera cars would go the other, so, in other
> words, you'd have a traveling train shot with a changing background. And
> on this flat car, he had marked out 8 positions, and so you had 8 camera mount-
> ing areas. And we shot it from every plausible angle—the whole thing—for
> 13 days to get that fight sequence. It shows you how well prepared Aldrich
> was: he had his angles figured out and he knew what he was doing. He was
> a very heavily-homeworked man. He was really prepared *all* the time.

The painstaking preparation and the Marvin-Borgnine chemistry paid
off: their fight sequence is one of the most exciting, gripping scenes
Aldrich has done.

Cigaret has remained uninvolved during the fight, but now he tries
to share A No. 1's victory. "Yes, sir, me and you, if we ain't the team,"
he says, to which A No. 1 answers, "Kid, you got no class," and throws
him off the train into a river. The film ends with A No. 1's disembodied
voice calling back to Cigaret as he struggles in the water: "You could
have been a meateater, kid. But you didn't listen. . . . You'll never be
Emperor of the North Pole. You had the juice, kid, but not the heart,
and they both go together. You're all gab and no feel and no one can teach
you that—not even A No. 1. So stay off the track."

There is a definite ambiguity to this ending. Although the temporary
victory belongs to A No. 1, both sides will surely lick their wounds and
prepare to fight again. And it is equally likely that Cigaret will be on
the trains again as well, lying and assuming his way. Still, there is a
satisfaction in the meeting out of justice here. In describing an earlier
ending to the film, Aldrich emphasized the rightness of the revised conclusion:

> The story used to end with Borgnine getting killed in the fall from the train
> and Marvin falling off the train with him. So the boy was left on the train.
> Being the King of the Mountain and the only one left, he prevailed. I felt that

if you let the kid win, you would rob the audience of any—an old-fashioned word, but—any rooting interest. You would be saying the guy who waited and didn't fight himself and took the free ride would be the survivor and the other people wouldn't. I didn't think that worked. . . . What really happens is the audience wants to see [Shack] fail but since he lived within the framework of his own integrity, as corrupt as that may be . . . they don't take any particular enjoyment out of it. So they hold back their release of satisfaction until Marvin throws off the young hobo.[18]

Thus Cigaret, the kid who is unwilling or unable to learn or mature, is the film's ultimate goat. Although thematically this idea is in keeping with Aldrich's usual way of seeing things, it may have been a reason for the film's lack of success. By casting Cigaret in such a harsh light, the film apparently alienated a large part of the youth audience, a group to which a picture of this sort would normally appeal. In Cigaret, however, Aldrich was, in part, expressing his disappointment with this generation, as he indicated in his comment on the "post-Vietnam" era. Today's youth, Aldrich said, is "too smart . . . and they're opportunistic. And their ideals? They left them in the closet."[19] There is no Lieutenant De-Buin in this picture, no young man of good intentions and a need to understand, however awkwardly or unsatisfactorily he goes about it. There is finally only the Emperor himself, who struggles to maintain his self-esteem. In the end, as Aldrich has noted, "perhaps [A No. 1] hasn't really prevailed over anything," but "it's the costs that make it into a gallant struggle."[20] And that, ultimately, is what the picture is about: a moral tall tale told big and spoken loud.

Aldrich was baffled by the failure of Emperor, which met not with the antagonism he might have expected but rather with mass indifference. "We misjudged the audience, or misjudged the application of those stories," he said, referring to the films immediately prior to and including Emperor. "We misjudged something."[21] Marvin speculated that the film's failure might be related to its setting in the Great Depression: "Don't forget: you're going into the Depression and situations people would prefer not to remember. Maybe it stirred too many memories of hard times in the audience."

By now Aldrich had "stayed at the table" through six years of financial and critical setbacks. Although he had reached a new level of artistic maturity and had made two of his finest films during this period, he desperately needed an unqualified hit, not only to regain his bargaining leverage, but, one suspects, to restore a certain degree of self-confidence. His next film, although artistically inferior and less demanding than either *The Grissom Gang* or *Ulzana's Raid*, would give him that boost he sought.

The Longest Yard (1974)

The New York premiere of *Emperor of the North* was discouraging, drawing a less than enthusiastic response from critics and crowds alike. Because Aldrich had learned from experience to trust in his axiom that "you're only as good as your last picture," he could hardly have been surprised at what happened next. Having already been announced by Warner Brothers as the director of *The Yakuza*, a film about the secret Japanese underworld organization, Aldrich—because of the poor showing of *Emperor*—found himself suddenly on very shaky ground: the film's star, Robert Mitchum, with whom Aldrich had worked fifteen years earlier on *The Angry Hills*, rejected the studio's choice of Aldrich as director.[22] But fortune was to smile on Aldrich in other ways. *The Yakuza* went on to become an unremarkable film directed by Sydney Pollack, and Aldrich himself was assigned to direct *The Longest Yard*, his biggest commercial success since *The Dirty Dozen*. This change in luck came about partly because Aldrich was a self-proclaimed sports fanatic—his first feature film, *The Big Leaguer*, was a baseball movie—and partly because Al Ruddy, who originated the idea for *The Longest Yard*, with its emphasis on football, was currently a hot Hollywood prospect (Ruddy had recently produced *The Godfather*).

Originally, Aldrich had intended to shoot the film at Oklahoma State Penitentiary—which already had a semi-pro football team and a stadium—but before filming began, the inmates rioted and burned the prison down, forcing Aldrich to change his plans. With the help of then-Governor Jimmy Carter, Aldrich arranged to do the film at the maximum security prison in Reidsville, Georgia. Prison officials cooperated fully, giving Aldrich more freedom than perhaps he had bargained for: "I didn't realize until after we'd completed the film that we had had no real protection from any prisoners who might have acted against us. By giving us total flexibility of movement the authorities also gave us total vulnerability. Had I known that, I might have approached the problem differently."[23] Script supervisor Alvin Greenman, working on his first Aldrich film, echoed those thoughts: "Every day we were locked into that prison, escorted in and out of the cell blocks. Some members of the crew left because they could not stand the claustrophobia of that situation."[24] But Aldrich was determined to maintain good relationships with the prisoners—his personal secretary Joan Bennett said he was "adamant" about it—and, as it happened, the inmates behaved as graciously as the prison authorities. In fact, Aldrich used several prisoners to help with set construction and to play minor parts—Greenman recalled, for example, the contingent of gay prisoners who were cast as cheerleaders in the game sequence—and when filming was over, he left behind the completed stadium for the prisoners' recreational use.

Aldrich did *The Longest Yard* with a script by Tracy Keenan Wynn, with Burt Reynolds, ex-Florida State halfback, in the hero's role, Eddie Albert as the villain, and several professional football players in minor parts. The film opened to largely rave reviews. *Variety* called it "an outstanding action drama, combining the brutish excitement of football competition with the brutalities of contemporary prison life."[25] Charles Champlin, who found all the acting performances strong, hailed *The Longest Yard* as "popular entertainment at its rousing best, with Aldrich at the top of his showmanly, audience-grabbing form."[26] Still, despite such accolades, the film got off to a sluggish start, what Aldrich termed a "very nervous first few weeks."[27] Aldrich attributed the initial poor showing at the box office to a preposterous advertising campaign created by studio executives: "The studio's ad on *The Longest Yard* was unbelievable. It was Burt Reynolds in a helmet with bars in front and a lock on it. Nobody understood what it meant, but we were assured by Paramount that the public would understand what it meant. Well, the picture opened in New York with that ad, and nobody went to see it. The picture opened in the rest of the country without the ad and everybody went to see it."[28]

What everybody went to see (the new ad for *The Longest Yard* featured Burt Reynolds posed to reveal what Pauline Kael insisted was a padded crotch, and padded or not, everybody knew what *that* meant)[29] was a tragi-comedy about sports and prison life. Paul "Wrecking" Crewe (Reynolds) is a former professional football player whose point-shaving escapade in a title game has gotten him drummed out of the sports business and into the gigolo business, a super-star turned super-stud who, in a fit of pique, borrows a client's Maserati, ditches it in the water, punches out some cops, and is sentenced to eighteen months hard labor at Citrus State Penitentiary—all before the opening credits are complete. The man in charge at Citrus State is Warden Hazen (Eddie Albert), a megalomaniac who has pulled strings to get Crewe assigned to his prison. Hazen, general manager of the prison guards' semi-pro football team, hopes that the addition of the former NFL MVP to his coaching staff will bring him, at long last, a national title. Anticipating Hazen's move, player-coach Captain Knauer (Ed Lauter) has assaulted and battered Crewe into submission, warning him that he—Knauer—runs the football team and foresees no immediate need for Crewe's services. Crewe is thus forced to refuse the warden's offer of easy time and begins to serve out his term, doing what prison officials euphemistically refer to as "swamp reclamation."

Unable to endure Knauer's continued savage harassment of him in the swamp, Crewe slugs the captain with a nightstick. Knauer retaliates by stuffing Crewe in the prison's "hot box" for twenty-four hours of solitary confinement. Crewe is rescued by Warden Hazen, who proposes a deal: in exchange for a reduction in sentence (Crewe could do two to five years for striking Knauer) and an early parole, Crewe will put together a team of inmates to give the guards a pre-season tune-up game; the game will be played before a public audience in order to showcase the warden's team and to advertise his "progressive rehabilitation program." Crewe accepts the offer and begins the arduous task of assembling a team and recruiting players. One by one, they join up: Nate Scarboro (Michael Conrad), Samson (Richard Kiel), Schokner (Robert Tessier), Granville (Harry Caesar), and the others, all united in their contempt for the warden, the guards, and the system. The team quartermaster is Caretaker (James Hampton), who secures such essential supplies as game films, the guards' medical files, pain-killing drugs, and new equipment. Meanwhile, Unger (Charles Tyner), the warden's snitch and resident pyromaniac, applies for the position of assistant coach, the better to spy on the opposition. When Crewe rejects him, Unger plots revenge by rigging an incendiary device in Crewe's cell, but Caretaker is killed instead when he walks into the trap set for Crewe.

Inspired by Caretaker's death and his legacy—brand new "Mean Machine" uniforms and helmets—Crewe's team plays tough, holding the guards to a 15-13 halftime lead. Hazen is furious—the game is not the complete rout he had counted on. To prevent further embarrassment for his team and damage to his personal reputation, Hazen confronts Crewe at halftime in the locker room; he orders Crewe to lose the game by a 21-point margin or face life imprisonment as an accessory to Caretaker's murder (Unger has threatened to testify to that effect). Crewe submits to the blackmail on the condition that the guards ease up on the inmates after achieving their 21-point lead. Hazen gives his word to Crewe, but then turns around and orders the guards to inflict as much physical damage as possible on the inmates after the point spread is assured. Unaware of Hazen's intended treachery, Crewe fulfills *his* part of the bargain and throws the game in the second half, once again (as he did in the pro's) selling out his teammates. With the score 35–13 in favor of the guards, Crewe sees his team suddenly brutalized and realizes that he has been deceived. Angered and determined to get even, Crewe decides to play, rallies his squad around him, and leads "The Mean Machine" to a dramatic, come-from-behind victory in the game's closing seconds.

Even with its twists and turns, its reversals and *Dirty Dozen* gimmickery, the plot of *The Longest Yard* moves swiftly along, the suspense effectively sustained until the narrative arrives at its rowdy resolution. One finds here a vitality and spontaneity, an energy and exhilaration, which give every indication that Aldrich did indeed have a "marvelous" time making the film. His daughter, Adell Aldrich, confirmed that impression: "He was 'coach'! He loved that picture and the guys loved him." As a former athlete and a football fan (he once flew from London to Los Angeles to watch the Rams play the 49ers), Aldrich had obviously taken full advantage of this opportunity to convey, in carefully choreographed slow-motion and split-screen images, in soundtracks filled with every conceivable crunch and groan and obscenity, the sheer spectacle and gut-wrenching thrill of a sporting event. The game sequence indeed is quintessestial Aldrich direction.

But *The Longest Yard* expresses more than a sports enthusiast's self-indulgent reverence for the genre. It is also a showcase for some of Aldrich's favorite themes. As a professional player, Crewe shaves points, for example, for his father's sake. Crewe sees his scam as a one-time opportunity to make a big killing and then to get out and take care of his father—who is blind, who cannot see him play—for the rest of his life. But before either man can profit from it, the plan backfires: his father dies and Crewe gets caught. The son fails to win the father's approval. There are other major themes as well. In his determination to win despite the costs, in his readiness finally to incur Hazen's authoritarian wrath, Paul Crewe manages to salvage his pride and earns the respect not only of his teammates but also of the guards themselves. He tells Hazen: "I'm just trying to give you a football team, Warden. And, along the way, maybe give the men some pride and some dignity—of course, only for a little while." Ultimately, of course, he gives *himself* dignity. When, in the film's final scene, Crewe walks off the field to retrieve the game ball, Hazen hysterically commands Knauer to shoot him down. But Knauer hesitates, as much out of growing disgust for Hazen as grudg-

Burt Reynolds and Eddie Albert after the big game in *The Longest Yard*. Used by permission of the Museum of Modern Art/Film Stills Archive, courtesy of Paramount.

ing admiration for Crewe (one guard has remarked to the cons, "You know, you guys ain't half bad!"). Crewe delivers the ball to the stunned warden and invites him to "stick this in your trophy case," and we recognize in this gesture, in this courageous risk-taking, a moment of personal triumph. The "trophy" belongs to the cons, to Crewe. The film ends with a freeze frame of Crewe and "Pop" (John Steadman)—another con with integrity, doing thirty years for punching the warden in the mouth—on their way to the locker room, walking side by side down a darkened, deserted corridor. They face an uncertain future, a vaguely ominous fate. But it is the victory itself, no matter how fleeting or ephemeral, that ultimately counts.

Aldrich admitted to lifting this ending from *Body and Soul*: "There the Garfield character had thrown everything away and had to redeem his self-esteem more than anything else. Without the switch, without the main character having to regain his self-esteem after having sold everybody out, there's no pull, you don't care. So I just stole from Polonsky, stuck it on, wrote in the story of Jimmy's [Caretaker's] burning to death, and the funeral. None of that was in the script. And that kind of movie lent itself better to audience identification than *Body and Soul*. . . ."[30] In an even more explicit analysis of the film's theme, Aldrich told Stuart Byron that *The Longest Yard* embodied his most cherished convictions about the possibilities for individual human redemption:

> I like to believe that my indelible trademark is my affection for the struggle to regain self-esteem. Now, the likelihood of doing that is remote. Still, it's the costs that make it into a gallant struggle. In *The Longest Yard*, perhaps Burt Reynolds is not going to have a happy prison life; perhaps he's not going to go on living at all. And in *Emperor*, perhaps Lee Marvin hasn't really prevailed over anything. But in each case a man has fallen from grace, done something he's ashamed of, and then struggled to recapture his opinion of himself. Now, I think the odds against succeeding in doing that are overwhelming. It's not in the cards that that's probably going to happen. But I think you admire the people beside you who say, "The hell with it. I'm not going to quit. I don't give a shit what other people think about me. I'm going to try and hold myself in esteem." That's what all these pictures are really about.[31]

For Aldrich, the football game in *The Longest Yard*—like the baseball game in *The Big Leaguer*, the war games in *The Dirty Dozen*, and the survival games in *The Flight of the Phoenix*—functions both as a social ritual by which men test and define themselves and also as a metaphor for teamwork and camaraderie: the working together to achieve a common goal, a common purpose. In *The Longest Yard*, Crewe and his cohorts cooperate in a collective attempt to strike back at the "Establishment" which oppresses them and whose figurehead and proprietor is Warden Hazen. In Hazen—their nemesis—the power structure has reposited its absolute authority, and "The Mean Machine" means to challenge and disrupt that authority. Hazen's platitudes about the value of "achievement and teamwork" and his pretense that "the game embodies what has made our country great" mask a more sinister theory of power, what Nate Scarboro describes as the warden's "fear and violence philosophy." Eddie Albert plays Hazen precisely in that fashion: "A man who believes he's doing right is a far more dramatic villain than a cardboard villain. That's what the warden in *The Longest Yard* was all about. He was going to show these prisoners what discipline was—he was doing it for their own good." In fact, when Hazen orders Knauer's men to brutalize the inmates, it is a bullying show of force—power politics pure and simple: "I want everybody in this institution," intones Hazen, "to know about power and who controls it." And the inmates' satisfaction at having successfully resisted Hazen's power, at having effectively opposed his will, is apparent after the game when a "Mean Machine" player taunts the warden: "Where's your damn power theory now?" Interestingly, Aldrich had intended the film to be a contemporary allegory about power and corruption, but few people caught what he regarded as obvious and timely parallels to the current political scene: "Eddie Albert is Nixon! When I put him in those clothes, and put the flag in there, and had the football talk, and the guy turning on and off the tape recorder—on the set, everybody said, 'You can't do that, Bob; you're going too far.' I must say I thought I did go too far but obviously I didn't go half far enough, because nobody, nobody understood. Jesus, except for having a wife named Pat, we had everything in the picture. But nobody picked up on it."[32] Albert and Aldrich had discussed the advantages of playing the warden as Nixon, and Albert agreed to do so, though he tried to make Hazen more strong, "less whining and whimpering" than his San Clemente counterpart. And he came away from that performance with a renewed respect for Aldrich's skill in developing a character in film.

Like most of his other action-adventure films, *The Longest Yard* featured virtually an all-male cast. Only two women appear, both in minor parts: Anitra Ford as the wealthy socialite whom Crewe slaps around in the opening scene, and Bernadette Peters in the comic role of the warden's secretary. (In a scene set in the warden's office, Peters does a wonderful parody of the "Rosemary Woods stretch," made famous by the Watergate hearings—Aldrich did indeed put "everything" Nixonian in the film.) Most of the attention, however, focused on Burt Reynolds, whose career was rapidly on the rise after his breakthrough role in *Deliverance* (1972). Reynolds reflected on his part in the film:

> *The Longest Yard* had an atmosphere of fun. Also, Bob kept the game very competitive. The members of the two teams didn't socialize during filming, just as they wouldn't have socialized in the fictional setting. We would run plays the defense knew. Then I would call plays that they didn't know about and those takes were generally what ended up in the movie because they looked so much more real. Bob was not unlike Woody Hayes. We discussed my character a lot, and, fortunately, completely agreed. He was [to be] a combination of Joe Namath and Bobby Lane. Bob wanted me to have fun with the role and to feel free to improvise—an actor's dream. Bob and I both felt that this All-Pro, All-American had learned nothing in his life, but a rag-tag band of convicts finally taught him a lesson about humanity.[33]

Aldrich thought that Reynolds had done fine work in his film, and he was surprised by the undeserved attacks on the actor by such critics as Pauline Kael and Vincent Canby.[34] Indeed Aldrich and Reynolds had enjoyed working together, and they planned a second collaboration, a detective film more serious than *The Longest Yard* and, though less successful commercially, one that ranks among Aldrich's best.

Hustle (1975)

Aldrich's and Reynold's second project together originated when Reynolds received a script from writer Steve Shagan, author of the 1972 film *Save the Tiger* (for which Jack Lemmon had won an Academy Award as Best Actor). The story (which went through title changes of *Home Free* and *City of the Angels* before its final designation, *Hustle*) concerned a Los Angeles police detective who is appalled by the sordidness of his personal and professional life and yearns for romantic escape. Aldrich and Reynolds formed a co-production company, RoBurt, to make the film. What attracted Aldrich to the script was not so much the police angle (which he called "second-rate Kojak") as the unusual love interest, for the policeman lives with a highly-paid professional prostitute who works out of their shared apartment. Aldrich agreed to do the film with Reynolds on one condition: that the role of the call girl be played not by an American, as indicated in the script, but by Catherine Deneuve (or "Miss Chanel," as Aldrich called her, in reference to her Chanel No. 5 perfume commercials then popular on television). Aldrich felt, and Reynolds agreed, that an American audience would be more willing to accept the relationship if the woman were foreign, an off-handed concession to the vestigial Puritanism with which Aldrich had often butted heads. Aldrich and Reynolds jointly bought the property, each putting up $12,500 for the rights against a total payment of $150,000. Then together they went to Paris to convince Deneuve to do the film.[35] Shooting began on November 20, 1974 and ended on February 11, 1975.

Its tight script and excellent performances would seem to indicate that the *Hustle* set was a relatively tranquil one, but Aldrich apparently had trouble both with Shagan and Deneuve. Script supervisor Alvin Greenman recalled that Shagan and Aldrich did not get along. According to Greenman, their disagreements arose from Shagan's insistence that his screenplay be filmed exactly as written, a stipulation Aldrich found both unrealistic and impractical. "Bob's contention," Greenman explained, "was this: 'Look, you've made a lot of money on this property. Now it's my turn. I can't promise you that every word is going to be the way it is in the script. Words are changed for a hundred reasons. It happens all the time.' " Greenman also observed Aldrich's growing displeasure with Deneuve's performance and with her behavior on the set, an opinion shared by cinematographer Joseph Biroc. "She was constantly complaining about how she looked in the daily rushes," said Biroc. "But Aldrich told me: 'The hell with her. You do what I want.' "

As Aldrich noted, the script of *Hustle* was composed of two story lines. The detective story concerns the apparent murder of a young girl, Gloria Hollinger, whose body is found washed up on the beach by a group of school children. The coroner's verdict is death as a result of drug overdose, but he also notes that the girl was sexually misused shortly before dying. Because she is linked with the sex and pornography trade, the police are inclined to pass her death off as accidental and unimportant. However, the girl's father, Marty Hollinger (Ben Johnson), an unstable Korean war veteran, insists that his daughter has been murdered and is determined to find and punish those responsible if the police refuse. Because of the father's obsession, Phil Gaines (Burt Reynolds), the detective in charge of the case, finds himself drawn deeper into an affair he would rather have avoided.

The second—and, in some ways, parallel—story line deals with Gaines' private life. Having divorced his wife after finding her with another man, Gaines now has a "relationship" with the prostitute Nicole Britton (Catherine Deneuve), one which allows them to live together without stated commitments. Although Gaines is disturbed that Nicole sleeps with other men, he tries to accept it as part of the "deal" they have made. Nicole points out the hypocrisy of his attitude: "I'm a whore, so it's all right. But it's not all right for your wife." She has, moreover, made it clear that she would give up her work if Gaines would admit his love for her and "take care of her," but he is emotionally unable to do so. Gaines is a self-described "student of the 30's," one who dotes on old movies, old music, old heroes. He has set up the city of Rome (which he once visited while on a narcotics investigation) as representative of his ideal world, a place of love. Thus Gaines uses a fantasy life to shield himself from the tawdriness of his real world.

Hustle views this world as shot through with corruption and callousness. Near the beginning of the film, as Gaines and Nicole prepare to attend a Rams-Vikings football game, Phil rather bitterly reflects that Nicole, for all her beauty and sophisticated charm, can be bought and sold. "She's for sale," he says. "So is everybody else in the stadium," Nicole answers. To Nicole, everyone is a whore, everyone has a hustle, but some are simply more honest about it than others. When Gaines is called in on the Hollinger case, he is literally knocked into this awareness when Marty Hollinger, horrified at the sight of his naked daughter lying uncovered in the morgue, slugs him. "You bastards could have covered her up," he shouts. "You're right," Gaines answers, nursing his jaw. "We should have covered her up." Later he tries to explain, "Sometimes we don't have time to care," but he fails to convince either Hollinger or himself of the validity of his statement. Hollinger knows how the system really works. "The only thing that's on [the death certificate] is what *they* want to put on there," Hollinger says. "And everybody knows that it's just a damn pack of lies . . . . If I had turned up with a high-priced lawyer, things would be different." Hollinger sees a society that protects the powerful and ignores the "nobodies," which encourages evasion, distortion, and cruelty. And Hollinger's view reflects Aldrich's own that "we're living in a two-tier system of justice and a two-tier system of influence. It's more than the have and have-nots, it's a whole combination of inequality, and inequality has nothing to do with black anymore or brown or yellow. It has to do with who gets favored treatment and who doesn't."[36]

As a part of this system, Phil Gaines is a divided character, one torn between what he knows to be the truth and what he would like for the

Burt Reynolds and Catherine Deneuve in *Hustle*. Used by permission of the Museum of Modern Art/Film Stills Archive, courtesy of Paramount.

truth to be. He lives a life of compromise, deluding himself into thinking that by going along with the small corruptions, he can still maintain his overall integrity. Thus, his initial reaction in the Hollinger case is to avoid complications. "A wasted little girl on the beach. . . . Is that the way you want it, Lieutenant?" Marty Hollinger asks. "Yes, that's the way I want it," Gaines answers. But Paula Hollinger (Eileen Brennan) tells Gaines, "You live in a right-wrong world," and Nicole says that he "is always concerned with being right." Both comments suggest a simplicity and order in Gaines' life which do not exist. The Hollinger case, with all of its ramifications, soon becomes a mirror in which Gaines is forced to see the all-too-accurate reflection of his own confused situation.

In order to emphasize the connections between the two story lines in this film, Aldrich employs a suggestive doubling motif. For example, our first view of Gloria Hollinger's dead body on the beach comes in a crane shot from above. It is immediately followed by a similar shot which descends through the air to Nicole Britton, standing on the balcony of the apartment she shares with Gaines. These shots link the two women in our minds, especially when we learn more about them. Both are whores, but one is more highly paid, runs in fancier social circles than the other. Where do we draw the moral line between party girl and courtesan? The lawyer Leo Sellers (Eddie Albert) is the embodiment of corruption rather than justice: his very name underlines the fact that money brings power in this society. Sellers is connected, ironically, to Gaines' superior officer in the police department, Santoro (Ernest Borgnine). Both men drink carrot juice and both ask Gaines the same question about Hollinger: "That kid's father, was he anybody?" Sellers and Santoro use the law for personal and political reasons, hide behind it for their own gain.

The most complete pattern of doubling, however, is indicated between Phil Gaines and Marty Hollinger. Each has been twisted emotionally by the sexual infidelity of his wife. Both are infuriated by the callousness of the system, yet each feels impotent before it. More specifically, both men have been manipulated and abused by Leo Sellers. The last sex party that Gloria Hollinger attended before her death was at Sellers' home, and his picture is found among her belongings, making him a suspect even though his influence reaches into the police department itself. But Sellers is also one of Nicole's clients. He even uses her as an alibi during Gaines' investigation. Sellers—and the society he represents—has, in a sense, cuckolded them both. Thus, although Gaines' search for a possible killer logically takes him to Sellers, his motives are complicated by his emotional involvement with Nicole. Both Hollinger and Gaines make Sellers the focus of their general outrage.

Marty Hollinger is a man obviously out of control, but the film suggests that Gaines is potentially as dangerous. Both men take the law into their own hands, and their actions are presented in morally ambiguous terms. Gaines' explosive moment of violence comes when he confronts the psychopath Jerry Bellamy (David Speilberg). Bellamy has murdered two women and is holding a third hostage, threatening her death unless Gaines shows up. Since Gaines originally sent him to prison, from which he has now been released, Bellamy clearly wants revenge. Ranting hysterically, he forces Gaines to kneel before him and prepares to kill him, but Gaines is able to shoot Bellamy when his partner Louis Belgrave (Paul Winfield) jumps through a skylight, diverting Bellamy's attention.

Gaines, however, must shoot *through* the hostage, must wound her in order to hit Bellamy. When he finds that the madman is apparently still alive, Gaines completes the execution by emptying his gun into the prone body. He tells Belgrave that he is only finishing a job which Justice has botched, but he is also venting his anger and despair. Marty Hollinger's parallel moment of violence comes when he finally tracks down Leo Sellers and confronts him as the murderer of his daughter. Sellers tries to talk him out of the act by claiming a kind of innocence: "Your daughter was involved with a lot of people. Why single me out?" "Because I can't kill everyone," Hollinger simply replies. Then he shoots him. There is some irony in that, although Sellers is a murderer (he has arranged for the bombing death of a union leader earlier in the film), he *is* apparently innocent of Gloria's death (which is, as suspected, a suicide) except in a most general way. Thus, while both Jerry Bellamy and Leo Sellers deserve their fates, they also serve as targets for Gaines' and Hollinger's greater, deeper-seated frustrations.

"Every man is in search of a whale," Gaines tells Belgrave in one of his frequent philosophical moments, "and when he finds it, it kills him." When Gaines discovers what Hollinger has done, he decides that "there comes a time when you've got to try to turn the whale around." He once again twists the system by cleaning up for Hollinger. He makes the murder appear self-defense by wounding Hollinger, just as he had wounded the innocent hostage. By covering up for Hollinger, Gaines is, as he sees it, doing "all the wrong things for the right reasons" in order to "put mercy in the system," but he is also justifying his own earlier excesses. Indeed, what becomes clear to us is that Gaines, despite his heroic stance as a modern-day Ahab decrying the monstrous unfairness of the universe, is, like the mad captain, also seeking his own humiliation and death. This masochism is yet another—and perhaps the central—bond he shares with Hollinger. Both men wallow in self-pity and self-inflicted pain. Certainly this is true of Gaines' relationship with Nicole. He tells her that he "doesn't know how to love her," but he continues to live with her and even listens tormentedly while she conducts her business over the telephone. When he finally admits the truth—"We made a deal. I do what I do, and I know what you do, and it's killing me because I love you"—she answers, "I knew it. But I never thought you'd ever say it." Yet saying it is not enough. It is not until Gaines acts in Hollinger's—and his own—behalf that he decides to chance emotional commitment once again.

According to Aldrich, the ending of the film comprised one of the few major changes from Shagan's original script.[37] Shagan had had Gaines arrive at the airport to meet Nicole so that they might "bust out" of the corruption together, only to find that she isn't there: she can't leave her world of hustling. Aldrich opted for a more dramatic and more ambiguous ending. In the film, Gaines, on the way to the airport where Nicole *is* waiting, is caught in the middle of a liquor store robbery. Aldrich described what he was after in some detail:

> If the viewer doesn't understand that when Burt's in that liquor store and the guy tells him to get his hands up, and he looks at the gun, he is thinking of what his own self-esteem means and of what's on the line, and that he has an opportunity just to play melody and avoid the unpleasant, then the director has failed. There are three cuts: Burt in medium shot, an insert of the gun, and a big, big head of Burt. The audience should realize that he's making up his mind whether to get involved or not get involved, knowing what getting involved would mean. And that he thinks, "Fuck it, I've lived a particular way, and it's my job not to let people really get hurt. I can look the other way and nobody's going to be critical. But if I do, I will have lost my self-esteem and without my self-esteem, what difference does it make that she's at the airport?" And he elects to act out what he is.[38]

Gaines tries to stop the robbery and is shot dead. It is an ethical and courageous act, but it is also his final act of masochism, or, if one prefers, of absolution. Surely Aldrich is correct when he says the audience must see this act as more than mere bravado in the midst of a third-rate heist, but Gaines' response should also be seen as a logical result of his private as well as professional dilemma.

Hustle was a moderate box office success for Aldrich, largely because of Burt Reynolds' drawing power. Reynolds discussed the film and the controversial ending: "Bob and I knew going in that *Hustle* was not a commercial picture, but believed it was a story that should be told. I always believed that if the guy had not died, it would have made another twenty million dollars. Everyone at Paramount wanted us to change the ending. By his death, Gaines demonstrated he was a dedicated law enforcement officer. Regardless of what was going down, he was not going to walk away from it. I think we opted for the most provocative ending."[39] It serves the film well. A tight, sharply focused film, *Hustle* is much closer to the economy of Aldrich's earlier works than to the loose quality of some of his more contemporary films. Here, Aldrich chooses his camera shots and movements for their utility and for their thematic importance: the parallel crane shots which link Gloria Hollinger and Nicole Britton, for example, or the incessant use of close-ups of Reynolds and

Robert Aldrich, his son William, his daughter Adell, and his son Kelly on the set of *Hustle*. Used by permission of Adell Aldrich.

Deneuve which imprison us in their claustrophobic relationship. Sound overlaps move us, sometimes abruptly, from one scene to another, but further suggest the thematic connection between the two stories. Aldrich often lets the background business comment on the main action. The football game which Gaines and Nicole plan to attend (Nicole's "stadium full of hustlers") can be heard on the radio at the police station and in the morgue while Hollinger (who has been at the game) identifies the body of his daughter. The policemen are more interested in the score than in Marty's grief or the possibility of murder. When Nicole and Gaines have their talk in the bar, discussing the seeming impasse in their relationship, *Mission: Impossible* blares out from the television. When Gaines' investigation takes him to the "Scanty Clad Club," a strip joint where Gloria Hollinger once worked, *The Dating Game* is on the set, a cruel but accurate evaluation of our social mores and hypocrisies. As the film ends, with Gaines dead, the constant flow of romantic music is finally ended, replaced by the desolate howl of blowing wind, the same sound which began the picture and foreshadowed the discovery of Gloria's body.

Tom Milne, in his perceptive essay on Aldrich, calls *Hustle* a "remarkable film" which "deserves to rank with *Ulzana's Raid* as Aldrich's best to date."[40] This is high praise, perhaps more than the film can bear. But Milne is, as usual, right in his general appreciation. *Hustle* should earn our respect, and it does deserve critical reappraisal. In its questioning of the nature of courage and of justice, it is yet another of Aldrich's works which expands the boundaries of the genre it represents.

Hustle was the last film Aldrich would do with Eddie Albert, who had previously played major roles in *Attack!* and *The Longest Yard*. For more than twenty-five years, Aldrich and Albert remained good friends who respected and admired one another. Albert considered him a "splendid director":

I was the kind of actor he liked—professional, grown-up, responsible—just like he was. He was a terribly strong man, perhaps too inflexible, too hot-tempered. He might have saved himself some harm had he been more flexible. But he did not suffer fools gladly. He was an intelligent, compassionate man, with genuine sympathy for the underdog. He found much wrong in the world and he hated it. He was a hard worker and he loved conflict. On the set, he was a great general, like Zanuck and Wilder; the set was professionally run and you were expected to do your job. He would listen to me, but he wasn't one for talk. He was not one of those directors who talk through a scene; to him, that was a kind of artistic masturbation. He was too intense. He was a man of action. He wanted to get on with it. It would take a smart director to study Aldrich's films and learn from them, and there aren't too many of those around. I owe him a lot, and I can never repay him.

Far more complicated, far more turbulent, was the relationship between Aldrich and Burt Reynolds, whose collaboration also ended with *Hustle*. The two men were remarkably alike. Both were self-made men who loved film and who were professional filmmakers (as a director—his first film was *Gator* in 1976—Reynolds modeled himself on Aldrich to some extent). Both conceived of the film crew as an extended family bound together by trust and loyalty. Both believed that to betray that trust was unforgivable. Both had tremendous egos. The bond between Aldrich and Reynolds, signified by their partnership RoBurt, was not unlike that which exists between father and son, a relationship both men must have cherished. Thus, the rift between them—perhaps inevitable given each man's pride and independence, given their similarities—was doubly unfortunate. They had planned another film for their production company, but then the trouble started, as William Aldrich explained:

> There was a third picture called *Stand On It* that I had found and I was going to produce and Bob was going to direct and Burt was going to star in. This was an action picture about car racing. We took the book to Universal and made a development deal there, and they wanted Paul Newman to star in it. We talked to Paul and he liked the book, but Paul eventually turned down the screenplay. We went right away to Burt, whom we wanted to do the picture with in the first place. Burt said that he'd like to do it, but we got into a lot of problems at United Artists. Burt wasn't happy with United Artists. He had a three picture development deal there and knew he had to go there, but there were some restrictions or the picture wouldn't get made by us. We got a phone call a year and a half ago from Dick Clayton, who is Burt's manager, saying *they're* going to go ahead and make the picture—this is some five years later—at Universal where we had developed it. And *we're* obviously going to have nothing to do with it. It was just terrible.

Their relationship suffered. There was probably over-reaction and misunderstanding on both sides—each man believed he was right— and it is impossible to know whether Aldrich ever felt completely reconciled to Reynolds. For his part, Reynolds seemed to have come to terms with his mentor. He wrote: "Bob was an uncompromising individual. He did not make movies for studios or for anyone else. His works were personal statements that he felt should go on record. I always admired him. In these times, and in this business, it is not easy to be true to yourself. He was one of the most true-to-himself, uncompromising individuals I have ever encountered."[41]

Twilight's Last Gleaming (1977)

In his article on "Aldrich's *Twilight*," Richard Combs writes, "Ever since he unleashed the Atom bomb at the end of *Kiss Me Deadly*, Robert Aldrich seems to have been looking for creative ways of confronting the apocalypse."[42] The "apocalypse" of *Hustle* had been played on a minor scale: the death quest of one man disillusioned by the realities of a corrupt world. In *Twilight's Last Gleaming*, Aldrich expanded his scope once more to the image of global suicide, to the image of a real world held for ransom. As the title itself indicates, this was a film about endings, the fading of light, the passing of hope.

Twilight begins at full throttle. Former Army General Lawrence Dell (Burt Lancaster) and three other cohorts have escaped from a Montana state prison. Dell is a former prisoner of war, having been captured and held by the Viet Cong for five years. Upon his release, he threatened to reveal certain political secrets about U.S. military policies in Vietnam, to show that the war had been purposefully begun and then prolonged by the Pentagon to demonstrate America's willingness to fight ruthlessly and to sacrifice its men in the struggle against Communism. The war was, in other words, a deliberate exercise in death. But before Dell can make known these assertions, he is set up, convicted of a trumped-up murder charge, and again jailed, this time in his own country. In order to get this information finally before the American public, Dell, using his knowledge of military security, leads his men in a takeover of an underground Titan missile installation. In the initial skirmish, some soldiers are killed, and Dell himself shoots one of his fellow convicts, Hoxey (William Smith), for disobeying Dell's orders. When Dell and his two remaining men—Willis Powell (Paul Winfield) and Augie Garvas (Burt Young)—have secured the silo, Dell makes his demands. Speaking directly to the President of the United States, David Stevens (Charles Durning), Dell lists his requirements: (1) $10 million; (2) transportation out of the country on Air Force One, the President's personal airplane; (3) the President himself as hostage; and, most importantly, (4) a public revelation of the National Security Council Document 9759, which proves Dell's contentions about the military's manipulation of the war and implicates a former U.S. President as an accomplice in the plan. If these demands are not met, Dell threatens, he will fire the nine ICBMs already aimed toward Russia and thereby start World War III.

The military's initial reaction to Dell's nuclear blackmail is to see it as a bluff. SAC's commanding general, Martin MacKenzie (Richard Widmark), is a former colleague of Dell and may have been a part of the conspiracy against him. MacKenzie doubts that Dell has the necessary information needed to launch the missiles and argues for an attack on the silo with the careful placement of a miniature atomic bomb which will destroy the men and missiles with limited fallout. Dell, however, *does* have the information, tricked from two soliders captured in the takeover. When he realizes MacKenzie's plan, Dell sets the rockets in motion toward launch (in a suspenseful and dramatic scene which Aldrich brilliantly intensifies through the use of the split screen technique). Although Garvas is killed in this foiled attack, Dell's determination is made clear, and the President realizes that he has no choice but to meet the demands. Before he gives himself over to Dell and Powell, President Stevens reads the NSC document and learns for the first time of the government's horrifying duplicity. Recognizing the possibility that he could be killed, Stevens asks the secretary of defense, Zachariah Guthrie (Melvyn Douglas), to make public the document should Stevens die, and Guthrie agrees. When Stevens delivers himself to Dell, the former general apologizes and treats the President with respect despite the fact that he is their hostage; Powell, on the other hand, is confounded that Dell still retains so many patriotic illusions. What Dell cannot comprehend—but what Powell all too clearly sees—is that the government will sacrifice any President in order to hide its secrets. And indeed, when Dell, Powell, and Stevens emerge from the bunker under a promise of safety, they are all three shot down by military snipers under the direct orders of General MacKenzie. Dell and Powell are killed outright. As the President lies dying, Defense Secretary Guthrie slowly bends over him to hear Stevens' last pleadings to reveal the contents of the document. But the secretary never answers, the President dies, and we are left to interpret the look on Guthrie's face.

   Twilight's Last Gleaming was based on the novel *Viper Three* by Walter Wager. The film rights had been purchased by Lorimar Production Company in 1971. Lorimar had, until this time, concentrated largely on television (*The Waltons*) but wished to expand into theatrical releases. They announced shortly after purchase that a screenplay was to be written by Tom Mankiewicz and that the film would be directed by Jay Sandrich.[43] But Lorimar, apparently, was unable to find the necessary financial backing for the project, and nothing further came of the film until 1975, when Aldrich was brought in. When Aldrich was offered the picture, now called *Silo III*, he disliked the script given him. "It was an action melodrama—and if you hadn't already seen it, you were going to see it. Or you knew one or two pictures that were kind of like it," Aldrich remembered. In the script (and in the novel), money is the main reason for the takeover:

> There was no social impact. The kidnappers had no interesting motivation. I wondered what would happen if you had an Ellsberg mentality, if you had some command officer who came out of Vietnam and who was soured not by war protesters but by the misuse of the military. The military, really, has had a unique relationship with this country; they've really done what they

were supposed to do—stayed out of politics, and protected the country. Now in Vietnam, they were there for political and not defensive reasons. . . . What would happen if you had a general who was angry at the political use of the armed forces?[44]

Aldrich agreed to direct the film if a new script were written with the added political motivation and implications, and if Burt Lancaster would star as Lawrence Dell. Lancaster had already turned down the Dell role in the original script, but Aldrich had worked with Lancaster now in three films (*Apache*, *Vera Cruz*, and *Ulzana's Raid*), and when he explained his new ideas about Dell, Lancaster agreed even before seeing a revised script.[45] Aldrich modeled *his* version of Dell on a Navy admiral he had met, a former POW deeply disturbed by America's involvement in Vietnam. Aldrich suspected the man "was certainly going to have some kind of breakdown. He just couldn't reconcile the radical views he held with the uniform he wore."[46] Lancaster liked this "new idea" about the Dell character. Lancaster already shared a number of Aldrich's liberal leanings, and *Twilight*, with its novel twist, had the kind of social theme he could enthusiastically endorse: "People today have a despairing picture of democratic life in America. Some people will take *Twilight's Last Gleaming* as entertainment, others will come away saying there's an element of truth there. The world changes slowly. But you have to keep making an effort. Societies have to. Otherwise there is no change."[47] With Lancaster committed as star and with a powerful script by Ronald M. Cohen and Edward Huebsch, Lorimar was able to finance the picture through an agreement with the West German company Geria, which picked up two-thirds of the cost, thus enabling Aldrich to realize a longstanding dream to make a "really tough political picture . . . . a totally honest political film."[48]

Twilight was shot in West Germany in and around Munich, largely with a German film crew instead of Aldrich's usual group. Unlike his experience with *Ten Seconds to Hell*, however, Aldrich was pleased with the work done by the Germans. Indeed, the Germans were able to construct not only an enlarged and exact replica of the President's Oval Office, but also an approximation of the underground silos which seemed extremely authentic because, as Aldrich wryly remarked, they "had better research than we have. They had all the photographs down to the minutist detail. I don't know if they got it from the East Germans or where they got it, but they had it."[49] Remarkably smooth and professional conditions prevailed on the set. Script supervisor/dialogue

Burt Lancaster, Alvin Greenman, and Robert Aldrich on the set of *Twilight's Last Gleaming*. Used by permission of Alvin Greenman.

director Alvin Greenman remembered it as "the best picture I ever worked on." Richard Jaeckel called it "a terrific film to be in . . . the whole atmosphere was terrific." And Charles Durning described *Twilight* as the "best film I've been in and the best cast I've worked with."[50] As always, much of the credit for the film's smooth running belonged to Aldrich. Durning recalled, for example, the deference with which Aldrich treated the elderly members of the cast (who largely made up the President's cabinet), particularly Melvyn Douglas, ill at the time with pneumonia. Durning was "shocked, literally shocked" at how frail and weak Douglas appeared. To accommodate him, Aldrich shot many of the cabinet scenes early in the morning, when these actors worked best, and shot Douglas frequently from behind, so a double could be used.

Some responsibility for occasional conflicts on the set also belonged to Aldrich, however. At one point, he became upset with a German camera operator working under the film's cinematographer Robert Hauser. Aldrich was convinced that the cameraman, Dieter Matzka, had made a mistake in the framing composition and lighting of a certain set-up. Although he was intimidated by Aldrich, Matzka held his ground. Aldrich was furious and, to prove the man wrong, sent the film secretly to Los Angeles for processing. The exposed film indeed vindicated the cameraman. To set things straight, Aldrich called the entire cast and crew together, confessed his secret effort to prove his point, and apologized publicly to the man. His sense of fairness demanded the act.[51]

Although the film was a long one, running approximately 145 minutes, *Twilight* is one of Aldrich's tightest and most handsomely produced. As the reviewer in *Variety* put it, "Aldrich manifests an assurance and command of his medium that comes across forcefully; you know that someone's in charge here, someone who respects the need for a vital story as the base for cinematic wonders which bring it alive."[52] Richard Combs called it "as austere and pungent as anything Aldrich has done" and especially praised the director's use of the split screen technique.[53] Although there were several splendid reviews of the film, however, most critics were confused by just what Aldrich wanted to say in it. Lancaster's General Dell should be our ostensible hero. He is, after all, attempting to reveal the corruption and tell the truth; he is the man most betrayed by the country. Indeed, he seems the typical Aldrich hero—Lt. Costa of *Attack!*, for example, pushed to the frightfully logical extremes. But Dell's method—to destroy the world if he cannot cleanse it, in his words to "perpetuate a theatrical holocaust for credibility"—is surely mad. As Aldrich said at the time, "I think you have to understand that in the Lancaster character there is a degree of imbalance, because he's willing to do an insane thing to prove a point. . . . My hope was that you gradually came to understand that Lancaster is crazy. But I don't think we did it."[54] The military, led by Widmark's General MacKenzie, is trying to prevent nuclear war, but they are also covering up their own dirt. MacKenzie is, in his own way, just as rash and violent as Dell, and he certainly does not gain our support. Presumably, it is this moral ambiguity, the feeling that we are often morally adrift in the film, which accounts in part for the critical confusion surrounding *Twilight's Last Gleaming*.

The man who comes most to demand our sympathies is the President, David Stevens. Aldrich had originally wanted "a Camelot kind of President" and had offered the Stevens role to Paul Newman, but

Newman had declined. Then, according to Aldrich, "we thought, 'Hell, we'll write the picture the way it should be and worry about casting it later.' And my idea of the President was really that of a smart, classy uptown Daley. Catholic origins. Maybe Holy Cross as a school. His mother wanted him to be a Jesuit, but he liked politics, became a lawyer, was really a pol, never pretended to be a statesman—very pragmatic man."[55] It was a fine idea and gave the picture both its emotional center and its devastating ending.

Durning indicated that he and Aldrich had spoken at length about the part of President Stevens, about his emotions and motivations, and that he found Aldrich's advice and direction quite beneficial: "He said that the President became heroic through the office, not because he was heroic, but because the office *made* him heroic. He would tell me those little gems which cleared up a lot of problems for me." Cut from the final film were scenes involving the President's wife (Vera Miles) and his secretary (Pippa Scott) with their implications of presidential infidelity, a subplot deleted—and properly so, Durning thought—owing to *Twilight's* excessive length. *Twilight* was Durning's first film with Aldrich. They had become acquainted through Eileen Brennan, who had worked with both men (Durning in *The Sting*, and Aldrich in *Hustle*) and who had first suggested Durning for the role of Hollinger in *Hustle*. Although Aldrich had already promised that part to Ben Johnson, he agreed to use Durning in *Twilight* despite Gregory Peck's interest in the part of Stevens. Durning held Aldrich in awe and admitted to being afraid of him: "He was very volatile. He had a volatile temper and when he said something, he meant it. There was no bullshit about him. He was adamant about certain things and if you disagreed with him, that was your tough luck." Yet on the set, Durning found Aldrich to be a "benevolent" director—intelligent, energetic, and encouraging: "After the dailies, he would say to me, 'Go, you Irish bastard, go!' " Once, following a particularly bad series of nosebleeds, which twice held up production, Durning offered his apologies to Aldrich, to which Aldrich replied: "You can have all the nosebleeds in the world as long as you keep doing scenes like that." But one of Durning's most memorable moments of filming occurred when he first confronted his cabinet:

> It was a scene in which I face all these legends—Melvyn Douglas on my left, Joseph Cotton, Scott Simon, William Marshall, Charlie McGraw and Leif Erikson—and I had to call them all pricks and assholes. And I turned to Bob and I said, "I can't *do* this." Well, Joseph Cotton kept calling me "the kid":

"Come on, kid; let's do it, kid." And about 10 days into the show he started calling me "Mr. President," and I knew that I had gotten to them, that I had crossed some kind of barrier. At first I could see them judging me and then I could see the change. I don't know what happened; I don't know if Bob talked to them or if they said, "Well, we gotta help this idiot out."

Charles Durning's excellent performance makes the President an ordinary man placed in extraordinary circumstances. We first see him acting as a professional politician—relatively honest, cunning, a compromiser, but a man having what Aldrich termed "very idealistic views of good and bad."[56] Because he is ordinary—one of us—we accept the fact the he could have served as President and yet not known about Document 9759, and that he could be honestly shocked to discover that such shenanigans could have occurred in the highest realms of government. President Stevens can be manipulated just as the American public was manipulated during the Vietnam War. And yet, when faced with the truth and with the need to act with courage—and perhaps with sacrifice—Stevens is ready. It is appropriate that when Stevens gives himself up as hostage, he and Dell quickly develop an understanding and respect for one another, indeed, become allies, for the military surrounding them, in league with the National Security Commission, has become their common enemy. Aldrich has said that he intended for the picture to end in an ambiguous manner with two possible readings: "first, that they really intended to kill the President all along, and second, that the President was killed by accident because it was more important that the terrorists not get away."[57] Aldrich told Durning during filming, however, that the President *was* deliberately killed, and the film's strong implication is that Stevens had been murdered because he now knew too much. William Aldrich explained that his father hoped the audience would arrive at that interpretation: "I think *he* thought he was being ambiguous, but I don't think he was. It was his point of view that the President was murdered by the government, but he didn't want to *say* that in the picture. He wanted somebody else to say that, the person who paid the $2.50. But *he's* telling the story so he's going to stack it the way he wants it stacked. That's the privilege he earned."

Aldrich later wished that he had been more subtle with the film's ending, but the film's final power comes from just the realization that the corruption is so widespread, that good men can so easily be dismissed. Stevens dies in despair, faced with the proof of his betrayal. "I didn't trust anybody else in the cabinet except the Melyvn Douglas character, my advisor," Durning remembered, "and then I realized that he also did it to me and betrayed me in the end. I realized it *after* I got shot, and I played it that way."

The devastating ending—Dell and Powell dragging President Stevens from the silo to Air Force One parked on a nearby runway, twisting and turning to avoid giving military sharpshooters a clear target—was entirely Aldrich's idea. The scene had to be choreographed and was very difficult to shoot. Durning remembered that, despite the intensity of the scene, there was still a spirit of fun on the set. "All the while Lancaster was turning me around, circling me, he was joking with me, saying: 'Ten years ago, you wouldn't get away with this. Ten years ago, it would have been my picture. I would have the last shot in this picture. But now I'm an old man and I don't care any more.' He was telling me all this stuff and I could hardly keep from laughing. It broke me up a couple of times and Bob would say, 'What the hell is going on? Let's do this scene and get out of here. It's cold!' "

General Dell and President Stevens are naive characters. In Aldrich's own words, they are "idealistic innocents." As such, they must die. "What you discover," Aldrich said, "is that there is no room for purity at either end of the spectrum. You're not going to get through the game if you don't find a middle ground. Also, treachery comes from the most unexpected quarters." The intentions of both men are honorable (despite Dell's insanity), but both become "unwise martyrs": "There's nothing wrong with being a martyr if you know beforehand that being a martyr is going to advance the cause, which most martyrs don't. Life, it seems to me, is filled with knowing that you can rock the boat just so far; if you rock it beyond that, you're not really going to make any substantial change because they're going to get rid of you . . . they're going to find a way to excommunicate you from that society. . . . You have to come right up to that edge."[58]

The pervading bleak tone of *Twilight*, plus its disquieting touches of black comedy (Lancaster's Dell becomes more and more ludicrous, a variation on Sterling Hayden's General Jack D. Ripper in *Dr. Strangelove*) and savage irony (Billy Preston's bluesy singing of "My Country 'Tis of Thee" during the opening credits is both irreverent and extremely moving, perhaps an anticipation of the singing of "God Bless America" at the end of *The Deer Hunter*) made the film difficult to take in 1977, a time when America was trying to pull itself together after the paroxysms of Vietnam and Watergate. Perhaps, like *Too Late the Hero*, its release was poorly timed. Perhaps audiences found un-

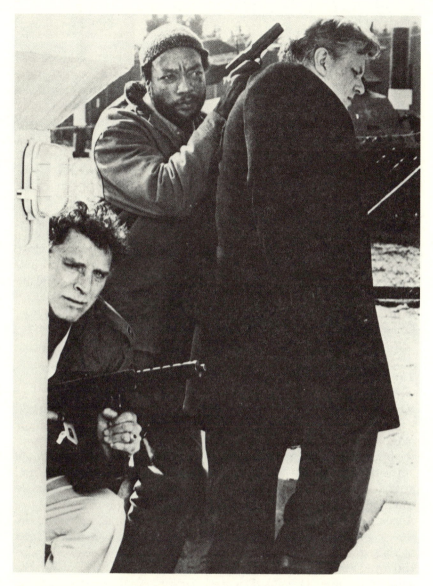

Burt Lancaster and Paul Winfield hold the President, Charles Durning, hostage in *Twilight's Last Gleaming*. Used by permission of the Museum of Modern Art/Film Stills Archive, courtesy of Allied Artists.

palatable the unrelieved gloom of the ending. In any event, Aldrich was terribly disappointed with the failure of *Twilight*, one of his most personal films: "I was more involved in it and producer of it than I think any [film] I'd ever done. I felt it had something to say; I thought it was desperately important, because I'm fearful that one of these days somebody just might capture a nuclear silo and hold the world at ransom. . . . But it died; it was a disaster. It wasn't the critics, wasn't the campaign. It just plain died because nobody damned well wanted to know. They just didn't want to know."[59] Foreign distributors were particularly disturbed by the political implications. The British version, for example, was cut by twenty-six minutes, omitting the more earthy aspects of the President's character and, incredibly, the contents of the secret document itself. Aldrich himself cut the television version of the film, which is close to full-length and retains the original's impact (minus much of its profanity). Although *Twilight's Last Gleaming* was not a success critically or commercially upon release, it seems one of Aldrich's best films today, more perceptive—and perhaps more despairing—than was clear in 1977. Of his many films, Aldrich ranked it among his personal favorites.[60]

The Choirboys (1977)

It is impossible to discuss the failure of *The Choirboys* without first taking into account the controversy which accompanied it during all stages of production. In retrospect it seems one of those projects doomed from the beginning, and yet the subject must have appeared ideal for Aldrich at the time. After all, Joseph Wambaugh's novel was a best seller, and critics had applauded it as his best work to date. It was a study of male camaraderie, detailing the experiences of a group of men on the Los Angeles police force—the pressures they faced, the violence they feared, the escapes they sought. The book, episodic in structure, contained scenes of high excitement, bawdy humor, and, at times, great despair. It also conveyed a sense of authority and credibility, since Wambaugh was a veteran member of the LAPD when he wrote the novel. It was in every way a hot property. In view of Aldrich's past successes with such similar material in *The Dirty Dozen* and *The Longest Yard*, there was little reason to foresee the debacle which was to follow.

Wambaugh was hired to write the screenplay for *The Choirboys* and finished the first version, he claimed, in nineteen days, in May 1976. According to Aldrich, Wambaugh went through "six or seven scripts" in all,[61] but the results were still not satisfactory. Thus, when Aldrich began filming in March 1977, he and screenwriter Christopher Knopf (who had written *Emperor of the North*) began to make changes, as was typical of Aldrich's style on any project. Wambaugh felt that his contract prevented such tampering without his personal agreement, and in June 1977 he filed suit against Lorimar for $1 million, claiming that his screenplay had been "drastically and crudely" altered. Moreover, Wambaugh demanded that his name be removed from the credits, as he wished to disassociate himself from the film as much as possible.

Wambaugh's suit exacerbated an already tense situation on the set of *The Choirboys*. Lorimar Productions had hired Aldrich to direct *The Choirboys* on the assumption that *Twilight's Last Gleaming* (which Aldrich had also done for Lorimar) would be a box-office hit. When *Twilight* failed to take off as expected, Lorimar's enthusiasm for Aldrich diminished noticeably. Charles Durning said that "you could see the change. They [Lorimar Studio heads Merv Adelson and Lee Rich] were a little less cordial, a little more businesslike and straightforward. They felt they had made a mistake. I think they got anxious, lost their urge for Aldrich." Aldrich got anxious too—conceivably, he felt betrayed both by Lorimar and Wambaugh—and his attitude toward making the film was different from the outset. William Aldrich observed the change: "We certainly noticed at the beginning of *The Choirboys* that there was something different. He wasn't doing what he usually did when he made movies. He just wasn't taking the time and his enthusiasm dropped from a 9.9 to a 7.0." To make things worse, Lorimar wanted to settle the suit immediately, a move Aldrich violently opposed because it ran counter to his deepest convictions as a director. As William Aldrich explained: "That really didn't jive with Dad's opinion of film making. A writer was going to get rewritten by somebody. If Dad was told, 'You'll just have to do this screenplay and you can't change it,' he'd just walk away. It was not just for himself as much as it was for the Guild. He wanted every director to have that right, not just himself. Every director." And while there must have been other pressures associated with the subject matter itself—vulgar, depressing, sleazy material which, as script supervisor Alvin Greenman recalled, "brought everybody down"—the script remained the main source of Aldrich's discontent.

There were basically four points of contention in Wambaugh's suit over the changed script. First, in his novel, the characters were clearly members of the Los Angeles police force, but in the film this reference was changed to the more general "Metropolitan Police." Wambaugh wanted to maintain the specific identification, but Aldrich was opposed, explaining that such a use would not be allowed by the film's insurance company, an explanation which Mr. Wambaugh did not accept. In connection with this complaint, Wambaugh wanted those scenes set in MacArthur Park (where, in the book, the "choirboys" met for "choir practice" and where the climactic events occur) to be filmed on location. Aldrich opted for a studio set and at one point even gave a press luncheon on the set to demonstrate that a realistic equivalent to MacArthur Park could be created within the confines of the studio. Again, however, the effect was to make the picture a little less obviously about Los Angeles in particular, as Wambaugh wanted.

These two differences, however, were relatively minor when compared to the other, more crucial, objections. One of the scenes Wambaugh found especially "demeaning" portrayed the policeman Baxter Slate (Perry King) being discovered by two of his fellow officers, Sam Lyles (Don Stroud) and Harold Bloomguard (James Woods), in the apartment of a prostitute who specializes in sadism and bondage. Slate has been leashed, masked, and whipped by the prostitute. When he is found, he reaches out to Lyles for help and understanding, but Lyles is unable to respond and retreats, horrified. Later that night, Slate commits suicide, and this burden lies heavily on Lyles thereafter. The scene and its consequences are found in Wambaugh's book; indeed, Slate's discovery is central to the further development of the plot and leads directly to the tragic ending. The difference is that in the novel the reader is prepared for this scene. Slate's background—his home life, his early failure in police work, his sense of guilt—helps explain his need for this humiliation. Such an explanation, however, is only hinted at in the film, with the result that Slate's actions seem rather more perverse than Wambaugh intended. Moreover, the same problem exists for other characters as well. They appear in the film with little or no past; their behavior is thus explained only by the odd twists of their characters and the pressures of their lives and job.

This lack of exposition is definitely a flaw, one which Aldrich recognized and addressed. Part of the problem apparently lies in the cutting of the film. Aldrich started off with over four hours of film, which he then cut to two hours and sixteen minutes for the preview showings. Lorimar and Universal (the distributor), on the basis of the first preview, found this version still too long, and Aldrich then cut the sixteen minutes which contained most of the background material on the major characters. As Aldrich explained:

[Cut were] a marvelous scene between Don Stroud and his wife; two marvelous scenes between Bloomguard and his Vietnam buddy [Lyles]. And even more important, two long scenes with the eventual suicide, Perry King, to explain where his head was at, so you didn't think, as you do in the picture, that he committed suicide only because he got caught in some deviant sex act. . . . But without those character insights—and you know much more about Spermwhale [Charles Durning]—it is truly episodic and just for laughs.[62]

Durning made practically the same point: "The only thing the audience saw was the choir practice; you never saw *why* they became what they became. You never saw any of their sensitivity." The whole story of *The Choirboys*, told in the longer print which Durning saw, was more sympathetic to the police. But it was simply not possible, Durning stressed, to squeeze ten fully developed characters into a two-hour film.

Wambaugh's fourth complaint concerned the ending of the film, and this was certainly the most divisive issue of them all. Wambaugh's book ends with Sam Lyles's hysterical killing of a young homosexual in MacArthur Park. In an attempt to cover up Lyles's guilt, the other choirboys agree to lie about what happened. However, when threatened with the loss of his pension, only a few months away, the unofficial leader of the group, Spermwhale Whalen, breaks under interrogation and betrays his friends. The book ends with this recognition of despair. The system—represented by corrupt, fatuous officers and politicians—has prevailed; even the best of the choirboys has been unable to stand against them. This was obviously an important reality that Wambaugh wanted to stress, for it re-emphasized his view of these men as martyrs and victims who were, in effect, dying for our sins.

But this was a view which Aldrich could and would not hold. To him it undermined all that had come before. Wambaugh's ending, he felt, was a false one; "pablum Sartre," he called it, a "frontal lobotomy" on what had been up to that time a loud, vulgar, crudely upbeat comedy. Thus, Aldrich had Knopf rewrite the ending so that Whalen, after his initial betrayal, rethinks his decision, faces his superiors, and backs them down. Slate is still a suicide, Lyles has suffered a mental collapse, and the others have been discredited, but Whalen undoes what he can. The film ends with a freeze frame of Whalen and Potts (Louis Gossett, Jr.) laughing and slapping hands in apparent victory and celebration. "By extending the picture to a hopeful resolution, certainly not a happy one, you have a chance to expand the character of Durning and give him some redemption and self-esteem," Aldrich explained.[63] In a letter to Lorimar Productions proposing the new ending, Aldrich (with *Twilight's* failure in mind, perhaps) suggested that a redemptive resolution might enhance *The Choirboys* commercial appeal: "To avoid the terrible depression and unrelieved melancholy of the ending, and to shortcut the unforgivable—the turning of a hero into an informer—a change *must* be made . . . it seems to me we could save the movie, save the commercial possibilities, and save Spermwhale."[64]

Aldrich and Wambaugh were obviously at loggerheads over this issue; there was little or no ground for compromise, and neither was willing to give way. Because the new ending had "changed the intent of the work," as the Writers Guild ruled in their arbitration of the dispute, Wambaugh was allowed to remove his name from the film, thus giving Knopf full credit for the screenplay, although, as Aldrich pointed out, Knopf contributed only about 10 percent of the script.[65] Wambaugh also settled his suit with Lorimar in January 1978, soon after the film's release, and achieved most of his demands. The film itself met with some of Aldrich's worst reviews. Richard Schickel in *Time*, for example, called it the year's "most repulsive release,"[66] and others followed much the same line. The film was condemned by the Legion of Decency, and, although it did hold some appeal for the "broad-based audience" Aldrich had aimed for, it is considered one of his least memorable films.

It is probably useless to debate either side of this argument with too much fervor. Aldrich's insistence on the revised ending underlines his continued faith in man's ability to regain grace. The nihilism of Wambaugh's ending ran counter to Aldrich's central philosophy, and the director refused to budge. And certainly Aldrich is correct to accuse Wambaugh of pretentiousness and romanticism, for each is a primary ingredient of Wambaugh's prose style. Still, the anger and regret which also infuse Wambaugh's books, and especially *The Choirboys*, suggest that his writing, on some level, might be both exorcism and *mea culpa* for him. In either case, Aldrich's ending would have to be anathema to Wambaugh, since it implies that the system can be, if not defeated, then at least held at bay.

Also it should be stressed that this revised ending is not particularly convincing. Although it is in keeping with the darkly comic tone already established, it seems nonetheless forced. No one has actually won anything. The victims have been sacrificed, but the corruption remains, so why all the laughter? The ambiguity of justice which makes the endings of such films as *Attack!*, *The Grissom Gang*, and *The Longest Yard* so powerful is missing, and we are left feeling neither elated nor incensed.

Basic to the problem of *The Choirboys* is Aldrich's attitude toward the central characters in the film. In a patrol picture, the audience must *want* the men to survive, must care what happens to them. Aldrich had proved his ability to call forth this emotion in any number of films, some dealing with the most disreputable sorts. And, in part, Aldrich was able to do this because of his own strong sympathy with these characters, who represent in various forms the outlaws and outcasts of society. But in *The Choirboys*, he is dealing with those *in authority*, and although there is some attempt to make them less reprehensible than their superiors, Aldrich cannot bring himself—and therefore us—to *like* these men. Aldrich made these feeling clear in an interview given before the release of the film:

> I think Mr. Wambaugh is going to be very unhappy with this film of his work. . . . You see, I think Wambaugh's feelings for the "problems of the cop" are probably genuine . . . but I don't feel the same way. I don't find the fact that cops can't "cope" particularly rewarding; I can't relate to it. It's a volunteer force. You're not drafted to become a cop. So you've got to take some of the heat if you don't like what people think about you. . . . In fact, I disagree with Wambaugh to such an extent that I don't think people really *like* cops. . . . And he certainly wouldn't agree with me that the Los Angeles police force is murderous in terms of their attitude towards the public, particularly when the public is black or minority. . . . So I think you've got to show L.A. cops as brutal as they really are. And Wambaugh can't face that problem, so it's never touched in the book.[67]

Despite Aldrich's adamant position, the film does display a certain ambivalence on the subject. Thus, we have the recurring scene of the policemen in the squad room preparing to go out on detail, with the camera *outside* the building, looking in through the barred and screened window. Such a shot suggests both the tragic entrapment of their lives *and* their unusual relationship with the very criminals they have themselves imprisoned. There are also a few characters who transcend the stereotypes. Spermwhale Whalen, as played by Charles Durning, reveals his basic goodness despite his overall crudity; and James Woods' characterization of Harold Bloomguard is successfully gentle, comic, and believable. But, on the whole, the other men are held at a distance from us, either by their unrelieved vulgarity, cruelty, or silliness; or by the incompleteness of their characters.

The Choirboys lacks the cohesive "ensemble" spirit Aldrich so brilliantly achieved in *The Dirty Dozen* and his other patrol pictures, a deficiency Greenman and Durning attributed to the uncooperativeness of the young members of the cast. Greenman reported that the young

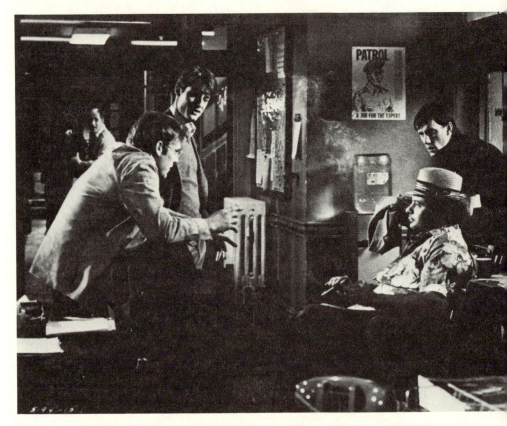

Don Stroud, Perry King, Burt Young, and James Woods confer in *The Choirboys*. Used by permission of the Museum of Modern Art/Film Stills Archive, courtesy of Universal City Studios.

actors had become so jealous of each other, so obsessed with who was getting the most close-ups, that they finally were unable to work closely together. Nor did they get along with Aldrich, whom they treated, Durning said, with extreme disrespect: "When you're young, you are macho and impolite and late a lot. And some of those kids would come in late and unprepared and be irreverent toward him." At first, when these rebellious actors—unhappy with the scripts they'd been given—began to rewrite their own scenes, Aldrich took his usual hard line: "Get straight or see your lawyers." But eventually, Durning believed, their insubordination simply wore him out: "He began to give up the ghost in that film. Toward the end, he got so much flak from those kids—some of them, not all of them—that he began to mistrust their loyalty. And he began to allow them to do things that were not right for the picture. He was tired of it all. It was such a very hard shoot for him—ten weeks dealing with those incredible egos." Ironically, Aldrich had thought *The Choirboys* might do for its ensemble what *The Dirty Dozen* had done for Lee Marvin and company. He told Durning that the ten men in *The Choirboys* were at virtually the same point in their careers as were the men in *The Dirty Dozen*, and that *The Choirboys* might prove the blockbuster hit they'd been waiting for. Unfortunately, as it turned out, *The Choirboys* helped no one's career very much, least of all Aldrich's.

Through it all, Aldrich retained his customary sense of humor on the set, as Durning recalled: "Bob would have me start a scene; then, once I got into it, he'd stop it—without saying 'cut'—and tell everybody but me to break for lunch. And the next thing I knew, I'd turn around and there wouldn't be anybody there. He did that to me twice on *The Choirboys*. And I was petrified. I thought, 'Well, there goes my career, and everybody else is on their way to lunch.' " Like Burt Lancaster, Eddie Albert, and Burt Reynolds, Charles Durning found Aldrich a strong-willed man, but very fair and very professional. In the final days before his death, Aldrich phoned Durning in Florida to say good-bye, a gesture Durning regarded as an honor: "He was a man I respected, a man I admired, a man I loved."

To see this film, as has one critic, as a "desperate assault on the box office"[68] is to imply undue cynicism on Aldrich's part. It seems clear that his intentions were more honorable than that, although the hope of a box office success was surely uppermost in his mind. His failures with this film were more the fault of strongly-held beliefs and, perhaps, a kind of perverse stubbornness rather than an unprincipled desire to cash in on the latest sex-and-violence fad. Thematically, *The Choirboys* is very much an expression of Aldrich's lifelong tenets. As a film, however, it remains a disappointment.

Aldrich as Politician

Robert Aldrich was a politician at heart. Politics ran in his blood, as in the blood of the Aldrich-Rockefeller family in which he had been raised. Politics, William Aldrich recalled, was his father's "second" love: "If he weren't a director, then certainly he'd have been a politician, but he would have been a very tough one, I think. He would have been a backroom politician—like his father. Whatever time he didn't spend thinking, talking, and making movies, he spent thinking, talking politics. Those were the two passions in his life." With those actors who would listen, whom he trusted, Aldrich shared his political predilections. "We discussed politics all the time," Lee Marvin said. "He was a raving maniac on that subject." Throughout their friendship, Aldrich discussed politics with Abraham Polonsky, even during the final days of his life: "When I received a call from his family on the first of the last three occasions on which I saw him, he was at the hospital, and when I arrived there he wanted to talk about something. And I said, 'What do you want to talk about?' and he said, 'Politics.' He says, 'What's going on?' Well, of course, he didn't want an answer from me. He wanted to tell *me* what was going on. And he did."[69] It was that same impulse that inspired him on occasion to call Pat Brown and instruct him to instruct his son Jerry how to govern the state of California. To express his political vision, to vent his political passions, Aldrich made his share of political films—*Apache, Kiss Me Deadly, The Big Knife, Attack!, The Dirty Dozen, The Longest Yard, Twilight's Last Gleaming*—and he dreamed of making, with Polonsky as screenwriter, a radical political blockbuster, "bigger than *Twilight,* more athletic than *Twilight,*" a film "that said to you that the American People lost control of the Revolution. And it doesn't look like they're going to control it. . . . And the only solution for this is some kind of benign 'ism'—I don't care what you call it: socialism, fascism, statism—to take over for a ten-year period to get at the root causes of all our problems. . . ."[70] Aldrich often opened himself to charges of political extremism—charges to which he had grown accustomed since his early years in Hollywood—and there were those in the industry, as Lukas Heller explained, who judged Aldrich a communist. Heller thought him a "radical," but in the more refined, British sense of the word, as "a sort of broad, humanitarian, being-on-the-side-of-the-underdog type of thing, which in some ways is quite conservative." Aldrich's broad humanitarian concerns, his streetwise political toughness, his integrity, his interest, as Polonsky put it, in "very specific answers to the problems that face us,"[71] made him a natural, perhaps inevitable candidate for president of the Directors Guild of America, a post to which he was elected in July 1975.

When Aldrich arrived in Hollywood in 1941 to begin his career, he had chosen to work his way up the studio organization, from the lowest possible position to the highest, developing at each step—as Franklin Shaffner emphasized—"that intimate knowledge and special feeling for those

above and below the line"[72] As he had moved upward through the ranks
of the Hollywood hierarchy, so too had he risen through the ranks of
the Directors Guild. He joined the Guild as a junior assistant in 1942.
For ten years he was a member of the Assistant Directors Council of
the Guild, and he served that council both as president and vice-president.
He was also a member of the council's Negotiating Committee, By-Laws
Committee, Television Committee, and Veterans Welfare Committee.

From 1971 to 1975, Aldrich served as first national vice-president of
the Directors Guild, and from 1975 to 1979, he served two terms as president. As Shaffner later described Aldrich's tenure, "His was a Jeffersonian
concept of the Guild, Lincolnian in passion with more than a little of
Teddy Roosevelt in representing the Guild."[73]

Aldrich considered himself to be the first truly "political" president
the Guild had had, although he acknowledged the strong leadership provided by such men as King Vidor and George Stevens before him. "The
other ones have been very loyal, helpful, dedicated men," he noted, "But
they have not thought of the Guild as a political instrument for the bet-
terment of the members." Aldrich explained:

> For a long time [the Guild] was run by big-name directors in a benign,
> thoughtful, conservative way, but for their best interests. It was very difficult
> to make them understand that it was a vertical union, that they had to con-
> sider the welfare of a second assistant who was being exploited, who was not
> being paid proportionately to other craftsmen. It was very hard for them to
> come by the fact that, having involved the assistants, it was their respon-
> sibility to care for the assistants' concerns and welfare just as they cared for
> their own.[74]

Aldrich knew the Guild, and Hollywood, from top to bottom. He had
experience as a writer and as a producer, he had formed his own production company, he had owned—and lost— his own studios, and he had
worked with most of the giants of the industry. It was this knowledge
and experience that made him so active and effective a leader. During
his two terms in office, Aldrich instigated radical changes and instituted
major reforms which benefited the entire Guild membership: the closing
down of the old *Action* Magazine and the initiating of the new *Action*
and the DGA *Newsletter*; the reforming of the DGA Trust and Retirement Fund; the overhauling of the Health and Welfare system; the
launching of the Special Projects Committee, begun during the Robert
Wise administration, charged with establishing creative and cultural
programs within the Guild; the settling of the dispute with the Writers

Guild of America over the issue of possessory screenplay credit; and the negotiating of a new contract with the Alliance (a bargaining unit formed by Paramount Studios and Universal-MCA) and the Association of Motion Picture and Television Producers (AMPTP).

Of these, the latter two represent perhaps Aldrich's most significant accomplishments in office. The DGA's widely publicized debate with the Writers Guild, which dominated Aldrich's first term as president, focused on the screenwriters' contention that their creative rights, in effect, were abrogated by the changes directors routinely made in the shooting script during production. The writers sought a contractual agreement with producers that would grant them full autonomy over the final shooting script and prevent directors from changing screenplays during filming. Aldrich, who never worked that way—"everybody's going to get rewritten by somebody"—and who realized that few directors could operate under such restrictions, threatened to strike if such provisions were accepted by the Alliance and the AMPTP. The writers backed off and withdrew their demands. (A short time later, Wambaugh filed suit against Aldrich over the changes Aldrich had made in the screenplay for *The Choirboys.*) Aldrich's second term as DGA president was no less demanding and controversial. The major issue facing the Guild at that time was the negotiation of a new contract between the DGA and the two producers' associations. With his characteristic passion and panache, Aldrich went to the table with a professional bargaining team and a pledge of support from the Guild to strike if necessary; he hammered out a landmark contract for the Guild membership. Franklin Shaffner observed that "by the awesome muster of his talents, the President, along with his colleagues . . . delivered the most remarkable gains to the membership in dollars, residuals and creative rights. Robert Aldrich set the tone and purpose for those negotiations, melding an economic and creative impact which affected the texture and the substance of our working lives as never before."[75] For directors in particular, Aldrich secured entitlements allowing them far more access to—and control over—the final version of their films. As Aldrich told an AFI Seminar in 1978:

> So now in the latest contract, we have a provision whereby your employer, the studio, cannot dispense with your physical presense. A, you get to cut the picture first, nobody [else] cuts the picture. They will have to stay back and wait until you're through. B, they can't dispense with your body anymore. If they're going to cut it, you've got to be there. If somebody else is going to dub it, you've got to be there. If somebody else is going to score it, you've got to be there. If somebody else is going to take it to preview, you've got to be there. But . . . that's a minimum contract.[76]

Aldrich hadn't forgotten the lesson in auteurism he had learned in an Italian court over *Sodom and Gomorrah*; nor had he forgotten his battle over *The Garment Jungle* with Harry Cohn at Columbia, a fight that taught him that no matter how much power a director *thinks* he has, the studio has more. Aldrich understood power. He wanted that kind of power for himself, for the Guild. He wanted directors to remain competitive with their employers in that power struggle.

Aldrich's tenure as president of the DGA was unprecedented; his was a landmark administration. Lukas Heller called him a "great, a tremendous" president. Franklin Shaffner suggested that "his indelible stamp had brought the Guild closer to the 21st century than even he believed possible."[77] Aldrich had been tough, innovative, bold, and outspoken. But in the exercising of power and in the playing of the game, Aldrich had antagonized important men who could make it difficult for him to find work. "He loved running that Guild," his children said, "but it cost him physically, financially, psychologically. It cost all of us. When it came contact time, it didn't matter who was across the table. Now, you walk over later, with a project, and they don't want to see you. They say you're too much trouble." Aldrich was willing to make the personal and professional sacrifices necessary to do that job well, to do any job well. He applied to the business of running the Guild the same axiom of survival that he brought to his work: "If you can somehow manage to stay at the table long enough, you will prevail."

7. What Ever Happened to Robert Aldrich?

The Frisco Kid (1979)

The making of *The Choirboys* and its aftermath marked the nadir of Robert Aldrich's career. It had drained him emotionally and hurt him creatively. The savage reviews made his name anathema among the major studios. He had neither the influence nor the resources to start his own projects, and he was not offered jobs by those who did. In one sense he was paying the price for his independence and forthrightness. As Lukas Heller put it, "Mind you, he asked for it. He was very contemptuous—and rightly so, in my opinion—of a large number of people in Hollywood. And he wasn't afraid of saying so, and he was frequently quoted in high places. You can do that as long as you're being successful. But, of course, once you start being not successful, it may come back."

He was well aware of his reputation of not abiding fools, of being difficult, and he often exacerbated the problem in moments of anger. His personal secretary, Joan Bennett, would sometimes try to protect him against himself on these occasions. She would ask Aldrich to tone down his letters, or she would hold them back a day before mailing and then ask him to reconsider. "Sometimes he would think it over and make changes," she recalled, "but other times he would say, 'Fuck him, he deserves it, the son of a bitch.' " The general word on Aldrich in Hollywood was that he was too hard, too tough, too involved in all aspects of production. "This guy is easier—why do we want to put up with Aldrich?" they would ask. "Dad wouldn't check himself," William Aldrich remembered. "I was pulling him away from meetings for years to *not* have him say things or do things to people that he shouldn't say or do. He didn't care."

But Aldrich's failure at this time was due to more than personal animosity. He had in a sense lost touch with the viewing public. A number of his friends and co-workers were aware that his choice of subjects was uncertain and erratic. Charles Durning, for example, who greatly admired Aldrich, felt that "the edge was off; his finger was no longer on the pulse." Aldrich knew it as well. The director, he said, the "guy who makes the movie," has "got to run out of gas sooner than the guy sitting under the umbrella, drinking lemonade."[1] Thus, for long days he would stay in his North Larchmont office, developing ideas, optioning projects, talking with friends like Richard Jaeckel or members of his staff, waiting for the chance to get back into the game.

That chance came with *The Frisco Kid*, an unlikely project for Aldrich. He had been preparing a football film called *Sudden Death* for Warner Brothers/Orion. When that film was delayed (it was never made), Warner Brothers asked that he take over this trouble-plagued comedy western. The original screenplay of *The Frisco Kid* (called *No Knife* at this time) had made the studio rounds for years. At one point it was apparently intended for Mike Nichols to direct. Aldrich was brought in late on the picture. Despite his reputation as a demanding director, he was still also known as a sure professional who could organize, refocus, and save a film. Although he felt that the film would not work and even warned Warner Brothers that it would likely lose money, he finally agreed to give it a try. When he replaced the original director, the picture was already two weeks behind schedule. It was budgeted at $10 million, but the projections showed that it would probably come in at closer to $14 million. Aldrich met with Gene Wilder, the star of the film, and liked him. Then he cut about $3,500,000 from the budget, which again made it a feasible picture to make. He was back at work.

The plot of *The Frisco Kid* concerns the misadventures of Polish rabbi Avram Belinski (Gene Wilder), sent by his superiors to America in 1850 to take charge of a congregation in San Francisco. Avram's overland travels from Philadelphia to San Francisco comprise an allegory of the innocent abroad: he is the naive idealist adrift in a land of duplicity and corruption, and the disparity between his expectations of life in the Old West and his actual experience of that reality provides for the comic tone and context of the film. Belinski's troubles begin when, after landing in Philadelphia, he misses the boat which was to take him around the Cape to San Francisco. Committed to a cross-continental odyssey, Avram joins forces with the Diggs brothers, Darryl and Matt (George Di Cenzo and William Smith) and their henchman Jones (Ramon Bieri), but the Diggs gang robs him and leaves him to die on the prairie. Avram is rescued by Amish farmers (whom he assumes mistakenly to be Jewish). They care for him, give him money, and place him on a train to Akron. But on the train also is Tommy Lillard (Harrison Ford), a charming outlaw who robs the other passengers and makes his escape while Avram is in

Harrison Ford and Gene Wilder in *The Frisco Kid*. Used by permission of the Museum of Modern Art/Film Stills Archive, courtesy of Warner Brothers.

the restroom, unaware of what is happening. After leaving the train—it being against his religion to ride on Sabbath's eve—Avram works for a while on the railroad, buys a horse, and continues his westward journey.

Coincidentally—as is the case in all good picaresque tales—Belinski meets Lillard on his journey, and Lillard elects to guide the wayward rabbi to the West Coast. Along the way, the two men rob a bank (Avram is, of course, an unsuspecting accomplice in the affair), cross the Rockies in mid-winter, are captured by Indians (they are released when Avram proves his courage and faith by his willingness to endure torture rather than see his Torah burned), ambushed by the Diggs gang (Avram kills Darryl in the ensuing shoot-out), and arrive finally in San Francisco at the home of Samuel Bender (Jack Somack), the head of the local Jewish community. Although with some reluctance (Belinski, after all, has killed a man), the Jewish leaders accept him as rabbi, and his credibility as moral leader, both in his own eyes and in the eyes of the community, is assured when he refuses to engage in further gunplay with Matt Diggs, who reappears to exact vengeance for his brother's death, and also prevents a gunfight between Tommy and Diggs. All ends well when Diggs is run out of town and Avram is joined in marriage to Bender's beautiful daughter Rosalie (Penny Peyser).

Aldrich had problems in the making of *The Frisco Kid*. He enjoyed working with Gene Wilder and felt they had a good understanding during rehearsals. But Wilder was also interested in directing, and while he worked hard to learn from Aldrich, once filming began, he made numerous suggestions as to how the film should be made, rethought certain aspects of his role, and invented new routines to strengthen the comedy. Although Wilder's comedic knowledge surely helped the picture (after the film was released, Wilder complained that Aldrich had no feel for this kind of comedy, which may have been true), his changes upset Aldrich. Still, Aldrich appreciated Wilder's dedication. He found Harrison Ford much less willing to devote himself to the film. Ford, extremely popular from his role in *Star Wars*, was not Aldrich's choice for the part of Tommy Lillard, but Warner Brothers insisted, and Aldrich had to oblige.

Predictably, critics pounced upon this eccentric and off-beat film with a vengeance. Gary Arnold, describing the film as "westward hokum," decried the picture's heavy-handedness: "The finished film obliterates whatever promise of novelty and human interest existed in the basic idea of Belinski's culture shock. If the rabbi's odyssey was embryonically appealing, the filmmakers have nurtured it along with the sort of finesse one might expect from an elephant trying to hatch a robin's egg."[2] Vincent Canby also complained of the mismatch between director and material: "Asking Robert Aldrich to direct a sentimental Jewish comedy on the order of *The Frisco Kid* is like putting the late Gen. George S. Patton, Jr. in charge of a tap-dancing class for tiny tots. Not knowing exactly what to do, he doesn't seem to do very much at all. The result is harmless chaos."[3]

Although Canby is probably correct when he asserts that Aldrich was an inappropriate choice to direct such a comedy, the film is better than he judges. The pace is easy and controlled, the humor is often quite funny, and the themes are recognizably Aldrichian. *The Frisco Kid* is finally about personal integrity and the need, upon occasion, to compromise one's scruples within limits—to practice, in effect, a kind of situational ethics. As in so many Aldrich works, the film gives us two opposites who need each other to survive. Avram is a naif; Tommy is a rogue. Avram is religious; Tommy is skeptical. But this gentle film shows the rewards of friendship, the possibility of brotherhood. Neither Avram nor Tommy has to die. Their conflict can be resolved and turned into trust. Tommy Lillard is basically a good man who, despite his loud cynicism, takes pity on the innocent Avram. And Avram, who seems so incompetent in a new and foreign land, proves himself able to act with purpose when the situation demands it—to grow up, take responsibility, and behave courageously.

Avram Belinski does not abandon his principles, as his non-violent resistance to Matt Diggs near the film's end nicely illustrates. But earlier, when he kills Darryl Diggs to save Tommy Lillard, Belinski demonstrates an awareness of the need to compromise those principles should circumstances require it. And what better set of circumstances than those which place the life of one's friend in jeopardy? By thus acknowledging the prior, more urgent claims of friendship, Avram reveals the moral flexibility which makes him a variation of the changing Aldrich hero, comic, unwitting, and reluctant though he may be.

Although Aldrich did not have high hopes for this film before he started it, he was gradually won over by the picture. Its very sentimentality and good will were perhaps a necessary antidote to the bitterness and rancor and ugliness of *The Choirboys*. Thus, when the picture failed, Aldrich was doubly hurt. "I think he was very disappointed that the picture wasn't more successful," William Aldrich said. "He fell in love with his movies, you know, but he fell in love with that one more than others."

. . . *All the Marbles* (1981)

As Robert Aldrich approached what would be his last film, he knew he had lost much of the bargaining power which had enabled him to make so many of his best works. *The Frisco Kid* had come to him at least third hand, and he had done with it what he could. According to the rules of the game, he had to have a financially successful picture to regain a position of strength and independence. Thus, . . . *All the Marbles* was intended, in Aldrich's words, to be "an out-and-out commercial movie. No messages, just a comedy."[4] Given the list of failures he had experienced in the late 1970s, it is not surprising that he should have downplayed the significance of this film, and perhaps entertainment is all we should look for in it. But this reading seems all too easy. Aldrich, despite his disclaimers, too often proved himself an original who flouted conventions, who subverted genres. And, indeed, although this film *looked* like a curiously old-fashioned and conventional picture, there was something deceptive about it. For a comedy, it was surprisingly downbeat. For a film with "no messages," it telegraphed a number of serious ideas. It returned yet again to the Aldrich theme of compromise and integrity. And in a curious twist, it brought his career full circle, returning him to MGM and the world of professional sports such as he had explored in his first feature film, *The Big Leaguer*, twenty-seven years earlier. It looked back at his own work, and in that sense proved to be a very personal movie.

The personal nature of the film was evident from the start. The title *All the Marbles* had first been used on a project Aldrich tried to develop in 1974. At this time, the story was a soldier-of-fortune, double-cross, adventure film which Aldrich wanted to make with Lee Marvin, Burt Reynolds, George Kennedy, Alain Delon, and Woody Strode. Although this film never materialized, the title—with its meaning of going for broke—stayed with Aldrich, and he now applied it to Mel Frohman's screenplay of an entirely different subject. In a "Prologue" Aldrich wrote to the screenplay, he explained, in a question-and-answer format, what he saw in this script. "I do know more about this movie than one could glean from reading the script . . . no matter how carefully; no matter how many times," he wrote. What makes it special? he asked himself. His answer:

> I can't remember a picture that views the lives of three people, not particularly unusual people, but three people who, because of their own needs to survive, are basically selfish, uncaring, greedy and really impervious to the well-being of anyone other than themselves. . . . These three people learn through the most personal kind of defeat and despair that their happiness and emotional well-being are totally tied to the mutual success and well-being of two other people. . . . It has to do with the redemption of self-esteem, the rediscovery of one's self-respect.[5]

Aldrich was determined to emphasize the characters' selfishness throughout most of the film: ". . . the inherent sentimentality of the piece will not be allowed to catch up to the telling of the story until long after each one of the principals has concluded that it 'can't be made alone' . . . [that] without mutual trust and mutual regard, there is no road to the redemption of self-esteem."[6]

Dealing with the unusual subject of lady wrestlers, . . . *All the Marbles* stars Peter Falk as Harry Sears, the fast-talking, conniving manager of the California Dolls, two beautiful young women who travel the grunt-and-groan circuit looking for a shot at the North American Tag Team Championship. Iris (Vicki Frederick) is a dedicated professional: she takes pride in her skills, in working "without gimmicks." She is Harry's former lover, and although their romance has cooled, they still feel obvious affection for one another. Molly (Laurene Landon) is less confident of her abilities and depends on Iris's guidance. The demands of their life on the road are difficult to accept, and she dreams of a better future; but without even a high school education, she recognizes the futility of these dreams. Thus, she takes pills to escape, to cope, but that hackneyed and potentially melodramatic subplot is never explored, and by the final match she has resolved to "work without a net." The second potential complication—the suggestion that Molly is romantically attracted to Iris and feels left out of Iris and Harry's more intense relationship—is largely subsumed in the general sense of healthy camaraderie which exists among the three. "The three of us are a team," Iris says. "I love you, Moll. And so does the son-of-a-bitch. He'll never admit it, but he does."

Aldrich wisely played down these side issues of drugs and lesbianism (they were explored more fully in the script but omitted from the final cut) in order to concentrate on the central theme of the film, the idea of personal redemption. The first half of the film details the depressing mundaneness of their life on the road; the second half rescues them by means of a miracle championship match. This, then, would appear to be another variation on the classic come-from-behind story made so popular by the *Rocky* movies—and anticipated by Aldrich's own *The Longest Yard*. But, if so, this is an underdog story with a difference. Set in the world of wrestling, the film admits from the very beginning the basic falseness of its premise, for what other spectator sport is more obviously theater? Much of the sport's attraction comes from the audience's recognition of its Three Stooges' brand of violence, from the knowledge that all is pre-ordained, pre-scripted. Wrestlers are actors, with personae, make-up, and costume. How, then, are we to take such a subject seriously?

Indeed, Aldrich gives us every opportunity *not* to be suckered in by this tale. The bouts are clearly choreographed, the abuse stylized, the sound and action amplified to cartoon level. No one is ever really hurt, nor is there ever any real danger, despite the apparent viciousness of the fights. From a *sporting* point of view, we should have no emotional stake in the contests. Moreover, there is little apparent moral justification for the Dolls to win. In other such films, we have reason to pull for the underdogs because of their integrity or pride, but these were the virtues Aldrich wanted to downplay through most of the film. Harry is willing to lie, cheat, scheme, and steal to get to the top. He *wants* gimmicks. "There are only so many brass rings," he warns, emphasizing that integrity should have its limits. "You should have fought dirty," he tells them after they lose an important fight. And although Iris and Molly at first insist on maintaining their "dignity," refuse to become "sideshow freaks," they are also finally willing to do what they must to get ahead. Thus, while they refuse to tattoo themselves or dye their body hair, as Harry suggests, Iris does agree to sleep with the repulsive Eddie Cisco (Burt Young), albeit without Harry's knowledge, because he can get them in the championship match. When he tries for a second time, however, Iris coldly replies, "We both know why we're here. You got what you wanted and I got what I wanted." Then she pushes him aside. Despite all of the girls' vocal abhorrence of gimmicks, their championship match is nothing but one vast public relations display, the epitome of tinsel glamour. In its own sneaky way, . . . *All the Marbles* becomes a parody of all the other come-from-behind, spiritually-invigorating films which feed our national mythos. Once again, Aldrich undermines the very genre he seems to employ, at least to a degree.

Furthermore it is clear that Aldrich's main interest in the film is not the *sport* of wrestling—we learn nothing about holds, tactics, rankings— but the show business which surrounds it. In this sense, . . . *All the Marbles* fits neatly into the category of his "Hollywood" films. We are encouraged to see Harry and his Dolls as entertainers. Harry constantly plays a tape of *Pagliacci* and identifies with the weeping clown. He tells the Dolls that Pagliacci is a "strolling player. He goes from town to town entertaining people, even though his heart is breaking. That's why you've got to keep going, keep trying." By the time of the championship match, however, Harry has turned the Dolls from mere wandering vaudevillians into a sure enough *Act*, with costumes straight from the latest Vegas floor show, a theme song ("Oh, You Beautiful Doll"), and a publicity barrage suitable for the Super Bowl (even "Mean" Joe Green makes an appearance). Harry orchestrates their arrival at the arena, organizes the audience to sing, to chant, to boo or cheer. He bribes the organist and light operator to dramatize their entrance when they, dressed in pure white, are carried in by seven large muscular men costumed in Eastern garb. It is hype at its best and worst, and it all takes place at MGM's flashy

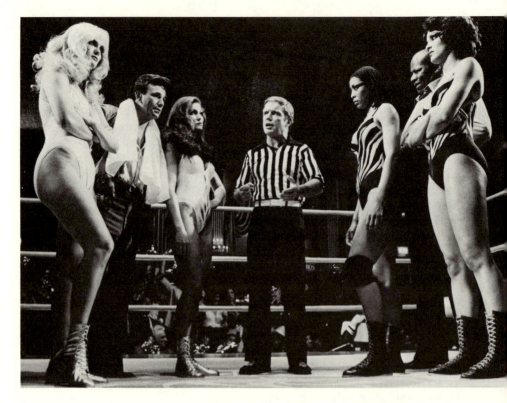

The championship match between the California Dolls and the Toledo Tigers in . . . *All the Marbles*. Used by permission of the Museum of Modern Art/Film Stills Archive, courtesy of United Artists.

Grand Hotel in Reno. Although the Grand represents the big time to Harry, Aldrich shows us that this monument to man's greed, tastelessness, and gullibility is also an extension of the corruption that has surrounded Harry from the beginning. The sleazy Cisco continues to call the shots. Once the match begins, there is no discernible difference between the Grand's luxurious setting and the crummy arenas in which the girls have been fighting. It's all dirty and cheap. Since Aldrich made this film at MGM, this choice of location was probably conceived by the studio as an easy bit of self-promotion; but what Aldrich does to it is an act of audacity comparable to his having filmed *The Big Knife*, with its partially Cohn-inspired villain, under Harry Cohn's own nose.

Although the film makes us aware of Harry Sears' many shortcomings and limitations, it seems probable that Sears acted, in part, as a kind of surrogate for Aldrich, for they shared many of the same characteristics. Both were skilled promoters, but both wanted to maintain their independence. When Eddie Cisco offers Harry a job within his organization, Sears insults him and is virtually blacklisted for a time, much as was Aldrich. Harry's references to Clifford Odets (Harry's immigrant father supposedly learned English by reading Odets, Will Rogers, and the *New York Times*) recall Aldrich's own relationship with the dramatist and, as well, his early association with the idealistic projects at Enterprise Studios in the late 1940s, when he worked with Robert Rossen and Abraham Polonsky on such films as *Body and Soul* and *Force of Evil*. (Indeed, as with *The Longest Yard* and other films, Aldrich claimed that for . . . *All the Marbles* "we stole the whole psychological drive and ending" from *Body and Soul*.)[7] But . . . *All the Marbles* indicates that these days of idealism are long past. In lines Aldrich himself inserted, the Dolls admit to never having heard of Rogers and Odets. "They're a dance team," Harry says in disgust. "They worked the Catskills." The rules have changed, and Harry is willing to play dirty if necessary to stay in the game. You simply don't make it on talent alone any more, the film seems to say; and since the audience demands the gimmick, the special effect, the promotion, then you give it to them in spades. But you don't always have to like it.

"The customers don't give a damn," Eddie Cisco tells Harry after the film's first match. "All they want is tits and ass." The film maintains this belligerent attitude toward the spectators throughout. Out-of-work steelworkers or Vegas highrollers, they are interchangeable once the bout begins, shouting for the faked violence, demanding to be fooled. Nowhere do they show sympathy or humanity. This contempt for the audience is most clearly seen when Aldrich finally *does* show us the tits and ass we have, after all, been waiting for. Harry is offered $500 if the girls will take part in a mud wrestling contest at a third-rate Kiwanis Club carnival, held somewhere in conservative middle-America. The girls object, but Harry convinces them that no one in the "real" business need know, that the money is double their going rate, and that they can use the larger fee as a base in future negotiations. During the match, it becomes impossible to tell which beslimed girl is which. Although breasts are bared, the scene is not erotic because of the Dolls' sense of shame and abasement, and because of the pure hatred they have for the audience. Even as the scene changes and the girls are once again washed clean, the shouts and cries of the crowd continue to echo nightmarishly on the soundtrack. "You did this to me," Iris yells at Harry. "You turned me into a freak. They laughed at me. I can take anything, but they laughed at me." Since most of the theater audience has been laughing right along with the boors at the fair, the accusation is aimed at us as well as them.

But perhaps the best expression of Aldrich's attitude is the fact that, despite all the sham and compromise and unsavoriness, he is still able to manipulate us even while revealing to us the mechanics of his manipulation. What Harry does to the championship crowd, Aldrich does to the theater audience. Aldrich makes it both a Christmas match and a winner-take-all. "We're fighting for the title," Harry tells the Dolls. "We're fighting for our lives." The ringside announcer blatantly tells us what to think, directs our emotional shifts during the fight. The sequence is expertly paced, moving from crisis to crisis in the ring, from certain defeat to sudden and joyous victory. Although there is never any question who will win, we are exhilarated by the outcome. But then Aldrich does a strange thing. In the middle of the celebration, he cuts to the just-defeated champions, the Toledo Tigers, whose manager tells them that in three months *they* will be back on top. This dialogue is not in the script, and it should effectively undercut our sense of celebration. Nobody wins for long in this game.

The picture Aldrich actually made was not exactly the one he had initially envisioned. Peter Falk was not his choice for Harry Sears, and Aldrich found him uncooperative. Falk was basically uncomfortable with the unsympathetic characterization of Sears. He wanted Sears to be a "nicer" man from the beginning, while Aldrich wanted to hold off this transformation until the end and even then to mute it as much as possible. This conflict caused difficulties on the set and delays in filming. Falk was being paid $1 million for his role. At one point Aldrich, in disgust at what he considered Falk's unprofessional manner, totalled up the time Falk had kept them waiting at two hours and twenty-two minutes and played with the idea of billing him for $6,250 before he was dissuaded.

The film was also not as comic as Aldrich had first planned. When they went to Ohio for location shooting, Aldrich was shocked at what he saw and tried to reflect it in the film. "It was not a sophisticated movie," William Aldrich, its producer, explained, "but it was what this country was going through at the time. The recession was terrible, inflation was terrible, people were out of work. It was miserable back there in Youngstown. It was devastating, all the factories shut down. And that's why he kept changing little bits of the story, and that's why all that car stuff is in there, to show, 'This is a rough world out here, where people are trying to struggle their way through.' " Aldrich told Frank DeVol to score the film with an old-fashioned sound. He wanted the music to trigger off echoes of the Depression era, to indicate in this way as well as visually that the country was in serious trouble.

The film received some exceptionally good reviews—Andrew Sarris, for example, called it the director's "most enjoyable entertainment since *Ulzana's Raid*" and praised its warmth,[8] while Vincent Canby exulted that "you should have a ball with this slam-bang, wisecracking, fanciful comedy"[9]—but most critics dismissed . . . *All the Marbles* as a crudely-made film on an unpleasant subject. MGM tried to sell it as a comedy, while Aldrich wanted to aim the advertising at the "six-pack" crowd, the average guy who might be out of work and who needed some hope. He told Charles Durning that he had advised MGM to release it after the World Series, for then the national mood would be more in synch with the film. MGM did not listen, and the film was not a success. Aldrich agonized over its failure for months, reviewing it, rethinking it. It had been, to him, a heartfelt and ultimately positive film. If he tempered its warmth with a dose of irony and cynicism, it was still a testament to his sense of humanity, although one buffeted by the realities and cruelties of a hard world.

The Unmade Films

The failure of . . . *All the Marbles* sealed Aldrich's fate in Hollywood. There had been talk that Paramount was considering him for head of the studio, but nothing came of the idea. He was unable to get new films started. As Alvin Greenman saw it, "He was very concerned about his loss of power, and it was wearing him down." Charles Durning felt that Aldrich "was more hurt than bitter. But he realized that his term in Hollywood was drawing to a close." Still, he had numerous projects in different stages of development. Among them were three scripts written by Lukas Heller: *Stand On It*, the project which had caused the break with Burt Reynolds; *Seven Day Soldiers*, a story of a group of men who tap into the Swiss bank accounts of a Batista-like dictator; and *Twin*, a murder mystery which Heller described as "a very good thing that unfortunately never got made because nobody would touch Aldrich." Of the three, *Twin* probably came closest to being filmed. Peter O'Toole visited the set of . . . *All the Marbles* to discuss the lead with Aldrich, and Cheryl Ladd was considered for the co-star. Other projects in development were *Dial Tone*, an original mystery written by Keats Leigh; *Man on Fire,* based on the novel by A.J. Quinnell; *The Sheltering Sky,* Paul Bowles's novel of Africa which Aldrich had owned for over twenty years; and *Noble House,* James Clavell's novel of the Orient.

And there were other projects which were even closer to Aldrich at this time. *For Export Only* was a screenplay which Aldrich himself wrote after . . . *All the Marbles.* Basically a comedy, it tells of nine men, all minor criminals, who are arrested and deported to Naples, Italy, since none of them are naturalized citizens. The story line is similar to *The Dirty Dozen* in that, as part of their sentence, they are forced to live together, work together, and depend on each other in order to fulfil their debts to justice. If they break no laws during these ten years, then they may be readmitted to the United States and apply for citizenship. But if any one of them does break a law or the conditions of the punishment, then *all* will serve twenty years at hard labor in Italian prisons. The screenplay details their attempts to survive in Italy, where they are innocents in comparison with the truly corrupt gangsters (including Lucky Luciano) and slippery characters they come in contact with. There would again be a largely all-male cast, with Anthony Quinn, Charles Bronson, Tony Danza, Abe Vigoda, Burt Young, James Coco, and others envisioned in the lead roles.

The plot probably developed from an early script entitled *Vengeance is Mine* that Aldrich co-wrote with A.I. Bezzerides in 1963. The story dealt with a deported gangster in Italy during World War II. Yet another version of the same idea could be found in a screenplay entitled *Charlie Casbah,* which Aldrich had written in the early 1970s. A parody of *Casablanca,* *Charlie Casbah* again told of a minor gangster, Beshara Bezzerides (a nod to his co-writer on *Vengeance is Mine*), who is deported to Algeria just before the outbreak of World War II. There he becomes known as "Charlie Casbah," a comic version of Bogart's Rick. Charlie's line is "Here's seeing through you, Kid," which appropriately reflects his surface cynicism, but he also helps needy Americans passing through, and he ends up fighting against the Nazis. *Charlie Casbah* is a bizarre work, obviously modeled on the Mel Brooks-type of humor, and Aldrich thought of actors like Jerry Lacy, Madelyn Kahn, Arte Johnson, Tim Conway, and Charo to act in it. It ended in a fantastic dream sequence inspired, one imagines, by the absurd ending of *Blazing Saddles,* although Aldrich described it as "Bunuelish" in the screenplay.[10] There was also a strong vein of political satire running through the story. One character is a "Monsieur Richard," to be played by David Frye as a French Richard

Nixon, who is given a chance to reconstruct himself by working for the French underground and bugging Nazi bathrooms.

For all their vulgarity and coarse humor, both *Charlie Casbah* and *For Export Only* apparently grew out of Aldrich's feelings concerning the House Un-American Activities Committee in the early 1950s. "You gotta understand," Charlie cries at his deportation hearing, "this is my country, too."[11] And Ernest Pastore, the leader of the nine men in *For Export Only*, declares, "We're 100% American."[12] There is, in fact, in both screenplays a strong patriotic message. Charlie Casbah says, "There is only one advantage to being an exile, and that is you have a better perspective on just how much your own country really means to you."[13] *Charlie Casbah* ends with Billy Preston's bluesy version of "My Country 'Tis of Thee," which, Charlie says, is "a song you have all heard a hundred times. But the *way* he sings it is brand new . . . perhaps you will understand how I feel about my country and how I suspect you feel about your country."[14] Aldrich did, of course, later use this version of the song in *Twilight's Last Gleaming*, in which it very effectively counterpoints the treachery and despair which mark that film.

Of Aldrich's unmade films, the most important to him was undoubtedly *Kinderspiel*. He had first considered making it in 1955, the same year he made his first statement on the insanity of nuclear war in *Kiss Me Deadly*, and he came close to filming it a number of times. "If you talked to him any time when he was working on that, that's all he would talk about," William Aldrich recalled. "That was the story that he really wanted to tell more than any other. He was very frightened that we were going to blow ourselves up, and what could he do to prevent that? 'Make this movie—that's all I can do.' "

In *Kinderspiel*, the children of all nations band together in some mysterious way and leave their homes and parents to form a kind of children's crusade. The various governments declare states of emergency, and some use force to make the children return. But the children are willing to die, for they see no future as things stand under the threat of nuclear war. Because the adults of the world act like children, the children take on the role of adults. In Aldrich's description, they "start out gently but adamantly refusing to accept the authority of their parents, and then eventually of 'authority' itself. . . ."[15] When Aldrich last worked on the project, he had seen Steven Spielberg's *E.T.*, a film he dearly loved, and he clearly wanted a kind of childlike magic in this film as well. He saw *Kinderspiel* as a "wonderfully exciting and affirmative screenplay that deals convincingly with [nuclear war], not in the doom-laden manner that has heretofore been the hallmark of such stories, but in a positive, dramatic, and humorous way that will, above all, be deeply moving and leave an audience feeling that it has experienced an exciting and truly life-enhancing two hours in the theatre."[16] Whether Aldrich could have achieved such a response is debatable. As Lukas Heller, who wrote a treatment of the subject, said, "I don't know if his particular sensibilities would in fact have made it a great movie or not, but it was a massive subject . . . and he got fairly close with it with a number of people."

On His Own Terms

Aldrich was unwell during the summer of 1983. In August, he entered the hospital in Los Angeles to have his gall bladder removed. It was considered a simple procedure with few risks. After he returned home, however, he failed to recover as expected. Alvin Greenman visited him in his home. "Now they think that maybe it's my spleen," Aldrich told him. After some debate with his family, Aldrich agreed to reenter the hospital to have the spleen excised. Again, everyone felt that it was a common operation and no cause for alarm. Nevertheless, few people in Hollywood actually knew that Aldrich was ill. He feared that any rumors of incapacity would simply compound the problems he was having in the business. He was less likely than ever to be offered jobs if there were any doubt of his physical ability to fulfill his obligations.

The serious health problems began after the second operation. His kidneys went into shock and stopped functioning. Even then his doctors were not overly concerned. They explained to the family that such an occurrence was common and that the kidneys should "kick back in" after several days. During that time he was placed on a dialysis machine to clean his blood of the impurities the kidneys could not handle. But the kidneys did not reactivate themselves, and soon Aldrich began to experience problems with his liver as well. Finally his doctors told him that his kidneys had failed and that he would be dependent on the dialysis machine for the rest of his life. At first a machine was placed in his home, but such an arrangement proved inadequate. Then Aldrich tried to alternate three days at home with trips to the UCLA Dialysis Center. He told Alvin Greenman, "You don't know what these machines are like. They are terrible, just terrible." During the Fall of 1983, he was in and out of the hospital many times, and finally he had had enough. As Greenman recalled, "Ultimately what he said was, 'If I can't make movies and I can't do anything constructive with my life, if my life is now reduced to going three days a week to a dialysis center, then that's not living for me. I choose to die on my own terms.' He said, 'Take me off and let me go home.' Once he realized that he was not going to get better, that was it."

It was entirely in keeping with Aldrich's philosophy that he should choose to die "on his own terms," with his family, rather than depend on a machine to keep him alive. Once he refused further treatment, however, he was faced with another problem. Before the hospital would allow him to leave, he had to prove that he was capable of making his own decision on the matter. A meeting was arranged in his hospital room. Gathered there would be members of the family, his attorney, his doctors and a psychiatrist. William Aldrich came to his father before the meeting. "I said, 'This is going to happen this afternoon. You've been asking to get out of this place. Now all you have to do is say yes, you want to go home. That's *all* you have to do. Don't argue with anybody; don't fight with anybody; don't *say* anything else. OK?' He said, 'OK.' I said, 'Really, Dad, *don't*, because they're going to have shrinks here and doctors here and the head of the department—don't fuck around with these guys. Let's just go home.'"

Aldrich agreed to cooperate with the doctors. That afternoon the group gathered in his room. At first Aldrich was controlled and answered their questions calmly. But when the psychiatrist asked him, "Do you know *why* you want to go home?" Aldrich exploded. "I don't want to talk to you," he shouted. "I didn't ask you to come see me!" He turned to his doctors. "You," he pointed, "you're killing me, and you're taking me away from my family, and I want you to pay for this!" He tried to get out of bed, but he was too weak, and for a time he slipped between rationality and tremendous anger. William Aldrich remembered:

> He was *so* angry and *so* mad, and he just would not shut up. All he wanted to do was go home, but he was center stage again. And there was nothing you could do. You just sat there and sort of cried. But you also said, "This is the last hurrah; this is the last battle, and he's going to have it. You can't deny him that. He's going to have *a fight* before he dies, and this is it. This is the enemy—the distributors, the executives at the studios: this is Authority."

Aldrich fired his doctors, checked out of the hospital, and went home to die. During the five days before his death, he asked to see certain people in order to say good-bye to them. Abraham Polonsky visited him three times. At the end of the second visit, Aldrich, who had been alert and at peace, smiled at him and said, "Remember me this way." At the third meeting, on the day before he died, he was drifting in and out of consciousness—"in and out of the flutter of knowing who you are," in Polonsky's words—but just before his old friend left, Aldrich focused on him for one last time, pleased to see him in the room.[17] Burt Lancaster also came to the Aldrich house. Although Aldrich was only partly coherent, Lancaster stayed with him for an hour and a half. "He didn't discuss his problems," Lancaster recalled, "but you knew that Bob didn't want to stick around any longer, that he wanted to go. It was as if he had had enough." Among the other people Aldrich saw were Alvin Greenman, Michael Luciano, Lukas Heller, and Burt Young. When Heller saw him, Aldrich's mind was still on his films. "Jesus," he told Heller, "*Kinderspiel* would have made a great movie." As Heller left, Aldrich stopped him. "You can help Abe Polonsky write my obituary," he said. "I'll be happy to do that," Heller answered, "but it's going to be a while before that happens." "Oh, do you think so?" Aldrich quietly replied.

During these last days, Aldrich also placed calls to friends who were not in Los Angeles. He tried unsuccessfully to call Lee Marvin, who was on location and knew nothing of his illness. He did talk with Charles Durning, who was filming with Burt Reynolds in Florida on Reynolds' film *Stick*. He also called Elia Kazan, who was receiving the Life Achievement Award at the Kennedy Center in Washington, D.C. They had sometimes been on opposite sides of political questions, but Aldrich was reaching out as a final gesture of friendship.

Before he died, Aldrich described the kind of service he wanted. There should be no open casket or public funeral as such. He did want the Directors Guild to hold a memorial service, however, and "If people want to say a few words about me, that's terrific," he said. "Then I want you to invite people back to the house and have lots of good things to eat and music and lots to drink." He was a director to the end, in charge of it all.

In the early morning of December 5, 1983, he died, at home, with his family.

Epilogue

Two days following Aldrich's death, the Directors Guild of America held a memorial service for its former leader at the DGA Theater in Los Angeles. The service was led by Robert Wise, Aldrich's old friend from RKO Studios and also a past president of the Guild. The eulogy was delivered by Abraham Polonsky, who recalled his forty-year association and friendship with Aldrich. In words of great feeling he captured the essence of Aldrich's life:

> He didn't divide the world up into Good and Evil. He didn't see it that simply. He found himself as someone who knew that his idea of himself was why he existed, and that his self-esteem and respect for himself could never be jeopardized—and he could never jeopardize it—by any compromise that involved that deep portion of his nature. . . . In the deeper part of human life, one just doesn't want to get things done. One wants to live as things *should be* done. And I think he lived that way.

Polonsky movingly described his last visits with Aldrich and concluded, "I, like Bob, believe that almost anything in life is bearable in one way or another, but some of the things that are bearable are *un*-bearable, and his death to me is that."[1]

Following Polonsky was director Franklin Schaffner, who spoke of Aldrich's accomplishments as a filmmaker and as a leader of the Guild. Gilbert Cates, then the president of the Guild, and Jud Taylor, the recent past-president, also spoke. "In a business that has its share of duplicity," Taylor said, "Bob always tried, in his own way, to speak the truth as he saw it. No man can do more."[2]

At this point in the service, according to Aldrich's wishes, the floor was open to anyone in the audience who might want to remember the man, and slowly, from varied voices, a composite picture of Aldrich began to appear. Among the speakers were A.I. Bezzerides, his co-writer on *Kiss Me Deadly, The Angry Hills*, and other projects; Louis Champ, a black electrician whom Aldrich put in charge of the electrical department at the Aldrich Studios, the first black to hold such a position in the Hollywood studios; Frank DeVol, who had scored sixteen of Aldrich's films; Harry Caesar, a character actor who claimed Aldrich had saved him from the penitentiary by giving him roles in *Emperor of the North* and *The Longest Yard*; a stunt man who had been touched to see Aldrich pay his respects at the funeral of another stunt man and had concluded, "There's a man who cares, who takes the time for the little people in the business"; producer Howard Koch, who had worked with Aldrich on *4 For Texas* and recalled Aldrich's battles with Frank Sinatra; Aldrich's transportation captain, who had been with him from near the beginning; Michael Luciano, Aldrich's favorite editor; and an anonymous boom man, who claimed to have been fired and rehired by Aldrich more than any other man in the business.

The thoughts that held all these memories together were centered on Aldrich's loyalty, his courage, and his honesty. He was clearly one of the last of his breed, a man who lived and worked on a grand scale. Both his successes and his failures were colossal. He inspired great affection and admiration among many, but he also inspired great anger as well. "He had an enormous presence," his secretary Joan Bennett recalled. "Whether you were agreeing or disagreeing with him, you always knew he was there." His concern for the "little people" in Hollywood was legendary. "The actors have their agents," he would say. "The crew has nobody but me." He felt responsible for the people who worked for him, and he quietly, behind the scene, helped an untold number of them. Perhaps in one respect he needed others to depend on him, to give him a sense of belonging that he may have missed as a child. "He asked only for loyalty," Alvin Greenman said, "but he was unforgiving if you weren't loyal." Nevertheless, he also felt a very real obligation to make life a little better for those who would have otherwise found the world a colder place. "It all falls on my shoulders," he liked to say.

Aldrich's public reputation, one he encouraged, was that of the tough, hard-boiled variety. He talked rough; he yelled; he got in fist fights and shoving matches; he stood toe-to-toe with anyone. "If he started to get angry, he just *got* angry and he blew," William Aldrich recalled. "He was a big man, a powerful man. You knew he was going to come across the table at you. And you had better know that. He just didn't care who it was." Aggression was an important part of Aldrich's style. As his daughter Adell noted, her father had a strong sense of masculine pride and judged others from that standpoint. He felt more comfortable in an all-male situation. In men, he appreciated physical courage *and* courage of conviction, whatever that conviction was. Thus, he greatly liked Lee Marvin, although their political beliefs rarely coincided. He enjoyed the challenge of working with tough men, men like Burt Lancaster, Jack

Palance, Burt Reynolds, Jim Brown, Richard Jaeckel, Robert Mitchum, and Lee Marvin. He wanted the dangerous edge. In women, he appreciated intelligence. "We fought about this all the time," Adell remembered. "He was very compassionate to women he respected and liked. If the woman had a brain, if she knew what she wanted, that was o.k. But the poor little things that weren't so bright, well, he didn't have much use for them." Thus, he admired and enjoyed working with a smart, dedicated actress like Bette Davis, but he often had trouble with women he considered weak or precious, and he rarely got their best work from them. "I don't think he was doing anything intentionally," William Aldrich said. "It was just his limited knowledge of women."

In general, however, he respected his actors if they behaved in a professional manner. "He gave them everything they wanted, but ultimately they had to understand that his word was the final one," Alvin Greenman said. Aldrich had a ritual which illustrated his position, as Greenman described. "He would give his actors two weeks of rehearsals to work through every nuance of character, to make themselves at ease with each line. Then, on the last day of rehearsals, he would place a dime at each actor's place at the rehearsal table. 'If we are not in agreement now, if we don't understand how each other works now,' he would say, 'the dime there is for you to call your agents and get off the picture.' " He would tell his writers, "If you want to write what you want to write, then you should become a novelist or a poet. You know who you work for." In the editing room he would listen to Luciano's suggestions, but "the vote in here is always one to nothing," he would say.

Given his desire for a close-knit group, it is not surprising that he employed his own children in his films. His daughter Adell worked as script supervisor on a number of his films before becoming a director on her own. His son William had bit roles in *What Ever Happened to Baby Jane?* and *The Flight of the Phoenix* and then took on the responsible jobs of manager of the Aldrich Studios and producer of . . . *All the Marbles*. His younger son Kelly also worked at various jobs on the set before becoming a transportation captain in the film business. "He was really tough to work with," William Aldrich said. "If anybody was around, he was really tough. It was just going to be harder for any of his kids or people who were social friends of his to work for him. He didn't want anybody to *ever* say there was favoritism here, or nepotism. Of course, there *was* nepotism, but you *earned* it." Adell Aldrich remembered her first job as script supervisor on *Baby Jane*. "I was really trained. Bette Davis and Joan Crawford were horrendous to me, but they had been told to do that. At that time, when you're eighteen or nineteen or twenty years old and go home crying . . . well, it was hard. And if you were late, there'd be a Mickey Mouse alarm clock there the next morning for you to turn off so you'd be there in time for your call. It was great training, but it was tough to understand when it was professional and when it was personal." For Aldrich, life was a challenge, and everyone—especially his children—had to be disciplined enough to face it. "It was not easy," Kelly Aldrich recalled. "He just knew everything about the business. There were no corners you could hide behind. There was no toleration for mistakes."[3] When others did their jobs, he was ready to give credit and appreciation. As Joan Bennett put it, "You were determined to do the best job possible for Mr. Aldrich. A simple thank-you from him was worth eight paragraphs from anybody else." But Alida Aldrich, the only one of his four children not to enter the motion picture business, felt that his children "could not fulfill his expectations. The accolades and pride of a parent were not forthcoming."[4]

The reverse side of Aldrich's toughness was his strong vein of sentimentality. "He was overly sentimental to a fault," Alvin Greenman said. "He could become teary at nothing at all. You could really get to him if you knew how." The extreme masculinity and cynicism of many of his films can, in part, be seen as a defense against this aspect of his personality. Violence and coarseness were acceptable conduits for these more confusing emotions. Both *The Frisco Kid* and . . . *All the Marbles* showed a mellowing in his subject matter; both expressed a real warmth and tenderness for the main characters. For his memorial service, he requested that two of the songs to be played be "I've Written a Letter to Daddy" from *What Ever Happened to Baby Jane?* and the title song to *Hush . . . Hush, Sweet Charlotte*, in both cases a mixture of the beautiful and the banal, the weird and the wonderful.

It is difficult to judge Aldrich's eventual position among the leading Hollywood directors. Michael Luciano, and others, still feel that Aldrich was never honestly appreciated by the film industry, that his talent was never acknowledged because of his unpopular stands. And Aldrich even today evokes strong reactions from both his supporters and detractors. He made his share of bad movies, as he well knew, but he also made movies which exploded genres and challenged viewers. He could sometimes joke about his films and the readings they received. While making *The Frisco Kid*, for example, he was trying to get in a final series of shots before a storm broke. "You know something," he told Alvin

Greenman. "The French critics are going to go on and on about this shot—the hidden signficance of why we made it with the dark clouds coming in. We know we've got to get it before it starts to pour and get back to the hotel. But just wait and see." On the other hand, if there is such a thing as an *auteur*, Aldrich was surely it. "One thing I can honestly say is that there's not a picture that he made, that he worked on as a director, where his stamp is not on it," William Aldrich has said.

Robert Aldrich never won a major American film award, was never even nominated for an Academy Award as best director. He took his independent stance and he paid for it, as he fully expected to do. He understood the nature and the cost of rebellion. At the present time, his reputation still seems to rest on *Kiss Me Deadly, The Big Knife, Attack!, What Ever Happened to Baby Jane?, The Dirty Dozen,* and *The Longest Yard*. A re-evaluation of such major but under-appreciated films as *The Flight of the Phoenix, Ulzana's Raid, The Grissom Gang, Hustle,* and *Twilight's Last Gleaming* is surely due.

People tap me on the shoulder all the time and ask, 'Are you Bob Aldrich's kid?' " Kelly Aldrich said. " 'He was a good person to work for,' they say. 'He gave people a lot of breaks. He was one of those guys that you liked to be around.' " When asked, however, about Aldrich's present reputation in Hollywood, Burt Lancaster made a candid but perceptive assessment. "Everybody is forgotten sooner or later," he said. "Unless we can be commercialized like Elvis or Marilyn, we will all be forgotten, and I think Bob will be forgotten, too. And that's the way it should be. We must not look for immortality. But the films are something else. I would like to think that, in the future, people will look at these films we did and be moved by them. *That's* the memory we should hope for."

It is a judgment with which Aldrich would surely have agreed.

Notes

Chapter One

1. Charles Higham and Joel Greenberg, "Robert Aldrich" in *The Celluloid Muse: Hollywood Directors Speak* (London: Angus and Robertson, 1969), 22.

2. See Nathaniel Wright Stephenson, *Nelson W. Aldrich: A Leader in American Politics* (New York: Scribner's 1930; rpt. Port Washington: Kennikat Press, 1971), 6–7. Also see Peter Collier and David Horowitz, *The Rockefellers: An American Dynasty* (New York: Holt, Rinehart and Winston, 1976), 92–93.

3. See Stephenson for a thorough discussion of Nelson Aldrich's career.

4. Edward Aldrich's life is summarized in his obituary in the *New York Times*, 26 Oct. 1957, p. 21.

5. See the *New York Times*, 13 Aug. 1960, p. 15; 5 June 1966, p. 86; 26 Dec. 1941, p. 13; and 26 Feb. 1974, p. 40.

6. Lucy T. Aldrich, "A Week-End with Chinese Bandits," *The Atlantic Monthly*, Nov. 1923, pp. 672–86.

7. See Mary Ellen Chase, *Abby Aldrich Rockefeller* (New York: Macmillan, 1950) for an account of Abby Rockefeller's life.

8. William and Adell Aldrich interview with authors, 24 May 1984. All subsequent remarks by William or Adell Aldrich are taken from this interview.

9. Letter dated 28 Sept. 1977. A copy of the letter was included in the Aldrich papers as part of a proposal to make a film entitled *Rebellion*, which Apstein would write.

10. *Who's Who in America* 1982–1983, 42nd ed. (Chicago: Marquis Who's Who, 1982), I, 37.

11. Taken from unpublished notes dictated by Aldrich in 1978 for biographical press release, p. 2 of seven-page typescript. Hereafter referred to as Aldrich "Notes."

12. Pierre Sauvage, "Aldrich Interview," *Movie*, no. 23 (Winter 1976–77), 56.

13. Higham and Greenberg, 22.

14. Aldrich took with him a wife, Harriet Foster, whom he had known since childhood in Rhode Island. They would be married from 1941 to 1965. In 1966 Aldrich married Sibylle Siegfried.

15. See Betty Lasky, *RKO: The Biggest Little Major of Them All* (New York: Prentice-Hall, 1984).

16. Higham and Greenberg, 22.

17. James Powers, "Dialogue on Film: Robert Aldrich," *American Film*, IV (Nov. 1978), 60.

18. Aldrich "Notes," 4.

19. Powers, 57.

20. Robert Aldrich, "The High Price of Independence," *Films and Filming*, IV (June 1958), 35.

21. Sauvage, "Aldrich Interview," 56.

22. Ibid.

23. Francois Truffaut, "Rencontre Avec Robert Aldrich," *Cahiers du Cinema*, no. 64 (Nov. 1956), 3.

24. Unpublished transcript of the American Film Institute Seminar with Robert Aldrich held 2 Nov. 1971 at the Center for Advanced Film Studies, Beverly Hills, Calif., p. 26.

25. AFI Seminar, 2 Nov. 1971, p. 27.

26. Taken from speech delivered by Aldrich at the DGA tribute to Lewis Milestone, Aug. 1979.

27. Sauvage, "Aldrich Interview," 56.

28. Allen Eyles, "Films of Enterprise," *Focus on Film*, XXXV (April 1980), 13. Much of the following discussion is based on Eyles' article.

29. Higham and Greenberg, 23.

30. Eyles, 25.

31. Higham and Greenberg, 22.

32. Lukas Heller interview with authors, 25 May 1984. All subsequent remarks by Lukas Heller taken from this interview.

33. Higham and Greenberg, 23.

34. Eyles, 23.

35. Taken from Polonsky's eulogy for Aldrich, delivered at the DGA Memorial Service for Aldrich, 7 Dec. 1983.

36. Higham and Greenberg, 24–25.

37. Ibid.

38. For a discussion of Rossen's role in the HUAC hearings, see Victor S. Navasky, *Naming Names* (New York: Viking Press, 1980), 302–304.

39. Quoted in ibid., xix.

40. Letter from Robert Aldrich to authors, 22 Sept. 1982.

41. Alain Silver, "Mr. *Film Noir* Stays at the Table," *Film Comment*, VIII (Spring 1972), 19.

42. Aldrich "Notes," 2.

43. Robert Aldrich, "TV Techniques in Feature Making," *Studio Review*, no. 2739 (31 March 1960), 3.

44. Ibid.

45. We are indebted to Howard H. Prouty of the Meyer Library, AFI, Los Angeles, Calif., for sharing his findings on Aldrich's work in early television. The episodes of *Four Star Playhouse* directed by Aldrich were "The Squeeze" (1 Oct. 1953; repeated 1 June 1954; also repeated on NBC's *The Best in Mystery* series, 20 June 1956); "The Witness" (22 Oct. 1953; repeated 22 June 1954); "The

Hard Way" (19 Nov. 1953; repeated in *The Best of Mystery*, 13 June 1956 and 31 Aug. 1956); "The Gift" (24 Dec. 1953; repeated 22 Dec. 1955); and "The Bad Streak" (14 Jan. 1954; repeated 2 Sept. 1954). "The Squeeze" and "The Hard Way" were written by Blake Edwards.

46. Sauvage, "Aldrich Interview," 56.

47. Powers, 52.

48. Silver, 15–16.

49. Richard Jaeckel interview with authors, 18 Aug. 1984. All subsequent remarks by Richard Jaeckel taken from this interview.

50. Unedited transcript of AFI Seminar with Robert Aldrich, 26 April 1978, held at the Center for Advanced Film Studies, Beverly Hills, Calif., p. 10. The edited version of this seminar appeared as the Powers interview in *American Film*.

51. Aldrich, "High Price," 7.

52. Sauvage, "Aldrich Interview," 57.

53. Higham and Greenberg, 26.

54. Sauvage, "Aldrich Interview," 57.

55. Higham and Greenberg, 26.

56. Aldrich, "High Price," 7.

57. See Philippe Demonsablon's review of *World For Ransom* in *Cahiers du Cinema*, no. 50 (Aug.–Sept. 1955), 49–50; and Roger Tailleur, "Avènement de Robert Aldrich," *Positif*, II (May 1956), 12–15. Francois Truffaut also expressed great admiration for the film. See Truffaut, "Rencontre Avec Robert Aldrich," 4.

58. Richard Combs, "Robert Aldrich (1953–1961)" in Combs, ed., *Robert Aldrich* (London: British Film Institute, 1978), 6.

59. Aldrich, "High Price," 7.

60. Ibid. Aldrich further discussed this scene with Truffaut in "Rencontre Avec Robert Aldrich," 4–5.

61. *New York Times*, 5 June 1954, p. 11.

62. Higham and Greenberg, 26. Also see James Morgan, "Hecht-Lancaster Productions," *Sight and Sound*, XXV (Summer 1955), 38–42, 55.

Chapter Two

1. Higham and Greenberg, 26.

2. Burt Lancaster interview with authors, 19 July 1984. All subsequent remarks by Burt Lancaster taken from this interview (unless otherwise noted).

3. André Bazin, *What is Cinema?*, trans. Hugh Gray, II (Berkeley: Univ. of California Press, 1971), 123.

4. For further discussion of the "pro-Indian" western, see Robert Larkins, "Hollywood and the Indian," *Focus on Film*, XV, no. 2 (March–April 1970), 44–53.

5. Higham and Greenberg, 26–27.

6. "Apache," *Time*, 9 Aug. 1954, p. 84.

7. Aldrich, "High Price," 7.

8. Tailleur, "Avènement de Robert Aldrich," 11–12.

9. Flora Lewis, "Cameras Capture 'Vera Cruz' in Cuernavaca," *New York Times*, 11 April 1954, II, p. 5.

10. Ian Cameron and Mark Shivas, "Interview with Robert Aldrich," *Movie*, no. 8 (April 1963), 9.

11. Andrew Sarris, *The American Cinema: Directors and Directions 1929–1968* (New York: Dutton, 1968), 84.

12. Combs in Combs, ed., *Robert Aldrich*, 13.

13. As Burt Lancaster recalled, "It was a film that had quite a number of people who went on to bigger things. Borgnine went on to get the part of *Marty*. We were impressed with his good humor and gave him the job." Lancaster interview.

14. Aldrich said, "I think Peckinpah is a fine director. I don't think he's as good as I am, but I think he's a sensational director . . . some of his . . . pictures, like the Mexican picture with the Borgnine/Holden stock company [*The Wild Bunch*], I liked. But I think we did it before, with *Vera Cruz*." Quoted in Harry Ringel, "Up to Date with Robert Aldrich," *Sight and Sound*, XLIII (Summer 1974), 169.

15. Francois Truffant, "Le Derby des Psaumes," *Cahiers du Cinema*, no. 48 (June 1955), 42–45.

16. Jean-Pierre Coursodon with Pierre Sauvage, *American Directors*, II (New York: McGraw-Hill, 1983), 3.

17. Truffaut, "Le Derby des Psaumes," 44.

18. Aldrich, "High Price," 7.

19. Tailleur, "Avènement de Robert Aldrich," 15.

20. For a fuller discussion of this aspect of the film, see Michael Wood, *America in the Movies* (New York: Dell, 1975), 85–86.

21. Higham and Greenberg, 27.

22. Ibid.

23. Aldrich interview in *Film Index*, May 1971. Quoted in Combs, ed., *Robert Aldrich*, 54.

24. Truffaut, "Rencontre Avec Robert Aldrich," 4.

25. Higham and Greenberg, 28.

26. Quoted in Murray Schumach, *The Face on the Cutting Room Floor* (New York: William Morris, 1964), 177.

27. John Calendo, "Robert Aldrich Says, 'Life is Worth Living,' " *Andy Warhol's Interview*, III (Aug. 1973), 30.

28. *New York Times*, 22 Dec. 1954, p. 22.

29. Aldrich quoted in "Sex and Violence 'Justified,' " *America: The National Catholic Weekly Review*, 5 March 1955, pp. 583–84.

30. Ibid., 584.

31. Higham and Greenberg, 27.

32. Michael Luciano interview with authors, 25 May 1984. All subsequent remarks by Michael Luciano taken from this interview.

33. The crucified position is repeated throughout the film, in a painting found in Christina's apartment, for instance, and in Hammer's own position when he is tied to a bed for torture.

34. Calendo, 30.

35. *The Complete Poems of Christina Rossetti: A Variorum Edition*, ed. R.W. Crump, I (Baton Rouge: Louisiana State Univ. Press, 1979), 37.

36. "That devilish box . . . an obvious atom bomb symbol—was mostly [Bezzerides'] idea," Aldrich said. Quoted in Higham and Greenberg, 27.

37. Several writers on the film maintain that Hammer and Velda escape from the exploding beach house. See, for example, the plot synopsis in Alain Silver and Elizabeth Ward, *Robert Aldrich: A Guide to References and Resources* (Boston: G.K. Hall, 1979), 22–23; and Francois Truffaut's section on *Kiss Me Deadly* in *The Films in My Life* (New York: Simon and Schuster, 1978), 93–94. In neither of the two prints of the film we have seen, however, does such a scene appear. In a letter to the authors (22 Sept. 1982), Aldrich commented on this discrepancy: "I have never seen a print without, repeat, without Hammer and Velda stumbling in the surf. That's the way it was shot, that's the way it was released; the idea being that Mike was left alive long enough to see what havoc he had caused, though certainly he and Velda were both seriously contaminated."

38. Truffaut, "Rencontre Avec Robert Aldrich," 4.

39. Calendo, 30.

40. Higham and Greenberg, 28.

41. Sauvage, "Aldrich Interview," 57. For a full discussion of the stylistic complexities of this film, see Alain Silver, "*Kiss Me Deadly:* Evidence of a Style," *Film Comment*, X (March–April 1975), 24–30.

42. AFI Seminar, 2 Nov. 1971, p. 36.

43. Luciano interview.

44. Schumach, 177–78.

45. Charles Bitsch, "Surmultipliée," *Cahiers du Cinema*, no. 51 (Oct. 1955), 42–43.

46. Claude Chabrol, "Evolution du film policier," *Situation* (Christmas 1955), 27–33.

47. Truffaut, *The Films in My Life*, 94.

48. Paul Schrader, "Notes on *Film Noir*," *Film Comment*, VIII (Spring 1972), 12.

49. Sauvage in Coursodon with Sauvage, *American Directors*, 4.

50. Truffaut, "Rencontre Avec Robert Aldrich," 11.

51. G. Moskowitz, "Le Petit Journal du Cinema," *Cahiers du Cinema*, no. 61 (July 1956), 33.

52. Clifford Odets, "In Praise of a Maturing Industry," *New York Times*, 6 Nov. 1955, II, p. 5.

53. Aldrich, "High Price," 7.

54. Silver, 17.

55. Tailleur, "Avènement de Robert Aldrich," 21.

56. Truffaut, "Rencontre Avec Robert Aldrich," 10.

57. Aldrich, "High Price," 7.

58. Calendo, 30.

59. Luciano interview.

60. See the comments on this aspect of the film in George Robinson, "Three by Aldrich," *The Velvet Light Trap*, XI (Winter 1974), 48.

61. Silver, 17.

62. Tailleur, "Avènement de Robert Aldrich, " 23.

63. Jean-José Richer, "La Quatrieme Vitesse," *Cahiers du Cinema*, no. 53 (Dec. 1955), 50–51.

64. Aldrich, "High Price," 7.

65. Higham and Greenberg, 30.

66. *New York Times*, 9 Nov. 1955, p. 41.

67. Aldrich, "Notes," 4.

68. "Robert Aldrich" in Richard Roud, ed., *Cinema: A Critical Dictionary, Vol I: Aldrich to King* (London: Secker and Warburg, 1980), 23.

69. Higham and Greenberg, 30.

70. Aldrich, "High Price," 7.

71. Truffaut, "Rencontre Avec Robert Aldrich," 8.

72. Ian Jarvie, "Hysteria and Authoritarianism in the Films of Robert Aldrich," *Film Culture*, nos. 22–23 (1961), 106.

73. Combs in Combs, ed., *Robert Aldrich*, 18.

74. Aldrich had problems with Joan Crawford on the picture. She first of all insisted that her own writers rework the script, a demand Aldrich refused. Then she threatened not to appear on the set, but Aldrich held firm. Finally she did show but refused to talk to Aldrich for several days. See Higham and Greenberg, 30–31. Although they became friends by the end of the picture, Aldrich wrote, "I admired Joan Crawford . . . but I could not get her to be a drab, aging woman, which threw off the balance of the picture." Aldrich, "High Price," 7.

75. R. Lachenay, "Le Petit Journal du Cinema," *Cahiers du Cinema*, 33.

76. One of Aldrich's projects at this time was a story entitled "Kinderspiel," which he planned to film in Germany with Anthony Quinn. He described it as "a story of the rebellion of the world's children against their parents in view of an impending nuclear war." See George N. Fenin, "An Interview with Robert Aldrich," *Film Culture*, II (1956), 9. Although the film was never made, Aldrich returned to the project at various times throughout his career. See Ch. 7.

77. This scene contains conscious echoes of the famous Burt Lancaster-Deborah Kerr episode in *From Here to Eternity* (1953).

78. Combs in Combs, ed., *Robert Aldrich*, 19.

79. Ibid.

80. Lachenay, "Le Petit Journal du Cinema," 33.

81. Jacques Rivette, "Notes Sur Une Révolution," *Cahiers du Cinema*, no. 54 (Christmas 1955), 17–21.

82. Quoted in Richer, "La Quatrieme Vitesse," 50.

83. Oscar Godbout, " 'Fragile Fox' Foments Fireworks," *New York Times*, 19 Feb. 1956, II, p. 5.

84. Arthur Knight, "Aldrich Against the Army," *Saturday Review*, 1 Sept. 1956, p. 25.

85. "Pentagon is Called Censor of War Film," *New York Times*, 31 Aug. 1956, p. 7.

86. Truffaut, "Rencontre Avec Robert Aldrich," 8.

87. Godbout, 5.

88. Lee Marvin interview with authors, 16 Sept. 1984. All subsequent remarks by Lee Marvin taken from this interview.

89. Eddie Albert interview with authors, 6 Aug. 1984. All subsequent remarks by Eddie Albert taken from this interview.

90. Joseph Biroc interview with authors, 19 July 1984. All subsequent remarks by Joseph Biroc taken from this interview.

91. Higham and Greenberg, 31.

92. Fenin, 8.

93. Robinson, 48.

94. According to Albert, this striking pose was Palance's idea. "I think Jack had worked in the mines and had seen men killed, and he was drawing on his recollection of death."

95. Truffaut, "Rencontre Avec Robert Aldrich," 8.

96. Sauvage, "Aldrich Interview," 55.

97. Truffaut, "Rencontre Avec Robert Aldrich," 7–8.

98. Aldrich, "High Price," 7.

99. *New York Times*, 20 Sept. 1956, p. 29.

100. Norman Kagan, *The War Film* (New York: Pyramid Communications, 1974), 97.

Chapter Three

1. Silver and Ward, *Robert Aldrich: A Guide*, 29.

2. Joel Greenberg, "Interview with Robert Aldrich," *Sight and Sound*, XXXVIII (Winter 1968–69), 10.

3. Fenin, 9.

4. Sauvage, "Aldrich Interview," 59.

5. Greenberg, 10.

6. Sauvage, "Aldrich Interview," 59.

7. Greenberg, 10.

8. Truffaut, "Rencontre Avec Robert Aldrich," 8.

9. Aldrich, "High Price," 7, 35.

10. Greenberg, 10.

11. Silver, 20.

12. Ibid.

13. Ibid.

14. Aldrich, "Learning from My Mistakes," *Films and Filming*, VI (June 1960), 9.

15. Ibid.

16. Ibid.

17. Cameron and Shivas, 10.

18. Aldrich, "Mes Déboires en Europe," *Cahiers du Cinema*, no. 107 (May 1960), 3.

19. Harry Ringel, "The Director as Phoenix," *Take One*, IV (Sept. 1974), 11.

20. Silver and Ward, *Robert Aldrich: A Guide*, 14.

21. Higham and Greenberg, 33.

22. *New York Times*, 18 July 1959, p. 6.

23. Greenberg, 10.

24. Paul Mayersburg, "Robert Aldrich," *Movie*, no. 8 (April 1963), 4.

25. Silver, 20.

26. Higham and Greenberg, 32–33.

27. Aldrich, "Learning from My Mistakes," 9.

28. Higham and Greenberg, 32.

29. Cameron and Shivas, 10.

30. Jarvie, 108.

31. Aldrich, "Learning From My Mistakes," 9.

32. Chris Petit and Richard Combs, "Interview with Robert Aldrich," in Combs, ed., *Robert Aldrich*, 41.

33. Greenberg, 12.

34. Ringel, "The Director as Phoenix," 11.

35. See, for example, T.J. Ross, "Dark Legend," *December Magazine*, XIII (Fall 1971), 196–201.

36. Combs, in Combs, ed., *Robert Aldrich*, 19.

37. Ross, "Dark Legend," 197.

38. Sarris, *The American Cinema*, 85.

39. Cameron and Shivas, 8.

40. Ibid.

41. Sauvage, "Aldrich Interview," 60.

42. Petit and Combs in Combs, ed., *Robert Aldrich*, 44.

43. Charles Champlin, "Aldrich: He Spreads the Credits Around," *Los Angeles Times Calendar*, 26 June 1977, p. 13.

44. Letter from Robert Aldrich to authors, 22 Sept. 1982. Aldrich's obsession with *Taras Bulba* is apparent in an oftquoted remark he made in an interview with Harry Ringel: "But I will film *Taras Bulba* because I have to and I

have to because . . . I *am* Taras Bulba!" The picture was eventually made in 1962 by J. Lee Thompson with Yul Brynner in the title role. It was not a blockbuster hit. See Ringel, "The Director as Phoenix," 12. For a more lengthy discussion of the financial exigencies which led to Aldrich's loss of the property, see Ringel, "Up to Date with Robert Aldrich," 169.

45. Ringel, "The Director as Phoenix," 11.

Chapter Four

1. Higham and Greenberg, 33.
2. Robert Aldrich, "The Care and Feeding of 'Baby Jane,' " *New York Times*, 4 Nov. 1962, X, p. 1.
3. Cameron and Shivas, 9.
4. Higham and Greenberg, 35.
5. Charles Derry, "Aldrich Interview," *Cinefantastique*, III (Fall 1974), 19.
6. Sauvage, "Aldrich Interview," 62.
7. Ibid.
8. Letter from Robert Aldrich to authors, 22 Sept. 1982.
9. Higham and Greenberg, 36.
10. Sauvage, "Aldrich Interview," 62.
11. Peter John Dyer, "Meeting Baby Jane," *Sight and Sound*, XXXII (Summer 1963), 118.
12. Derry, "Aldrich Interview," 19.
13. Cameron and Shivas, 9.
14. Jean Boreil, "Doctor Jekyll and Mr. Hyde: Qu'est-il Arrive a Baby Jane?," *Positif*, no. 56 (Nov. 1963), 67.
15. Charles Derry, "The Horror of Personality," *Cinefantastique*, III (Fall 1974), 17.
16. Boreil, "Doctor Jekyll and Mr. Hyde," 67.
17. Arthur Knight, *Saturday Review*, 10 Nov. 1962, p. 27.
18. Dyer, 119.
19. Higham and Greenberg, 37.
20. Daniel Bates, *Film Quarterly*, XVII (Spring 1964), 62.
21. AFI Seminar, 2 Nov. 1971, p. 28.
22. Greenberg, 12.
23. Derry, "Aldrich Interview," 19.
24. Higham and Greenberg, 36.
25. Derry, "Aldrich Interview," 19.
26. Aldrich quoted in biographical publicity release (c. 1967) issued by Jerry Pam and Associates, pp. 7–8. Included in Aldrich Papers.
27. Bette Davis quoted in "Film Clips," *Sight and Sound*, XXXIV (Summer 1965), 151.

28. Calendo, 30.

29. Written by Frank DeVol and sung by Patti Page, the title "Hush . . . Hush, Sweet Charlotte" was a hit in 1964.

30. Robert Aldrich, "Portrait de Bette," *Cahiers du Cinema*, nos. 166–67 (May–June 1965), 113.

31. *Variety*, 5 Jan. 1966, p. 6.

32. AFI Seminar, 2 Nov. 1971, p. 19.

33. Ringel, "Up to Date with Robert Aldrich," 167.

34. "Man-Made Myth," *Time*, 4 Feb. 1966, p. 103.

35. Brendan Gill, "New Crusoes," *New Yorker*, 12 Feb. 1966, p. 140.

36. In filming this scene, the stunt pilot Paul Mantz was killed and another stunt man, Bobby Rose, seriously injured in a crash of the plane. See Peter Bart, "Paul Mantz, Stunt Pilot, Is Killed in Crash During Filming of Movie Scene in Arizona," *New York Times*, 9 July 1965, p. 14.

37. Charles Higham, "Robert Aldrich," *Action*, IX (Nov.–Dec. 1974), 16.

38. Ringel, "Up to Date with Robert Aldrich," 167.

39. Greenberg, 12.

40. "Kenneth Hyman made enormous contributions to *The Dirty Dozen* and if it hadn't been for Kenneth Hyman, I don't think I would have directed *The Dirty Dozen*. However, *The Dirty Dozen* was at MGM long before Kenneth Hyman brought it to their attention." Letter from Robert Aldrich to authors, 22 Sept. 1982.

41. Greenberg, 12.

42. AFI Seminar, 2 Nov. 1971, p. 6.

43. Greenberg, 13.

44. Higham and Greenberg, 38.

45. AFI Seminar, 2 Nov. 1971, p. 16.

46. The film was plagued by problems. It ran several weeks over schedule, came in $1 million over budget. Also, late in filming, the chateau used in the final scenes mysteriously burned down. See Allen Eyles, "The Private War of Robert Aldrich," *Films and Filming*, XIII (1967), 4–9.

47. Bosley Crowther, *New York Times*, 16 June 1967, p. 36.

48. Penelope Gilliatt, *New Yorker*, 22 July 1967, p. 70.

49. "Dialogue: Bertolucci and Aldrich," *Action*, IX (March–April 1974), 24.

50. Sauvage, "Aldrich Interview," 59.

51. AFI Seminar, 2 Nov. 1971, p. 11.

52. Sauvage, "Aldrich Interview," 59.

53. Robert Windeler, "Aldrich: To Shut Up and Take Your Lumps," *New York Times*, 3 Sept. 1967, II and X, p. 9.

54. AFI Seminar, 2 Nov. 1971, p. 16.

55. Ibid.

56. Ibid., p. 3.

57. Ibid., pp. 13–14.

58. Calendo, 32.
59. Ibid., 33.
60. Ibid., 32.
61. Higham and Greenberg, 38.
62. Ibid.
63. AFI Seminar, 2 Nov. 1971, p. 35.
64. Ibid., p. 36.
65. Calendo, 32.
66. Given the carnivorous conditions which prevail in Aldrich's vision of Hollywood, it is difficult to see how Andrew Sarris could contend in his review of *Lylah Clare* that "Aldrich is as interestingly ambivalent as ever about Hollywood." See *The Village Voice*, 3 Oct. 1968, p. 45.
67. Calendo, 33.
68. Ibid., 32.
69. Richard Schickel, "Cornball Son of Sunset Boulevard," *Life*, 27 Sept. 1968, p. 8.
70. *New York Times*, 23 Aug. 1968, p. 33.
71. Ringel, "Up to Date with Robert Aldrich," 167.

Chapter Five

1. *Daily Variety*, 8 June 1967, pp. 1, 4.
2. Information taken from "Studio History and Fact Sheet," publicity release issued by Jerry Pam and Associates (c. 1968). Included in Aldrich Papers.
3. Ibid., 4.
4. Robert Aldrich, "Why I Bought My Own Studio," *Action*, IV (Jan.–Feb. 1969), 8.
5. Ibid., 10.
6. Ibid.
7. "Robert Aldrich Takes Stand for Hollywood-Made Movies," *The Independent Film Journal*, 6 Aug. 1968, p. 23.
8. Charles Champlin, "Aldrich Weighs Hollywood's Future," *Los Angeles Times Calendar*, 24 Aug. 1969, p. 18.
9. "Robert Aldrich Takes Stand," 23.
10. Robert Aldrich, "Film-Making in Era of New Liberality," *Los Angeles Times Calendar*, 15 Dec. 1968, p. 36.
11. Aldrich, "Why I Bought My Own Studio," 9–10.
12. Aldrich, "Film-Making in Era of New Liberality," 36.
13. "Robert Aldrich Takes Stand," 23.
14. Vito Russo, *The Celluloid Closet: Homosexuality in the Movies* (New York: Harper and Row, 1981), p. 173.
15. Ringel, "The Director as Phoenix," 13.

16. Calendo, 33.

17. DGA Memorial Service for Aldrich, 7 Dec. 1983.

18. For a fuller discussion, see "Curb on Ads for X-Pix Cues 'Sis' Suit by Aldrich," *Variety*, 5 Feb. 1969, pp. 1, 70.

19. Russo, 174.

20. Calendo, 33.

21. Indeed, it might be argued that the scene was shot so that it could be easily excised from the film.

22. Russo, 173.

23. Ibid., 172.

24. Silver and Ward, *Robert Aldrich: A Guide*, 49–51.

25. Silver, "Mr. *Film Noir*," 21.

26. Ibid.

27. Ringel, "The Director as Phoenix," 14.

28. "Robert Aldrich Brings World War II Excitement To The South Pacific," publicity release issued by Cinerama Releasing Corporation (c. 1970), p. 3.

29. Joan Bennett interview with authors, 25 Oct. 1984. All subsequent remarks by Joan Bennett taken from this interview.

30. Ringel, "Up to Date with Robert Aldrich," 168.

31. Higham, 20.

32. Tom Milne, "Robert Aldrich (1962–1978)" in Combs, ed., *Robert Aldrich*, 29.

33. See review in *Variety*, 26 May 1971, p. 13, for example.

34. *New York Times*, 29 May 1971, p. 10.

35. See Orwell's essay "Raffles and Miss Blandish" in *As I Please: 1943–1945*, vol. III of *The Collected Essays, Journalism and Letters of George Orwell*, ed. Sonia Orwell and Ian Angus (New York: Harcourt Brace Jovanovich, 1968), 212–24.

36. Ringel, "Up to Date with Robert Aldrich," 168.

37. AFI Seminar, 2 Nov. 1971, p. 64.

38. Ringel, "Up to Date with Robert Aldrich," 168.

39. Ibid., 169.

40. Ibid., 166.

41. Powers, 52.

42. Ringel, "Up to Date with Robert Aldrich," 166.

Chapter Six

1. Powers, 52.

2. Alan Sharp, "White Man Unforks Tongue for 'Ulzana'," *Los Angeles Times Calendar*, 14 May 1972, p. 20.

3. Ringel, "Up to Date with Robert Aldrich," 168.

4. Sharp, "White Man Unforks Tongue," 20.

5. For a fuller discussion of this aspect of the film, see Jack Nachbar's essay "*Ulzana's Raid* (1972)" in *Western Movies*, ed. William T. Pilkington and Don Graham (Albuquerque: Univ. of New Mexico Press, 1979), 139–47.

6. Ringel, "Up to Date with Robert Aldrich," 168.

7. Petit and Combs, in Combs, ed., *Robert Aldrich*, 39–40.

8. Martin Levine, *Newsday*, 16 Nov. 1972, p. 9.

9. "Sharp, Lancaster and I totally believed in the parallel with Vietnam. The producer [Carter DeHaven] thought the public would see it immediately and if they did that would lessen the film's chances of economic survival. We tried to do it all the same." Aldrich quoted by Petit and Combs, in Combs, ed., *Robert Aldrich*, 40.

10. Vincent Canby, "How the West was Brutal," *New York Times*, 3 Dec. 1972, II, p. 1.

11. Ringel, "Up to Date with Robert Aldrich," 168.

12. AFI Seminar, 26 April 1978, pp. 42–43.

13. Milne, in Combs, ed., *Robert Aldrich*, 32.

14. Calendo, 30.

15. Stuart Byron, " 'I Can't Get Jimmy Carter to See My Movie': Robert Aldrich Talks with Stuart Byron," *Film Comment*, XIII (March–April 1977), 51.

16. Calendo, 30.

17. Ringel, "The Director as Phoenix," 16.

18. Calendo, 30.

19. Byron, 51.

20. Ibid., 52.

21. Ibid., 51.

22. Ibid., 50.

23. Higham, 21.

24. Alvin Greenman interview with authors, 28 May 1984. All subsequent remarks by Alvin Greenman taken from this interview.

25. *Variety*, 20 Aug. 1974, p. 8.

26. Champlin, "Cons vs. Guards in *Longest Yard*," *Los Angeles Times*, 25 Sept. 1974, IV, p. 1.

27. Byron, 51.

28. Powers, 59.

29. Pauline Kael, "The Actor and the Star," *New Yorker*, 14 Oct. 1974, p. 179.

30. Sauvage, "Aldrich Interview," 62.

31. Byron, 52.

32. Sauvage, "Aldrich Interview," 62.

33. Letter from Burt Reynolds to authors, 1 May 1984.

34. Vincent Canby wrote, "Burt Reynolds may be the phoniest love object to be foisted on the American public since Jayne Mansfield," *New York Times*, 15 Sept. 1974, II, p. 1.

35. Byron, 52.

36. Sauvage, "Aldrich Interview," 53.

37. Ibid., 52.

38. Ibid., 55.

39. Reynolds letter to authors, 1 May 1984.

40. Milne in Combs, ed., *Robert Aldrich*, 36.

41. Reynolds letter to authors, 1 May 1984.

42. Richard Combs, "Aldrich's *Twilight*," *Sight and Sound*, XLVI (Summer 1977), 186.

43. *Daily Variety*, 11 April 1972, p. 16.

44. Byron, 47.

45. Ibid.

46. Bart Mills, " 'Last Gleaming' of Admiral X—Overlay of a Crackup," *Los Angeles Times Calendar*, 6 June 1976, p. 36.

47. Quoted in ibid., 36.

48. John Huddy, "Robert Aldrich Needs Hit," *Miami Herald*, 28 July 1974, Sec. H, p. 7.

49. Byron, 48.

50. Charles Durning interview with authors, 27 May 1984. All subsequent remarks by Charles Durning taken from this interview.

51. Joan Bennett, Michael Luciano, and Alvin Greenman all recalled this incident.

52. *Variety*, 2 Feb. 1977, p. 22.

53. Combs, "Aldrich's *Twilight*," 187.

54. Byron, 48.

55. Ibid., 47.

56. Petit and Combs, in Combs, ed., *Robert Aldrich*, 47.

57. Byron, 48.

58. Petit and Combs, in Combs, ed., *Robert Aldrich*, 38–39.

59. Champlin, "He Spreads the Credits Around," 13.

60. Combs, ed., *Robert Aldrich*, 71.

61. Petit and Combs, in Combs, ed., *Robert Aldrich*, 43.

62. Ibid.

63. Ibid., 42.

64. Letter to Merv Adelson and Lee Rich, 18 Aug. 1976. Included in Aldrich Papers.

65. Petit and Combs, in Combs, ed., *Robert Aldrich*, 42.

66. Richard Schickel, *Time*, 16 Jan. 1976, p. 82.

67. Byron, 49.

68. Milne in Combs, ed., *Robert Aldrich*, 36.

69. DGA Memorial Service for Aldrich, 7 Dec. 1983.

70. Byron, 49.

71. DGA Memorial Service for Aldrich, 7 Dec. 1983.

72. Ibid.
73. Ibid.
74. Powers, 61.
75. DGA Memorial Service for Aldrich, 7 Dec. 1983.
76. AFI Seminar, 26 April 1978, p. 13.
77. DGA Memorial Service for Aldrich, 7 Dec. 1983.

Chapter Seven

1. Calendo, 33.
2. Gary Arnold, "Westward Hokum," *Washington Post*, 27 July 1979, B3.
3. Vincent Canby, "Polish Rabbi Out West," *New York Times*, 6 July 1979, C–14.
4. Bernard Drew, "Leo Roars Again," *Film Comment*, XVII (Sept.–Oct. 1981), p. 38.
5. Aldrich, "Prologue" to Mel Frohman, . . . *All the Marbles* (screenplay), p. C.
6. Ibid.
7. Drew, 38.
8. Andrew Sarris, "What Ever Happened to Bobby Aldrich?" *The Village Voice*, 28 Oct.–3 Nov. 1981, p. 49.
9. Vincent Canby, "Rough and Tumble," *New York Times*, 16 Oct. 1981, C8.
10. Robert Aldrich, *Charlie Casbah* (screenplay), 154.
11. Ibid., 10.
12. Robert Aldrich, *For Export Only* (screenplay), 6.
13. *Charlie Casbah*, 156.
14. Ibid., 156–57.
15. Robert Aldrich, *Kinderspiel* (Suggested Revisions—An Overlay), 4. Included in Aldrich Papers.
16. Ibid., 1.
17. DGA Memorial Service for Aldrich, 7 Dec. 1983.

Epilogue

1. DGA Memorial Service for Aldrich, 7 Dec. 1983.
2. Ibid.
3. Kelly Aldrich interview with authors, 29 July 1985. All subsequent remarks by Kelly Aldrich taken from this interview.
4. Alida Aldrich interview with authors, 29 July 1985.

Filmography

Films Directed by Robert Aldrich

The Big Leaguer (1953). Released by MGM. Producer: Matthew Rapf. Screenplay: Herbert Baker, based on story by John McNulty and Louis Morheim. Cinematographer: William Mellor. Editor: Ben Lewis. Art Direction: Cedric Gibbons and Eddie Imazu. Music: Alberto Colombo. Cast: Edward G. Robinson (John B. Lobert), Vera-Ellen (Christy), Jeff Richards (Adam Polachuk), Richard Jaeckel (Bobby Bronson), William Campbell (Julie Davis), Carl Hubbell (himself), Paul Langton (Brian McLennan), Lalo Rios (Chuy Aguilar), Bill Crandall (Tippy Mitchell).

World For Ransom (1954). Released by Allied Artists. Producers: Robert Aldrich and Bernard Tabakin. Screenplay: Lindsay Hardy and Hugo Butler [uncredited]. Cinematographer: Joseph Biroc. Editor: Michael Luciano. Art Direction: William Glasgow. Music: Frank DeVol. Cast: Dan Duryea (Mike Callahan), Gene Lockhart (Alexis Pederas), Patric Knowles (Julian March), Reginald Denny (Major Bone), Nigel Bruce (Governor Coutts), Marian Carr (Frennessey), Arthur Shields (Sean O'Conner).

Apache (1954). Released by United Artists [Hecht-Lancaster Productions]. Producer: Harold Hecht. Screenplay: James R. Webb, based on novel *Bronco Apache* by Paul I. Wellman. Cinematographer: Ernest Laszlo. Editor: Alan Crosland, Jr. Art Direction: Nicolai Remisoff. Music: David Raksin. Cast: Burt Lancaster (Massai), Jean Peters (Nalinle), John McIntire (Al Sieber), Charles Buchinsky [Bronson] (Hondo), John Dehner (Weddle), Paul Guilfoyle (Santos), Morris Ankrum (Dawson), Monte Blue (Geronimo).

Vera Cruz (1954). Released by United Artists [Hecht-Lancaster Productions]. Producer: James Hill. Screenplay: Roland Kibbee and James R. Webb, based on story by Borden Chase. Cinematographer: Ernest Laszlo. Editor: Alan Crosland, Jr. Music: Hugo Friedhofer. Cast: Gary Cooper (Ben Trane), Burt Lancaster (Joe Erin), Denise Darcel (the Countess), Cesar Romero (the Marquis), Sarita Montiel (Niña), George Macready (Maximilian), Ernest Borgnine (Donnegan), Charles Buchinsky [Bronson] (Pittsburgh), Henry Brandon (Danette), Jack Elam (Tex), Charles Horvath (Reno).

Kiss Me Deadly (1955). Released by United Artists [Parklane Productions]. Producer: Robert Aldrich. Screenplay: A.I. Bezzerides, based on novel *Kiss Me, Deadly* by Mickey Spillane. Cinematographer: Ernest Laszlo. Editor: Michael Luciano. Art Direction: William Glasgow. Music: Frank DeVol. Cast: Ralph Meeker (Mike Hammer), Albert Dekker (Dr. Soberin), Paul

Stewart (Carl Evello), Wesley Addy (Pat), Marian Carr (Friday), Maxine Cooper (Velda), Cloris Leachman (Christina), Gaby Rodgers (Lily Carver/-Gabrielle), Nick Dennis (Nick), Jack Lambert (Sugar), Jack Elam (Charlie Max), Percy Helton (Morgue Doctor), Juano Hernandez (Eddie Yeager).

The Big Knife (1955). Released by United Artists [Associates and Aldrich Production]. Producer: Robert Aldrich. Screenplay: James Poe, based on play *The Big Knife* by Clifford Odets. Cinematographer: Ernest Laszlo. Editor: Michael Luciano. Art Direction: William Glasgow. Music: Frank DeVol. Cast: Jack Palance (Charlie Castle), Ida Lupino (Marion Castle), Wendell Corey (Smiley Coy), Shelley Winters (Dixie Evans), Jean Hagen (Connie Bliss), Rod Steiger (Stanley Hoff), Ilka Chase (Patty Benedict), Everett Sloane (Nat Danziger), Wesley Addy (Hank Teagle), Paul Langton (Buddy Bliss), Nick Dennis (Nick).

Autumn Leaves (1956). Released by Columbia Studios [William Goetz Productions]. Producer: William Goetz. Screenplay: Jack Jevne, Lewis Meltzer, and Robert Blees. Cinematographer: Charles Lang, Jr. Editor: Michael Luciano. Art Direction: William Glasgow. Music: Hans Salter. Cast: Joan Crawford (Millicent Weatherby), Cliff Robertson (Burt Hanson), Vera Miles (Virginia), Lorne Greene (Mr. Hanson), Ruth Donnelly (Liz), Maxine Cooper (Nurse Evans).

Attack! (1956). Released by United Artists [Associates and Aldrich Production]. Producer: Robert Aldrich. Screenplay: James Poe, based on play *Fragile Fox* by Norman Brooks. Cinematographer: Joseph Biroc. Editor: Michael Luciano. Art Direction: William Glasgow. Music: Frank DeVol. Cast: Jack Palance (Lt. Joe Costa), Eddie Albert (Capt. Erskine Cooney), Lee Marvin (Col. Clyde Bartlett), William Smithers (Lt. Woodruff), Robert Strauss (Pfc. Bernstein), Richard Jaeckel (Pfc. Snowden), Buddy Ebsen (Sgt. Tolliver), Peter Van Eyck (German officer).

The Garment Jungle (1957). [Aldrich replaced by Vincent Sherman during filming]. Released by Columbia Studios [Harry Kleiner Production]. Producer: Harry Kleiner. Screenplay: Harry Kleiner, based on articles "Gangsters in the Dress Business" by Lester Velie. Cinematographer: Joseph Biroc. Editor: William Lyon. Art Direction: Robert A. Peterson. Music: Leith Stevens. Cast: Lee J. Cobb (Walter Mitchell), Kerwin Mathews (Alan Mitchell), Gia Scala (Theresa Renata), Richard Boone (Artie Ravidge), Valerie French (Lee Hackett), Robert Loggia (Tulio Renata), Joseph Wiseman (Kovan), Harold J. Stone (Tony), Wesley Addy (Mr. Paul).

Ten Seconds to Hell (1959). Released by United Artists [Seven Arts-Hammer Production]. Producer: Michael Carreras. Screenplay: Robert Aldrich and Teddi Sherman, based on novel *The Phoenix* by Laurence P. Bachmann.

Cinematographer: Ernest Laszlo. Editor: Harry Richardson. Art Direction: Ken Adam. Music: Kenneth V. Jones. Cast: Jack Palance (Eric Koertner), Jeff Chandler (Karl Wirtz), Martine Carol (Margot Hofer), Robert Cornthwaite (Loeffler), Dave Willock (Tillig), Wesley Addy (Sulke), Jimmy Goodwin (Globke).

The Angry Hills (1959). Released by MGM [Raymond Stross Productions]. Producer: Raymond Stross. Screenplay: A.I. Bezzerides, based on novel *The Angry Hills* by Leon Uris. Cinematographer: Stephen Dade. Editor: Peter Tanner. Art Direction: Ken Adam. Music: Richard Bennett. Cast: Robert Mitchum (Michael Morrison), Elisabeth Mueller (Lisa), Stanley Baker (Konrad Heisler), Gia Scala (Eleftheria), Theodore Bikel (Tassos), Sebastian Cabot (Chesney), Peter Illing (Leonidas), Leslie Phillips (Ray Taylor), Donald Wolfit (Dr. Stergiou).

The Last Sunset (1961). Released by Universal-International [Brynaprod S.A.]. Producers: Eugene Frenke and Edward Lewis. Screenplay: Dalton Trumbo, based on novel *Sundown at Crazy Horse* by Howard Rigsby. Cinematographer: Ernest Laszlo. Editor: Michael Luciano. Art Direction: Alexander Golitzen and Alfred Sweeney. Music: Ernest Gold. Cast: Rock Hudson (Dana Stribling), Kirk Douglas (Brendan O'Malley), Dorothy Malone (Belle Breckenridge), Joseph Cotton (John Breckenridge), Carol Lynley (Missy Breckenridge), Neville Brand (Frank Hobbs), Jack Elam (Ed Hobbs).

Sodom and Gomorrah (Filmed in 1961, released in 1963). Released by 20th Century-Fox [Titanus Production]. Producer: Goffredo Lombardo. Screenplay: Hugo Butler and Giorgio Prosperi. Cinematographer: Silvio Ippoliti, Mario Montuori, and Cyril Knowles. Editor: Peter Tanner. Art Direction: Ken Adam and Giovanni D'Andrea. Music: Miklos Rozsa. Cast: Stewart Granger (Lot), Pier Angeli (Ildith), Stanley Baker (Astaroth), Rossana Podesta (Sheeah), Anouk Aimee (Bera).

What Ever Happened to Baby Jane? (1962). Released by Warner Brothers [Associates and Aldrich-Seven Arts Production]. Producer: Robert Aldrich. Screenplay: Lukas Heller, based on novel *What Ever Happened to Baby Jane?* by Henry Farrell. Cinematographer: Ernest Haller. Editor: Michael Luciano. Art Direction: William Glasgow. Music: Frank DeVol. Cast: Bette Davis (Jane Hudson), Joan Crawford (Blanche Hudson), Victor Buono (Edwin Flagg), Marjorie Bennett (Della Flagg), Maidie Norman (Elvira Stitt), Anna Lee (Mrs. Bates), Barbara Merrill (Liza Bates), Dave Willock (Ray Hudson).

4 For Texas (1963). Released by Warner Brothers [The S.A.M. Company and Associates and Aldrich Production]. Producer: Robert Aldrich. Screenplay: Teddi Sherman and Robert Aldrich, from original story by Aldrich. Cinematographer: Ernest Laszlo. Editor: Michael Luciano. Art Direction: William Glasgow. Music: Nelson Riddle. Cast: Frank Sinatra

(Zack Thomas), Dean Martin (Joe Jarrett), Anita Ekberg (Elya Carlson), Ursula Andress (Maxine Richter), Charles Bronson (Mastson), Victor Buono (Harvey Burden), Edric Conner (Prince George), Nick Dennis (Angel), Richard Jaeckel (Mancini), Mike Mazurki (Chad), Wesley Addy (Trowbridge), Jack Elam (Dobie), Marjorie Bennett (Miss Emmaline).

Hush . . . Hush, Sweet Charlotte (1964). Released by 20th Century-Fox [Associates and Aldrich Production]. Producer: Robert Aldrich. Screenplay: Henry Farrell and Lukas Heller, from original story by Farrell. Cinematographer: Joseph Biroc. Editor: Michael Luciano. Art Direction: William Glasgow. Music: Frank DeVol. Cast: Bette Davis (Charlotte Hollis), Olivia de Havilland (Miriam Deering), Joseph Cotton (Drew Bayliss), Agnes Moorehead (Velma Cruther), Cecil Kellaway (Harry Willis), Victor Buono (Sam Hollis), Mary Astor (Jewel Mayhew), Wesley Addy (Sheriff Luke Standish), William Campbell (Paul Marchand), Bruce Dern (John Mayhew), George Kennedy (Foreman).

The Flight of the Phoenix (1966). Released by 20th Century-Fox [Associates and Aldrich Production]. Producer: Robert Aldrich. Screenplay: Lukas Heller, based on novel *The Flight of the Phoenix* by Elleston Trevor. Cinematographer: Joseph Biroc. Editor: Michael Luciano. Art Direction: William Glasgow. Music: Frank DeVol. Cast: James Stewart (Frank Towns), Richard Attenborough (Lew Moran), Peter Finch (Captain Harris), Hardy Kruger (Heinrich Dorfmann), Ernest Borgnine (Trucker Cobb), Ian Bannen (Crow), Christian Marquand (Dr. Renaud), Ronald Fraser (Sergeant Watson), Dan Duryea (Standish), George Kennedy (Bellamy), Gabriele Tinti (Gabriele).

The Dirty Dozen (1967). Released by MGM [MKH Productions]. Producer: Kenneth Hyman. Screenplay: Nunnally Johnson and Lukas Heller, based on novel *The Dirty Dozen* by E.M. Nathanson. Cinematographer: Edward Scaife. Editor: Michael Luciano. Art Direction: W.E. Hutchinson. Music: Frank DeVol. Cast: Lee Marvin (Major Reisman), Ernest Borgnine (General Worden), Charles Bronson (Joseph Wladislaw), Jim Brown (Robert Jefferson), John Cassavetes (Victor Franko), Richard Jaeckel (Sgt. Bowren), George Kennedy (Major Armbruster), Trini Lopez (Pedro Jiminez), Ralph Meeker (Captain Kinder), Robert Ryan (Colonel Everett Dasher Breed), Telly Savalas (Archer Maggott), Clint Walker (Samson Posey), Donald Sutherland (Vernon Pinkley), Robert Webber (General Denton), Tom Busby (Vladek), Ben Carruthers (Gilpin), Stuart Cooper (Lever), Al Mancini (Bravos), Colin Maitland (Sawyer).

The Legend of Lylah Clare (1968). Released by MGM [Associates and Aldrich Production]. Producer: Robert Aldrich. Screenplay: Hugo Butler and Jean Rouverol, based on teleplay by Robert Thom and Edward de Blasio. Cinematographer: Joseph Biroc. Editor: Michael Luciano. Art Direction: George W. Davis and William Glasgow. Music: Frank DeVol. Cast: Kim

Novak (Lylah Clare/Elsa Brinkman), Peter Finch (Lewis Zarkan), Ernest Borgnine (Barney Sheean), Milton Selzer (Bart Langner), Rossella Falk (Rossella), Gabriele Tinti (Paolo), Michael Murphy (Mark Peter Sheean), Coral Browne (Molly Luther), Valentina Cortese (Countess Bozo Bedoni), Nick Dennis (Nick), Dave Willock (Cameraman).

The Killing of Sister George (1968). Released by ABC Palomar International [Associates and Aldrich Production]. Producer: Robert Aldrich. Screenplay: Lukas Heller, based on play *The Killing of Sister George* by Frank Marcus. Cinematographer: Joseph Biroc. Editor: Michael Luciano. Art Direction: William Glasgow. Music: Gerald Fried. Cast: Beryl Reid (June Buckridge/"Sister George"), Susannah York ("Childie" McNaught), Coral Browne (Mercy Croft), Ronald Fraser (Leo Lockhart), Patricia Medina (Betty Thaxter).

Too Late the Hero (1970). Released by Cinerama Releasing Corporation [ABC-Palomar, Associates and Aldrich Production]. Producer: Robert Aldrich. Screenplay: Robert Aldrich and Lukas Heller, based on original story by Aldrich and Robert Sherman. Cinematographer: Joseph Biroc. Editor: Michael Luciano. Art Direction: James Vance. Music: Gerald Fried. Cast: Michael Caine (Pvt. Tosh Hearne), Cliff Robertson (Lt. jg Sam Lawson), Henry Fonda (Capt. John G. Nolan), Ian Bannen (Pvt. Thornton), Harry Andrews (Lt. Col. Thompson), Denholm Elliott (Capt. Hornsby), Ronald Fraser (Pvt. Campbell), Ken Takakura (Major Yamaguchi).

The Grissom Gang (1971). Released by Cinerama Releasing Corporation [ABC Pictures, Associates and Aldrich Production]. Producer: Robert Aldrich. Screenplay: Leon Griffiths, based on novel *No Orchids for Miss Blandish* by James Hadley Chase. Cinematographer: Joseph Biroc. Editor: Michael Luciano. Art Direction: James Vance. Music: Gerald Fried. Cast: Kim Darby (Barbara Blandish), Scott Wilson (Slim Grissom), Tony Musante (Eddie Hagen), Irene Daily (Ma Grissom), Robert Lansing (Dave Fenner), Connie Stevens (Anna Borg), Joey Faye (Woppy), Don Keefer (Doc), Ralph Waite (Mace), Wesley Addy (John Blandish), Dave Willock (Rocky), Matt Clark (Bailey).

Ulzana's Raid (1972). Released by Universal Pictures [Carter DeHaven, Associates and Aldrich Production]. Producer: Carter DeHaven. Screenplay: Alan Sharp. Cinematographer: Joseph Biroc. Editor: Michael Luciano. Art Direction: James Vance. Music: Frank DeVol. Cast: Burt Lancaster (McIntosh), Bruce Davison (Lt. Garnett DeBuin), Jorge Luke (Ke-ni-tay), Richard Jaeckel (the Sergeant), Joaquim Martinez (Ulzana), Lloyd Bochner (Captain Gates), Douglass Watson (Major Wainwright), Karl Swenson (Rukeyser), Dran Hamilton (Mrs. Riordan).

Emperor of the North (1973). Released by 20th Century-Fox [Inter-Hemisphere Productions]. Producer: Stanley Hough. Screenplay: Christopher Knopf. Cinematographer: Joseph Biroc. Editor: Michael Luciano. Art Direction:

Jack Martin Smith. Music: Frank DeVol. Cast: Lee Marvin (A No. 1), Ernest Borgnine (Shack), Keith Carradine (Cigaret), Charles Tyner (Cracker), Harry Caesar (Coaly), Matt Clark (Yardlet), Elisha Cook (Gray Cat), Dave Willock (Groundhog).

The Longest Yard (1974). Released by Paramount. Producer: Albert S. Ruddy. Screenplay: Tracy Keenan Wynn, from story by Albert S. Ruddy. Cinematographer: Joseph Biroc. Editor: Michael Luciano; Frank Capacchione, Allan Jacobs, and George Hively for football sequences. Music: Frank DeVol. Cast: Burt Reynolds (Paul Crewe), Eddie Albert (Warden Hazen), Ed Lauter (Capt., Knauer), Michael Conrad (Nate Scarboro), James Hampton (Caretaker), Harry Caesar (Granville), John Steadman (Pop), Charles Tyner (Unger), Richard Kiel (Samson), Ray Nitschke (Bogdanski), Mike Henry (Rassmeusen), Joe Kapp (a Guard), Bernadette Peters (Warden's secretary), Anitra Ford (Melissa).

Hustle (1975). Released by Paramount [RoBurt Productions]. Producer: Robert Aldrich. Screenplay: Steve Shagan. Cinematographer: Joseph Biroc. Editor: Michael Luciano. Art Direction: Hilyard Brown. Music: Frank DeVol. Cast: Burt Reynolds (Lt. Phil Gaines), Catherine Deneuve (Nicole Britton), Ben Johnson (Marty Hollinger), Paul Winfield (Sgt. Louis Belgrave), Eddie Albert (Leo Sellers), Eileen Brennan (Paula Hollinger), Ernest Borgnine (Capt. Santoro), Jack Carter (Herbie Dalitz), Catherine Bach (Peggy Summers), David Spielberg (Bellamy), James Hampton (Bus Driver).

Twilight's Last Gleaming (1977). Released by Allied Artists [Lorimar Presentation of a Geria Production]. Producer: Merv Adelson. Screenplay: Ronald M. Cohen and Edward Huebsch, based on novel *Viper Three* by Walter Wager. Cinematographer: Robert Hauser. Editor: Michael Luciano. Art Direction: Werner Achmann. Music: Jerry Goldsmith. Cast: Burt Lancaster (Lawrence Dell), Richard Widmark (Gen. Martin MacKenzie), Charles Durning (President David Stevens), Melvyn Douglas (Zachariah Guthrie), Paul Winfield (Powell), Burt Young (Garvas), Joseph Cotton (Arthur Renfrew), Gerald S. O'Loughlin (Gen. Michael O'Rourke), Richard Jaeckel (Capt. Towne), Roscoe Lee Browne (James Forrest), William Marshall (William Klinger), Leif Erickson (Ralph Whittaker), Charles McGraw (Gen. Crane), William Smith (Hoxey).

The Choirboys (1977). Released by Universal—M.C.A. [Lorimar-Airone Production]. Producer: Merv Adelson, Lee Rich. Screenplay: Christopher Knopf and [uncredited] Joseph Wambaugh, based on novel *The Choirboys* by Joseph Wambaugh. Cinematographer: Joseph Biroc. Editor: Maury Winetrobe, William Martin. Art Direction: Bill Kenney. Music: Frank DeVol. Cast: Charles Durning (Spermwhale Whalen), Louis Gossett Jr. (Calvin Motts), Perry King (Baxter Slate), Clyde Kasatsu (Francis Tanaguchi), Stephen Macht (Spencer Van Moot), Tim McIntyre (Roscoe

Rules), Randy Quaid (Dean Proust), Don Stroud (Sam Lyles), James Woods (Harold Bloomguard), Burt Young (Scuzzi), Robert Webber (Riggs), Blair Brown (Kimberly Lyles), Barbara Rhoades (Hadley), George Di Cenzo (Lt. Grimsley), Charles Haid (Nick Yanov), David Spielberg (Lt. Finque), Jim Davis (Capt. Drobeck), Phyllis Davis (Foxy/Gina).

The Frisco Kid (1979). Released by Warner Brothers. Producer: Mace Neufeld. Screenplay: Michael Ellis and Frank Shaw. Cinematographer: Robert B. Hauser. Editor: Maury Winetrobe, Irving Rosenblum, Jack Horger. Production Design: Terence Marsh. Music: Frank DeVol. Cast: Gene Wilder (Rabbi Avram Belinski), Harrison Ford (Tommy Lillard), Ramon Bieri (Jones), George Di Cenzo (Darryl Diggs), William Smith (Matt Diggs), Val Bisoglio (Chief Gray Cloud), Penny Peyser (Rosalie), Jack Somack (Samuel Bender).

. . . *All the Marbles* (1981). Released by United Artists. Producer: William Aldrich. Screenplay: Mel Frohman. Cinematographer: Joseph Biroc. Editor: Irving C. Rosenblum and Richard Lane. Music: Frank DeVol. Cast: Peter Falk (Harry Sears), Vicki Frederick (Iris), Laurene Landon (Molly), Burt Young (Eddie Cisco), Richard Jaeckel (Referee).

Selected Bibliography

Books, Articles, Interviews

Aldrich, Robert. "Director's Formula for a Happy Cast." *Los Angeles Times Calendar*, 6 Feb. 1966, pp. 13, 29.
_____. "Film-Making in Era of New Liberality." *Los Angeles Times Calendar*, 15 Dec. 1968, p. 36.
_____. "La Fonction de Producer: Cinq Questions a Robert Aldrich." *Cahiers du Cinema*, nos. 150–51 (July–Jan. 1963–64), 79–84.
_____. "Learning From My Mistakes." *Films and Filming*, VI (June 1960), 9, 33.
_____. "Mes Déboires en Europe." *Cahiers du Cinema*, no. 107 (May 1960), 2–6.
_____. "Portrait de Bette." *Cahiers du Cinema*, nos. 166–67 (May–June 1965), 113.
_____. "The Care and Feeding of 'Baby Jane'." *New York Times*, 4 Nov. 1962, Sec. X, p. 1.
_____. "The High Price of Independence." *Films and Filming*, IV (June 1958), 7, 35.
_____. "TV Techniques in Feature Making." *Studio Review*, no. 2739 (31 March 1960), 3, 10.
_____. "What Ever Happened to American Movies?" *Sight and Sound*, XXXIII (Winter 1963–64), 21–22.
_____. "Why I Bought My Own Studio." *Action*, IV (Jan.–Feb. 1969), 7–8, 10.
Byron, Stuart. " 'I Can't Get Jimmy Carter to See My Movie!': Robert Aldrich Talks with Stuart Byron." *Film Comment*, XIII (March–April 1977), 46–52.
Calendo, John. "Robert Aldrich Says, 'Life is Worth Living.' " *Andy Warhol's Interview*, III (Aug. 1973), 30–33.
Cameron, Ian, and Mark Shivas. "Interview with Robert Aldrich." *Movie*, no. 8 (April 1963), 8–11.
Champlin, Charles. "Aldrich: He Spreads the Credits Around." *Los Angeles Times Calendar*, 26 June 1977, pp. 1, 13, 45.
_____. "Aldrich's Safari in Mogul Country." *Los Angeles Times Calendar*, 25 Aug. 1974, pp. 36–38.
_____. "Aldrich Weighs Hollywood's Future." *Los Angeles Times Calendar*, 24 Aug. 1969, p. 18.
Combs, Richard. "Aldrich's *Twilight*." *Sight and Sound*, XLVI (Summer 1977), 186–87.

_____ , ed. *Robert Aldrich*. London: British Film Institute, 1978.

_____ . "Robert Aldrich (1953–1961)" in Combs, ed., *Robert Aldrich*, pp. 3–20.

_____ . "Worlds Apart: Aldrich Since *The Dirty Dozen*." *Sight and Sound*, XLV (Spring 1976), 112–15.

Coursodon, Jean-Pierre, with Pierre Sauvage. *American Directors*, II. New York: McGraw-Hill, 1983.

Derry, Charles. "Aldrich Interview." *Cinefantastique*, III (Fall 1974), 19.

_____ . "The Horror of Personality." *Cinefantastique*, III (Fall 1974), 15–18.

"Dialogue: Bertolucci and Aldrich." *Action*, IX (March–April 1974), 23–25.

Duval, Bruno. "Aldrich Le Rebel." *Image et Son*, no. 306 (May 1976), 25–44.

Dyer, Peter John. "Meeting Baby Jane." *Sight and Sound*, XXXII (Summer 1963), 118–20.

Eyles, Allen. "Films of Enterprise." *Focus on Film*, XXXV (April 1980), 13–27.

_____ . "The Private War of Robert Aldrich." *Films and Filming*, XIII (1967), 4–9.

Farber, Stephen. "New American Gothic." *Film Quarterly*, XX (Fall 1966), 22–27.

Fenin, George N. "An Interview with Robert Aldrich." *Film Culture*, II (1956), 8–9.

Greenberg, Joel. "Interview with Robert Aldrich." *Sight and Sound*, XXXVIII (Winter 1968–69), 8–12.

Higham, Charles. "Robert Aldrich." *Action*, IX (Nov.–Dec. 1974), 16–21.

_____ , and Joel Greenberg. *The Celluloid Muse: Hollywood Directors Speak*. London: Angus and Robertson, 1969.

Huddy, John. "Robert Aldrich Needs Hit." *Miami Herald*, 28 July 1974, Sec. H, 1, 7–8.

Jarvie, Ian. "Hysteria and Authoritarianism in the Films of Robert Aldrich." *Film Culture*, nos. 22–23 (1961), 95–111.

Kagan, Norman. *The War Film*. New York: Pyramid Communications, 1974.

Larkins, Robert, "Hollywood and the Indian." *Focus on Film*, XV, no. 2 (March–April 1970), 44–53.

Legrand, Gerard. "Robert Aldrich et l'incompletude du nihilisme." *Positif*, no. 181 (May 1976), 1–5.

Mayersburg, Paul. "Robert Aldrich." *Movie*, no. 8 (April 1963), 4–5.

Milne, Tom. "Robert Aldrich (1962–1978)" in Combs, ed., *Robert Aldrich*, pp. 23–36.

Morgan, James. "Hecht-Lancaster Productions." *Sight and Sound*, XXV (Summer 1955), 38–42, 55.

Parish, James Robert, and Michael R. Pitts with Gregory W. Mank. *Hollywood on Hollywood*. Metuchen, N.J.: Scarecrow Press, 1978.

Petit, Chris, and Richard Combs. "Interview with Robert Aldrich" in Combs, ed., *Robert Aldrich*, pp. 37–48.

Powers, James. "Dialogue on Film: Robert Aldrich." *American Film*, IV (Nov. 1978), 51–62.

Ringel, Harry. "The Director as Phoenix." *Take One,* IV (Sept. 1974), 9–16.

————— . "Up to Date with Robert Aldrich." *Sight and Sound,* XLIII (Summer 1974), 166–69.

Robinson, George. "Three by Aldrich." *The Velvet Light Trap,* XI (Winter 1974), 46–49.

Roud, Richard, ed. *Cinema: A Critical Dictionary, Vol. I: Aldrich to King.* London: Secker and Warburg, 1980.

Sarris, Andrew. *The American Cinema: Directors and Directions 1929–1968.* New York: Dutton, 1968.

————— . "What Ever Happened to Bobby Aldrich?" *The Village Voice,* 29 Oct.–3 Nov. 1981, p. 49.

Sauvage, Pierre. "Aldrich Interview." *Movie,* no. 23 (Winter 1976–77), 50–64.

Schrader, Paul. "Notes on *Film Noir.*" *Film Comment,* VIII (Spring 1972), 8–13.

Sharp, Alan. "White Man Unforks Tongue for 'Ulzana'." *Los Angeles Times Calendar,* 14 May 1972, p. 20.

Sherman, Eric, ed. *Directing the Film: Film Directors on Their Art.* Boston: Little, Brown, 1976.

Silver, Alain. "Mr. *Film Noir* Stays at the Table." *Film Comment,* VIII (Spring 1972), 15–23.

————— , and Elizabeth Ward. *Robert Aldrich: A Guide to References and Resources.* Boston: G.K. Hall, 1979.

Tailleur, Roger. "Avènement de Robert Aldrich." *Positif,* II (May 1956), 11–23.

Truffaut, Francois. *The Films in My Life.* New York: Simon and Schuster, 1978.

————— . "Le Derby des Psaumes." *Cahiers du Cinema,* no. 48 (June 1955), 42–45.

————— . "Rencontre Avec Robert Aldrich." *Cahiers du Cinema,* no. 64 (Nov. 1956), 2–11.

Unedited transcript of the American Film Institute Seminar with Robert Aldrich, held at the AFI Center for Advanced Film Studies, Los Angeles, California, 2 Nov. 1971.

Unedited transcript of the American Film Institute Seminar with Robert Aldrich, held at the AFI Center for Advanced Film Studies, Los Angeles, California, 26 April 1978. For edited version of this seminar, see Powers, "Dialogue on Film: Robert Aldrich," *American Film,* 51–62.

Personal Interviews, Letters, and Tapes

Albert, Eddie. Telephone Interview. 6 Aug. 1984.

Aldrich, Alida. Telephone Interview. 30 July 1985.

Aldrich, Kelly. Telephone Interview. 29 July 1985.

Aldrich, Robert. Telephone Interview. 10 Sept. 1982.

————— . Letter to the authors. 22 Sept. 1982.

Aldrich, William, and Adell Aldrich. Personal Interview. 24 May 1984.

Bennett, Joan. Telephone Interview. 25 Oct. 1984.
Biroc, Joseph. Telephone Interview. 19 July 1984.
Directors Guild of America Memorial Service for Robert Aldrich. Cassette tape.
    7 Dec. 1983.
Durning, Charles. Personal Interview. 27 May 1984.
Franklin, Michael. Telephone Interview. 6 Sept. 1984.
Greenman, Alvin, and Jean Greenman. Personal Interview. 28 May 1984.
Heller, Lukas. Personal Interview. 25 May 1984.
Jaeckel, Richard. Telephone Interview. 18 Aug. 1984.
Lancaster, Burt. Telephone Interview. 19 July 1984.
Luciano, Michael. Personal Interview. 25 May 1984.
Marvin, Lee. Telephone Interview. 22 Aug. 1984.
_____ . Cassette Tape. 16 Sept. 1984.
Reynolds, Burt. Letter to the authors. 1 May 1984.
Young, Burt. Letter to the authors. 12 June 1984.

Index

Aadland, Beverly, 151
Abbott and Costello Meet Captain Kidd (1952), 8
Action magazine, 215
Addy Wesley, 8, 39, 47, 80, 109, 158
Adelson, Merv, 207, 254n
Adler, Renata, 139
Adler, Stella, 63
Adventures in Paradise (t.v. show), 15
Aimee, Anouk, 96
Air Force Motion Picture Unit, 6
Albert, Eddie, 8, 62, 63, 64, 65, 74, 181, 186, 191, 195, 213, 247n
Aldrich, Adell (daughter), 4, 183, 217, 236, 237, 241n
Aldrich, Alida (daughter), 238, 255n
Aldrich, Edward (father), 3, 4–5, 53, 58, 241n
Aldrich, Harriet Foster (1st wife), 241n
Aldrich, Kelly (son), 237, 238, 239, 255n
Aldrich, Lora (mother), 4
Aldrich, Lucy T. (aunt), 3, 241n
Aldrich, Nelson Wilmarth (grandfather), 2–3, 241n
Aldrich, Richard Steere (uncle), 3
Aldrich, Robert Burgess
—ambiguity in films of, 24–25, 30, 36, 42, 49–50, 51, 59–60, 72–73, 94, 105–107, 116, 121, 138, 146, 154, 163, 173, 178–79, 185, 191, 201, 203, 210–11, 245n
—apprenticeship of, 5–14
—background, 1
—censorship, 21, 43, 62, 127–28, 147–48, 151

Aldrich, Robert Burgess *(cont.)*
—education of, 5
—exile from Hollywood, 15, 76–98
—European critical attitudes toward, 19, 23, 42, 43–44, 49, 60–61, 80, 238–39
—filmmaking "family" of, 8, 19, 63–64, 80, 109, 136, 141–43, 147, 163–64, 165, 236
—genre, use and subversion of, 19, 32–36, 43, 57–58, 59–60, 62, 75, 85, 90, 95, 96, 100, 107, 108–109, 115, 116, 118, 123–25, 132, 136–37, 151, 156–57, 159, 165–67, 173, 175, 180–81, 183, 195, 196–97, 206, 214, 219, 222–23, 225, 228–29
—hero and anti-hero in films of, 2, 21, 29–30, 34–35, 37, 39–41, 49, 74, 81–84, 87–89, 91–94, 97, 104, 107–108, 110, 119–20, 125, 128–30, 154–55, 158–59, 160–61, 169–71, 173, 176–78, 189, 190–91, 201, 202, 211, 222, 223
—Hollywood and film industry, 46, 47–48, 76–77, 79, 99, 100, 102–103, 108, 132, 134–35, 136, 138, 140–41, 142–43, 150–51, 165, 179–80, 196, 217, 218–29, 229
—illness and death, 232–34
—politics and political views, 4, 12, 13–14, 37, 49, 75, 189, 198–99, 213–17, 230–32
—power, importance of, 4, 8, 51–52, 95–96, 109, 141, 143, 147, 169, 175, 179–80, 217
—preparation and rehearsals, 6–7, 14–15, 31–32, 63, 86, 122, 130–31, 237

Aldrich, Robert Burgess *(cont.)*
—professionalism, 16, 63, 64, 137, 152,
   165, 178, 188, 199, 201, 204, 218–19,
   221, 228–29, 236–39
—prologues in films of, 65–66,
   114–15, 117–18, 144, 181, 197
—relationship with actors and
   crew, 7–8, 31, 63, 64, 74, 80, 89–90,
   91, 102, 110–11, 130–31, 138–39, 147,
   152, 175, 178, 186, 187, 188, 195, 200,
   202–204, 211–13, 246n
—relationship with his children,
   237–38
—relationship with family, 3–5
—sex in films of, 21, 40–41, 57–59,
   91–94, 97, 143, 144, 146–47, 148–49,
   150–51, 160–61, 191
—television experience, 14–15, 18
—themes and motifs in films of:
   the "atomic" world, 21, 42, 43, 49,
      61, 97, 196, 231
   authority, 2, 4, 48–49, 69–70, 74,
      75, 121, 125–27, 168, 176–77, 186,
      210, 233
   claustrophobia, 30, 50, 119
   compromise, 28, 30, 49–50, 66–67,
      72, 77–79, 120–21, 190, 204,
      221–22, 225
   courage and cowardice, 30, 74,
      93, 121–22, 129, 151–52, 154-55,
      163, 202
   double-cross and duplicity, 24, 27,
      32–34, 35, 42, 43, 65, 69, 71, 84,
      88, 96, 105–106, 109, 112–14, 119,
      125, 146, 150–51, 155–56, 157–58,
      182–83, 186–87, 189, 190–91,
      197–98, 201, 203–204, 209–10, 219,
      224–26
   the game, 32, 33, 67–68, 81, 109,
      126–27, 131, 177, 185, 224–25
   group solidarity, 17–18, 65, 71, 72,
      80, 118, 123, 127, 129–30, 186, 206,
      224

Aldrich, Robert Burgess *(cont.)*
   integrity and self-respect, 10, 17,
      28, 30, 34–35, 49–50, 53, 71–73, 75,
      77–79, 82–84, 89, 121–22, 125,
      129–30, 155, 171, 177, 178–79, 183,
      185, 190, 193, 209–10, 223, 224–25,
      235
   parental figures, 4, 17, 35, 58, 74,
      77, 97, 104–105, 114, 150–51,
      159–60, 162–63, 171–72, 176, 183
   rebellion, 4, 24, 30, 107–108, 124,
      125–27, 173–74, 176
   responsibility and maturity, 28,
      30, 34–35, 49, 58, 59, 82–84,
      87–89, 97, 103, 105, 107–108,
      120–21, 155, 159, 160–63, 167–68,
      171–72, 176, 178–79, 187, 192–93,
      222
   the "rightful battle," 2, 21, 30,
      34–36, 49–50, 73, 75, 87–89, 122,
      155, 179, 185, 204, 209, 211
—unmade films, 229–232
—violence in films of, 37–38, 53, 61,
   64, 77, 94, 97, 104, 109, 114–15,
   127–29, 156, 158, 161–63, 166–67,
   168–69, 173, 178, 224
—women, attitude toward, 107, 110,
   147, 149, 160–61, 237
Aldrich, Sibylle Siegfried (2nd wife),
   241n
Aldrich, Stuart M. (uncle), 3
Aldrich, William (son), 3, 4, 7, 13, 117,
   122, 142, 148, 163–64, 165, 196, 203,
   207, 213, 217, 218, 222, 228, 231, 233,
   236, 237, 239, 241n
Aldrich, William Truman (uncle), 3
Aldrich, Winthrop William (uncle),
   3, 5
Aldrich, family, 1, 2–5, 213
"Aldrich Plan, The" (U.S. Senate),
   2–3
Aldrich Studios, the, 11, 140–44, 149,
   150, 151, 156, 163–64, 165, 237

All the King's Men (1949), 13
All the Marbles (unmade film), 223
. . . *All the Marbles* (1981), 132,
    222–29, 237, 238, 262–63
Alliance, the, 216
Allied Artists, 19
Altman, Robert, 175
*America: The National Catholic
    Weekly Review*, 38, 244n
ABC-Palomar Pictures, 143, 148, 150,
    151, 152, 163
Anderson, Warner, 14
Andress, Ursula, 109
Andrews, Harry, 152
Angeli, Pier, 96
Angry Hills, The (1959), 85–90, 94, 99,
    129, 150, 180, 235, 259
Apache (1954), 2, 22, 23–30, 36, 75,
    109, 120, 173–74, 199, 214, 257
Apstein, Theodore, 4, 150
Arch of Triumph (1948), 7, 11, 15
Arnold, Gary, 221, 255n
Associates and Aldrich, The, 46, 54,
    61, 79, 99, 111, 112, 116, 143
Association of Motion Picture and
    Television Producers (AMPTP),
    216
Astaire, Fred, 6
Astor, Mary, 116
Attack! (1956), 2, 47, 50, 51, 58, 60–75,
    76, 80, 117, 120, 126, 129, 130, 146,
    195, 201, 210, 214, 239, 258
Attenborough, Richard, 117, 122, 123
Attica State Prison riots (1971), 4
Autumn Leaves (1956), 14, 53–60, 76,
    100, 107, 258

Bachmann, Laurence, 80
"Bad Streak, The" (t.v. show), 243n
Baker, Herbert, 16
Baker, Stanley, 87, 96
Bannon, Ian, 122, 123
Bart, Peter, 250n

Bates, Daniel, 110, 249n
Battle Cry (1955), 62
Bazin, André, 23, 60, 243n
Beat the Devil (1954), 19
Bennett, Joan, 152, 181, 218, 236, 238,
    252n, 254n
Bergman, Ingrid, 9
Berry, John, 1, 12
Bertolucci, Bernardo, 128, 250n
Bezzerides, A.I., 38, 39, 41, 42, 86, 150,
    230, 235, 245n
Bieri, Ramon, 219
"Big Four, The" (U.S. Senate), 2
Big Knife, The (1955), 2, 46–53, 54, 59,
    73, 75, 76, 79, 80, 107, 132, 140, 146,
    214, 226, 239, 258
Big Leaguer, The (1953), 16-18, 20, 60,
    180, 223, 257
Bikel, Theodore, 87
Biroc, Joseph, 8, 19, 109, 111, 139, 142,
    147, 150, 152, 188, 247n
Bitsch, Charles, 43, 245n
blacklisting, political, 1, 10, 12–14, 75,
    90, 133
Blake, Walter, 14, 142
Blazing Saddles (1974), 230
Blumenthal, A. Pam, 9
Bochner, Lloyd, 166
Body and Soul (1947), 1, 10–11, 51, 185,
    227
Bogart, Humphrey, 230
Bonnie and Clyde (1967), 157, 159
Boone, Richard, 48, 77
Boreil, Jean, 105, 107, 249n
Borgnine, Ernest, 8, 32, 119, 123,
    132, 133, 175, 176, 177, 178, 191,
    244n
Bowles, Paul, 230
Boyer, Charles, 15
Brennan, Eileen, 190, 202
Bringing Up Baby (1938), 6
Broken Arrow (1950), 23
Bronco Apache (novel), 24

Bronson, Charles (Buchinsky), 8, 26, 32, 109, 110, 124, 129, 130, 131, 230
Brooks, Mel, 230
Brooks, Norman, 61
Brooks, Richard, 61
Brown, Jerry, 214
Brown, Jim, 129, 130, 237
Brown, Pat, 214
Brown vs. *Board of Education* (1954), 24
Browne, Coral, 135, 144, 146
Brynner, Yul, 249n
Bunuel, Luis, 230
Buono, Victor, 104, 109, 110
Butler, Hugo, 19, 54, 133
Byron, Stuart, 185, 253n, 254n

Cabot, Sebastian, 87
Caesar, Harry, 182, 235
Cagney, James, 159
Cahiers du Cinema, 42, 43, 57, 61, 82, 116
Caine, Michael, 152, 153, 155
Calendo, John, 244n, passim
Cameron, Ian, 244n, 248n, 249n
Campbell, William, 17
Canby, Vincent, 156, 173, 187, 221, 229, 253n, 255n
Carol, Martine, 81
Carr, Marian, 19
Carradine, Keith, 175, 176
Carter, Jimmy, 180
Casablanca (1942), 230
Cassavetes, John, 130, 131, 140
Cates, Gilbert, 235
Caught (1949), 12
Celluloid Closet, The (book), 148
Chabrol, Claude, 43, 60, 245n
Champ, Louis, 235
Champlin, Charles, 96, 181, 248n, 251n, 253n, 254n
Chandler, Jeff, 81, 82

Chandler, Raymond, 37
Chaplin, Charles, 7, 16, 23
Charlie Casbah (screenplay), 230, 231
Charly (1968), 152
Charo, 230
Chase, Borden, 31
Chase, Ilka, 48
Chase, James Hadley, 157
Chase, Mary Ellen, 241n
Chase Manhattan Bank, 3
China Smith (t.v. show), 15, 18, 19, 123
Chinatown (1974), 45
Choirboys, The (1977), 2, 206–13, 216, 218, 222, 262
Citizen Kane (1941), 6
Clavell, James, 230
Clayton, Dick, 196
Clouzot, Henri-Georges, 114
Cobb, Lee J., 76, 77
Coco, James, 230
Cohen, Ronald M., 199
Cohn, Harry, 48, 54, 76–77, 79, 217, 226
Cole, Nat "King", 54
Collier, Peter, 241n
CBS, 15
Columbia Studios, 48, 54, 76, 79, 217
Combs, Richard, 20, 32, 59, 92, 94, 196, 201, 243n, 244n, 246n, 248n, 253n, 254n
Communist Party (American), 12–14
Conrad, Michael, 182
Conway, Tim, 230
Cooper, Gary, 31, 32, 34, 110
Cooper, Maxine, 39
Cooper, Merian C., 5
Corey, Wendell, 47
Cotton, Joseph, 91, 112, 116, 202, 203
Coursodon, Jean-Pierre, 244n
Crandall, Bill, 17

Crawford, Joan, 54, 98, 99, 100, 102, 103, 112, 116, 237, 246n
Cross of Iron (screenplay), 100
Crowded Bed, The (screenplay), 143
Crowther, Bosley, 21, 37–38, 53, 74, 127, 250n
Cukor, George, 5
Culp, Robert, 152
Curtiss, Ursula, 150

Daily, Irene, 157
Danza, Tony, 230
Darby, Kim, 157
Darcel, Denise, 32
Davis, Bette, 99, 100, 102, 103, 112, 115, 116, 144, 237, 249n
Davison, Bruce, 166
Deer Hunter, The (1978), 204
de Havilland, Olivia, 112, 116
DeHaven, Carter, 253n
Dehner, John, 26
Dekker, Albert, 42
Deliverance (1972), 187
Delon, Alain, 223
Demonsablon, Philippe, 243n
Deneuve, Catherine, 188, 189, 194
Dennis, Nick, 109
Denny, Reginald, 19–20
Depression Era, 229
Dern, Bruce, 112
Derry, Charles, 107, 249n
de Toth, André, 9
Devil's Doorway (1950), 23
DeVol, Frank, 8, 19, 147, 228, 235, 250n
Diabolique (1955), 107, 114
Dial Tone (screenplay), 229
Di Cenzo, George, 219
Dies, Martin, 14
Dietrich, Marlene, 21
Directors Guild of America (DGA), 96, 207, 214, 215–17, 234, 235

DGA Memorial Service for Aldrich, 11, 235–36, 252n, 254n, 255n
Dirty Dozen, The (1967), 2, 18, 65, 109, 123–32, 140, 151, 155, 175, 176, 180, 185, 206, 213, 214, 230, 239, 250n, 260
Dirty Dozen, The (novel), 123, 125
Dmytryk, Edward, 6
Doctor, The (t.v. show), 14, 15, 18
Dr. Strangelove (1964), 45, 204
"Don't Sit Under the Apple Tree" (song), 132
Douglas, Kirk, 90–91, 94
Douglas, Melvyn, 198, 200, 202, 203
Drake, Alfred, 133
Drew, Bernard, 255n
Drum Beat (1954), 23
Dunnock, Mildred, 149–50
Dupont "Play of the Month" (t.v. show), 133
Durning, Charles, 197, 200, 202, 203, 204, 207, 209, 211, 212, 213, 218, 229, 234, 254n
Duryea, Dan, 15, 19, 123
Dyer, Peter John, 249n

Eastwood, Clint, 95
Ebsen, Buddy, 62
Edwards, Blake, 15, 243n
Einfeld, Charles, 9
Eisenhower, Dwight D., 3
Ekberg, Anita, 109
Elam, Jack, 32
Elliott, Denholm, 153
Ellsberg, Daniel, 198
Emperor of the North (1973), 174–80, 185, 207, 236, 261
Enterprise Studios, 1, 9–14, 16, 19, 141, 142, 227
Erikson, Leif, 202
Errol, Leon, 6
E.T. (1982), 231
Exodus (1960), 90

Eyles, Allen, 9, 11, 242n, 250n

Falk, Peter, 224, 228
Falk, Rosella, 136
Farrell, Henry, 99, 111
Faulkner, William, 7, 160
Faye, Joey, 157
Fenin, George N., 246n, 247n
film noir, 43, 45
Finch, Peter, 119, 122, 123, 133, 150, 151
First Time, The (1952), 22
Fistful of Dollars, A (1966), 95
Fleischer, Richard, 8, 11
Flicker, Theodore, 143
Flight of the Phoenix, The (1966), 18, 65, 117–23, 124, 175, 176, 185, 237, 239, 260
Flynn, Errol, 151
Fonda, Henry, 152
For Export Only (screenplay), 230, 231
Forbidden Garden, The (novel), 150
Force of Evil (1948), 1, 11, 227
Ford, Anitra, 186
Ford, Harrison, 219, 221
Ford, John, 5, 147, 171
Foreman, Carl, 12
Forsyth, Rosemary, 149
4 For Texas (1963), 109–11, 236, 259
Four Star Playhouse (t.v. show), 15, 16, 242–43n
Fragile Fox (play), 61
Fraser, Ronald, 119, 123, 144, 156
Frederick, Vicki, 224
Frisco Kid, The (1979), 218–22, 238, 262
Frohman, Mel, 223
From Here to Eternity (1953), 246n
Frye, David, 230
Fuller, Robert, 150

Garfield, John, 1, 9, 10, 11, 12, 13, 46, 185
Garment Jungle, The (1957), 76–79, 258

Gateways Club, 144
Gator (1976), 195
Gay Divorcé, The (1934), 6
German Club, 5
"Gift, The" (t.v. show), 243n
Gill, Brendan, 118, 250n
Gilliatt, Penelope, 127, 250n
Glasgow, William, 8, 19, 142, 150
Godbout, Oscar, 247n
Godfather, The (1972), 1, 180
Godfrey, Arthur, 110
Goetz, William, 54
Goodwins, Leslie, 6
Gordon, Ruth, 149, 150
Gossett, Louis Jr., 209
Granger, Stewart, 96
Grant, Cary, 6
"graylisting," 16
Greatest Mother of 'Em All, The (1969), 143, 150–51
Green, "Mean" Joe, 225
Green Berets, The (1968), 125
Greenberg, Joel, 241n passim
Greene, Lorne, 55
Greene, Nathanael, 2
Greenman, Alvin, 180–81, 188, 200, 207, 211, 229, 232, 234, 236, 237, 238, 239, 253n, 254n
Griffiths, Leon, 150, 161
Grissom Gang, The (1971), 45, 58, 60, 123, 150, 156–64, 165, 175, 180, 210, 239, 261
Gunga Din (1939), 6

Hagen, Jean, 47
Hammer Studios, 79
Hammett, Dashiell, 37
Hampton, James, 182
"Hard, Way, The" (t.v. show), 242–43n
Hardy, Lindsay, 19
Hauser, Robert, 201
Hawks, Howard, 6
Hay, Alexandra, 150, 151

Hay, Alexandra, 150, 151
Hayden, Sterling, 204
Hayes, Woody, 187
Hecht, Harold, 22, 23, 24
Hecht-Lancaster Productions, 21–22, 23, 25, 36, 98
Heller, Lukas, 8, 10, 11, 60, 90–91, 99, 100, 104, 109, 111, 114, 116, 118, 122, 124–25, 133, 143, 144, 146, 148, 149, 152, 214, 217, 218, 229, 232, 234, 242n
Hepburn, Katharine, 6
Hersey, Geraldine, 99
Higham, Charles, 241n passim
Hill, James, 31
Hitchcock, Alfred, 38, 59
Holliman, Earl, 15
Hollywood witch hunts, 12–14, 37
Hopper, Hedda, 48
Horowitz, David, 241n
Horung, E.W., 157
Horvath, Charles, 31
Hubbell, Carl, 17
Huddy, John, 254n
Hudson, Rock, 91
Huebsch, Edward, 199
Hunchback of Notre Dame, The (1939), 6
Hush . . . Hush, Sweet Charlotte (1965), 14, 60, 102, 107, 111–17, 124, 150, 238, 260
"Hush . . . Hush, Sweet Charlotte" (song), 238, 250n
Hustle (1975), 2, 45, 187–96, 202, 239, 262
Huston, John, 19
Hyman, Ken, 124, 125, 250n

"I Can't Give You Anything But Love, Baby" (song), 160, 163
"I Wouldn't Trade My Daddy" (song), 105
Informer, The, 5
"I've Written a Letter to Daddy" (song), 105, 238

Jaeckel, Richard, 8, 16, 17, 62, 63, 64, 109, 110, 129, 130, 165, 166, 200, 219, 237, 243n
Jarvie, Ian, 246N, 248n
Johnson, Arte, 230
Johnson, Ben, 188, 202
Johnson, Nunnally, 124

KMPC (radio station), 148
Kael, Pauline, 181, 187, 253n
Kagan, Norman, 74, 247n
Kahn, Madelyn, 230
Katzin, Lee H., 150
Kazan, Elia, 234
Keefer, Don, 157
Kellaway, Cecil, 116
Kennedy, Edgar, 6
Kennedy, George, 123, 223
Kennedy, Joseph P., 5
Kentuckian, The (1955), 36
Kerr, Deborah, 246n
Kibbee, Roland, 31
Kiel, Richard, 182
Killing of Sister George, The (1968), 50, 51, 54, 60, 132, 143–49, 260–61
Kinderspeil (screenplay), 231, 234, 246n
King, Perry, 208, 209
King Kong (1933), 5
Kiss for Corliss, A (1949), 8
Kiss Me Deadly (1955), 36–45, 46, 47, 61, 82, 86, 117, 136, 140, 150, 156, 196, 214, 231, 235, 239, 245n, 257–58
Kiss Me, Deadly (novel), 36, 37, 38, 42, 156
Kleiner, Harry, 76
Knight, Arthur, 62, 109, 247n, 249n
Knopf, Christopher, 175, 176, 207, 209, 210
Knowles, Patric, 19
Koch, Howard 236
Kruger, Hardy, 117, 122, 123
Kubrick, Stanley, 45

Lachenay, R., 57, 60, 246n
Lacy, Jerry, 230
Ladd, Cheryl, 229
Lady From Shanghai (1948), 43
Lamont, Charles, 8
Lancaster, Burt, 8, 21–22, 23, 24–25,
  30, 31, 32, 34, 36, 46, 98, 110, 165,
  166, 173, 174, 197, 199, 201, 204, 213,
  234, 236, 239, 243n, 244n, 246n,
  253n
Landon, Laurene, 224
Lane, Bobby, 187
Langton, Paul, 47
Lansbury, Angela, 144
Lansing, Robert, 158
Lardner, Ring, 12
Lardner, Jr., Ring, 13, 14
Larkins, Robert, 243n
Lasky, Betty, 241n
Last Sunset, The (1961), 90–95, 100,
  107, 259
Laszlo, Ernest, 26, 31, 50, 80, 109,
  110–111
Lauter, Ed, 182
Leachman, Cloris, 39
Legend of Lylah Clare, The (1968),
  2, 132–39, 140, 143, 146, 150, 251n,
  260
Legion of Decency, 43, 210
Leigh, Keats, 229
Lemmon, Jack, 187
Leone, Sergio, 95, 109
Levine, Joseph E., 95, 99
Levine, Martin, 173, 253n
Lewin, Albert, 8
Lewis, Florà, 244n
Limelight (1952), 7
Little Women (1933), 5
Lockhart, Gene, 19
Loggia, Robert, 76
Longest Yard, The (1974), 18, 65,
  180–87, 195, 206, 210, 214, 224, 227,
  236, 239, 261–62
Lopex, Trini, 130,132

Lorimar Production Company, 198,
  199, 207, 208, 209, 210
Los Angeles Police Department,
  206, 207, 211
Losey, Joseph, 7
Lowe, David L., 9
Luciano, Lucky, 230
Luciano, Michael, 8, 19, 43, 50, 122,
  136–37, 140, 234, 236, 237, 238, 244n,
  245n, 254n
Luke, Jorge, 166
Lupino, Ida, 15, 46
Lynley, Carol, 91, 94

M (1951), 7
McCarthy, Senator Joseph, 12, 14, 37,
  48, 75, 90
McCrea, Joel, 9
McGraw, Charles, 202
McIntire, John, 28
Macready, George, 32
Mailer, Norman, 62
Malone, Dorothy, 91
Man on Fire (screenplay), 229–30
Mankiewicz, Tom, 198
Mann, Anthony, 61
Mantz, Paul, 250n
Marcus, Frank, 143, 146, 149
Marshall, William, 202
Martin, Dean, 109, 110
Marty (1955), 244n
Marvin, Lee, 8, 62, 63, 64, 66, 124, 125,
  127, 130–31, 174, 175, 176, 177, 178,
  179, 185, 214, 223, 234, 236, 237, 247n
Marx Brothers, 6
Mary of Scotland (1936), 6
Mathews, Kerwin, 76, 77
Matzka, Dieter, 201
Mayer, Louis B., 15, 48
Mayérsburg, Paul 248n
Mayflower, the, 2
Medina, Patricia, 149
Meeker, Ralph, 38, 39, 41
Metro-Goldwyn-Mayer, 5, 9, 15–16

Metro-Goldwyn-Mayer, *(cont.)*
  85, 86, 124, 125, 139, 140, 143, 223,
  225, 226, 229
Michener, James, 15
Miles, Vera, 55, 202
Milestone, Lewis, 7, 8, 9, 11, 242n
Miller, Henry, 45
Mills, Bart, 254n
Milne, Tom, 174, 195, 252n, 253n,
  254n
Miner, Alan, 79
Mr. Roberts (1955), 62
Mitchum, Robert, 85–85, 89–90, 180,
  237
Monroe, Marilyn, 239
Montiel, Sarita, 31, 32
Moorehead, Agnes, 116
Morgan, James, 243n
Morocco (1930), 21
Moses Brown School, 5
Moskowitz, G., 245n
MPAA (Motion Picture Association
  of America), 37, 43, 148
Mueller, Elizabeth, 87
Murphy, Michael, 135
Musante, Tony, 157
"My Country 'Tis of Thee" (song),
  204, 231

NBC, 14
Nachbar, Jack, 253n
Naked and the Dead, The (novel),
  62
Namath, Joe, 187
Nason, Richard, 85
Nathanson, E.M., 123
National Association of Theater
  Owners, 140
Navasky, Victor S., 242n
New Mexico (1951), 8
New York Giants (baseball team),
  16–17
Newman, Paul, 196, 202
Nichols, Mike, 219

Nicholson, Jack, 45
Niven, David, 15
Nixon, Richard, 186, 187
No Orchids For Miss Blandish
  (novel), 157, 158, 160
Noble House (novel), 230
Norman, Madie, 104
Novak, Kim, 133, 138–39

Odets, Clifford, 46, 48, 227, 245n
Of Men and Music (1950), 8
"Oh You Beautiful Doll" (song), 225
On the Waterfront (1954), 77
One Flew Over the Cuckoo's Nest
  (1975), 130
Ophuls, Max, 9, 12
Orwell, George, 157, 252n

Page, Geraldine, 149, 150
Page, Patti, 250n
Pagliacci (opera), 225
Palance, Jack, 8, 46, 53, 62, 64, 65, 80,
  81, 125, 237, 247n
Paramount Studios, 181, 193, 229
Parrish, Robert, 10
Patton, Jr., General George A., 221
Peck, Gregory, 202
Peckinpah, Sam, 32, 244n
Penn, Arthur, 159
Peters, Bernadette, 186
Peters, Jean, 26
Petit, Chris, 248n, 253n, 254n
Peyser, Penny, 221
Phoenix, The (novel), 80
Podestra, Rossana, 96
Poe, James, 46, 61, 74
Polanski, Roman, 45
Pollack, Sydney, 180
Polonsky, Abraham, 1, 9, 10, 11, 12, 13
  185, 214, 233, 234, 235, 242n
"Pop Goes the Weasel" (song), 158
Powell, Dick, 15

Powers, James, 241n, 242n, 243n, 252n, 253n, 255n
Preminger, Otto, 90
Presley, Elvis, 239
Preston, Billy, 204, 231
Price, Rep. Melvin, 62
Private Affairs of Bel Ami, The (1947), 8, 9
Prouty, Howard H., 242n
Prowler, The (1951), 7
Psycho (1960), 38, 59, 60, 107

Quinn, Anthony, 79, 230, 246n
Quinnell, A.J., 230

RCA (Radio Corporation of America), 5
RKO (Radio-Keith-Orpheum) Studios, 1, 5–6, 62, 89, 235
Raiders of the Lost Ark (1981), 45
Rapf, Matt, 16
Ray, Nicholas, 61
Reagan, Ronald, 14
Red Pony, The (1949), 7, 89
Reid, Beryl, 144
Reis, Irving, 8
Renoir, Jean, 6–7
Reynolds, Burt, 181, 187, 188, 193, 195, 196, 213, 223, 229, 234, 253n, 254n
Rich, Lee, 207, 254n
Richards, Jeff, 17
Richer, Jean-José, 51, 246n, 247n
Riddle, Nelson, 109
Ride Back, The (1957), 79
Rigsby, Howard, 91
Ringel, Harry, 84, 151, 244n, passim
Rios, Lalo, 17
Rivette, Jacques, 61, 247n
Roberts, Bob, 9, 11
Robertson, Cliff, 54, 58, 152, 155
Robinson, Edward G., 16, 17
Robinson, George, 246n, 247n

Ro-Burt Production Company, 187, 195
Rockefeller, Abby Greene (Aldrich), 3
Rockefeller, John D., Jr., 3
Rockefeller, Nelson, 3, 4
Rockefeller, Winthrop, 3
Rockefeller family, 1, 3, 4, 5
Rocky (1976), 224
Rogers, Gaby, 41
Rogers, Ginger, 6
Rogers, Roy, 15
Rogers, Will, 227
Romero, Cesar, 32
Room Service (1938), 6
Ross, Barney, 10
Ross, T.J., 94, 248n
Rossen, Robert, 1, 9, 10, 11, 12–13, 75
Rossetti, Christina, 39, 41
Rouault, Georges, 51
Roud, Richard, 246n
Rouverol, Jean, 54, 133
Ruddy, Al, 180
Rudolph, Oscar, 109
Run of the Arrow (1957), 23
Russo, Barry, 151
Russo, Vito, 148, 149, 251n, 252n
Ryan, Robert, 132

Sanctuary (novel), 160
Sandrich, Jay, 198
Sarris, Andrew, 32, 53, 94, 173, 229, 244n, 248n, 251n, 255n
Sauvage, Pierre, 32, 45, 241n, passim
Savalas, Telly, 125, 130, 131
Save the Tiger (1973), 187
Saville, Victor, 36
Scala, Gia, 76, 87
Schary, Dore, 15
Schickel, Richard, 139, 210, 251n, 254n
Schoedsack, Ernest B., 5
Schrader, Paul, 45, 245n

Schumach, Murray, 244n, 245n
Scott, Pippa, 202
Searchers, The (1956), 171
Selzer, Milton, 133
Seven Arts Company, 79, 99
Seven Day Soldiers (screenplay), 229
Shaffner, Franklin, 214, 215, 216, 217, 235
Shagan, Steve, 187, 188, 192
Sharp, Alan, 166, 167, 171, 252n, 253n
Shaw, Irwin, 62
Sheltering Sky, The (novel), 230
Sherman, Bob, 151
Sherman, Teddi, 80, 109
Sherman, Vincent, 77
Shields, Arthur, 19
Shivas, Mark, 244n, 248n, 249n
Silver, Alain, 84, 242n, passim
Simon, Scott, 202
Sinatra, Frank, 109, 110, 236
Sirk, Douglas, 57
Sloane, Everett, 48
Smith, William, 197, 219
Smithers, William, 62, 66
So This Is New York (1948), 8, 11–12
Sodom and Gomorrah (1963), 45, 95–97, 99, 109, 259
Somack, Jack, 220
"Sons of the Pioneers, The" (MGM Production Group), 15–16
Southern, Ann, 150
Southerner, The (1945), 6–7, 9
Speilberg, David, 191
Spielberg, Steven, 45, 231
Spillane, Mickey, 36, 37, 38, 39, 40, 42, 157
"Squeeze, The" (t.v. show), 242n, 243n
Stand On It (screenplay), 196, 229
Stanwyck, Barbara, 9
Star Wars (1977), 221
Steadman, John, 185
Steiger, Rod, 46, 48
Stephenson, Nathaniel Wright, 241n

Stevens, Connie, 158
Stevens, George, 215
Stewart, James, 117, 122
Stick (1985), 234
Sting, The (1973), 202
Story of G.I. Joe, The (1945), 7, 62, 89
Strange Love of Martha Ivers, The (1946), 7
Strategic Air Command (1955), 62
Strauss, Robert, 62
Strode, Woody, 223
Stross, Raymond, 85, 86
Stroud, Don, 208, 209
Sudden Death (screenplay), 219
Sundance Kid, The (pilot for *Hotel de Paree*, t.v. show), 15
Sundown at Crazy Horse (novel), 91
Sutherland, Donald, 124, 130, 131

Tabakin, Bernie, 19
Tailleur, Roger, 30, 34, 35, 49, 51, 60, 243n, 244n, 246n
Takakura, Ken, 153
Taras Bulba (1962), 98, 248–49n
Tatzloff, Ted, 8
Taylor, Jud, 235
Ten Seconds to Hell (1959), 79–85, 99, 109, 120, 199, 258–59
Ten Tall Men (1951), 22
Tessier, Robert, 182
Thompson, J. Lee, 249n
Three Stooges, The, 110
Tinti, Gabriele, 119
To Hell and Back (1955), 62
Too Late the Hero (1970), 123, 129, 143, 151–56, 175, 204, 261
Top Hat (1935), 6
Touch of Evil (1958), 45
Trevor, Elleston, 122
Truffaut, Francois, 32, 34, 37, 42, 43–44, 49, 54, 60, 61, 62, 73, 74, 77, 242n, passim
Trumbo, Dalton, 13, 14, 90, 92
20th Century-Fox, 112, 174

Twilight's Last Gleaming (1977), 2, 196–206, 207, 214, 231, 239, 262
Twin (screenplay), 229
Tyner, Charles, 182

UFA Studios, 79, 80
Ulzana's Raid (1972), 30, 165–74, 175, 176, 180, 195, 199, 229, 239, 253n, 261
United Artists, 9, 24, 25, 43, 61, 79, 80, 196
U.S. House Armed Services Committee, 62
U.S. House Un-American Activities Committee, 12–13, 231
Universal Studios, 165, 196, 208
University of Virginia, 5
Uris, Leon, 86

Velie, Lester, 76
Vengeance is Mine (screenplay), 230
Vera Cruz (1954), 31–36, 37–38, 43, 46, 82, 98, 107, 109, 110, 120, 199, 257
Vera-Ellen, 17
Vidor, King, 215
Vietnam War, 173, 176, 179, 197, 198, 199, 203, 204
Vigoda, Abe, 230
Viper Three (novel), 198
von Sternberg, Josef, 21

Wager, Walter, 198
Waite, Ralph, 157
Walker, Clint, 129, 130, 131
Wallace, Richard, 8
Wambaugh, Joseph, 206, 207, 208, 209, 210, 211, 216
Ward, Elizabeth, 245n, 247n, 248n, 252n
Warner, Jack L., 48
Warner Brothers, 180, 219, 221
Watergate, 187, 204
Watts, Douglass, 166
Wayne, John, 125

Webb, James R., 24, 31
Weld, Tuesday, 133
Welles, Orson, 6, 43, 45, 61
Wellman, Paul, 24
Wellman, William, 7
What Ever Happened to Baby Jane? (1962), 14, 54, 60, 98, 99–109, 111, 112, 114, 115, 116, 117, 120, 124, 132, 150, 161, 237, 238, 239, 259
What Ever Happened to Baby Jane? (novel), 99
Whatever Happened to Aunt Alice? (1969), 143, 149–50
White Feather (1955), 23
White Tower, The (1950), 8
Who's Who in America (Aldrich entry in), 4
Widmark, Richard, 197, 201
Wild Bunch, The (1969), 32, 244n
Wilder, Billy, 195
Wilder, Gene, 219, 221
Williams, Roger, 2
Willock, Dave, 80
Wilson, Scott, 157
Windeler, Robert, 250n
Winfield, Paul, 191, 197
Winters, Shelley, 47
Wise, Robert, 215, 235
Wiseman, Joseph, 76
"Witness, The" (t.v. show), 242n
Wood, Michael, 244n
Woods, James, 208, 211
World For Ransom (1954), 19–22, 257
Writers Guild, 124, 210, 215, 216
Wynn, Tracy Keenan, 181
Yakuza, The (1975), 180
York, Susannah, 144, 146, 147, 149
Young, Burt, 197, 225, 230, 234
Young Lions, The (novel), 62

Zanuck, Daryl F., 195